ORWELL: THE WAR BROADCASTS

ORWELL
THE WAR
BROADCASTS

Edited with an Introduction by

W.J. West

Duckworth/
British Broadcasting Corporation

First published in 1985 by
Gerald Duckworth & Co Ltd
The Old Piano Factory
43 Gloucester Crescent, London NW1
and the British Broadcasting Corporation
35 Marylebone High Street, London W1M 4AA

ISBN 0 7156 1916 0 (cased) (Duckworth)
ISBN 0 563 20327 7 (cased) (BBC)

British Library Cataloguing in Publication Data

Orwell, George
  Orwell: the war broadcasts.
  Rn: Eric Blair   I. Title
  II. West, W.J. (William John)
  828'.91208   PR6029.R8

  ISBN 0-7156-1916-0

Photoset in North Wales by
Derek Doyle & Associates, Mold, Clwyd
Printed and bound in Great Britain by
Billing & Sons Limited, Guildford, London and Worcester

Contents

For Tom and Richard West

Preface

The sudden discovery in 1984 of a large number of unknown writings by George Orwell is a happy coincidence, coming as it does in the year that Orwell was to make his own. That these writings bear directly on the genesis of *Animal Farm* and *Nineteen Eighty-Four* confirms that the event is one of major literary significance.

The quantity of material discovered is large, but it falls readily into two categories: first Orwell's literary and other talks, with the letters and scripts relating to them, most of which he actually broadcast himself and which are published in this volume; and secondly the weekly war commentaries written by Orwell, but mostly broadcast by others, which will be published in a second volume.[1] All of these texts have remained unpublished until now.[2] Fifteen of the 75 Orwell wartime scripts and a handful of letters were deposited by BBC Archives in the Orwell Archive, University College London, but the very existence of the remainder was unsuspected by scholars.

The Introduction that follows describes in some detail how Orwell came to be broadcasting to India during the war, how the British Broadcasting Corporation was organised then, particularly with reference to censorship and Orwell's struggles against it, how Orwell fared in his two years working for the Corporation, and lastly the significance of that experience for his later work. The accepted verdict that these years were largely wasted is decisively overturned.

The discovery of the scripts was not made by serendipity or mere chance but by a lengthy process of search through a large number of documents in the BBC Written Archives after a clue was found to their likely existence. Exactly how they were found, especially as they are in what is, in effect, a public archive, perhaps needs some explanation in detail here.

The BBC Written Archives Centre at Caversham Park, Reading, houses the vast mass of printed papers, letters, programmes, scripts and data of every kind that the Corporation has produced since its earliest days. Originally in one of the main BBC buildings in central London, it was moved to its present location in 1969 when it was realised that the ever-increasing bulk of material could not be made properly available in the existing premises.

All the earlier academic research on Orwell's years in the BBC appears to have been based on information about him released from the Archives when

---

[1] *Through Eastern Eyes: Orwell's War Commentaries*, edited by W.J. West.

[2] One (No. 6) was printed in a censored form in the BBC's official magazine the *Listener* within two weeks of broadcasting.

they were in London. At that time, while a lot of Orwell material was kept conveniently to hand, much more was inaccessible for physical or other reasons. With the move to Reading the entire mass of Orwell's work for the BBC became potentially available for study.

Unfortunately, however, neither scholars nor successive BBC staff were fully aware of how much Orwell had actually done or where it was to be found. This was not the fault of the staff at the archive. A great deal of Orwell's work had been filed according to administrative, rather than research, criteria.

Earlier this year I visited the Reading Archives to check on certain references to Basic English in papers from the C.K. Ogden archive that had come into my possession. The relationship to Orwell's 'Newspeak' was self-evident but, surprisingly, the Basic file at Reading revealed some unrecorded letters, a War Cabinet report recommending that Basic should be adopted by the BBC Overseas Services, including the section where Orwell worked, and a script that Orwell had commissioned on the subject for one of his Indian programmes. The talk was filed, somewhat mysteriously, under the name of the Indian lady who introduced the talk rather the author and broadcaster of it, Leonora Lockhart, or Orwell or Ogden.

A visit to the Orwell Archive at University College London established that this information was unknown to the standard authorities. It seemed to be a worthwhile project, therefore, to search the BBC Archives more thoroughly. As it was known from the beginning that filing had been illogical, without cross-referencing, the only way to conduct the research was to go through the administrative records for every day's broadcasts for the period when Orwell was at the BBC, noting everyone who had had anything at all to do with each programme and checking the files under all these headings.

At the end of many weeks' search through the bound volumes of roneoed sheets that contain this information, the essential outlines of Orwell's contribution began to emerge. The discoveries continued, culminating in the appearance of over sixty scripts or war commentary by Orwell which, again, had been filed under the names of the Indians who had read them over the air. Many letters were found, more straightforwardly, in the files of the people to whom they had been sent, whose names had also been discovered by this search of the day-to-day records.

It can hardly be possible, certainly not within the space of a few months, to feel that an archive of such immense scope as the BBC's has been in any sense exhausted. A few scripts that are known to have once existed and been broadcast are still missing despite thorough search. In any event it would not be the place of a work at this stage, so soon after such major discoveries, to aim at absolute completeness.

This fresh material about a neglected period of Orwell's life also enabled me to undertake the very pleasant task of seeking out and interviewing those people, mentioned in my acknowledgments below, whose place in Orwell's life has likewise not been fully recognised. The perspectives gained from these interviews were supplemented by the extensive collection of Orwell's letters, work and diaries published in the four volumes of *Collected Essays, Journalism and Letters of George Orwell*, edited by Sonia Orwell and Ian Angus (1968), referred to hereafter as *CE*, and other published sources to produce a radically new understanding of Orwell's work which I have described in the Introduction.

I am grateful to the staff at the BBC Written Archives, Caversham Park, Reading, particularly the Archivist, Mrs Jacqueline Kavanagh and her assistant Miss Guiniver Jones, but not least Mr Denis Perry and Miss Amanda Mares, who watched my first simple request for material on Basic English grow into a full search of large parts of the archive with commendable patience. Without their swift location and vetting of the many files called for and the excellent copying service, the search for scripts and letters could never have been accomplished as rapidly as it has been. Secondly I am grateful to the staff at the University College London rare books room, including Miss Jill Furlong, and Mrs Janet Percival, who is in charge of the Orwell Archive there, the most complete collection of published work on Orwell.

I should like to thank Dr Mulk Raj Anand, Orwell's friend from his days in Spain and close collaborator on many of the programmes published here, for his help and encouragement; Desmond Hawkins, who first brought Orwell to the microphone and worked with him on programmes while he was at the BBC, for his recollections and help in understanding the atmosphere at the BBC in those days; Douglas Cleverdon, who produced many of Orwell's scripts including his adaptation of Ignazio Silone's 'The Fox' which inspired Orwell to write *Animal Farm*; Laurence Brander, Intelligence Officer for the Indian Section, who worked closely with Orwell and obtained information for him in India; T.R. Fyvel, who knew Orwell during those years and later and who has written an invaluable memoir of Orwell; Sir Osbert Lancaster for identifying the subjects of his cartoon 'Figures in a landscape'; Sir Stephen Spender for confirming a number of impressions of wartime literary London; John Lehmann and Lettice Cooper for their memories of the period; and Kathleen Halpin for identifying Dorset Chambers. I was sad that an appointment with Sir William Empson was forestalled by his death, and I am grateful to Lady Empson for her help at this difficult time.

I am grateful to Sheila Ableman at BBC Publications for her tact and efficiency in smoothing my path in all dealings with the BBC. Finally I owe a very great debt of gratitude to Colin Haycraft, my publisher and editor at Duckworth, whose shrewd questions about a letter of Brendan Bracken's to C.K. Ogden on Basic English that I happened to show him started me off on this trail, and whose unfailing scholarly instincts have sustained and encouraged me throughout.

Exeter, July 1984   W.J.W.

Illustrations

between pages 188 and 189

20. The Barcelona Restaurant today, then a haunt of Spanish Civil War veterans and one of Orwell's favourite meeting places. Photo: W.J. West
21. Senate House, Malet Street, wartime headquarters of the Ministry of Information and model for the 'Ministry of Truth' in *Nineteen Eighty-Four*. It was visible to Orwell from Langford Court. Photo: W.J. West
22. A wartime Home Guard exercise of the kind Orwell strongly supported. The figure fifth from the right looks remarkably like Orwell. Photo: Hulton Picture Library
23. An autograph letter from Forster to Orwell (see p. 272).

Introduction

I

George Orwell is now one of the best-known English writers of the twentieth century and his last two books, *Animal Farm* (1945) and *Nineteen Eighty-Four* (1949), are acknowledged as master works of their era. But at the beginning of the Second World War his reputation was not nearly so well established. He was known to a small audience as the author of a number of novels and books of social reportage, his deeply felt *Homage to Catalonia* (1938), based on his experiences in the Spanish Civil War, being seen as the best of them. When war broke out in 1939, like many little-known authors writing from a left-wing standpoint, he found himself without a clear role; and yet he ended the war, almost alone of his literary contemporaries, with extraordinary achievements. He had written *Animal Farm*, whose unique quality was recognised almost from its first appearance, and he was working on *Nineteen Eighty-Four* which was to give him the place in English literature that he holds today. Although much has been written of these two books, little attention has been paid to the wartime experience which formed their background, or to the great gulf which separates them stylistically and thematically from the work that went before.

The key to Orwell's evolution from the slightly pedantic and unpolished author of pre-war days lies in the two years he spent as a Talks Producer in the Indian Section of the BBC's Eastern Service from August 1941 until November 1943. The received view is that these were lost years for Orwell the writer.[1] But this is far from the case. Orwell did not cease writing while he was at the BBC, nor did his creative talents lie unused. There were constraints and frustrations certainly, but, besides commissioning, editing and rewriting a vast mass of work by leading English and Indian writers, he wrote a number of key talks himself. None of this work involved any 'black' propaganda. The Indian Section and the BBC generally were seen by Orwell as essentially truthful. The work entailed nothing less than the setting up of what was in effect a 'university of the air' for students of the Punjab and other Indian universities, coupled with weekly news broadcasts that enabled educated Indians generally to follow the progress of the war around the world.

The Second World War began, for Britain, as a propaganda war. The BBC, which had always prided itself on its political neutrality, found that it was to be put under the control of the Ministry of Information and used in the

[1] Bernard Crick, *George Orwell: a life* (1982), p. 413: '... for two precious years his talents were mainly wasted.'

13

front line in a radio battle against a country whose foreign propaganda, directed by Goebbels, was the most sophisticated in the world. Germany's victories in Europe were heralded by intense radio campaigns, and a similar onslaught on the British listening public soon began. But the Germans did not confine themselves to broadcasts in Europe. One of their main targets was the British in India. There were two million Indian troops fighting for Britain, all volunteers.[2] Their loyalty was vital for Britain, and the Germans knew that if they could be alienated in any way, most obviously by a civil breakdown in India itself, Britain's position could become precarious, especially in the Middle East. There were many Indian political leaders bitterly opposed to the British; some were imprisoned, but others had made their way to Japan and Germany where they had been given a warm welcome. The most important of these was the military insurgent Subhas Chandra Bose who came to the microphone in Berlin and ranted against the British with considerable effect.[3] To spice these tirades the programmes broadcast books by English authors which had attacked the British presence in India, notably E.M. Forster's *A Passage to India*, about which Orwell later remarked: '... so far as I know they didn't even have to resort to dishonest quotation.'[4]

The effect of these broadcasts in India was immediate. The *Daily Telegraph* correspondent cabled home on 6 October 1939: 'German propaganda in English excellently received. Listeners await vainly for refutation from London or Delhi'; and these and other reports which circulated in London with their implied criticism of the BBC and the Ministry of Information did produce some result. A section was set up within the Eastern Service of the BBC to broadcast to India in English and Hindustani. Known as the Indian Section, it was run by Sir Malcolm Darling, a recently retired civil administrator and Vice-Chancellor of the University of the Punjab, who, it was hoped, would be able to gather round him influential Indian authors of the same standing as Bose and his friends to act as a direct counter to them. But the matter was not so easily arranged. Darling approached the Indian novelist Mulk Raj Anand, author of *Coolie* and *Untouchable*, a veteran of the struggle against Franco in Spain (where he had been a close friend of Orwell's), with the suggestion that he might like to work for the BBC. Anand, a graduate of Punjab University, had known Darling in India and held him in high regard, but he did not wish to become involved. His letter declining Darling's offer says a great deal about the delicate position of Indians in England, many of whose works were banned in India and who would have found themselves in prison if they returned home:

---

[2] 'India has two million volunteers fighting in the Allied cause. It is the largest – and, I think, the least publicised – army of volunteers ever gathered under any flag.' F.Yeats-Brown, *Martial India* (1945), p.13.

[3] Subhas Chandra Bose (1897-1945). A violently anti-British member of the Indian Nationalist Congress Party, his movements during the war were a mystery to the British authorities (*CE* II, pp.476-7). There is no doubt that he broadcast from Berlin, but he seems also to have established the Indian National Army from a Japanese base.

[4] *Tribune*, 23 November 1945, in his article 'Through a Glass Rosily'. *CE* IV, pp.54ff.

8, St Georges Mews,   22 March 1941
Regent's Park Road, N.W.1

Dear Sir Malcolm,
   Your kind letter of the 8th has followed me about from London to Devon to
Surrey and, finally, back to London, where I have ended up for the duration
after all my peregrinations. Hence the delay in answering it.
   Now, I don't know how to explain my position in the face of your generous
suggestions, without complicating matters and seeming ungrateful.
   Briefly, as you know, since the breakdown of negotiations between the
Viceroy and Gandhiji, the position of Indians in this war has become very
invidious. Particularly is this so with regard to the Indians resident in England
at the moment. Because, even those who have the most distant affiliations with
the Congress, are bound to feel a certain sense of national humiliation if, with
full awareness of the internment of hundreds of their compatriots and the
savage sentence on Pandit Nehru, they do anything to help the war effort. My
own connections with the Congress are rather more intimate. And the one
question that has been taxing my mind all these months is how to reconcile that
affiliation with my belief that fascism would destroy all I stand for. I am afraid
the British Government has done nothing which may help to solve the dilemma
which faces some of us: It has declared neither its war aims nor its peace aims –
and India seems to be its one blind spot. This enforces on us a kind of vague
neutrality, the strain of which can be very harrowing for the more timid
individual, who is torn between conflicting loyalties. I, for instance, have
friends in this country with whom I have worked in the anti-fascist struggle for
some years ...
   I don't want to bore you with these personal and ideological difficulties, but I
hope, from what I have said, that you will see how difficult it is for me to
associate myself with the work of the Indian broadcasting section in any way. I
want to assure you that nothing I have said above detracts from my personal
respect for you and your writing, and I hope that you will understand and
forgive me for my disability to take your offer.
   With our kindest wishes for you and April,
   Yours sincerely,
   Mulk Raj Anand

Sir Malcolm Darling did in fact gather together a group of Indian
broadcasters and administrators for the Indian Section of the Eastern
Service, but they were headed by a BBC-trained man brought over from
India, Z.A. Bokhari.[5] Bokhari came with the highest recommendations from
his friend Lionel Fielden,[6] then the controller of broadcasting in New Delhi,
and between them Darling and Bokhari soon established the station as a
working unit. Because of lack of funds and other constraints, however, a large

---

   [5] Zulfaqar Ali Bokhari, Indian Programmes Organiser for the Indian Section from its
foundation. After the war he became Director General of Pakistan Radio.
   [6] For Lionel Fielden (1896-1974) see below, p.57, and his autobiography, *The Natural Bent*
(1960).

part of the station's first output consisted of music and comedy shows borrowed from the Home Service. Bokhari and his team contributed a weekly news report and an occasional cultural programme for which they sought the advice of Desmond Hawkins, a well-known contributor to the Home Service programmes who had the reputation of being able to get good authors to the microphone where others had failed.

George Orwell's first broadcast had been on Hawkins's programme 'The Writer in the Witness Box' in a discussion with Hawkins on 'Proletarian Literature'. The series was the highlight of the BBC autumn programmes in 1940 and introduced Orwell to a much wider audience. It was followed by a discussion between Orwell, Hawkins and V.S. Pritchett on 'What's Wrong with the Modern Short Story?',[7] and at about the same time Hawkins introduced Orwell to T.S. Eliot, another noted broadcaster.[8] Clearly both Darling and Bokhari wanted Orwell for their programmes, and Hawkins was happy to introduce him to them; Orwell's close friendship with Anand, which had continued from Spanish Civil War days, was no doubt an added incentive. Bokhari went ahead and commissioned a series of four talks from Orwell on literary themes.[9] As Orwell was a novice at the microphone, this was a substantial commission, but he had created a good impression within the BBC when working on 'The Writer in the Witness Box'. C.V. Salmon, the producer who commissioned Orwell's talk, said, writing to Hawkins: 'Here is Orwell's draft, too political and not dealing enough, I think, with the literary side. Will you try to put this right by raising the questions he can answer? He will obviously be charming to work with and as amenable as possible.'[10] The final talk had been good enough to appear in the *Listener*.[11]

From Orwell's point of view working for the BBC was not a sacrifice of principle, as it might have been for other writers thought to be of left-wing opinions. Orwell in fact approved of the BBC; in a typically back-handed compliment to them in his bi-monthly newsletter to *Partisan Review* he had written: 'I believe that the BBC, in spite of the stupidity of its foreign propaganda and the unbearable voices of its announcers, is very truthful. It is generally regarded here as more reliable than the press.'[12]

The four talks came at an opportune moment for Orwell. Like all full-time writers he had been badly affected by the war. Many of the usual channels

[7] It has not been possible to locate any surviving copy of this script.

[8] T.S. Eliot, as a Director of Faber and Faber, had rejected the manuscript of Orwell's first book *Down and Out in Paris and London* (1933) and was later to reject *Animal Farm*. Each had separately suggested to Hawkins that they might meet. The meeting did not, however, produce any immediate result. Eliot had broadcast for India before Orwell joined the section and he mostly dealt with Bokhari. Orwell later asked him to be the guest of honour on his magazine 'Voice'.

[9] The commission went ahead and all four talks were printed in the *Listener* after broadcasting. Their titles were 'The Frontiers of Art and Propaganda', 'Tolstoy and Shakespeare', 'The Meaning of a Poem (by Gerard Manley Hopkins)' and 'Literature and Totalitarianism'. They were reprinted in *CE* II, pp.149-64.

[10] See below, p.21.

[11] Broadcast on 6 December 1940 and printed in the *Listener* for 19 December. The discussion is printed as Orwell's work in *CE* II, pp.54-61, but for the true status of this text see below, p.21.

[12] *Partisan Review*, 13 April 1941. *CE* II, p.139.

open to him had been closed through cut-backs in normal publishing, and in any case there may not have been a ready market for the sort of thing he wanted to say. To those who knew Orwell by sight it must have been surprising that he had not been swept up immediately into some sort of active service. Of commanding appearance, well over six feet tall, with a background of Wellington, Eton and the Burma Police, he would have seemed an ideal recruit for any branch of the services. Those who knew him better realised that his health had never been good and that he had been seriously wounded fighting in Spain when a bullet passed through his neck. The wound had healed, but his health had not improved. The disease of the lungs which eventually killed him was already so serious that no medical board would pass him for any military duty whatsoever. Orwell was greatly disappointed. 'What is so terrible about this kind of situation is to be able to do nothing. The government won't use me in any capacity, not even a clerk, and I have failed to get into the Army because of my lungs. It is a terrible thing to feel oneself useless and at the same time on every side to see half-wits and pro-fascists filling important jobs.'[13]

This depression held him for quite some time. After the outbreak of war he first stayed at the smallholding and village shop which he and his wife Eileen O'Shaughnessy had run in Hertfordshire before the war. Eileen soon got a job in London in a censorship department,[14] leaving Orwell alone at the shop during the week, a situation that clearly could not last. In May 1940 they moved into a small flat in Dorset Chambers, Chagford Street,[15] ostensibly so that Orwell could be in London to do weekly theatre and film reviews for *Time and Tide*. In fact he threw himself into any activity he could find. The Local Defence Volunteers, precursor of the Home Guard, had been formed on 10 May in response to a radio broadcast by Anthony Eden, and Orwell immediately joined his local group. He proceeded to take part in their famous camp at Osterley Park, a sort of guerilla training-school founded by the magazine *Picture Post*[16] and run by veterans of the Spanish Civil War under Tom Wintringham.[17] Among the lecturers who visited were Guy Burgess and Hugh 'Humphrey' Slater.[18]

[13] Letter to John Lehmann, 6 July 1940. *CE* II, pp.44-5.
[14] *CE* II, p.34, n.7. In which Ministry is not recorded.
[15] The building began life as dwellings for working men in the 1860s. It has recently been totally refurbished, and the name changed to Chagford House. It can never have been as described in *George Orwell: a Life* (p.389): '... above shops backing onto garages in a mews ...' The garages which Orwell describes in his war diary as burning (*CE* II, p.453) were further along.
[16] See, for example, *Picture Post*, vol.8, no.12, 'The Home Guard can Fight'.
[17] Thomas Wintringham (1898-1949), author of *Freedom is Our Weapon: a Policy for Army Reform* (1941), published in the series 'The Democratic Order', edited by Francis Williams, and other books. He had fought in Spain, starting as a journalist and ending up in charge of the British Battalion of the International Brigade. His activities at Osterley Park were a development of his role in Spain but did not reach their logical conclusion as there was no English revolution. In his London Letter for *Partisan Review* in November 1942 (*CE* II, p.266) Orwell describes Wintringham as a 'useful demagogue' and reports his joining Sir Richard Acland's Commonwealth Party (for which see below, n.98).
[18] Hugh 'Humphrey' Slater (1906-1958), painter and journalist, had been a chief of operations in the Spanish Civil War. He later edited *Polemic*, to which Orwell contributed.

On the literary side his most fruitful project arose from discussion with the publisher Fred Warburg and their mutual friend T.R. Fyvel. Fyvel, in his excellent book on Orwell,[19] has described the evolution in the summer of 1940 of a series of 'Searchlight Books', to be edited jointly by Orwell and himself, and the decision to start the series with Orwell's *The Lion and the Unicorn* (1941). Subtitled 'Socialism and the English Genius', the book identifies essential characteristics of English life and at the same time looks forward optimistically to 'The English Revolution', of which Orwell thought he saw signs around him; his formal programme for this revolution included the granting of immediate Dominion Status to India, with power to secede once the war was over, and the formation of an Imperial General Council in which the coloured peoples, as he called them, would be represented.[20]

Work on this started in 1940 during the Battle of Britain and kept Orwell occupied for most of the later part of the year, but he kept up connections with the wartime literary scene, especially with the group that gathered around Cyril Connolly, fellow-Etonian and a life-long aquaintance, and his monthly magazine *Horizon*. Orwell was a signatory of the 'War Writers Manifesto' which appeared in *Horizon*,[21] but was not totally committed to the group or its attitudes. Unlike the others, for instance, he did not haunt the Café Royal in Regent Street. Sir Osbert Lancaster, who portrayed the world of *Horizon* in his cartoon 'Figures in a Landscape', is certain that he never saw Orwell there.[22] Mulk Raj Anand recalls that Orwell regularly referred to the group as 'that Café Royal set', and that on one of the few occasions when he was lured there his plain-speaking in a discussion with Stephen Spender and others caused a row.[23]

None the less Orwell did write for two of the habitués who feature in the centre of Osbert Lancaster's cartoon, Cyril Connolly and Kingsley Martin, editor of the left-wing *New Statesman*; and it was through Kingsley Martin that he got to know Desmond Hawkins, who shared a review spot in the *New Statesman* with Orwell and Connolly. It is an indication of the immediacy of radio that, though Orwell did no work for his talk with Hawkins until he had finished *The Lion and the Unicorn*, both the broadcast and its publication in the *Listener* occurred months before the book appeared. Extraordinary prestige attached to radio in those days. Broadcasters received the same attention as television performers receive today, and the greatly improved financial status of anyone entering that world affected Orwell as it did others. By the time of his first talk for Bokhari, 'The Frontiers of Art and Propaganda', Orwell had moved to an expensive mansion block, Langford Court, in St John's Wood, then one of the most desirable areas of London. The move probably reflected concern for his wife's health and safety and the need for a normal family life. Eileen gave up her job when they moved, and it was well known that the new mansion blocks were relatively safer than ordinary houses. Orwell's famous

[19] T.R. Fyvel, *George Orwell: a personal memoir* (1982), ch.10.
[20] Reprinted in *CE* II, pp.119ff.
[21] *Horizon*, October 1941, pp.236-9.
[22] Personal communication.
[23] Personal communication.

remark, when a bomb blast had blown out the windows of a flat he and
Eileen were visiting, that if they had been in a working man's house at street
level they would all have been as dead as mutton, was that of a realist who
had fought in a war.[24]

Orwell's situation had now stabilised, and his work at the BBC had given
him much-needed reassurance. All these talks for the Indian Section were
printed in the *Listener*, and the éclat from that, with hopes for the future,
enabled him to view his position with equanimity. Writing to Dorothy
Plowman just after the last of the talks had appeared in the *Listener*, he said:
'It is hard to make much more than a living these days. One can't write books
with this nightmare going on, and though I get plenty of journalistic and
broadcasting work, it is rather a hand-to-mouth existence.'[25] There had
been no definite talk in the BBC either about the possibility of a regular series
of talks for Orwell, or even about employment, but the situation was suddenly
altered dramatically.

In the early hours of 22 June 1941 Germany invaded Russia and Russia
entered the war on the side of the Allies. Churchill welcomed the Russians in
the fight against a common enemy, despite his own detestation of Bolshevism
and all that Russia stood for. A similar change appeared throughout Britain,
and support for Russia in the popular press grew rapidly. The left-wing papers
which had been against the war as long as Germany and Russia were allies
now turned completely the other way and adopted an aggressive tone
demanding fresh action on all fronts and a stepping up of the propaganda war.
The Ministry of Information came in for especially strong criticism, and a
crisis within the Ministry soon developed. Kingsley Martin, in a crucial
editorial in the *New Statesman* of 5 July, headed 'Strategy of Propaganda',
launched a fierce attack on the Minister of Information, Duff Cooper, and his
running of the department. As the centrepiece of his attack, Martin chose the
Indian Section of the BBC:

Berlin war news is a great attraction to Indian listeners. The listening public in
India must not be judged by the number of Indians with radio sets since
considerable groups of Indians listen-in to every private set and coffee shop set.
Too often these groups of Indians prefer the racy style of Berlin to the British
solemnity. Anyone who follows British broadcasting to India will understand
why. British bulletins to India have included comments on the death of such
celebrities as Ethel M. Dell, and on the valuable contribution to British defence
afforded by a group of Australian footballers who filled some sandbags before
sailing for their homes. Before the war, and even after it, British broadcasting to
India consisted almost exclusively of British music hall, café orchestra music
and sentimental talks, in spite of the fact that Indians dislike European music
and think music hall entertainments vulgar. Plenty of educated Indians would
welcome serious talks on literature and other topics which recognise their
equality of interests. The Germans, who have made a special study of India,

[24] See Mark Benney, *Almost a Gentleman* (1966), pp.167-8. The customary view of the incident
is that it was class guilt on Orwell's part!
[25] 20 June 1941. *CE* II, p.165.

well understand how to meet Indian tastes and susceptibilities. Even after a Hindustani service from the BBC was established the usual news service was a literal translation into Hindustani of the overseas English bulletin, which consists of innumerable items which mean nothing at all to Indian listeners and which omit all the problems that would attract the attention of the Indian public. The average Indian wants a racy programme in his own tongue about things which concern him. No oriental translator, however experienced and adept, can produce this effect if he has to translate at speed an English news bulletin.[26]

Changes followed rapidly after this and other attacks. Brendan Bracken replaced Duff Cooper at the MOI, one of the best appointments ever made to the Ministry, and soon made his presence felt. There were many staff changes in the Ministry itself and others in the BBC, including the Indian Section. Since the BBC's personal files are closed to the public, we cannot know exactly how it happened,[27] but within a few days Orwell's name was put forward and he was accepted as an Empire Talks Assistant in the Indian Section. A letter was sent to him with a contract offering a salary of £680 a year, a not inconsiderable sum in those days, and he immediately accepted. He was appointed on 18 August.

II

Almost immediately Orwell was sent on a BBC staff training course. These courses were held twice yearly to teach the large number of wartime recruits the technicalities of broadcasting and the complexities of the administrative machinery. William Empson, writing many years later, referred to the scheme as 'the liars' school',[28] but others who attended say that the term was not current at the time and that there was no question of indoctrination or anything of the kind.[29] Orwell's own printed notes for the course, which have survived and are in the Orwell Archive at University College London, amply bear this out. The pile of roneoed sheets, two and more inches deep, was an augury of the bureaucracy to come; there was little time in two weeks

[26] It is tempting to see Orwell's hand in this passage: allusions to Ethel M. Dell and her mass fiction had been made by him before (e.g. 'Bookshop Memories', *Fortnightly* Nov. 1936.)

[27] The rules applying to the BBC Written Archives differ from those that apply to Government papers at the Public Record Office, for example. There is no 30-year rule, or any equivalent, but all papers have to be vetted before they can be seen by the public and all personal staff files are closed for 70 years. Apart from any other reasons for his appointment, Orwell must have been one of the few English writers of the time with an Indian background. He was born on 25 June 1903 at Motihari, Bengal, the son of a Bengal civil servant.

[28] 'William Empson and Orwell at the BBC', first published in Miriam Gross (ed.), *The World of George Orwell* (1971) and republished in Audrey Coppard and Bernard Crick (edd.), *Orwell Remembered* (1984).

[29] Personal communication from Douglas Cleverdon who attended the same course as Orwell, and Tom Chalmers who taught there.

for indoctrination. The only topic that would be strange today was censorship.

In peacetime censorship of the media is not tolerated; in war it is a vital means of protecting a nation's security. In the First World War, when radio did not exist, there had been no ready-made system of censorship and one was now rapidly evolved. The BBC was subjected to a censorship more thorough than that imposed on any other media.[30] It is important to realise that when Orwell joined the BBC he could not have known how extensive it was, or how authoritarian it could become. The totalitarian atmosphere of *Nineteen Eighty-Four* – of universal censorship that alters the past as well as the present and even attempts to alter the mind – was the ultimate development of Orwell's experience of censorship at the BBC at the hands of the MOI. At the beginning, in his talk on proletarian literature with Desmond Hawkins, Orwell would have been aware of it only when he saw the censors' stamps on the script he was reading into the microphone. He may not even have realised then that the censors operated from the Ministry of Information, situated in the white tower of London University's Senate House in Malet Street.

The basis of the system can be seen in what happened to this talk with Hawkins. Everything broadcast had to be submitted to the censor first; not a single word could be broadcast that had not been censored twice, once for security and once for policy. This meant that the apparently spontaneous talk between Orwell and Hawkins was in fact a construction written out beforehand. Orwell sent a draft essay on the subject (it was to this that Salmon referred in his letter), which Hawkins then worked up into a dialogue between himself and Orwell. Thereupon it was typed up as a script and sent to Orwell for his approval, and for any minor alterations that he thought necessary: extensive alterations were out of the question because of the exact running time of the script. When Orwell had agreed the script, Hawkins's producer sent it off to the censor, who cleared it. From a literary point of view the effect is rather weird. The dialogue between Orwell and Hawkins on the proletarian writer, which until now has been accepted at face value as Orwell's work and published as such in his *Collected Essays*,[31] is seen to be nothing of the sort. The direct result of the needs of the censor has been to create a situation in which, from the beginning, a visiting writer was liable to have words put into his mouth and his thoughts subtly reworked for him; or, at the very least, one in which everything he might have wanted to say was examined word for word for current political orthodoxy. As this procedure was simply a development of normal radio practice for scripted talks before the days of recording, and as it occurred at a time when broadcasting was a novelty and there was a danger that even the most fluent speaker might be at a loss for words when faced with a live microphone, few people saw anything sinister in it. In the months to come Orwell himself found that, in the same way, he had to write many scripts for people from essays they had written which then went out over the air as the original work of the person

[30] A full account of the system is given below in Appendix A.
[31] *CE* II, pp.54ff.

broadcasting. As the months turned into years and difficulties began to develop over particular scripts, Orwell's worries grew, as will become plain.

Orwell finally settled into the Indian Section on 23 September. When he arrived he found a letter from Bokhari, somewhat patronising in tone, outlining the work that was ahead of them. The BBC's programmes were planned by the quarter, and Bokhari summarised the plans already drawn up for the day-to-day broadcasts in the next quarter, which began on 5 October. He went on to ask Orwell's direct help for the future: 'I have received the syllabuses of various Indian Universities and I am negotiating with Herbert Read and trying to get a team of University dons to broadcast talks based on the books recommended for various examinations in India. It is all in the melting pot at the moment and as soon as I have a definite plan I shall let you know and we will get together to thrash it out.'[32] This academic approach tended to produce exactly the stale type of programme that had been criticised before Orwell's appointment. Bokhari was well aware of this, and of his own lack of overall perspective. He went on: 'These plans may seem haphazard to you and I dare say they are. I shall be delighted to have your suggestions ... We want ideas very badly. Could you kindly put your thinking cap on? We must start thinking now about our programmes for the quarter after ...'

For the next few months Orwell set about learning the wartime routine at the BBC. The Eastern Service was housed in a building by Oxford Circus, 200 Oxford Street, whose peacetime role was as a department store. The building's large rooms had been hastily converted into offices, consisting of small open-top cubicles with the sound of innumerable activities echoing around to create the hectic atmosphere which has often been described. The canteen on the ground floor was almost certainly the model for the canteen in *Nineteen Eighty-Four*; no doubt it was not very different from any other canteen acting as a centre for gossip and social life, but it would have been new to Orwell, who had never worked in an organisation of the kind before. Despite the descriptions of the food in *Nineteen Eighty-Four*, others remember the canteen as well run and well provisioned; in wartime London the BBC had considerable difficulty keeping people from other BBC departments away from it.[33] Besides the administrative buildings at 200 Oxford Street, there were also offices in the main BBC building at Portland Place and a large number of studios in other buildings all over London.

Orwell's actual work in these first months consisted mainly in writing introductions to talks and keeping contact with the authors he and Herbert Read had begun to get together for a literary programme called 'Turning over a New Leaf', devised by John Lehmann.[34] Orwell himself wrote a short talk for it based on the experiences recorded in his book *The Road to Wigan Pier*

[32] Memorandum, 'English Programmes to India', 23 September 1941. WAC: E2/403.

[33] No ration cards were needed in restaurants, but not everyone could afford to eat out. The BBC canteen was of course subsidised.

[34] For a brief period John Lehmann advised Bokhari on his literary programmes. He was followed by Desmond Hawkins, who also worked on a consultancy basis, until George Orwell was appointed to his full-time post and absorbed this work into it.

(1937).[35] He also began the delicate task of persuading Mulk Raj Anand and other Indian friends to the microphone.

Although Anand was more inclined to accept BBC work now that Russia had entered the war, he still held back. He was amused to see that the letter (see p. 176) came from 'Eric Blair' when, from his days in Spain onwards, he had only known Orwell previously as 'George Orwell'. Orwell explained that to the BBC he was known purely and simply as 'Eric Arthur Blair'.[36]

The question of Orwell's identity change from Blair to Orwell has caused some difficulty for interpreters of Orwell's life and work, especially as he did not legally adopt the name 'George Orwell' but nevertheless used the name in his private life. While he was at the BBC he used both names on his letters; there is even a legend within the BBC that he had both names sign-written on his door at Portland Place.[37] His own rule at first seems to have been to use his real name when writing formally, whether to strangers or to people he knew, and 'George Orwell' when writing informally or to close friends. On one day, 7 October 1942, he wrote two letters to Anand, one signed 'Blair' and the other, a more personal one, 'Orwell'. Usually he signed with his initials 'E.A.B.' above the typed name 'George Orwell'. The matter caused him considerable difficulty, and part of it may have stemmed from the fact that while 'Eric Arthur Blair' was a harmless person as far as the Government was concerned, 'George Orwell' was a seditious man whose book *Burmese Days* (1935) was strictly banned in India. Eventually, at the end of 1942, it was decided to take the risk of allowing Orwell to use his *nom-de-plume* and to broadcast to India over that name, but meanwhile the British Government preferred to conceal the odd fact that they had chosen to spearhead their propaganda campaign to India a man whose works they had actually banned. Whether there was more to it than this is open to conjecture. Orwell had written a clear and unambiguous statement of his position on India in *The Lion and the Unicorn*[38] and this cannot have changed in a few months. He was manifestly against the British Government's Indian policy root and branch, and yet his appointment to this most sensitive post had gone through. Possibly, in those dark days of the war, some long-term policy decision for India had already been taken and Orwell's appointment, and the tone of his articles, showed the way forward. For the moment 'George Orwell' sheltered in the obscurity of his own name.

III

By the end of 1941 Orwell had developed clearly the lines along which he intended to run the English-language broadcasts to India. Bokhari's role had

[35] This talk, 'From Colliery to Kitchen: a talk on how coal is produced', has not been discovered.

[36] Personal communication.

[37] Personal communication from Mrs J. Kavanagh (quoting Gordon Cox, a BBC engineer at the time).

[38] See above, p.18.

by now been confined to the Hindustani Section and to the more mundane matters of administration. By chance two of Orwell's internal memoranda about his future programmes have survived and give an idea of the wide range of work he commissioned and the depth of interest he developed in India and its problems.[39] The cornerstone of his personal contribution was the weekly news broadcast which he began at the end of 1941, but he also wrote a number of talks in the long-established series 'We Speak to India' and 'Through Eastern Eyes'. The first two talks were on subjects close to the life of wartime London, 'Money and Guns' and 'British Rations and the Submarine War' (nos. 1 and 2 below). Both show the development of interests which are clearly reflected in *Nineteen Eighty-Four*. The first mentions the fallacy of the 'Lebensraum' ('living-room') policy of the Nazi government, a search supposedly for unoccupied lands but actually, as shown, for densely populated areas whose inhabitants could be turned into proles or slaves working with the minimum of sustenance. It discusses also the advantages of inexpensive communal activities as substitutes for 'conspicuous consumption' which took money away from guns. The second, with its mention of rations that had been raised or reduced coupled with an announcement that this had been expected, echoes almost exactly the tone of *Nineteen Eighty-Four*, where good news means that rations are to be lowered as expected.[40]

The next two talks began a series on the meaning of new words which were gaining currency in the war in England and which would be unknown to intellectuals in India where a purer form of English was spoken. Orwell wrote again to Mulk Raj Anand, asking him to continue the series, and this time he was successful:

Mulk Raj Anand Esq.,   27th February 1942
8, St George's Mews,
Regent's Park Road, N.W.1

Dear Anand,

I wonder if you would like to do a series of talks on Sundays, which would mean recording the talks normally on Fridays? I recently wrote myself two talks explaining what is meant by scorched earth and by sabotage, and it afterwards occurred to me that as we have about five Sundays vacant, we might have a series, discussing similar phrases which have passed into general usage in the last year or two, and are flung to and fro in newspaper articles, broadcasts and so forth, without necessarily being well understood.

I would like you, if you would, to do these talks, starting with one on the phrase Fifth Column, and following up with talks discussing propaganda, living space, new order, pluto-democracy, racialism, and so on. I am sending you as a sort of guidance copies of the first two talks I did. You will see from these that our idea is to make these catch-phrases more intelligible, and at the same time,

[39] Printed below, Appendix B.
[40] George Orwell, *Nineteen Eighty-Four*, with a critical introduction and annotations by Bernard Crick (OUP 1984), pp.206-7.

of course, to do a bit of anti-Fascist propaganda. Could you let me know pretty soon whether this would interest you?

Yours,

Eric Blair

Talks Assistant

Indian Section

The first of these talks has not survived, but 'The Meaning of Sabotage' is printed here (no. 3). Orwell must have realised that this talk, ostensibly of literary interest to explain the origins of the word 'sabotage', could also act as an incitement to sabotage to any who heard it. Orwell's interest in Indian independence probably did not go so far as to suggest that Indians should sabotage Britain's war effort in India, but the talk could certainly have had that effect. In fact it probably harks back to Orwell's view of the political situation in the early days of the war: namely, that a revolution was imminent, and that the Local Defence Volunteers were a people's army which should be ready for every eventuality, sabotage included, if a German invasion should actually take place.[41]

The main threat to India was from Japan. Orwell therefore looked for someone to represent the people of China who could broadcast to India and explain what was happening and what it was like to be living under Japanese occupation. By chance the Chinese author Hsiao Ch'ien was in London during the war, and Orwell wrote to Ch'ien to ask for something he could broadcast.[42] He received some interesting material. Later Ch'ien sent Orwell a copy of his book *Etchings of a Tormented Age* (1942). Orwell acknowledged it later, asking him for more talks, but this time on literary, rather than political, themes:

13th March 1942

Dear Mr Hsiao,

I delayed writing to thank you for the copy you sent me of *Etchings of a Tormented Age* until I should read it. It interested me very much. It also has brought home to me how complete my ignorance of modern Chinese literature is. I wonder if you would agree to do two talks for us on this subject about the end of April? We are having a series of talks on contemporary literature and we are starting off with six talks on English literature, followed by four on Russian and two on Chinese. I am sure you would be exactly the person to undertake the latter; they are half-hour talks, i.e. not more than about 27 minutes each, and I should want the script in each case about a week before the date of the talk.

[41] The LDV would have been ready for revolution if Wintringham and the others had won the day, before or after a German invasion. Not since Cromwell and the days of the Levellers had social revolution been so real a prospect in England. Orwell's likely view is summed up in 'My Country Right or Left', *CE* I, pp.587ff.

[42] Hsiao Ch'ien (Xiao Qian) (1910-   ). After the war he returned to China, where, in 1957, he fell foul of the authorities and had to go and work on a state farm; he was not rehabilitated until 1979. In 1984 he made a visit to the United Kingdom and gave an interesting account of his life in a talk to the Great Britain-China Centre. The text is published in No.27 of their newsletter 'Britain-China' (1985).

Could you let me know whether you feel ready to undertake this, and if you do,
I can give you further details. In the case of your not being able to broadcast on
the actual days, we can easily record the talk beforehand.

Yours sincerely,

Eric Blair

Talks Assistant

Indian Section

Ch'ien replied with further suggestions, and Orwell answered frankly:
'What you said in your book opened up a completely new world to me which I
had hitherto known nothing about, and I think it will be the same with our
listeners. I want to bring home to them that there is a vigorous modern
Chinese literature which is most likely to be accessible to them through
English translations.'[43] He went on to confirm that he had seen the Chinese
stories in *Penguin New Writing* and that they were what had given him the idea
for the talks. It is ironic that today, with all that has happened since, we are as
ignorant of Chinese literature as Orwell was then.

In the first letter Orwell wrote to Hsiao Ch'ien, with its talk of atrocities,
there is a touch of the propagandist – which Orwell was aware of in himself.
In his war diary for 14 March he wrote: 'Our radio strategy is even more
hopeless than our military strategy. Nevertheless one rapidly becomes
propaganda minded and develops a cunning one did not previously have. E.g.
I am regularly alleging in all my news-letters[44] that the Japanese are plotting
to attack Russia. I don't believe this to be so ...',[45] and he went on to explain
why he was alleging this. A week later, on 22 March, he wrote: 'Empson tells
me that there is a strict ban by the Foreign Office on any suggestion that
Japan is going to attack Russia. So this subject is being studiously avoided in
the Far East broadcasts while being pushed all the time in the India
broadcasts.'[46] The threat seems to have been purely Orwell's invention, but
it was reality for those listening in India, a reality created as easily as
Winston Smith's invention of a non-existent hero and battle in *Nineteen
Eighty-Four*.[47]

Orwell did not give up his own real-life imaginary battles in the Home
Guard. Although the threat of invasion had ceased, he still took his voluntary
service very seriously; Mulk Raj Anand remembers that Orwell always
seemed to be in his sergeant's uniform when Anand called round in the
evenings.[48] On one occasion when a supply of ammunition was not
distributed for over four hours Orwell indulged in an 'Orwellian' joke,
sending a memo to Sir James Grigg, the Secretary of State for War, through

[43] Letter quoted in full below, *Letters*, p.182.

[44] Orwell refers here to the weekly news review he wrote for most of the time he was with the
Eastern Service. See *Through Eastern Eyes: Orwell's War Commentaries*, edited by W.J. West,
forthcoming.

[45] Wartime diary, 14 March 1942. *CE* II, p.465.

[46] Wartime diary, 22 March 1942. *CE* II, p.466.

[47] *Nineteen Eighty-Four* (ed.cit.), pp.196-7.

[48] Personal communication.

Tom Jones, Lloyd George's secretary, complaining strongly.[49] The joke was that Lady Grigg ran a weekly radio programme for the women of India under Orwell's nominal control. Sir James was a fairly frequent broadcaster on the programme and he usually contrived to speak uncensored, as did many of his wife's guests,[50] to the intense annoyance of Orwell, who was responsible for them (see below, p. 184).

Orwell did not take a purely literary or political view of the war. With his experience of the Spanish conflict behind him he realised that science was all-important in the development of modern warfare and also that all political questions in battle are subservient to the geography of warfare. He took a very modern view of these themes. Living in a modern building, fighting the most modern form of media war which depended on science absolutely, he saw matters in a severely realistic way, and over the next two years he commissioned a series of talks from leading scientists. Among the series titles were 'Science and the People' and 'Science and Politics'. Orwell's interest and what he learned foreshadow the scientific themes in *Nineteen Eighty-Four*, with their entirely political context, and mark the difference between it and the earlier science fantasies of H.G. Wells and others.[51]

His first series of talks were from J.F. Horrabin, familiar at the beginning of the war for his broadcasts on television. During the war Horrabin became equally well known as a cartoonist for the *Star* and *News Chronicle* but, as Orwell knew, he was also a serious man with important and far-reaching theories on the significance of geography for modern war.[52] Horrabin's writings were far more thorough and soundly based than the sensational works of James Burnham.[53] Orwell had a clear idea of what he wanted from Horrabin and wrote:

J.F. Horrabin Esq.,   3rd February 1942
16 Endersleigh Gardens,
Hendon, N.W.4

Dear Horrabin,
   Very many thanks for the synopses you sent me. I like them very well, my only criticism is that I would like the talks to be a little more definitely about

[49] Wartime diary, 27 March 1942. Bernard Crick (*George Orwell: a life*, p.425) discovered Tom Jones's reply to Orwell's letter in the Orwell Archive, University College London, but did not relate it to this diary entry or, apparently, know of the close connection between Orwell and Sir James and Lady Grigg that gave the joke its flavour.
[50] For the attitude of society ladies to this sort of programme, and to the war effort in general, see *Fare-ye-well with Ladies of the Realm* (1944), compiled by the Countess of Effingham (Proceeds to: Comforts and medical supplies for the children of Soviet Russia).
[51] Mulk Raj Anand recalls many week-end discussions between Orwell, Wells, himself and others on utopias, anti-utopias and other subjects connected with the state of western civilisation. Orwell defined his position over the months; a fierce argument occurred at one of the meetings, noted in *George Orwell: a life* (p.429), relying on an entry in Inez Holden's diary.
[52] See J.F. Horrabin (1884-1962), *An Atlas History of the Second Great War*, 10 vols. (1940-46).
[53] James Burnham (1905-   ), author of several popular books on the likely future course of world politics written from an American standpoint but equally talked about in England. Orwell reviewed *The Managerial Revolution*, and *The Struggle for the World: CE* IV, pp.192-215, 361-75.

geography, with less direct reference to the war situation. Of course, one must mention the war at every turn, but what I am chiefly after is to try to give people an interest in geography which may lead them to look at an atlas occasionally. I am trying to arrange with one or two Indian papers that at the time of your first talk they shall publish a map of the world and mention your forthcoming talks in connection with it. I should not actually refer to this in anything you say, but I think you can talk with the assumption that some of your hearers will be looking at the map as they listen ...

    Yours sincerely,
    Eric Blair
    Talks Assistant
    Indian Section

Horrabin went on to do more talks for Orwell, and there is no doubt that his views of the war greatly influenced Orwell's vision in *Nineteen Eighty-Four* of three great superpowers. In the BBC Written Archives there is a manuscript note from Orwell asking Horrabin questions about the possibility of colonising the poles and deserts,[54] and other matters, culminating in a discussion about subjects for future talks for which the title 'The War of the Three Oceans' was agreed. It was Horrabin who pointed out that Hitler's plan for Spain involved breaking it up into a number of autonomous regions, corresponding to the racial divisions of the population – Basque, Catalan, and so on – and this must have helped Orwell to a new perspective on the situation in Spain.

For purely scientific talks Orwell turned to J.D. Bernal, suggesting that he do all six of a series on the role of science in the modern world.

Professor J.D. Bernal,   6th March 1942
R. & E. Branch,
Forest Products Research Station
Prince's Risborough, Bucks.

Dear Professor Bernal,

    I wonder if you would consider doing a series of six half-hour talks for me in the Eastern Service? These talks are aimed mainly at the English-speaking Indian population in India. What I had thought of was a sort of history of the rise of modern science from the end of the Middle Ages onwards, and then followed by a discussion of the future of science and the position of the scientific worker under Capitalism, Fascism and Socialism. I have roughly sketched out the series of talks, but don't, of course, want to tie you down in any way. I would like to know first whether it would interest you to go further in the matter.

    Should you agree, the first of the talks would be due about the end of May. If you do not agree to undertake this, or haven't time to do so, I wonder if you

---

[54] See below, illustration 15.

could let me know of somebody else who you think would be interested?
    Yours sincerely,
    George Orwell
    Talks Assistant
    Indian Section

    There is no indication in the BBC records of how Orwell came to know
Bernal or to choose him for his first scientific talks. Like many scientists of
the time, Bernal was a great admirer of the Soviet Union, which Orwell most
definitely was not, and he carried his admiration to the point of fanatical
adherence to Soviet Communism. Major repercussions resulted from
Orwell's choice of Bernal, and this must have given him an insight, if he
needed one, into the inner workings of the Communist Party in London at
the time.
    At first things seemed to be going well. When they met it was agreed that
the series would go forward, but that Bernal would do only two of the talks
himself and nominate scientists from among his colleagues to do the
remainder.
    Then other factors intervened. Guy Burgess, fellow veteran of the Osterley
Park Guerilla Training School, was now also working for the BBC as
Orwell's opposite number in the Home Service talks department. Burgess
decided that he too wanted Bernal to do some talks.[55] He knew Bernal
well,[56] and he wrote a fulsome letter asking him to contribute a talk.

Professor J.D. Bernal F.R.S.,   13th April 1942
Birkbeck College
Fetter Lane, E.C.4

Dear Sage,
    What about meeting to have a talk sometime on the possibility of you giving a
broadcast on science in the USSR?
    The suggestion is that the talk should follow the lines of 'How is science
organised in the Soviet Union?' It will be necessary to take care as much as
possible of the more obvious political traps, for instance the implication that the
Soviet Union does everything much better than we do. On the other hand I do
not see how it would be possible to give this talk without making the point that
science occupies a very different place in the Soviet Weltanschauung to what it
does in ours.
    Crowther has covered a certain amount of the ground in a talk he did about
six months ago which mentioned a certain number of individual Soviet
organisations and scientific institutes – rather along the lines of his article in the
new scientific journal 'Endeavour'. But as I say, this was some time ago and if
the latest developments in the Soviet research appeal to you as a theme this

[55] *Sage: a life of J.D. Bernal* (1980) by Maurice Goldsmith draws a veil over the matters
mentioned here. Neither Orwell nor Burgess appears in the index.
[56] For their friendship and the circle in which they moved, see Andrew Boyle, *The Climate of
Treason* (1982).

might be quite a good line. We live in a technical age with an accompanying public appetite for and digestion of a surprising amount of technical detail. However, you certainly know more about this than I do and this letter is really only in the nature of a preliminary enquiry – and any suggestion would be welcome.

Yours ever,

Guy Burgess,

for Director of Talks

Faced with a choice, Bernal suddenly, without warning, withdrew from his commitment to Orwell, who was understandably annoyed: the series was to go on the air in two days, and he was being deprived of his anchor man. He even sent Bernal one of his rare telegrams asking for a substitute. No rational explanation for the switch reached Orwell, and the bitterness caused by the incident remained, surfacing again after the war in a well-documented row between them[57] over an article written by Bernal in the Marxist *Modern Quarterly*, calling for a new morality. Until now the background of this argument has remained unknown. Whether Orwell knew of the close connection between Burgess and Bernal – whether indeed Burgess warned Bernal about Orwell's total hatred of Russian Communism – is not clear. Certainly Orwell went on meeting Burgess in the normal course of work and some while later even took him along to meet Sir Stafford Cripps on Cripps's return from his mission to India. There was never any apology from Bernal, and Orwell at the last moment gave the series the title 'Science and Politics', including in it a talk by J.G. Crowther on 'Science in the USSR' and another by Joseph Needham on 'Science, Capitalism and Fascism'.

The connection between science and literature was always in the forefront of Orwell's mind, and he chose it as a theme of one of his talks in an otherwise purely literary series. He asked C.H. Waddington to do the talk. This time there was no difficulty, and Orwell and Waddington met at the Barcelona Restaurant to finalise details of the programme before recording. The talk provided a useful foil for the literary speakers whom Orwell chose from the *Horizon* group as typical of literary life in London. There is an interesting contrast between the patronage Orwell was able to offer and the sort he received from Connolly – the new world of radio paying homage to the old-fashioned world of letters.

Orwell asked Connolly for a straightforward essay on literature in the thirties, and makes no allusion in his letter to the reversal of their normal roles. Nor is there any mention of the other side of the coin, the difficulty which Orwell sometimes caused for *Horizon* and which he mentions in his diary: '*Horizon* was nearly stopped from getting its extra paper to print copies for export on the strength of my article on Kipling (all well at the last minute because Harold Nicolson and Duff Cooper intervened),[58] at the same time as

[57] *Polemic*, no.3, 1946. The unsigned editorial by Orwell describes the encounter. *CE* IV, pp.185ff.

[58] Duff Cooper had been Minister of Information; Harold Nicolson was a Governor of the BBC.

the BBC asked me to write a "feature" based on the article.'[59]

In the same series Orwell asked for a talk from Arthur Calder-Marshall, raising some interesting questions in his letter:

Arthur Calder-Marshall Esq.,   17th February 1942
c/o The Film Division,
Ministry of Information,
Malet Street, W.C.1

Dear Mr Calder-Marshall,

I wonder if you would like to do a talk for us in a series of talks on contemporary English literature which we are running for the English-speaking Indian public? These talks are supposed to cover the development of literature from about 1918 onwards, but we are not doing them by periods, but approaching certain aspects of literature separately. I thought that if you liked you might do the last talk in the series, and discuss the economic bases of literature (we can think of a suitable title later). In doing this, one would have to glance at the past, but of course we are chiefly interested in the present and to some extent, the future. With the gradual, or not very gradual, disappearance of unearned incomes and in general of privileged minorities, the economic background of literature is altering, and this is bound to have its effect on technique, subject matter, and so forth. This is the subject I want you to tackle, if it would interest you. Do you think you could let me know about this? It is to be a 28 minute talk, and it would be about 10 weeks from now.

Yours sincerely,
George Orwell
Talks Assistant
Indian Section

Calder-Marshall, with Tom Harrison of 'Mass Observation',[60] had been the driving force behind the *Horizon* War Writers' Manifesto with its unspoken question of how writers could earn a living and keep their integrity in wartime. Orwell, ironically, asked him now to write a talk on 'The Economic Basis of Literature', proceeding to mention as well the effect the new conditions would have on technique and subject-matter chosen by writers. Calder-Marshall, working for the Film Division of the Ministry of Information, would also be learning new techniques far removed from those envisaged in the Manifesto. Now even the freedom to write for Orwell had to be confirmed in writing by the MOI, including specific permission for him to accept the fee that Orwell was offering. The wider implication of Orwell's letter was, of course, that in wartime normal writing had ceased to exist and that at the end of the war there might be nothing but writing for radio and

---

[59] Wartime diary, 22 March. *CE* II, pp.466-7.
[60] For an account of Mass Observation see Tom Jefferey, *Mass Observation: a short history*, Birmingham University Centre for Contemporary Cultural Studies; also, for this period, Tom Harrison, *Living through the Blitz* (1979), based on unpublished material in the Mass Observation Archive at Sussex University.

films under government patronage.[61]

If literary independence survived in the war, Orwell felt it was perhaps to be found among the poets. For a talk on the most recent poets of the generation he turned to Herbert Read.

> Herbert Read Esq.,   6th March 1942
> Broom House
> Seer Green, Beaconsfield
>
> Dear Read,
>
> I wonder if you would like to do one more literary talk for us, to be delivered on April 7th? Following on the series 'Masterpieces of English Literature' which you introduced, I am having one on contemporary English literature, to be called 'Literature Between the Wars'. I want you, if you would, to deal with the new movement which has arisen in the last few years, starting I suppose with Dylan Thomas and George Barker. There is quite a group of young writers centering round the Apocalyptic movement who I think would make material for an interesting talk. I had tentatively named your talk Surrealism, but if you think that this term cannot be strictly applied to literature, we can easily change it. These are half-hour talks as before, i.e. anything up to 28 minutes, and the more you can break up the talk with quotations the better. I wonder if you could let me know about this fairly soon?
>
> Yours sincerely,
> Eric Blair
> Talks Assistant
> Indian Section

By the time Read came to give the talk he and Orwell had decided to change the name 'Apocalyptic Movement' to 'The New Romantics', an insight into the way literary movements get their names and lose them.

Orwell continued some of the features in the earlier Indian Section programmes, running them in parallel with the new talks he was arranging. Principal among these was a weekly political commentary 'The Debate Continues' run by Orwell's Parliamentary correspondent, Princess Indira of Kapurthala;[62] typical of her talks was an interview with Capt. Quintin Hogg (now Lord Hailsham)[63] on 'The work of the Indian troops in the Libyan campaign'. On the literary side there was a weekly review by E.M. Forster of new books published in England. Orwell now suggested that Forster might also like to do a talk in his literary series on modern Indian literature written in English.

While Orwell enjoyed the light relief of compiling literary programmes

[61] With the continuation of the wartime CEMA (Council for the Encouragement of Music and the Arts) as the post-war Arts Council, with close links with Russian culture in its early days, Orwell's fears might seem to have been vindicated.

[62] As the Parliamentary Correspondent of the Indian Section, Princess Indira was the only woman member of the House of Commons Press Lobby at the time. For details of the Kapurthala family, see Charles Allen and Sharada Dwivedi, *Lives of the Indian Princes* (1984).

[63] For Hailsham's views at the time, see *One Year's Work* (1944).

intended as set talks for Indian undergraduates reading English Literature, the political realities did not disappear. The Cripps mission to India, a determined attempt by the British Government to resolve the Indian question, brought fresh demands for action from the BBC. Cripps had been told on his arrival in India that German radio propaganda to counteract his visit was being very successful and that the BBC did not seem to be doing much about it. He cabled the BBC, and also Brendan Bracken at the Ministry of Information. Bracken immediately broke with protocol and telephoned the Director General of the BBC, Sir Cecil Graves, asking what could be done. The internal BBC memorandum of the telephone call is succinct:

Report of telephone conversation about broadcasts to India
Sir Cecil Graves & Mr Brendan Bracken   Private & Confidential
March 16th, 1942   [WAC: E2/361/2]

Mr Bracken rang up to say that some action was needed in connection with BBC Indian broadcasters as the Germans were pumping in a tremendous amount of stuff into India to offset Cripps's visit. Sir Cecil said they had on Saturday received a cable in this sense from Cripps and had gone into that point. In addition, that morning, when seeing Sir John Anderson, they had mentioned this business as illustrative of matters with which the BBC was faced and he had instantly asked Mr Amery to come in and talk it over. Mr Amery had said that he must certainly see the BBC people responsible for the broadcasts to India. This was being arranged.

  Sir Cecil said he wished Mr Bracken to know that this crossing of official wires had never been intended as they had gone to see Sir John Anderson simply as the new D.G.s on a courtesy visit. Mr Bracken said he perfectly understood and was glad these conversations had taken place.

  G. Hope Simpson

Orwell took a special interest in the Cripps mission. He wrote in his diary: 'It has flopped after all. I don't regard this as final, however. Listened in to Cripps's speech coming from Delhi, which we were re-broadcasting for England etc. These transmissions which we occasionally listen-in to from Delhi are our only clues as to how our own broadcasts sound in India. Always very bad quality and a great deal of background noise which it is impossible to take out in recordings.'[64] He responded immediately to the call for additional programmes and organised a talk by Tom Harrison and 'Mass Observation' on 'Public Opinion and the Cripps Mission', a biographical talk on Sir Stafford Cripps by Sir Patrick Hastings and a talk in the studio between Bokhari and other members of the Indian staff. Since the exact nature of the proposals was a secret, it is difficult to see what more specific programmes Sir Malcolm Darling, L.F. Rushbrook-Williams, his deputy, or Orwell, who was actually responsible for any talks to be put out, could have done.

[64] Wartime diary, 11 April 1942. *CE* II, p.473.

When Cripps returned, Orwell went to listen to the debate in the House of Commons. Afterwards he went for a personal interview with Cripps: 'I saw Cripps on Wednesday, the first time I had actually spoken to him. Rather well impressed. He was more approachable and easy going than I had expected, and quite ready to answer questions ...'[65] Their discussion was mainly about the Indians broadcasting to India from Germany; Cripps had known Subhas Chandra Bose well in the past and thought him 'a thoroughly bad egg', but he differed from Orwell in thinking that the younger Communist and left-wing Indians were genuinely anti-fascist. A positive result of the visit was an invitation to Orwell to go with some of his literary and broadcasting colleagues to visit Cripps, which Orwell duly recorded in his diary for 7 June. He took along with him his colleagues William Empson from the Eastern Service and Guy Burgess from Home Talks; also the poet Norman Cameron and the writer Jack Common.[66] David Owen, Cripps's personal secretary, was also there, but not, it seems, George Strauss, Cripps's parliamentary private secretary who was the proprietor of *Tribune*, the left-wing newspaper that Orwell subsequently worked for. It is an interesting comment on his political perspectives at the time that Orwell didn't believe that Cripps appreciated the revolutionary implications of the war and its continuation.[67]

Orwell's weekly news summary was the only vehicle he had for his personal views, and thought of the censor no doubt restricted anything he might have wished to say. That, at least, is the most likely explanation for his reaction to a political event even closer to his heart, the campaign in Burma. By May it was clear that all was lost, and Orwell could not restrain himself from sending a very unusual internal circulating memo entitled 'Information re Burma Campaign', detailing who he felt was responsible for the catastrophe. He chose to make his points in the form of questions, eleven altogether:

BBC internal circulating memo   16.5.42
Information re Burma Campaign   [WAC: E1/475/1]

The questions which I think could usefully be asked of the Burma government are:

i. What number of Burmese voluntarily evacuated themselves along with British troops etc. leaving India, and what proportion of these were officials.

ii. Attitude of Burmese officials when breakdown appeared imminent. Whether there was a marked difference in loyalty between Burmese and Indian officials. To what extent Burmese officials are known to be carrying on under the Japanese occupation.

---

[65] Wartime diary, 15 May 1942. *CE* II, p.481.
[66] Jack Common (1903-1968) author of *The Freedom of the Streets* (1938) and of a brilliant vignette of Orwell, published in *Orwell Remembered* (pp. 139-43) as 'Jack Common's Recollections', which tells more of Orwell than almost anything else in that volume. He must have been glad to have met Cripps; Orwell knew how to repay a debt. Jack Common also did several talks for him for the Indian Section.
[67] Wartime diary, 7 June 1942. *CE* II, p.468.

iii. Behaviour under fire of the Burma regiments and military police. Whether any actual Burmese (not Kachins etc.) were fighting for the British.

iv. What difference appeared between political attitude of the Burmese proper and the Karens, Shans, Chins, Kachins.

v. What number of the Eurasian community, especially in Rangoon, Moulmein, Mandalay evacuated with the British and how many stayed behind under the Japanese occupation. Whether any who remained behind are known to have changed their allegiance.

vi. Behaviour of the Burmese population under bombing raids. Whether these produced resentment against the Japanese, admiration for Japanese air superiority, or mere panic.

vii. The native Christians, especially Karens. Whether interpenetrated to any extent by nationalist movement.

viii. Number of shortwave sets known to have been in Burmese, Indian and Eurasian possession before the invasion.

ix. Detailed information about the Burmese nationalist and leftwing political parties. The main points are:
   a. Numbers and local and social composition of the Thakin party.
   b. Extent to which Buddhist priests predominate.
   c. What affiliations exist between the Burmese nationalist parties and the Congress and other Indian parties.
   d. Burmese Communists, if any, and what affiliations.
   e. Extent of Burmese trade union movement and whether it has affiliations with trade unions in India or Europe.

x. Estimated number of Burmese actually fighting on side of Japanese. Whether people of good standing or mainly dacoits etc. Whether they are reported to have fought courageously.

xi. Extent of Japanese infiltration before the invasion. Whether many Japanese are known to speak local languages, especially Burmese, and to what extent they are likely to be dependent on Burmans for monitoring and interpretation generally.

   Eric Blair

In this memo Orwell's close knowledge of all aspects of Burma's affairs is evident everywhere, and it shows that his feelings for the country, and consequently his anger at the fate that had befallen it, had remained unchanged from his days in the Burma Police as a young man in the early twenties. No one in the BBC who saw the memo can have had any doubt of Orwell's view of what had happened. Those outside the BBC, however, chose this time to deliver a series of attacks on Orwell and his broadcasting work, making him out to be an old-style imperialist propagandist who had in effect sold out and reverted to type.

Two letters were sent to Orwell by *Partisan Review* in New York, one from the anarchist George Woodcock, the other from Alex Comfort. Woodcock's was the most aggressive, referring scathingly to 'Comrade Orwell, former fellow-traveller of the pacifists and regular contributor to the pacifist *Adelphi* which he now attacks! Comrade Orwell, former extreme left-winger, ILP [Independent Labour Party] partisan and defender of Anarchists (see *Homage to Catalonia*)! And now Comrade Orwell who returns to his old imperialist allegiances and works at the BBC conducting British propaganda to fox the Indian masses.'[68] We cannot tell when he received these letters, but it seems unlikely that he had them before him when he wrote his own critique of his position within the BBC in his diary entry for 21 June: 'The thing that strikes one in the BBC – and it is evidently the same in various other departments – is not so much the moral squalor and ultimate futility of what we are doing, as the feeling of frustration, the impossibility of getting anything done ... Our policy is so ill-defined, the disorganisation is so great, there are so many changes of plan and the fear and hatred of intelligence are so all pervading, that one cannot plan any sort of wireless campaign whatever. When one plans some series of talks, with some more or less definite propaganda line behind it, one is first told to go ahead, then choked off on the ground that this or that is "injudicious" or "premature", then told again to go ahead, then told to water everything down and cut out any plain statements that may have crept in here and there, then told to modify the series in some way that removes its original meaning; and then at the last moment the whole thing is suddenly cancelled by some mysterious edict from above ...'[69]

This seemingly all-embracing condemnation of the Indian Section did not prevent him, three weeks later, from launching an equally strong defence of his role within the BBC and of what, in spite of everything, he had managed to achieve. Writing on 12 July in reply to Woodcock and Comfort's letters, he said: 'Does Mr Woodcock really know what sort of stuff I put out in the Indian broadcasts? He does not – though I would be quite glad to tell him about it. He is careful not to mention what other people are associated with these Indian broadcasts. One for instance is Herbert Read whom he mentions with approval. Others are T.S. Eliot, E.M. Forster, Reginald Reynolds, Stephen Spender, J.B.S. Haldane, Tom Wintringham. Most of our broadcasters are Indian left-wing intellectuals, from Liberals to Trotskyists, some of them bitterly anti-British. They don't do it to "fox the Indian masses" but because they know what a fascist victory would mean to the chances of India's independence.'[70]

These two views are not incompatible. Orwell obviously felt acutely the ultimate futility, as he put it, of not being able to do anything – not being able to influence, say, the fate of Burma by any propaganda campaign that would pass the scrutiny of those who issued mysterious edicts from above. After the failure of the Cripps mission, the Government in India swung over to a harder line, which caused Orwell great personal anguish. To a background of extensive rioting Gandhi, Nehru and others were imprisoned. Orwell wrote in his diary: 'It is strange, but quite truly the way the British Government is

---

[68] Details of the controversy, with the text of the letters, may be found in 'Pacifism and War' in *CE* II, pp.254-65.
[69] Wartime diary, 21 June 1942. *CE* II, p.489.
[70] *CE* II, p.264.

now behaving in India upsets me more than a military defeat.'[71] Feelings within the Indian Section ran high; even Bokhari threatened to resign. Events were brought to a head by a speech of Leo Amery's which was broadcast over the Empire Service instead of the Indian Section. The staff had some difficulty getting Amery to talk in a way suitable for the microphone rather than a public hall. A despairing official wrote afterwards that he had made some attempt at coaching him but failed: 'There was nothing for it but to record him exactly as God and Harrow made him.'[72] The content of the speech matched its tone; Orwell wrote in the same diary entry: 'Ghastly speech of Amery, speaking of Nehru and Co. as "wicked men", "saboteurs" etc. This of course broadcast on the Empire Service and re-broadcast by All India Radio. The best joke of all was that the Germans did their best to jam it, unfortunately without success.'

IV

Orwell's sense of failure on the political front did not interfere with his literary work. He established two series on personalities: 'My Debt to India' with talks by E.M. Forster, F. Yeats-Brown, F.M. Birdwood, Gerald Nathan and others; and another, 'These Names Will Live', in which Stalin was described by Mulk Raj Anand, Edwin Muir by Narayana Menon, Abt Vogler by Edwin Muir himself,[73] with other unlikely combinations of hero and biographer. In a more definitely experimental vein, he proposed for the next quarter a poetry magazine to be broadcast with the poets themselves reading extracts from their works, to be called 'Voice'. Nothing like this had been done before on British radio. Desmond Hawkins recalls how very difficult it was before the war to get any live modern poetry on the air. It seemed at times as though the BBC regarded the phrase 'living poet' as a contradiction in terms.[74] Orwell must have been among the first to grasp what was possible, and to see the contrast between such a broadcast magazine and the old-fashioned literary review of the *Horizon* type. 'Voice' pointed the way to the sort of poetry programmes that finally reached the wider British public after the war on the Third Programme. Orwell evolved the details with Anand.[75] Anand also contacted likely contributors, whom Orwell then chased up.

He wrote to Connolly:

[71] Wartime diary, 19 August 1942. *CE* II, p.500.
[72] BBC internal staff memorandum. BBC Written Archives.
[73] In *George Orwell: a life* (p.263) it is suggested that Orwell at one time had such a low opinion of Muir that he crossed the street rather than talk to him and that this was an example of Orwell's dislike of the Scots. Obviously, by this time, Orwell had developed a more rational view of the world and was happy to make Muir both a contributor to his talks and the subject of one of them in his own right!
[74] Personal communication.
[75] Personal communication.

Cyril Connolly Esq.,   23rd July 1942
6, Selwyn House,
2, Landsdowne Terrace, W.C.1

Dear Cyril,
    As you lost our last letter, I will explain again about the magazine 'Voice'.
The lay-out of the first number is to be more or less as follows. First a sort of
editorial by myself, then a poem by somebody (we are going to have people
reading their own poems as much as possible), then a monologue by Inez
Holden and probably read by Vida Hope; then a poem by Herbert Read, and
then one by Henry Treece, in order to represent the newest school of poetry. We
shall then have a discussion of this poem by the four or five people present. And
then, in order to round off, I want you to read a poem of a different type, to make
a contrast, and I suggested your reading that one of Auden's first because I
heard you read it very successfully before, and secondly because it has a sort of
serene quality which would tone in rather well with the signature tune we
always put at the end of these programmes. With the audience that we are
aiming at, one need not bother about a poem of this sort being rather stale.
    The date of the first issue of 'Voice' is August 11th. I think this programme
will need at the least one rehearsal and then on a later day the recording of the
whole programme.
    In each case we shall, if possible, have to get all the contributors together at
one time, as we must, if possible, tie the thing together neatly. But I don't
suppose it means more than a couple of hours at each session. I will let you know
exact dates later
    Yours,
    George Orwell

    The sense of excitement in working in a new medium comes over strongly.
The aural possibilities, the choosing of a poem because someone had read it
well or because it toned with music that was to be used, are all things that
Connolly would have responded to immediately. He would have noted too the
contrast between the many weeks needed to get a magazine like *Horizon*
together and Orwell's breezy 'I don't suppose it means more than a couple of
hours at each session'.
    There were difficulties, however. There was an exchange of letters between
Orwell and Stevie Smith referring to arrangements made for a number of
'Voice' that had gone awry. The record bears out Orwell's view of the matter,
and the highly offensive letters from Stevie Smith were entirely
unwarranted.[76] On another occasion, when a monologue by Inez Holden[77]
had been chosen, it was realised that it would have to be adapted, and also
that as her voice was not suitable for broadcasting an actress would have to
be found to read it over the air. Orwell wrote to Vida Hope with some
misgivings. Asking anyone to do something entirely experimental within the

---

[76] The correspondence is reprinted in *George Orwell: a life*, pp.422-3 without mention of its
context.
    [77] Inez Holden (1906-1974), novelist, author *inter alia* of *Sweet Charlatan* (Duckworth 1929) and
Death in High Society and Other Stories (1933), written in Basic English.

BBC was always risky, and there was also the question of rapidly escalating costs when a large number of quotations were to be used. There were problems too, with a war on, in getting everyone together at the microphone on the same day. Henry Treece at one point could not make it, being otherwise employed on 'Course 13, School of Flying Control, Watchfield near Swindon'. Herbert Read was again an obvious choice, but he also lived out in the country, as Orwell realised when he wrote:

31st July 1942

Dear Read,

In furtherance to our conversation, we more or less got started on our radio magazine 'Voice' to-day, and we are very anxious that you should take part. This would mean two sessions, one the sort of final dress rehearsal, and the other the actual recording. I doubt whether it is feasible to telescope them into one, though it might be. If you can't make two visits to London for this, you could just record the two poems I want you to read; but I would like you, if possible, to be there to take part in the discussion. The poems I want you to read are your own poem, 'The Contrary Experience', which should come at the beginning of the programme, and at the end Wordsworth's sonnet 'The world is too much with us'. You could choose another if you like, but I think this will fit in well. Treece unfortunately cannot come, because he has an exam. or something, but his poems are being read by John Atkins,[78] who does them quite well. I will send you a copy of the script as soon as it is more or less in shape. Please let me know about this as soon as possible.

Yours,

George Orwell

Overall the series was a great success, running for six episodes, including one devoted entirely to American poetry at which T.S. Eliot was guest of honour. 'Voice' ended in late autumn 1942, and a further series was planned to start the following spring.

As if to strengthen his feeling that political propaganda was virtually powerless whereas literature could reach the heart of an audience, Orwell began another series called 'Books that have Changed the World'. Narayana Menon was invited to write the first talk on *Gulliver's Travels*. The choice was significant for Orwell since he regarded the book as one which, more than any other, had changed the world for him. Menon had been at Edinburgh University in the earlier part of the war but had recently come to London. He proved most useful to Orwell not only for literary programmes but also for choosing music which the Indian audience would find sympathetic. At one point someone within the BBC queried the necessity of paying someone for this, and Orwell, not for the last time, defended one of his writers (see p. 243f.).

The scientific series continued in parallel with these new literary ventures. A new programme 'A.D.2000' had begun at the end of June with a talk on the

[78] John Atkins (1916-). At this time Atkins was literary editor of *Tribune*, the job which Orwell took over when he left the BBC. T.R. Fyvel recalls vividly a visit with Orwell to *Tribune* in the spring of 1943 and a discussion then of the possibility of Orwell's taking Atkins' place (personal communication).

future of agriculture in India by Sir John Russell, Director of the Rothamsted Experimental Station. Others followed, with C.D. Darlington on 'India in the Steel Age' and Richard Titmuss on 'Four Hundred Million: the Population Problem'. Whether or not the abandonment by Japan of her attacks on Ceylon and the receding threat of an invasion of India itself had given rise to these optimistic glances at the future, they made a good propaganda point. They also show Orwell looking ahead at what the world might be like in the future, as he was to do in *Nineteen Eighty-Four;* one Indian contributor even mentioned the possibility of there being television in India by that time. This series again was a success, and Orwell encountered no trouble of the kind he had had with Bernal. Russell and the others did further talks for him on similar matters.

On the tricky ground, for Orwell, of politics a talk was commissioned from Harold Laski on the future of Parliament.[79] Orwell suggested that it should take the form of a discussion with Lord Winterton, one of the oldest members of Parliament.[80] Setting up the talk must have caused Orwell some amusement, as he knew that Laski, author of a number of books praising the regime in Russia, which Orwell detested, would be sure to attack this bastion of democracy on true Marxist lines. Winterton, for his part, was more than capable of defending himself and the institution of which he had been a staunch supporter for fifty years. Orwell obtained an essay from Laski in the normal way and gave it to Winterton, who wrote a reply. Orwell then composed a discussion for them from the material of these two essays. In sending Laski his script, Orwell made quite sure that Laski understood the position on any changes Laski might want to make:

Professor Harold Laski,   August 31st 1942
The Manor Cottage,
Little Bardfield,
near Braintree, Essex

Dear Professor Laski,

I am enclosing herewith a carbon copy of your discussion with Lord Winterton on 'The Future of Parliament'. Of course, you may want to make verbal alterations, but it would perhaps be better if you would not make any actual structural changes, unless you feel that in any place I have made you say something which does not represent your real opinion. In general, the less

---

[79] H.J. Laski (1893-1950), Professor of Political Science at the London School of Economics and Chairman of the Labour Party, author of *Faith, Reason and Civilisation* (1944) which Orwell described as 'pernicious tripe' (*CE* III, p.169, n.23).

[80] The Rt. Hon. the Earl Winterton P.C. (1883-1962), took his seat in the House of Commons in 1905, retiring in 1951. He was Under-Secretary for India 1922-4 and 1924-9. His account of his years in the House, *Orders of the Day* (1953), does not mention his talks for the BBC, but his description of Brendan Bracken is memorable: (p. 303) '... Mr Brendan Bracken floored each of his parliamentary critics in turn with an uppercut, usually to the delight of the House, whenever the actions of the Ministry of Information were questioned.' For his wife's role in the war see op.cit. in n.50, p.50.

alteration the better, as we shall not have too much time for the censorship, rehearsal and recording.

The recording will take place at 55, Portland Place, at 11.15 a.m. on Thursday, September 3rd. It should be over by 12.30. I shall meet you and Lord Winterton there on Thursday.

Yours sincerely,
George Orwell
Talks Producer
Indian Section

The progress of the war had changed Laski's views on censorship; on an earlier occasion, well remembered within the BBC, he had complained to the Director General when a single word of his script had been altered.[81] Now he was quite happy for Orwell to write an entire talk for him and read it out over the air, knowing that, while the sense might be his, the words were often Orwell's.

Towards the end of the year Orwell took the idea of putting words into people's mouths a stage further. If someone was prepared to write on a political topic to order, and have what they thought generally altered, could this principle not extend to a work of art, to fiction itself? The experiment of creating a fiction factory seemed worth trying, and in the autumn he gathered a group of writers to produce his 'Story by Five Authors'. The first episode he composed himself – almost the only fiction he wrote during the war, and clearly based on his earlier experiences in the Blitz. Elements appear, almost identically, in *Nineteen Eighty-Four*, and the writing of the story may have germinated the final book as we know it. As we shall see, the first sketch of *Nineteen Eighty-Four* was done at the end of 1943; in the story we note the woman who appears suddenly in blue overalls, with a face covered with plaster – echoes of Julia and Winston Smith suddenly caught in a bomb blast.[82]

For a continuation of the story Orwell approached Inez Holden, L.A.G. Strong and Martin Armstrong. The difficult task of ending it, and bringing it somewhere near the point he thought it ought to reach, he gave to E.M. Forster. He wrote Forster a somewhat wry letter, in the knowledge that Forster might well refuse.[83]

The idea of a fiction factory developed in Orwell's mind over the next few years. It is interesting to compare his polite request to Forster with the 'spoof' telephone call described by Orwell from someone in the Ministry of Information asking the BBC for a suitable piece of fiction: 'One can almost hear the tired, cultured voices from the MOI saying: "Hullo! Hullo! Is that you, Tony? Oh Hullo. Look here, I've got another script for you, Tony – 'A ticket to Paradise'. It's bus conductresses this time. They're not coming in. I believe the trousers don't fit or something. Well, anyway, Peter says make it sexy, but kind of clean – *you* know. Nothing extra-marital. We want the stuff

---

[81] A talk of his on Roosevelt had been banned by the censor in its entirety.
[82] *Nineteen Eighty-Four* (ed.cit.), p.267.
[83] See *Letters*, p.222.

in by Tuesday. Fifteen-thousand words. You can choose the Hero. I rather favour the kind of outdoor man that dogs and kiddies all love – *you* know. Or very tall with a sensitive mouth. I don't mind, really. But pile on the sex, Peter says".' Orwell then went on with the observation, harking back to his own 'Story by Five Authors': 'Something resembling this already happens with radio features and documentary films, but hitherto there has not been any very direct connection between fiction and propaganda.'[84] By *Nineteen Eighty-Four* the note of humour had vanished completely.

V

Towards the end of 1942 several things happened that caused Orwell to reassess his position within the BBC. Laurence Brander, the Intelligence Officer for the Eastern Service, had just returned from a six-month tour of India, and Orwell recorded in his diary the depressing results as they related to the Indian Section: 'Briefly – affairs are much worse in India than anyone here is allowed to realise. The situation is in fact retrievable but won't be retrieved because the Government is determined to make no real concessions. Hell will break loose when and if there is a Japanese invasion, and our broadcasts are utterly useless because nobody listens to them. Brander did say, however, that the Indians listen to the BBC news, because they regard it as more truthful than that given out by Tokyo or Berlin. He considers that we should broadcast news and music and nothing else.'[85] A few days later, in another talk with Brander, Orwell happened to mention that it was he who actually wrote the news broadcasts that so impressed the Indians. Brander thought it would be a good idea for Orwell to use his own name (that is his *nom-de-plume*), and sent a memo to the Eastern Services Director, Rushbrook-Williams:

From: Mr Brander, Indian Intelligence Officer, 217 Portland Place
Subject: Saturday Weekly News Letter   8th October 1942
To: Eastern Services Director, Oxford Street
    Copy to Mr Eric Blair   [WAC: R51/257/2]

In conversation with Mr Eric Blair this morning, I discovered that he writes our Saturday Weekly News Letter which is read by some Indian. The audience in India supposes that the reader is the composer, and the present audience is small. As you know, the universal demand amongst our Indian audience is for well-known Englishmen. If, therefore, it could be arranged that this News Letter be no longer anonymous, but the known work of 'George Orwell' instead of largely being ignored as at present, it would be looked forward to with the

[84] 'As I Please', *Tribune*, 25 February 1944. *CE* III, p.120.
[85] Wartime diary, 5 October 1942. *CE* II, p.507.

very greatest interest, as few names stand so high with our Indian audience at present as that of George Orwell.

L. Brander

Rushbrook-Williams in turn raised the matter with Orwell and sent a copy of Orwell's reply to R.A. Rendall, the Assistant Controller Overseas. Orwell's letter raised all the doubts about his double identity that had given him so much trouble in the past:

> With reference to the suggestion that I should write and broadcast the weekly news review in English over my own name, i.e. George Orwell. The four speakers who are at present doing this in rotation have contracts up to 7 November, after which I will be glad to take this on. But there are one or two points that it would be better to define clearly beforehand.
>
> If I broadcast as George Orwell, I am as it were selling my literary reputation, which so far as India is concerned probably arises chiefly from books of anti-imperialist tendency, some of which have been banned in India. If I gave broadcasts which appeared to endorse unreservedly the policy of the British Government I would quite soon be written off as 'one more renegade' and should probably miss my potential public, at any rate among the student population. I am not thinking about my personal reputation, but clearly we should defeat our own object in these broadcasts if I could not preserve my position as an independent and more or less 'agin the government' commentator. I would therefore like to be sure in advance that I can have reasonable freedom of speech. I think this weekly commentary is only likely to be of value if I can make it from an anti-Fascist rather than Imperialist standpoint and avoid mention of subjects on which I could not conscientiously agree with current Government policy.
>
> I do not think this is likely to cause trouble, as the chief difficulty is over Indian internal politics, which we rarely mention in our weekly news commentaries. These commentaries have always followed what is by inclination a 'left' line, and in fact have contained very little that I would not sign with my own name. But I can imagine situations arising in which I should have to say that I could not in honesty do the commentary for that week, and I should like the position to be defined in advance.

This letter is somewhat extraordinary in that several times Orwell talks about writing under his own name when he means the name 'George Orwell'. At this stage, clearly, that was the name he wanted as his own. Rushbrook-Williams, writing to Rendall, had translated this complex letter into a simple query whether it was in order for someone working for the BBC to use a *nom-de-plume*. Rendall replied that there was no objection, but said that the Controller of Overseas Programmes had suggested that the India Office be approached to ensure that there was no objection there. The request for approval received what Orwell would have called a typically 'Indian' reply:

I have consulted Mr Joyce and his colleagues (at the India Office) and they feel it would be useful to take advantage of Orwell's name. In view of the fact that several people whose books have fallen under the displeasure of the Government of India do in effect speak for us, and that their contributions are appreciated, Mr Joyce feels that it would be mistaken to refer the matter specifically to the G. of I. If asked the G. of I. might feel called upon to adopt a critical attitude. If the question is not raised Mr Joyce thinks they are very unlikely to object!
	L.F. Rushbrook-Williams. 29.10.42

This matter seemed to have been resolved without undue conflict, but within a few days Orwell had a very worrying shot fired across his bows that made him think he might well have to leave the BBC. The trouble stemmed, once again, from his political broadcasts. For some months these had been confined to commissioning a series of 'open letters' to various political parties. Anand had written a letter to a Chinese Guerilla; Tambimuttu[86] to 'A Marxist'; and so on. Then, in October, Orwell had set in train a series of lectures called 'The History of Fascism'. The speakers were Indian, and the series had gone forward without difficulty until it came to Anand's contribution on the Spanish Civil War. The BBC censor had been worried by this and had sent it to the Ministry of Information, who banned it entirely. This was the first time Orwell had had direct confrontation of this kind over one of his programmes. He stood by Anand and took the bold step of writing a memo insisting that Anand be paid for the work he had done:

From Eric Blair, Indian Section, 200 Oxford Street
Subject: Contract for talk by Dr Anand – scheduled for December 3rd 1942,
		1115 –1130 GMT, Eastern Service
To: Miss Boughen, Talks Bookings.			10th December 1942
									Confidential

Dr Mulk Raj Anand was commissioned to write a talk on 'The Spanish Civil War' – the fifth talk in the series 'History of Fascism', to be broadcast as above.
	Mr Anand submitted the script, but it was not passed by the censor. I suggest that as Dr Anand had taken a good deal of trouble over his talk, he might be paid a proportion of the fee. You will realise that this subject is a particularly delicate one at the present time, and we decided that rather than alter the whole angle of the talk, it would be better to abandon it altogether. A fill-up talk was therefore used.
	Eric Blair

The day after this cancellation Orwell wrote a letter to George Woodcock,[87] whom he had by this time befriended. For the first time he

---

[86] J.M. Tambimuttu (1915-1983), Ceylonese poet and editor of *Poetry London*. He did a number of broadcasts for Orwell, but he had never been to India and his voice was not easily understood there. No doubt Orwell would have involved him in the Indian Section more but for this.
[87] 2 December 1942. *CE* II, pp.306-7.

suggests that he might not stay long at the BBC, a change of mind which may reflect either disgust at the censor or worry about the significance for his own position as the person who had sponsored the talk. The reality of his concern is shown by his next step, which was to approach Edmund Blunden and ask him to prepare a whole series of six talks:

Edmund Blunden, Esq.,   3rd December 1942
Merton College
Oxford

Dear Mr Blunden,

    I think Brander will have rung you up before this letter reaches you. We would like it very much if you would compere a series of talks for us and deliver one in the series yourself. I should warn you, however, that it is all rather short notice and it is very important to get all the scripts in by the end of this month.

    I will explain the reason. We are proposing to have a series of six talks covering some of the set books in the B.A. course in English literature at Calcutta University. This will be more or less similar to the series you took part in before, but we propose this time to publish the six talks in the form of a pamphlet in Calcutta, so as to appear before the University examinations. This will mean that the scripts will have to be despatched from England early in January at latest, though some of them will not actually go on the air until a few weeks later. The six subjects are:

1. Shakespeare, with special reference to *Julius Caesar*.
2. Milton, with special reference to the shorter poems.
3. Hardy, with special reference to *Far from the Madding Crowd*.
4. Hazlitt - with some remarks about English essays in general.
5. Shaw - with special reference to *Arms and the Man*.
6. The Book of Job.

The speakers I have projected are E.M. Forster, F.L. Lucas, yourself, George Sampson, Bonamy Dobrée and T.S. Eliot, respectively. Of course you could alter this list as much as you wished, but the all important thing is to get things moving quickly. The first talk would be actually delivered on the 25th December (it can be recorded beforehand of course) but I should want to have all six manuscripts in by about that date.

These are 15 minute talks, which means approximately 1500 words.

Can you please let me know, as early as possible, whether you can undertake this.

    Yours sincerely,
    George Orwell
    Talks Producer
    Indian Section

Unusually the arrangement was made through Brander, although Orwell already knew Blunden and had used him in one of the 'Voice' programmes. The full sketch plan of the talks is interesting because it shows how Orwell normally went about planning his series. Two days later he wrote a further lengthy description of how the programme was to be carried out (see p. 233). He also wrote to Herbert Read about another series, postponing it for six weeks to allow Blunden's to go before it. The conclusion to be drawn from these letters is obvious: namely that Orwell was covering the BBC for the next three months' special talks in case he did actually have to leave.

The pressure on Orwell did not cease with the censor's remarks. One of his memoranda of his department's talks[88] provoked without warning a letter from Norman Collins, the Empire Talks Manager, who was highly critical:

From: Empire Talks Manager
Subject: Mr Blair's speakers in the Eastern Service
To: Eastern Services Director   8th December 1942

A copy of Mr Blair's memo of the 7th December (of which you have been sent a copy) has just reached me. I notice one thing in it which suggests that Blair is working rather too independently of the existing organisation.

On Tuesday, the 15th December there is a talk on Plastics by Dr Yarsley: on Monday of this week there was a talk on the same subject by C.F. Merriam. It may well be that Dr Yarsley's talk is better than C.F. Merriam's (or vice-versa), but it certainly seems extravagant from the point of view of the Corporation that we have paid for two talks on the same subject within little more than a week.

I wonder if the situation could be met by someone from Mr Blair's department attending the Daily Talks meeting. I had thought that Mr Weymouth would cover such points, but I gather that now Blair does not refer his arrangements to him.

Similarly, Blair's note of the 5th December regarding the new series of talks to cover the set books in the B.A. course in English Literature at Calcutta University mentions T.S. Eliot and refers to fixing up other speakers. To avoid duplication of approaches made I suggest that Blair should fall in with the usual procedure whereby talks producers refer to my office to know if anyone else is approaching these speakers round about the same time. (I know you will understand that this is simply not red tape, but to prevent one speaker from getting two letters from the Empire Service on the same day.)
Norman Collins

Orwell probably did not know of the existence of this memorandum. Those who were used to reading between the lines could see that the well-known bureaucratic method of dislodging someone who no longer fitted had perhaps begun. In his regular letter published in *Partisan Review* dated 3 January 1943 but probably written shortly before that, Orwell mentions that the atmosphere in Britain was changing: '... but over the whole year ... there has been visible a steady growth of blimpishness and a more conscious elbowing-out of the "reds" who were useful when morale needed pepping up

[88] See below, Appendix B.

but can now be dispensed with.'[89] And this was a fairly close reading of the situation Orwell now found himself drifting into. He could see the other side of things as well, and in the same piece wrote: 'As to the real moral of the last three years – that the right has more guts and ability than the left – no one will face up to it.'

There had been a further development in the Indian Section to enable talks to be brought under more effective control. A committee meeting had been called early in December under the chairmanship of Sir Malcolm Darling to consider the shape and content of a new series that was to be called 'Round Table Discussions'. There was even a formal paper prepared for the committee to work from entitled 'The Future of India'. The minutes of the meeting show that Orwell attended, as did Joyce from the India Office.[90]

There was no scope with this sort of arrangement for experiments such as 'Voice' or for arranging amusing confrontations between people as different as Laski and Lord Winterton. Indeed it began to look as though all Orwell's freedom of movement was about to be circumscribed. But his position within the BBC was still relatively sound. True he was of 'the Left', a *soi-disant* 'red', but he was of that unfashionable type of 'Anti-Stalin' red not unliked within the BBC. He was also known as an intellectual pure and simple with great interest in such abstruse subjects as Basic English, then one of the very fashionable concerns. He had even gone so far as to commission a talk on Basic in his series 'I'd Like it Explained' from Miss Leonora Lockhart.[91] William Empson had been first to arouse interest in the language within the BBC and had commissioned a talk the previous year called 'Wordsworth and Basic'.[92] He and Orwell must have had many discussions on the subject while they were at 200 Oxford Street, although Orwell makes it clear in a letter to the inventor of the language, C.K. Ogden, that he was not himself quite sure of the implications of Basic and the controversies surrounding it:

C.K. Ogden, Esq.,   16th December 1942
3 The Square,
Buxton, Derbyshire

Dear Mr Ogden,
    Many thanks for your letter. We didn't have any response to that talk on

[89] Reprinted in *CE* II, p.318.

[90] A.H. Joyce, Director of Information at the India Office. Before the war Orwell had corresponded with Joyce when Joyce had been asked for a reference for Orwell from a future employer in India. Orwell would have been aware that a similar reference would have been obtained when he joined the BBC. For the pre-war correspondence between them see *George Orwell: a life*, pp.254-5. See also WAC: E2/361/2.

[91] See above, p.8.

[92] In the original manuscript text of *Nineteen Eighty-Four* (Peter Davison (ed.), *George Orwell Nineteen Eighty-Four the Facsimile of the Extant Manuscript* (1984)) when Ampleforth is arrested for Thoughtcrime he imagines his fault to be that he used the word 'God' in a poem by 'Wordsworth' that he was 'rectifying' (p.221); in the published edition of the book (ed. cit., p.358) this has been changed to a poem by 'Kipling'. Whether this change indicates that the first part of *Nineteen Eighty-Four* was first thought of as a *roman-à-clef* or not, it is clear that if 'Wordsworth' had been allowed to stand in the text it could have been taken as a direct reference to Empson.

Basic English given by Miss Lockhart but that doesn't necessarily mean anything because we get very little response indeed to all our broadcasts and I understand that even in India, Indians are not very strong on writing to broadcasters to give criticisms or suggestions.

When we did Miss Lockhart's talk my idea was, if possible, to follow this up sometime later by a series of talks giving lessons in Basic English which could perhaps afterwards be printed in India in pamphlet form. I still have not given up this project but I must tell you that it has come up against a great deal of discouragement and opposition, some of which I understand and some not. You, no doubt, know the inner workings of this controversy better than I do. If, at any time, it seems possible to do something about Basic English on the air again I will of course get in touch with you. I am sorry not to be more helpful at this moment.

Yours sincerely,
George Orwell
Talks Producer
Indian Section

Whatever his reservations about the BBC or the pressures put upon him, Orwell continued working. He had always enjoyed putting out the programmes and commissioning them, and he continued as normal with the additional work of broadcasting the weekly news summary himself. The strain of this new work and of the new organisational pressures must have told on his health. Early in January and later in February he was away for considerable periods. The staff at the BBC may not have realised how ill he was – he always made light of his military exemption. The arrangements he had made with Blunden and Read against the possibility of his leaving meant that he was not missed too much; and he contributed a talk to each of their series. For Blunden he prepared a talk on Bernard Shaw (no. 8 below), for Read one on Jack London (no. 9). The talk on Jack London has some political overtones, but the two talks together form a strong contrast with the off-the-cuff near-revolutionary talks written a year before, such as 'Money and Guns' and 'The Meaning of Sabotage'.

Suspicions about Orwell's purposes grew; a perfectly harmless note about two new appointments in the series 'In Your Kitchen', for which, incidentally, Eileen Blair had made a broadcast before Christmas,[93] brought severe condemnation from Rendall, the Assistant Controller of Overseas Talks, who sent the note to the Eastern Services Director with a series of terse observations:

This is the third of these notes that I have received recently. I don't like the look of them because it suggests that Blair is setting up an independent business as an Eastern Talks Director. I have a high regard for his general abilities and I know that he would not deliberately attempt to do this in a self-advancing or

[93] Eileen Blair did several Kitchen Front talks for the Indian Section, usually with Dr Gangulee, a cousin of Rabindranath Tagore, and others. Unfortunately none of her scripts has been found.

separatist way: and I know that you have been badly affected with illness in your dept. But I must point out (i) that I have more than once asked to be consulted in advance on new series, (ii) that co-ordination and general notification is Collins's job and he really should be informed in advance ... (Note dated 3.2.42).

Orwell responded to these further warnings by sticking to the letter of the official procedure when approaching outside speakers, known as 'Approaching Eminent Speakers':

From: Eric Blair, Indian Section, 200 Oxford St.   24th Feb. 1943
Subject: Approaching Eminent Speakers
To: Mr Norman Collins, Eastern Talks Manager   [WAC: R51/257/2]

In connection with our new literary series ('Great Dramatists') to start in Week 11, on the completion of 'Landmarks in American Literature' we propose approaching Bernard Shaw for a talk on Ibsen. This would be the fourth talk in the series and would therefore be broadcast on Thursday of Week 17. It would be a ten minute talk and would go out on Thursday, April 29th. In the same series we also propose approaching T.S. Eliot and James Stephens. I do not know whether these two will come under the heading of 'eminent speakers'.
    Eric Blair

The irony in the last sentence of this minute stems from the fact that he had already used both T.S. Eliot and James Stephens before. Presumably he was given permission by telephone, for his letter to James Stephens is dated the same day (see p. 242).
    Although another series of 'Voice' was announced in the overseas programme guide *London Calling*, the proposal was scrapped and instead Orwell arranged a talk by Keidrych Rhys on 'Wartime Poetry'.[94] He also started a series of interludes of music and live poetry.
    In March Orwell wrote to Reg Reynolds, an old friend, who had asked if he could do something on the Russian discovery of Alaska (see p. 247). It is obvious from this letter that some running down of the Indian Section was being considered. Clearly the original purpose of the Indian Section to boost morale in India in case of a Japanese invasion was now gone and there was more danger from the Indian Independence Movement. The Indian Section that the MOI had created for themselves at the BBC was very likely to encourage such a movement rather than the other way around. Similar considerations held for the whole of the Eastern Service, as John Morris, a new colleague of Orwell's of a seemingly conventional colonial type, made plain in a memorandum.

[94] See also 'Poetry and the Microphone', *CE* II, pp. 374-82.

From: John Morris   13th March 1943
Subject: Overseas Planning Committee of Ministry of Information.
To: Eastern Services Director   [WAC: E2/403]

The following matters which were discussed at the above meeting, are placed on
record for your consideration.
1. It was decided to enlarge the existing broadcasting and research work of the
    Far Eastern Bureau to such an extent as would eventually make the Far
    Eastern Section of the BBC and A[ll]I[ndia]R[adio] redundant. The
    intention to bring this about was apparent in the discussion with regard to
    transmitters, personnel and policy.
2. The proposed new Service would be nominally under the control of the Far
    Eastern Section of the Ministry of Information. In this connection I would
    like to place on record that during our voyage home from Japan Mr Redman
    frequently stated in the course of conversation that he wished at all costs to
    obtain control of all broadcasting to the Far East.
        In actual fact, however, it would appear that the Far Eastern Bureau would
    itself direct radio policy throughout the Far East, for it is obvious that it would
    not be possible for London to exert more than a general supervision over their
    activities ...
        John Morris

John Morris did not get on well with Orwell and wrote a very one-sided
portrait of him some years later,[95] but on the question of the influence of the
Ministry of Information on the BBC he would have agreed with him
wholeheartedly. There is no doubt that the Ministry of Information,
especially under Brendan Bracken who agreed with Churchill's views on the
Indian question, would have been happy to have got complete control of the
BBC Eastern Service. Morris had the advantage of having attended meetings
at the MOI and could see clearly what for Orwell was an unknown force,
encountered directly only when someone ran foul of the censor.
    Meanwhile Orwell continued to arrange for new programmes for the next
quarter, starting with a scientific series with which he asked Horrabin to help
him:

J.F. Horrabin, Esq.,   7th April 1943
16 Endersleigh Gardens
N.W.4

Dear Horrabin,
    I wonder if you would like to do us another talk, about the same length as
you did before. I should be wanting the script not later than the middle of May.
    We now do series of Talks which are designed to be printed in India in
pamphlet form: in general six talks – 10,000 words make one pamphlet. I am
now sketching out a Scientific Series and the subjects of the six talks are to be:

[95] John Morris, 'That curiously crucified expression', published in *Penguin New Writing* no. 40
(1950) and republished in *Orwell Remembered*, pp.171ff.

Malnutrition, Soil Erosion, Genetics, Malaria, House-flies and Water. This sounds rather heterogeneous, but they all touch on problems important to India. Do you think you could do us a talk on 'Soil Erosion and Soil Deterioration' – its causes and prevention. The main thing that I think wants rubbing in to India is the disastrous effect of cutting down all the trees. There should be good illustrations for this in what has happened round the Mediterranean.

Could you let me know as soon as possible whether you will do this? I will let you know later the exact date of the talk, which will be sometime early in June. If that actual day is inconvenient to you, we can always record beforehand, but I am chiefly concerned to get the scripts in in good time, so that I can send them to India to be printed.

Yours

George Orwell

Talks Producer

Indian Section

Orwell's interest in trees was a clear forerunner of present ecological concerns, at least thirty years before they became a popular rallying cry. He also arranged for a set of talks on modern aircraft from E.C. Bowyer of the Aircraft Manufacturers Association, giving separate programmes to different types of plane – naval aircraft, gliders, transport planes and so on – and explaining their part in the war.[96]

Besides the regular book review by Forster, Orwell had introduced a weekly series commemorating the anniversaries of famous people, places or events which Desmond Hawkins was happy to write and broadcast. He wrote to Hawkins for a contribution to a series called 'Modern English Verse': '... I would like you to deal with ... new departures since the Auden school. There seem to be several trends and I am not sure that I know my way about them, but I have put Dylan Thomas, Rayner Heppenstall and George Barker in brackets because they seem to fall chronologically between this school and the previous one.'

Towards the end of May there were serious developments on the political scene both nationally and internationally. The Comintern, the organisation linking individual Communist parties with Russia, was dissolved and Orwell wrote about the likely effects of this in England. He drew no firm conclusions but pointed to the new Commonwealth[97] party founded by Sir Richard Acland[98] as a possible serious force. In describing Acland, Orwell gave a good insight into the English class system and his understanding of it: 'Although of aristocratic and agricultural background (he is a fifteenth

---

[96] There was a nod here in Cripps's direction – he was now Minister of Aircraft production.

[97] The Commonwealth Party did not respect the inter-party truce and won a number of seats at by-elections. It failed to make any impact with the electorate after the war.

[98] Sir Richard Acland Bt.(1906-), author of *Unser Kampf* and *The Manifesto of the Common Man* (1940). After the war he retired to private life, later making a contribution to the teaching at St Luke's Teacher Training College, Exeter (now part of Exeter University).

baronet) he has the manners and appearance of a civil servant, with a typical upper-class accent. For a popular leader in England it is a serious disability to be a gentleman, which Churchill, for instance, is not. Cripps is a gentleman, but to offset this he has his notorious "austerity", the Gandhi touch, which Acland just misses in spite of his ethical and religious slant. I think this movement should be watched with attention. It might develop into the new socialist party we have all been waiting for, or it might develop into something very sinister: it has some rather doubtful followers already.'[99]

The most real danger seen by Orwell, and by those in power, was of infiltration of the Labour Party and other organisations by members of the Communist Party, even though they were still at one with the Allies in the struggle against Germany and Japan. Censorship became even more rigorous and, almost inevitably, Orwell talked himself into the Ministry of Information's net.

VI

On 4 June 1943 the normal news broadcaster for the Malaysia News Service was unavailable and Orwell was asked to step into the gap, which he happily did, writing a newsletter that no doubt reflected his feelings on the situation in Burma and elsewhere. He probably relied on the censor to weed out his more outrageous statements as usual, but by chance the censor on duty was relatively new and thought that writers of the eminence of 'George Orwell' required no censorship, so that the talk went out as Orwell wrote it. The effect was instantaneous. Complaints were made at the highest level from the War Office and the Ministry of Information to the Director General of the BBC. They were relayed to J.B. Clark, Controller of Overseas Services, who immediately launched an investigation. His subsequent report to the Director General speaks for itself:

From: Controller (Overseas Services)   Private & Confidential
Subject: George Orwell's talk of June 4th
To: Director General   14th June 1943

I must apologise for several serious errors of judgment betrayed by this talk for which I accept responsibility. The broadcast in its final form was, in fact, the result of misunderstandings which will not recur.

(a)   It was the first talk of the kind censored for policy by one of the new senior members of our staff who had, with some justification, not realised properly the extent to which a talk provided for 'personality' reasons in the target area should be brought into line with general policy. I make no excuse for failing to ensure that he was properly briefed, but I am satisfied

[99] *Partisan Review*, May 1943. Reprinted in *CE* II, pp.327-34.

that the situation in this respect is secure for the future.

(b)   The accident would have been less likely to have happened if Tonkin our principal news specialist on the Far East had not been diverted from his specialist duties. This situation is not likely to recur and needless to say no blame whatever attaches to Tonkin in these circumstances.

It may be relevant to recall that these English broadcasts in what is known internally as the 'Malayan Band' were started in simple English by the Chinese who was engaged for the Hokkein broadcasts. It was thought that his English and accent would be suitable for the purpose they were intended to serve, but he proved unequal to the task. They are radiated on a single frequency used on other days of the week at the same time for miscellaneous minority languages. Orwell was allowed to step into the breach because there was strong external evidence that he was well known and trusted in Burma where it was hoped we would influence an important section of the potential audience.

Apart from other considerations which were neglected in this instance, the talks have been rather carefully related to the information available to us about Japanese propaganda in the somewhat prescribed target area.

    J.B. Clark

There were a few changes as a result of this event, although, of course, the absence of a censor was not in any way Orwell's personal responsibility. He was given the new job of broadcasting the Tamil Newsletter, which was repeated the following day as the Indonesia Newsletter; in both cases the broadcast was again announced as the work of Eric Blair, not George Orwell. Also for the first time Orwell is shown as having his own switch censor – a Church of England clergyman.[100]

Z.A. Bokhari, either because he could no longer stand the aimless programmes they had been doing and thought Orwell was the cause, or because he already realised that Orwell would leave, wrote a letter to Orwell with detailed proposals for future broadcasts, similar to the letter he had written to him when he first joined. He sent copies to everyone else in the department.

I think I have hit upon an idea. I will just give you the outlines of it. Please work it out and let us discuss it. I am sick of having unconnected talks; frankly I don't like living from day-to-day. Here is an idea for our new schedule:

'The World We Hope For.'

Politicians, scientists, religious leaders, poets, writers, workers, employers, painters, sculptors, architects, editors and newspaper owners, film and theatre directors, philosophers, radio chiefs, economists, farmers, soldiers, sailors, *ad nauseam*.[101]

---

[100] A switch censor, as the name implies, sat by the microphone and threw a switch to cut the speaker off if he departed from the censored script.

[101] Internal memorandum, June 1943. BBC Written Archives.

There then followed a list of people in all these categories, carefully graded according to their political beliefs, with the hope perhaps, that this would prevent Orwell from falling foul of the censor yet again by choosing someone from the wrong camp.

Orwell's reaction to the changed situation after he had provoked the direct wrath of the hidden forces in the Ministry of Information, perhaps even the anger of Brendan Bracken himself, was, as before, to carry on as normal. He commissioned a series of talks from L.A.G. Strong called 'In England Now', the first dealing with invasion exercises. Bokhari suggested a series reviewing highlights of the week's broadcasts to be called 'Backward Glance', which Orwell agreed to provided Desmond Hawkins agreed to do it.

Orwell then suggested another series to counter it called 'Glimpses of the Future', which featured a talk by C.E.M. Joad on the future of religion, one by C.M. Fletcher on the likely impact of penicillin, and various others of a politically neutral kind. But he also decided, once and for all, to raise the question of freedom of speech over the air. He did this by commissioning a series from Kingsley Martin.

Martin was still Editor of the *New Statesman*, then the principal critic of Government policy from the left, as it had been since the original outburst against the Ministry of Information in 1941 which had helped Orwell to his post at the BBC. When Orwell first started running his own talks he had wanted to use Kingsley Martin but soon discovered that he was on a black list of some sort.[102] In December 1941 Martin had agreed to do a talk for an overseas programme to America called 'Answering You' on the subject of 18B security regulations. His talk had caused such difficulty that a full report had had to be made to the Director General by R.A. Rendall.[103] Rendall made a courageous defence of the BBC's right to use whom it pleased from all shades of political opinion. The MOI and the Home Office disagreed. However right Rendall was in principle, the MOI won the day and Kingsley Martin did no more broadcasting.

In this context Orwell was clearly taking the bull by the horns in asking Kingsley Martin for a series of talks. Martin's first reply mentioned that he had thought he was going to broadcast a good deal after Orwell's appointment but that there appeared to be some prejudice against him.[104] He would not have known, of course, of the storm he had provoked before. With the lapse in time Orwell succeeded in getting agreement for a series of talks for him. The first two went off smoothly; Martin discussed the Labour Party Conference with Princess Indira and then did a programme of his own on exiled governments. J.B. Clark discovered that he was being used and asked for, and received, assurances that he was being properly supervised, in a letter of 23 July from the Eastern Services Director.[105] Seven days later Kingsley

[102] The black list was said not to exist, but Orwell was convinced it did and habitually referred to it even in official forms, requesting, for example, a talk by Sir Richard Acland and openly asking if Acland is 'off the black list' or not.

[103] See below, Appendix C.

[104] Letter in WAC: Contributors File, s.v. Martin. WAC: R51/257/2.

[105] See below, Appendix D.

Martin put out a talk which flouted every possible security rule and can be seen as a direct provocation, most probably with Orwell's agreement. Asked to speak about a particular report on education, he appeared at the microphone with a talk on education in general, slanted to the extreme left; Orwell made formal moves by telephone to get some form of censorship done immediately before broadcasting but failed. The inevitable storm followed. Rushbrook-Williams wrote an extensive letter to Clark explaining what had occurred. An exchange of letters ensued[106] culminating in a last desperate manuscript note from Rushbrook-Williams to Sir Malcolm Darling dated 16 August:

> Would you please keep a fatherly eye on this matter of briefing? We cannot risk any more trouble over Kingsley Martin: and I'd be grateful if you would get Blair's co-operation to ensure that the suggested precautions are in fact observed.[107]

This acute sensitivity extended to anyone who made the slightest variations from Government policy on India. Even the veteran broadcaster Vernon Bartlett, who had been used on countless occasions in all departments of the BBC, found himself in deep water over a talk on India. Harman Grisewood, then Assistant Controller of European Services, wrote to his controller:

> Newsome tells me that there is no prejudice against Bartlett and we expect to use him from time to time on suitable occasions, but he has during the last year become less easy to handle as a speaker and more and more attached to his own personal opinions. He dislikes more and more any alterations to his scripts and his own line on current affairs increasingly seems to differ from our own. As an example, we had difficulties with him over a script on Indian affairs in which he gave vent to views against the Prime Minister's handling of India.[108]

The talk referred to here was one with Princess Indira on 31 July in her regular parliamentary series. Interference of this type constituted a direct attempt to curtail a Member of Parliament's right to free speech. The crime, of which Orwell was also guilty, was that of 'becoming more strongly attached to his own personal opinions', the ultimate sin in a bureaucracy, the penultimate stage before 'thoughtcrime'.

Orwell did not stop using Kingsley Martin. Rather he drove the matter on until there was no real option but resignation, with other factors of course helping towards such a drastic step. Martin's next talk for Orwell was 'Journalism' on 12 August, and then, a final gesture on 30 August, one on 'The Freedom of the Press in Wartime'.[109] By this time Orwell had definitely decided to leave the BBC. He spent August working on what was

---

[106] See below, Appendix D.
[107] MS. note on internal memorandum printed below in *Letters*, p.299.
[108] 4 August 1943. WAC: Contributors File, s.v. Bartlett.
[109] This script is unique among those seen at the BBC Written Archives in having, besides the censor's stamps, the personal approval of two senior staff members, junior only to the Director General.

for him an entirely new type of broadcast, and one quite uncommon in the BBC generally, called 'featurizing' a story for radio. Orwell found these broadcasts a challenge and was pleased with the results he achieved, referring to them years later with some pride. For the first time in the war they gave him the opportunity for purely creative work, even if it was on others' original material. For us today their significance is that they probably gave Orwell the idea of writing a story suitable for broadcasting himself, and that one of the stories he adapted, 'The Fox' by Ignazio Silone (no. 12), directly inspired him to write it: *Animal Farm*.

Orwell adapted three stories in addition to 'The Fox': 'Crainquebille' by Anatole France, which he considered one of the best short stories he had ever read (no. 11); 'A Slip Under the Microscope' by H.G. Wells (no. 13), concerning a poor but honest student's momentary mistake and his guilt about it, which ruin his career – an ironical reference no doubt to Orwell's uncensored talk to Burma; and 'The Emperor's New Clothes' by Hans Andersen (no. 15). All four were produced for Orwell by Douglas Cleverdon. Orwell may have hoped to move to a job in Drama similar to Cleverdon's.[109a] In a letter to Rayner Heppenstall asking him if he would like to do some of these adaptations as well Orwell makes the first reference to his definite decision to leave:[110]

24th August 1943

Dear Rayner,

Thank you for yours. I hope your new post isn't too bloody. I'll try and fit in a talk for you in our next literary lot, but that will be 6 weeks or more from now – schedule is full up till then.

I wonder if you would feel equal to featurizing a story? We do that now about once in three weeks. I featurized the first myself, choosing Anatole France's Crainquebille and Ignazio Silone's The Fox (these are half-hour programmes). I am probably going to hand the job of featurizing future ones over to Lionel Fielden, but he won't necessarily do it every time. The chief difficulty is in picking suitable stories, as they must be (a) approximately right length, (b) have a strong plot, (c) not too many characters and (d) not be too local, as these are for India. Have you any ideas? I could send you a specimen script and no doubt you could improve on my technique of featurization.

Re cynicism, you'd be cynical yourself if you were in this job. However, I am definitely leaving it in about three months. Then by some time in 1944 I might be near-human again and able to write something serious. At present I am just an orange that's been trodden on by a very dirty boot.

Yours,
Eric

The definite decision to leave had already been taken, no doubt at the time of the Kingsley Martin row. Orwell was waiting for the right moment.

The general position in the office was not made any easier by the

---

[109a] Personal communication.

[110] *CE* II, pp.348-9. Rayner Heppenstall (1911-1981) later adapted *Animal Farm* for radio.

publication in *Horizon* of a savage review by Orwell of Lionel Fielden's book about India *Beggar My Neighbour*.[111] Fielden has been mentioned earlier as a friend of Bokhari, who, as controller of broadcasting in India, had recommended him for his post in London. But there was more to the situation than that. Fielden himself had been much favoured in Indian Government circles for the post which eventually went to Sir Malcolm Darling. Indeed he had gone to London on the understanding that the place was his, with an agreed salary of £1,000 a year. Unfortunately, when he arrived it was found that the BBC did not consider him suitable for the job. Despite cajoling from Leo Amery, Harold Nicolson and others, they stuck to their guns, until the Government of India capitulated and offered Sir Malcolm Darling instead. Fielden worked with Darling for a short while, but the position was impossible and he resigned after a few months. His influence on the Indian Section did not disappear, however, as Bokhari was a close personal friend of his, and indeed they shared a flat in Park Lane for the whole of Bokhari's stay in England.

Fielden's book on India was diametrically opposed to what Orwell felt about the country. Orwell did not let his day-to-day contacts with Bokhari stop him from saying what he felt about the book very plainly. But he went further, attacking an 'imaginary Indian' who appears in the book and could very plausibly be identified as Bokhari.[112] If Bokhari ever read the review it would have been difficult for him to continue normal office life. For Orwell's part he had been shocked to discover that Bokhari supported the idea of an independent Pakistan, of which Orwell disapproved. The review actually appeared at the beginning of September, by which time Orwell had gone off for two weeks' annual leave.

When he returned in the third week in September, his mind was made up. His decision was no doubt reinforced by a friendly memo from the intelligence officer Brander, dated 23 September, pointing out that the audience in India was almost as low as had been feared and that Orwell's own rating was well below that of J.B. Priestley and others. He spoke to Rushbrook-Williams on the following day, 24 September, and then wrote confirming his resignation:

Dear Mr Rushbrook-Williams,

In confirmation of what I said to you earlier in private, I want to tender my resignation from the BBC and should be much obliged if you would forward this to the proper quarter.

I believe that in speaking to you I made my reasons clear, but I should like to put them on paper lest there should be any mistake. I am not leaving because of any disagreement with BBC policy and still less on account of any kind of grievance. On the contrary I feel that throughout my association with the BBC I have been treated with the greatest generosity and allowed very great latitude.

[111] *Horizon*, September 1943. *CE* II, pp.349-59.
[112] '... an imaginary Indian who denounces Western civilisation with all the shrillness of a spinster of thirty-nine denouncing the male sex ...' *CE* II, p.350. The book was also dedicated to Bokhari.

On no occasion have I been compelled to say anything on the air that I would not have said as a private individual. And I should like to take this opportunity of thanking you personally for the very understanding and generous attitude you have always shown towards my work.

I am tendering my resignation because for some time past I have been conscious that I was wasting my own time and the public money on doing work that produces no result. I believe that in the present political situation the broadcasting of British propaganda to India is an almost hopeless task. Whether these broadcasts should be continued at all is for others to judge, but I myself prefer not to spend my time on them when I could be occupying myself with journalism which does produce some measurable effect. I feel that by going back to my normal work of writing and journalism I could be more useful than I am at present.

I do not know how much notice of resignation I am supposed to give. *The Observer* have again raised the project of my going to North Africa. This has to be approved by the War Office and may fall through again[113] but I mention it in case I should have to leave at shorter notice than would otherwise be the case. I will in any case see to it that the programmes are arranged for some time ahead.

Yours sincerely,
Eric Blair

The letter has a slightly strange tone when we know the events that went before it. The literal truth of the fact that he had not been made to broadcast anything he did not want to is in contrast with the seemingly equivocal references to the BBC as having given him great latitude. The matter becomes clear when we realise that the difficulties which Orwell and his speakers experienced were caused not by the BBC but by the censors at the quasi-totalitarian Ministry of Information. Six months after he left the BBC his opinion of it had not seriously changed from that expressed in his letter or, indeed, from his opinion of it in 1941. Writing in the weekly column 'As I please' that he did as part-time work for *Tribune*, he said:

> ... I repeat what I said before – that in my experience the BBC is relatively truthful and, above all, has a responsible attitude towards news and does not disseminate lies simply because they are 'newsy'.
>
> Of course, untrue statements are constantly being broadcast and anyone can tell you of instances. But in most cases this is due to genuine error, and the BBC sins more by simply avoiding anything controversial than by direct propaganda. Even in India, where the population are so hostile that they will not listen to British propaganda and will hardly listen to a British entertainment programme, they listen to BBC News because they believe it approximates to the truth.[114]

[113] As Orwell well knew, there was no possibility of any such journey being cleared on medical grounds. Perhaps it was a ploy to enable him to leave immediately rather than work through the two months' notice clearly mentioned in his contract with the BBC; if so it failed.
[114] *Tribune*, 21 April 1944. *CE* III, p.155.

And as he no longer attacks the BBC for the quality of its announcers' voices his feelings for it may even be said to have softened. Certainly there was no feeling here so strong that he would launch a parody of the BBC in the bitter terms used in *Nineteen Eighty-Four*, as has been suggested.[115]

Orwell's opinions of the Indians who broadcast from Berlin also mellowed after the war. 'What right have we to describe the Indians who broadcast on the German Radio as "collaborators"? They were citizens of an occupied country hitting back at the occupying power in the way that seemed to them best.'[116] His personal memories of his days at the BBC were often happy ones. Towards the very end of his life he wrote in his diary about an amusing incident involving Venu Chitale, his Talks Assistant, who had not revealed for some months that a certain Marathi news broadcaster could not actually translate Orwell's news script into his own language and so had got a man who was banned from the BBC to help him. The point that struck Orwell as particularly amusing was the delay of six months before anyone was told about it.[117]

There were also other sides to life in wartime London. Although he avoided the Café Royal whenever possible, Orwell did go to the well-known haunt of veterans of the Spanish Civil War, the Barcelona Restaurant, in Beak Street, Soho. It is still there today, just round the corner from the Café Royal and still selling the paella and Rioja that Orwell liked. Sir Stephen Spender, who had been in Spain, and also signed the War Writers' Manifesto, recalls that it was one of the few places where you could go in wartime London to get good Spanish food and wine.[118] Douglas Cleverdon remembers that, because of the strange hours that Indian programmes went out over the air, it was normal for scripts and talks to be discussed in the evening in one of the hostelries such as 'The George' that the BBC effectively made its own.[119] Tosco Fyvel, who recounts seeing Orwell in pubs in Fitzrovia,[120] also remembers taking him to a café known as 'The Café of Social Significance'. At first Orwell declined to go to a café with such a name or reputation, but he was eventually persuaded. When he got there he discovered to his amusement that it was simply a restaurant in Covent Garden patronised by market porters at all hours of the day and night. The memoirs of literary figures of the time contain many echoes of Orwell and his writings,[121] but very few reveal the use Orwell made of the powers of patronage which he found in his hands at a time when creative work was virtually unobtainable.

---

[115] E.g. by Crick in *Nineteen Eighty-Four* (ed. cit.), p.63.
[116] 'As I Please' *Tribune* 17 January 1947. *CE* IV, p.311.
[117] 12 March 1949. *CE* IV, pp.56-7.
[118] Personal communication.
[119] Personal communication.
[120] *George Orwell: a personal memoir*, p.118.
[121] For an average account of the war period, written without understanding of the role of the BBC, see, for example, Robert Hewison, *Under Siege* (1977).

VII

As soon as Orwell left the BBC he began work on the two books which have given him the reputation he has today. *Nineteen Eighty-Four* was only sketched in outline,[122] but *Animal Farm* was finished in a few months. The direct inspiration given to Orwell by his arrangement of 'The Fox', a political allegory set in a pig farm, is obvious to anyone who gives it even a cursory glance; as if to acknowledge it he includes at the end of the first chapter of *Animal Farm* the incident of a fox getting into a farmyard. Orwell had first got the idea for writing the book before the war, as he tells us in the preface he wrote for the Ukrainian edition of the book: '... the actual details of the story did not come to me for some time until one day (I was then living in a small village) I saw a little boy, perhaps ten years old, driving a huge cart-horse along a narrow path, whipping it whenever it tried to turn. It struck me that if only such animals became aware of their strength we should have no power over them, and that men exploit animals in the same way that the rich exploit the proletariat.'[123] Orwell may well have seen 'The Fox' at the same time, for it appeared first in *New Writing* (autumn 1937) edited by John Lehmann.[124]

Besides the allegory of a pig farm that Orwell found in 'The Fox', he might well have been taken back by the story to his own original idea and his pre-war literary purposes. He says in his essay 'Why I Write': '*Animal Farm* was the first book in which I tried, with full consciousness of what I was doing, to fuse political purpose and artistic purpose into one whole.'[125] We can see now how Orwell got this 'full consciousness'. For two years he had ranged over the whole field of English literature in preparing his broadcasts for the Indian University students, writing many of the talks and rewriting or editing every single one of those that were actually broadcast.[126] The emotional and intellectual energy created by this work needed only the right time and the right stimulus for a book like *Animal Farm* to be created.

In a letter to Rayner Heppenstall, written after the war from Jura, Orwell talked of 'The Fox' and the other stories he featurized: 'If anyone is interested enough to look up these scripts you might tell them that I had to write them in desperate haste, as I was overwhelmed with administrative work and in each case could only give a day to the job.'[127] We can see from

[122] The outline is mentioned here and subsequently because it makes very clear the link with Orwell's BBC days, having been written either while he was working through his last two months at the BBC or a few weeks later. It is published as 'Appendix A' in Crick's edition of *Nineteen Eighty-Four* (op.cit.).

[123] The text quoted here is the one reproduced in *CE*. As explained there, the original English version has not been traced and the version printed is a translation back from the Ukrainian. *CE* III, pp.455-9.

[124] Reprinted in *Penguin New Writing* no. 2 (1941). The translators were Gwenda David and Eric Mosbacher.

[125] *CE* I, p.29.

[126] It is to this work that Orwell refers in his occasional sarcastic references to having written 'shelves full of work' at the BBC, not, surely, his own writings.

[127] Unpublished letter, WAC: Orwell File.

this that the extraordinary pressure that he had been working under in the BBC is a complete explanation of the great speed with which he wrote *Animal Farm*. But the effect of his BBC work goes further than that, for the perfection of shape and form of the story is in complete contrast with anything he wrote before the war and clearly owes a great deal to his newly acquired skills in radio adaptation. It can only have been the smallest step for Orwell to have conceived of the idea of writing a story himself that would be suitable for broadcasting as a radio feature. The adaptation of *Animal Farm* for radio which he broadcast in 1946 is a close reworking of the book. Looking at the original manuscript in the BBC Written Archives, we see that the adaptation is worked on in such a way that the two texts, the published prose text and the radio script, can arguably be considered as equally authentic.[128]

Unfortunately, although *Animal Farm* was clearly a brilliant book – concise, with a clarity of purpose and style totally removed from anything he had done before – Orwell had great difficulty in finding a publisher for it. Now that he was no longer in the BBC, Orwell began to see the censorship he had been subjected to by the Ministry of Information in a clearer light. Whereas at the BBC he would have been told nothing of the details of the censorship,[129] the publishers who sent *Animal Farm* along to the MOI were quite happy to hint at what had been done. The facts were enough to provoke a typical piece of Orwellian journalism in *Tribune*:

> Nowadays this kind of veiled censorship even extends to books. The MOI does not, of course, dictate a party line or issue an *index expurgatorius*. It merely 'advises'. Publishers take manuscripts to the MOI and the MOI 'suggests' that this or that is undesirable or premature, or 'would serve no good purpose'. And although there is no definite prohibition, no clear statement that this or that must not be printed, official policy is never flouted.[130]

And the wartime Official Secrets Act operated even here; for, as Orwell well knew, there was indeed definite prohibition, and there was a party line even if it was the Communist Party line impartially administered, no doubt, on behalf of Britain's Russian allies by people from the Anglo-Soviet Division of the Ministry of Information.

That Orwell could not get the book published meant that his strategy of leaving the BBC for part-time journalism while continuing his more serious work had failed. With *Animal Farm* unsold he could not let his journalism go. *Nineteen Eighty-Four* – or *The Last Man in Europe*, to give it Orwell's working title at the time – remained in outline only until after the war ended. Instead

---

[128] As a single example on a complex question, Mollie has asked if there will be sugar after the Rebellion. Napoleon replies, in Orwell's radio version: 'No, certainly not. When we are in control of this farm, it will have to be self-supporting. We have no means of making sugar here' (original MS. p.10). The published version, in answer to the same question, is: 'No, we have no means of making sugar on this farm.' This is clearly an edited version of the radio script, not the other way round. Possibly the radio script was written by Orwell from an earlier version of the MS. of *Animal Farm*.

[129] See the censorship details of a talk by Barbara Ward in Appendix A.

[130] 'As I please', *Tribune*, 7 July 1944. *CE* III, p.212.

Orwell produced more of the journalism which some critics have seen as his best work but which, in reality, sapped his talents and energy at least as much as working for the BBC and without giving him any fresh experience of the world in exchange.

All the main features in the original sketch for *Nineteen Eighty-Four* survived in the finished work.[131] The first essential element mentioned was 'Newspeak'. The contemporary origins of this horrific totalitarian language have been examined by a number of writers, notably by Howard Fink,[132] but the political context has not been explored. It is clear that 'Newspeak' originated in the artificial language 'Basic English' invented before the war by C.K. Ogden, and it has long been known that Orwell was himself an enthusiast for the language. As we have noticed, he commissioned a talk on Basic for the Indian Section and often discussed it with others. The aspects of the idea which appealed to him were its inherent simplification of what people said (it used only 850 words), the potential abolition of jargon, and the suggestion that anything without real meaning was immediately seen to be nonsense when translated into Basic.[133]

There was some general interest in Basic at the BBC, but it took an unexpected turn in September 1943. Winston Churchill, in a speech at Harvard University, announced his conversion to the language. He had become convinced of the need for a *lingua franca* for use by the Allies; Stalin himself had shown interest in Basic English. Churchill went on: 'Such plans [for the introduction of Basic] offer far better prizes than taking away other people's provinces or lands, or grinding them down in exploitation. The empires of the future are the Empires of the Mind.'

When he returned from America, Churchill pursued the matter further by setting up a War Cabinet Committee to report on the swiftest and surest means of getting Basic accepted. The BBC was to play a central role from the first, and a request was sent to the Director General, which was duly forwarded to R.A. Rendall, for an immediate evaluation of the project. For the next few months Basic enthusiasts were in great demand within the BBC as Rendall and his team developed their paper for the War Cabinet. As one of three men in the BBC who had commissioned talks on Basic – Orwell, Empson and Guy Burgess – Orwell might well have been stopped in a corridor, like Winston Smith in *Nineteen Eighty-Four*, and praised for his interest in the language.

The Cabinet Committee report recommended that a substantial part of the BBC's daily output overseas should be translated into Basic English and that there should also be regular lessons given in the language.[134] Had Orwell stayed with the Indian Section, he would have found himself in the position that Empson soon got into. Winston Smith, or Orwell, might have enjoyed

[131] See 'Appendix A: The 1943 Outline of *Nineteen Eighty-Four*' in *Nineteen Eighty-Four* (ed. cit), pp.137-8.

[132] Howard Fink, 'Newspeak: the epitome of parody techniques in *Nineteen Eighty-Four*', *The Critical Survey*, vol. 5, no. 2, Summer 1971, pp.155-63.

[133] An echo perhaps from Orwell's schooldays, for the same thing used to be said of Latin.

[134] War Cabinet paper WP(43)551. Recommendation 15(F).

the task of translating news reports into 'Newspeak';[135] for Empson, the task was soon found to be impossibly difficult. In September 1944 he finally wrote a desperate appeal to Ogden for help:

C.K. Ogden, Esq.,   27th September 1944
3 The Square,
Buxton, Derbyshire

Dear Mr Ogden,

I have been asked by my BBC superiors to translate a weekly bulletin into Basic for West Africa, and I understand that they have talked over details with you. There were plans to do one for the East but they have been dropped at present. Of course I would be very pleased to make myself useful; the only reservation I made when asked to do it was that I could only do it for the African Service on the understanding that I was filling in a gap till they trained someone to do it regularly. My job is on the Eastern Service, and anyway you can't run a regular service with only one man to do it; he is bound to get ill or go on holiday or something. The idea that the BBC is training someone to write in Basic for the African programme was agreed to over the telephone, and I hope you will represent from your side that that ought to be done if the scheme is to be put on a steady footing.

I am still not clear what is to be put out, but I understand that it is most likely to be a news summary of the week. A weekly summary doesn't raise the problems about hot News in Basic, but I have been told to ask you *whether there is an agreed list of extra news words*, and anyway I want to ask that myself. The problem about news, especially from the BBC, which has a policy of being cautious about news, is that half the time you are quoting a communiqué or some text which is the only authority for the story, and that source is itself couched in vague or puzzling terms. If you can't get a form of words that gives the impression intended in Chinese (or whatever language you are broadcasting in) you had better leave it out anyway, but still you want to give as interesting a news bulletin as you can.

I always leave out the pet names of specialised aircraft in bulletins for translation into Chinese, and think the same could be done in Basic (*heavy and light bomber and fighter* are the only essentials) but suppose the Beaufighter has shot up a barge. What shooting up may be I have never got explained to me, but it would be positively false to say that the fighter had damaged a ship. What would a 'pincer movement' become in Basic? Are there stock agreed Basic forms for a jeep, bulldozer, duck, and so on?

Of course I would want to put up the problems to you later on as they arose, but a key factor, if the BBC use of Basic develops, is going to be convincing the news boys that the system is adequate to handle their professional crotchets, and these usually turn on leaving the cover off the necessary amount of vagueness while giving the interest of as much definiteness as can be risked.

This, I think, is the only important point, but I would like to give you a puzzle.

[135] *Nineteen Eighty-Four* (ed. cit.), p.189.

What would Basic have made of Churchill's statement that Italy would be left to stew in her own juice? We gave it as such to the Chinese translators. Two Chinese broadcasts took it on the same day, one billed for Chungking, the other for Japanese-occupied areas. The man billed for Chungking made it 'The Italians will be given time for natural political development among themselves in their present painful circumstances', and the man billed for Japanese-occupied areas made it: 'The Italians will be given opportunities later, but at present they will not be prevented from suffering for their crimes.' This may or may not have shown a spontaneous tact in translators, but might be a bit puzzling for any listener who heard both broadcasts. A survey of how the BBC translated that announcement to all its languages would, I think, be of linguistic interest. Of course, it would be absurd for me to ask you 'How would Basic do it?' The serious question is: 'How would the man putting it into Basic choose to do it?' He would be sure to argue that there wasn't any other way of putting it into Basic except the one that expressed his own opinions. However, that problem isn't the main one here.

I hope you are flourishing,

Yours very sincerely,

W. Empson

Orwell would have followed this stage of Basic/Newspeak's progress with laughter, especially as the reference in this letter to the dropping of the Eastern Service's plans referred to his no longer being there. But there was a more serious side to the problem which slowly grew in Orwell's mind until the full-fledged parody in *Nineteen Eighty-Four* was created. The advantage of having very few words also meant, as Empson found, that someone had to do the translations and that that person had to make fundamental decisions on the real meaning of what was being said. The Ministry of Information was to be responsible for propagating Basic, and someone was sure to put into practice literally Churchill's suggestion that the battles of the future were to be battles for the Empires of the Mind. The censor would find unlimited opportunities for his work in an entirely new dimension.

The War Cabinet Committee on Basic included Brendan Bracken, and the report was quite clear that the MOI was to have the fullest control over all aspects of the dissemination of the new language. To Orwell the idea that the same bureaucrats who had censored his broadcasts and prevented *Animal Farm* from being published should be entrusted with the job of translating, say, Wordsworth, into Basic English would have been material for a Swiftian satire indeed. There is no mention of 'Big Brother' in the first sketch of *Nineteen Eighty-Four*, but no satire of the Ministry of Information would have been complete without a portrait of the figure at its head known universally in the corridors of the Ministry as 'B.B.'. The telegraphic address for the Ministry of Information was MINIFORM; Newspeak for the Ministry of Truth in *Nineteen Eighty-Four* is MINITRUE. The building occupied by the MOI during the war was, as we have seen, London University's Senate House in Malet Street. This was the highest building in London during the war, and for some years after. It towered above surrounding London in a way which we today, surrounded by skyscrapers, can hardly imagine. From the roof of Orwell's block of flats in St John's Wood, Langford Court, Senate House is clearly visible, with the trees of Regent's Park before it, just as the Ministry of Truth could be seen by Winston Smith from his window in Victory Mansions.[136] There are many other parallels which become apparent when it is borne clearly in mind that the satire is directed not against the BBC, which Orwell defended, but against the Ministry of Information which had control of the BBC through its censorship departments. Elements of *Nineteen Eighty-Four* are taken from his general experience in wartime London, including such things as the canteen at 200 Oxford Street, but they are not what is being satirised.

It has been suggested that 'Room 101' was Orwell's room at the BBC, or a studio he used, or a number of other possible locations. So far as is known none of these suggestions is correct. Neither Orwell's room at Portland Place nor the room he later had at 200 Oxford Street, nor any other room he was likely to use, had that number. Perhaps Brendan Bracken's room at Senate House was the first room on the first floor, Room 101.

Another central theme mentioned in the first outline of *Nineteen Eighty-Four* is 'World Geography'. Until now critics have looked exclusively to literary sources for Orwell's idea of three great superpowers, usually referring to his interest in Burnham's work.[137] We have seen now that Orwell's interest in world geography developed through his relationship at the BBC with J.F. Horrabin, and that Horrabin's views were continually before Orwell during the crucial period before he came to write the first outline of *Nineteen Eighty-Four*. It was Horrabin who actually suggested the title for the series, 'The War of the Three Oceans'. Orwell's weekly news broadcasts follow the situation in India and the far East in precise geographical terms, rather than according to the simpler, more grand-scale, ideas of Burnham. When Orwell examines the evolution of the three superstates in *Nineteen Eighty-Four* he describes how two of them were formed immediately, Eurasia and Oceania. 'The third, Eastasia, only emerged as a distinct unit after another decade of confused fighting.'[138] It is obvious now that Orwell thought that the 'wars on the Malabar Front' and the 'fighting in south India' described in *Nineteen Eighty-Four* were real possibilities, as they had been during his two years at the BBC before he conceived the book. Although India has been spared that kind of war, others have not; *Nineteen Eighty-Four* anticipated the conflicts of Korea and Vietnam. Wars in the area covered by 'Eastasia' still continue, with the doubtful future of Hong Kong as a symbol of the complex reality there which Orwell, with Horrabin's help, saw as underlying its existence.

The list of themes in the 1943 outline of *Nineteen Eighty-Four* ends with the 'Two Minute Hate'. In the First World War the press is always considered to have stirred up irrational fears and hatreds much more than in the Second World War, but there were examples of intense feeling in the BBC's broadcasts, even in Orwell's Indian Section. J.B. Priestley did a programme

---

[136] Ibid., pp.158-9.
[137] See above, n.42.
[138] *Nineteen Eighty-Four* (ed. cit.), p.316.

called 'Hate' and, perhaps more important, Mulk Raj Anand did an adaptation for Orwell of Sholokhov's short story 'The Science of Hatred'. This had first appeared in an English translation in *Soviet War News*, which was published in London from an office in Trafalgar Square, and Anand adapted it successfully for a broadcast in two parts that went out in the autumn of 1942. Anand remembers also a story from the early years of the war, well known to Orwell, about the setting up of a 'Hate School' by a mutual friend of theirs under Churchill's auspices. The difference between this 'Hate' – the 'Hate' in *Nineteen Eighty-Four* – and the hatred in the First World War is the difference between a world that knew totalitarianism and an earlier world that did not. Orwell belonged to that earlier world, and it was the fear and hatred essential to the modern totalitarian states that Orwell saw, in 1943, as England's worst danger. As a writer he saw the steady growth of similar patterns of thought in the wartime world around him more clearly than others. At times he felt he was the only man who saw it. In the 1943 outline of *Nineteen Eighty-Four* there is a chapter heading: 'Loneliness of the writer. His feeling of being *the last man.*'

This feeling would nowadays suggest paranoia; the idea in *Nineteen Eighty-Four* that every member of the party is being spied upon, that every word and movement in every room is being monitored, would seem to be the creation of a mind under that type of pressure. But the pattern of this sort of fear can readily be found in Orwell's BBC experience. When recording studios were not as self-evidently studios as they are today but more like ordinary rooms, there was always a danger of speakers uttering in front of an open microphone without thinking even with a light on to remind them that the equipment was live. The most experienced broadcaster could make a personal remark to a colleague in an unguarded moment, and Orwell was just the kind of man to take that sort of worry home with him from the studio, even at an unconscious level.[139] Extension of this situation to a world where microphones could be concealed and even the new televisions could receive as well as transmit, so obvious to us now in these days of bugging and Watergate tapes, would have been a genuine fear for Orwell, not 'paranoia'.

In the manuscript of *Nineteen Eighty-Four* the origin of Ingsoc is described as being the amalgamation of the Socialist and the Communist movements.[140] That such a union should take place was a worry that had been with Orwell since the abolition of the Comintern. Both *Animal Farm* and *Nineteen Eighty-Four* are warning against this totalitarian danger, the first as a fairy story, the second with 'fantasmagoric effect'[141] as a novel set in the future. In *Animal Farm*, set in the country around the village of Willington where Orwell lived before the war, the story is seen as directly aimed at what had happened in Soviet Russia, but the language used by Squealer and the other pigs is also exactly the language of the demagogues of the British Communist Party at the time. It survived well after Orwell's death in that stock figure of fun, the

[139] For an account of just this point see Arthur Calder-Marshall, *The Changing Scene* (1936), p.88 and ch.5, 'Broadcasting'.
[140] *Facsimile* (ed. cit., n.92 above), p.211.
[141] Orwell's words: *Nineteen Eighty-Four* (ed. cit.), p.138.

militant Union leader pleading with his 'comrades' – a bitter parody to be sure, but one that Orwell must have feared acutely after his experience with the Communist Party in Spain. The idea of that sort of language being used in the farms and villages of the countryside he loved must have haunted Orwell, as well as striking him as inexpressibly alien to the ordinary Englishman.

Nineteen Eighty-Four was aimed at a more sophisticated target, the middle-class fellow-travellers and covert Communists who inhabited the wartime ministries and enjoyed the foretaste of absolute power they got there. The Labour Government after the war could make no impact on the squalor and poverty of wartime life; if anything, people thought things were worse after the war ended. What it did was to create large numbers of new ministries on the model of the ministries which had sprung up during the war, like the MOI, the neo-totalitarian model for the 'Ministry of Truth'. It seems now that many of the fears Orwell expressed in *Nineteen Eighty-Four* – and he always said it was a warning of what *could* happen – were ill founded. Thus his fears for the fate of the 'proles', as he called working-men, were certainly wrong.[142] But perhaps those fears of a totalitarian state run by ministries of the sort he saw blossoming around him were not so far off the mark. We can see the elements of truth in what he foresaw even though the Communist Party itself never got anywhere near the power he thought it would have. Orwell said after the publication of *Nineteen Eighty-Four* that he was not attacking socialism or the British Labour Party, and indeed he was not. He was giving a warning about deep-rooted fears for the very nature of English life, fears which stemmed largely from his wartime experience at the hands of the MOI. Perhaps his fears were closer to home than he knew. If he had wanted a person to act as a model for O'Brien in *Nineteen Eighty-Four*, a man who would betray him and anyone else for the Party, what better choice could he have made than his fellow-Etonian and fellow-veteran of Osterley Park, his former colleague and friend at the BBC, Guy Burgess?

VII

The essays which follow are those that Orwell wrote as his own contribution to the programmes he produced. They form only a small part of the output that he was actually responsible for. Some idea has been given of the scope of the talks he commissioned: in the case of dialogues and discussions such as that between Lord Winterton and Harold Laski, Orwell also wrote the entire text from their drafts; and even these were only a portion of the overall Indian Section programmes. There were also numerous broadcasts by Indian soldiers to their relatives at home, performances of popular and classical music, comedy shows and other general variety programmes, all of which Orwell could find himself involved in either administratively or through writing linking introductions and announcements – essential but soul-destroying work.

[142] Far from being ignored by the state they are numbered and controlled as much as any Party Member in *Nineteen Eighty-Four*.

Despite the prominence of radio at the time, few people knew what a talks producer was or what he did. The magazine editors such as Kingsley Martin and Cyril Connolly, the editors of famous papers such as Michael Foot at the *Evening Standard*, the great publishers of the day, have all of them left their mark on the cultural history of the time. Their opposite numbers in radio remain to this day largely unknown or, like Orwell, famous for other reasons. This ignorance has no doubt contributed to the extraordinary neglect by scholars of this important period of Orwell's life.

The work published here, for the first time, ranges from his earlier political talks such as 'Money and Guns', through his experimental programmes 'Voice' and 'Story by Five Authors' to his talks on famous authors and plays, ending with his adaptations of stories by Silone and others. Orwell's dialogue with Jonathan Swift was written for another producer, but the choice of Swift was Orwell's and emphasises once again the profound importance he attached to Swift's work. ('I believe *Gulliver's Travels* has meant more to me than any other book ever written.')[143] The texts are printed as Orwell wrote them. Alterations were frequently made by the censor, or by the studio staff to ensure exact running times of the programmes. Since it is rarely possible to distinguish one from the other, I have not thought it necessary to draw attention to them, or to provide any alternative readings written by third parties, even though these may have been the final versions as broadcast. Additions or corrections made by Orwell in his own hand to a typed script have however been incorporated.

The letters which end the text are a substantial selection from the large number written by Orwell over two years at the BBC, printed from the carbon copies. In most cases Orwell has signed the carbon in ink as well as the top copy. As a result of wartime conditions, not all of these letters may have reached their destination. Dr Mulk Raj Anand, reading copies of the letters to him, found several that he had not seen before. They had failed to reach him because of the Blitz, and he remarked on the extraordinary experience of reading a letter to him from Orwell for the first time some forty years after it had been written.[144]

The correspondence between Orwell and E.M. Forster is printed in full as perhaps the most complete correspondence Orwell had with any of the contributors extending over the full period of his work with the BBC.

[143] Below, p.112.
[144] Personal communication.

Part One

1

Money and Guns, by George Orwell

20th January 1942

Very often as you walk down the London streets you see side by side on a newspaper poster the news of a great battle in Russia or the Far East, and the news of a football match or a boxing contest. And maybe on a wall nearby you will see side by side a Government advertisement urging young women to join the A[uxiliary]T[erritorial]S[ervice] and another advertisement, generally rather grimy and tattered looking, urging the public to buy beer or whisky. And perhaps that makes you stop and ask yourself – how can a people fighting for its life find time for football matches? Isn't there something contradictory in urging people to give up their lives to their country's service, and at the same time urging them to spend their money on luxuries? But this raises the question of recreation in wartime, which is not quite so simple as it looks.

A people at war – and that seems, as a rule, a people that is working harder and under more trying conditions than usual – cannot get on without rest and amusement. Probably these things are more necessary in wartime than at ordinary times. And yet when you are fighting you cannot afford to waste precious material on luxury goods, because this is primarily a war of machines, and every scrap of metal used up in making gramophones, or every pound of silk used up in making stockings, means less metal for guns and aeroplanes, or less silk for parachutes and barrage balloons. We laughed at Marshal Goering when he said, some years before the war, that Germany had to choose between guns and butter, but he was only wrong in the sense that there was no need for Germany to prepare aggression against her neighbours and thus plunge the whole world into war. Once war has started, every nation has to choose between guns and butter. It is merely a question of proportion. How many guns do you need to defeat the enemy? And how much butter do you need to keep your home population healthy and contented?

Granted that everyone is sufficiently fed and rested, the main problem of war is to divert expenditure from consumption goods to armaments. The working population, including the armed forces when they are on leave or off duty, still need their amusements, but as far as possible they must make do with amusements that do not use up much material or labour time. Also, since England is an island and shipping is very precious, they must make do as far as possible with amusements that do not waste imported materials.

71

Beyond a certain point you cannot lower the spending capacity of the population. As a result of taxation very large incomes have almost ceased to exist, and wages have not kept up with prices, but the spending power of the mass of the people has perhaps actually increased, because there is no longer any unemployment. Boys and girls of eighteen are now earning the wages of adults, and when they have paid for their board and lodging they still have something over every week. The question is, how are they to spend it without diverting much-needed labour to the manufacture of luxury goods? In answer to this question one can see how the war is altering the habits and even the tastes of the British people.

To make a rough division: the luxuries which have to be discarded in wartime are the more elaborate kinds of food and drink, fashionable clothes, cosmetics and scents – all of which either demand a great deal of labour or use up rare imported materials – personal service, and unnecessary journeys, which use up such precious imported things as rubber and petrol. The amusements which can be encouraged, on the other hand, are games, sports, music, the radio, dancing, literature and the arts generally. Most of these are things in which you create your amusement for yourself, rather than paying other people to create it for you. If you have two hours to spare, and if you spend it in walking, swimming, skating, or playing football, according to the time of year, you have not used up any material or made any call on the nation's labour power. On the other hand, if you use those two hours in sitting in front of the fire and eating chocolates, you are using up coal which has to be dug out of the ground and carried to you by road, and sugar and cocoa beans which have to be transported half across the world. In the case of a good many unnecessary luxuries, the government diverts expenditure in the right direction by simply cutting off supplies. For nearly two years no one in Britain has seen a banana, for example, sugar is not too plentiful, oranges are seen only from time to time, matches are cut down to the point at which no one ever wastes a match, travelling is much restricted, clothes are rationed fairly strictly.

At the same time, people who are working all day cannot altogether create their amusements for themselves. It is desirable, therefore, that they should concentrate on the kind of recreation that can be enjoyed communally without much wastage of labour. That brings me back to the thing I mentioned a few minutes ago – the newspaper report of a football match side by side with the report of a battle. Is it not all wrong that ten thousand citizens of a nation at war should spend two hours in watching a football match? Not really, for the only labour they are monopolising is the labour of the twenty-two players. If it is an amateur football match, and it usually is nowadays – a match between the Army and the R.A.F for instance – these players are not even being paid. And if it is a local match, the ten thousand spectators have not even wasted any coal or petrol in getting there. They have merely had two hours' recreation, which they are probably in need of, almost without any expenditure of labour or material.

You can see from this the way in which the mere necessity of war is bringing about in the English people a more creative attitude towards their amusements. Something symptomatic of this happened during the big air raids. The people who were penned up in the Tube shelters for hours together had nothing to do, and there were no ready-made amusements available. They had to amuse themselves, so they improvised amateur concerts, which were sometimes surprisingly good and successful. But what is perhaps more significant than this is the greatly increased interest in literature that has appeared during the last two years. There has been an enormous increase in reading, partly owing to the great numbers of men who are in the army in lonely camps, where they have little or nothing to do in their spare time. Reading is one of the cheapest and least wasteful recreations in existence. An edition of tens of thousands of copies of a book does not use up as much paper or labour as a single day's issue of one newspaper, and each copy of the book may pass through hundreds of hands before it goes back to the pulping mill. But just because the habit of reading has vastly increased, and people cannot read without educating themselves in the process, the average intellectual level of the books published has markedly risen. Great literature, no doubt, is not being produced, but the average book which the ordinary man reads is a better book than it would have been three years ago. One phenomenon of the war has been the enormous sale of Penguin Books, Pelican Books and other cheap editions, most of which would have been regarded by the general public as impossibly highbrow a few years back. And this in turn reacts on the newspapers, making them more serious and less sensational than they were before. It probably reacts also on the radio, and will react in time on the cinema.

Parallel with this is the revival of amateur sport and amateur theatricals in the armed forces, and of recreations, such as gardening, which are not only not wasteful, but actually productive. Though England is not primarily an agricultural country, the English people are fond of gardening, and since the war the government has done everything to encourage this. Allotments are available almost everywhere, even in the big towns, and thousands of men who might otherwise have spent their evenings playing darts in the pub now spend them in growing vegetables for their families. Similarly, women who in peacetime might have been sitting in the cinematograph, are now sitting at home knitting socks and helmets for Russian soldiers.

Before the war there was every incentive for the general public to be wasteful, at least so far as their means allowed. Everyone was trying to sell something to everyone else, and the successful man, it was imagined, was the man who sold the most goods and got the most money in return. We have learned now, however, that money is valueless in itself, and only goods count. In learning it we have had to simplify our lives and fall back more and more on the resources of our own minds instead of on synthetic pleasures manufactured for us in Hollywood or by the makers of silk stockings, alcohol and chocolates. And under the pressure of that necessity we are rediscovering the simple pleasures – reading, walking, gardening, swimming, dancing, singing – which we had half forgotten in the wasteful years before the war.

2

British Rations and the Submarine War
by George Orwell

22nd January 1942

Probably you have read in the newspaper or heard on the radio the news that food rations in Britain have been reduced. Everyone was expecting this. The rations of certain foods had been raised in November in order to cover the worst period of the winter, but the public were warned that they would be cut down again when war broke out in the Pacific because of the increased need for shipping. The fat ration has been cut down from 10 ounces to 8 ounces a week, and the sugar ration from 12 ounces to 8 ounces. Other foodstuffs are not affected, though naturally there is a shortage in winter of certain unrationed foodstuffs, such as fish and fruit.

There is a great deal of evidence that food rationing has not so far done any harm to public health in Britain – rather the contrary, if anything. English people before the war usually ate too much sugar and drank too much tea, and were too inclined to look on meat as their staple food. The war has brought home to a lot of people the value of vegetables, especially raw vegetables. There have been no epidemics of any importance in Britain since the war – not even in the worst period of the air raids, when something of the kind might have been expected – and the figures for all infectious diseases are fewer now than they were at this time last year. But to get a true idea of the significance of food rationing in Britain, one has got to make two comparisons. One is with the corresponding rations in Germany, and the other is with the conditions that existed in England in the war of 1914-1918.

If you go through the published lists of British and German rations, you will notice that the only foodstuff in which the German ration is even claimed as being higher is fat. According to the official figures, the German citizen gets a weekly ration of 9 ounces of fat, whereas the British citizen now gets only 8 ounces. But this is misleading, because every British citizen also gets a ration of 4 ounces of bacon; any bacon the German gets is included in his fat ration. In every other rationed foodstuff the British and German allowances are either equal, or the British allowance is higher. Moreover, many substances are rationed in Germany which can be freely bought in any quantity in England. Bread is one example, cocoa is another, and coffee is another. Certain things, tea for example, are literally unobtainable in Germany. An even more important fact is that in Britain you do not have to surrender any of your food coupons if you eat a meal away from home, in a

74

restaurant or a factory canteen, for example. The rationing applies only to foodstuffs which are bought raw and taken home. In Germany this is not the case. And since owing to the conditions of war, in which nearly everyone goes out to work, more and more people eat at least one meal a day away from home, this distinction is a very important one.

To see the significance of this, one has got to remember that the Germans are masters of Europe from Norway to the Black Sea. All the food that Europe can supply is at their disposal, and we can be quite sure that they are not sacrificing their own population for the sake of the other Europeans. Indeed, they hardly even pretend to be doing so. It is openly admitted that everywhere in continental Europe food conditions are worse than in Germany, and in some countries, such as Greece, they amount almost to famine. The Germans are looting all Europe to feed themselves, and in spite of that they get less to eat, and less varied food, than we get in Britain.

And now one sees the significance of that other comparison I made – the comparison with conditions in this country in 1914-18. Of course, I was not in England then and I am not pretending to speak out of my own experience. But all English people over 35, or even over 30, have vivid memories of that other war, and I have discussed it with very many people. Without exception they say that food conditions then, at any rate in the second half of 1917 and in 1918, were far worse than they are now. Indeed, people who were children during the other war have told me that their chief memory of the war is a memory of being hungry.

The chief difference, and the reason why we are better off now than people were then, is that the danger of food shortage was foreseen. When the war of 1914 started no one realised that the German submarine warfare would be as successful as it turned out to be, and the food shortage became severe quite suddenly. All of a sudden, it was discovered that there were only a few weeks' food in stock – and you must remember that England is a very small island which probably could not feed itself entirely, even if every inch of it were under cultivation. No arrangements for rationing had been made beforehand, and methods of storing food were nowhere near so efficient as they are now. Nor had the science of food values been studied at that time, as it has during the past twenty years. And meanwhile there was a period about the end of 1917 when the German submarines were sinking twenty or thirty British ships every week. As a result, butter almost ceased to exist in England for about a year, sugar and jam were rarities, and the bread, which in any case was not plentiful, was a dirty grey colour, having been adulterated with potato flour. Meat had to be rationed much more strictly than it is now, for even if you had a meal in a restaurant or a canteen you still had to give up meat coupons. Also, food was not distributed so skilfully as it is now, and one result was enormous queues of women outside the food shops, who sometimes had to wait there for hours before being served. My English friends have often told me that those long queues are one of their principal war memories. I cannot say that you never see food queues now, but at any rate you don't see them very frequently.

This time much has been changed because the Government took the necessary step of rationing essential foodstuffs from the start, and because the submarine menace has been much more effectively dealt with. To realise the difference one has got to remember that in the last war the British navy had the French, Italian and Japanese navies to help it, and towards the end the American as well, whereas during more than a year of this war it had to operate alone, with the Italians as well as the Germans against it. There is no doubt that from the beginning the Germans placed great hopes on the chance of starving Britain into surrender. If you listen in to the German wireless you will hear every week enormous figures of the tonnage of British shipping supposed to have been sunk by German submarines. Some people, who have taken the trouble to keep a note of these figures from the beginning, have found that the Germans claim by now to have sunk far more shipping than Britain ever possessed. Even if the German submarines could not cause actual starvation in Britain, they might hope to sink so many ships that the import of war materials would have to stop, and all the available shipping would have to concentrate on carrying food. But nothing of the kind has happened. The flow of goods across the Atlantic – tanks and fighter planes, as well as wheat and beef – has never slackened, and during the last year the number of British ships sunk every month has decreased enormously. And this is in spite of the fact that German submarines can now operate from ports all the way from Norway to Spain, and not only from German and Belgian ports, as in the last war. The methods of detecting and destroying submarines have vastly improved, and with every German submarine that goes to the bottom, Germany's difficulty of finding trained men for this dangerous work becomes harder. In addition, part of Britain's food problem is being solved by the expansion of British agriculture. Two million extra acres were ploughed up during 1940, and another large area was ploughed up during 1941. The more food Britain can grow for herself, the less shipping she need use to import it. The extra labour for the land is being supplied partly by women volunteers, and partly by Italian prisoners. You can see from all this why our food situation in Britain – though I don't want to pretend to you that it is perfect – is far better than what English people had to put up with during the last war, and far better than it is in Germany, even though Germany is systematically robbing all Europe in order to feed herself.

3

The Meaning of Sabotage
by George Orwell

29th January 1942

Some time back I gave a talk on the scorched earth policy which plays such an important part in this war, and the subject of sabotage arises naturally out of this. Sabotage is the tactic of a conquered people, just as scorched earth is the tactic of an army in retreat. But one understands better how it works if one knows something about its origins.

Everyone has heard the word sabotage. It is one of those words that find their way into all languages, but not all of the people who use it know where it comes from. It is really a French word. In parts of Northern France and Flanders the people, at any rate the peasants and working people, wear heavy wooden shoes which are called sabots. Once, many years ago, some working men who had a grievance against their employer threw their sabots into a piece of machinery while it was running, and thus damaged it. This action was nicknamed sabotage, and from then onwards the word came to be used for any action deliberately intended to interfere with industry or destroy valuable property.

The Nazis are now ruling over the greater part of Europe, and one can hardly open a newspaper without reading that in France, or Belgium or Yugoslavia, or wherever it may be, several more people have been shot for committing sabotage. Now, one did not read these reports, or at any rate one did not read them in such numbers, at the beginning of the German occupation. They are a growth of the last year, and they have increased in number since Hitler attacked Soviet Russia. The increase of sabotage, and, still more, the seriousness with which the Germans regard it, tell one something about the nature of Nazi rule.

If you listen to German or Japanese propaganda you notice that a great deal of it is taken up with the demand for living space, or 'lebensraum' as the Germans call it. The argument is always the same. Germany and Japan are crowded overpopulated countries, and they want empty territories which their populations can colonise. These empty territories in the case of Germany are western Russia and the Ukraine, and in the case of Japan they are Manchuria and Australia. If you disregard the propaganda put out by the Fascists, however, and study what they have actually done, you find it is quite a different story. It seems that what the Fascist nations actually want is not empty spaces, but territories already thickly populated. The Japanese did

77

indeed seize part of Manchuria in 1931, but they have not made serious attempts to colonise it, and soon afterwards they followed this aggression up by attacking and overrunning the most thickly populated parts of China. At this moment, again, they are attacking and trying to overrun the very thickly populated islands of the Dutch East Indies. The Germans, similarly, have overrun and are holding in subjection the most thickly populated and highly industrialised parts of Europe.

In the sense in which the early settlers colonised America and Australia, it would be quite impossible for the Germans to colonise Belgium and Holland, or for the Japanese to colonise the valley of the Yang-tse-Kiang. There are far too many people there already. But of course, the Fascists have no wish to colonise in that sense. The cry for living-room is only a bluff. What they want is not land but slaves. They want control of large subject-populations whom they can force to work for them at very low wages. The German picture of Europe is of two million people all working from morning to night and turning over the products of their work to Germany, and getting in return just as much as will keep them from dying of starvation. The Japanese picture of Asia is similar. To some extent the German aims have already been achieved. But it is just here that the importance of sabotage comes in.

When those Belgian workmen flung their wooden sabots into the machinery, they showed their understanding of something that is not always recognised – the immense power and importance of the ordinary working man. The whole of society rests finally on the manual worker, who always has it in his power to throw it out of gear. It is no use for the Germans to hold the European peoples in subjection unless they can trust them to work. Only a few days of unchecked sabotage, and the whole German war machine would be at a standstill. A few blows from a sledge hammer in the right place, can stop a power station working. One tug at the wrong signal lever can wreck a train. Quite a small charge of explosive can sink a ship. One box of matches, or one match, can destroy hundreds of tons of cattle fodder. Now, there is no doubt that acts of this kind are being carried out all over Europe, and in greater and greater numbers. The constant executions for sabotage, which the Germans themselves announce, show this clearly. All over Europe, from Norway to Greece, there are brave men who have grasped the nature of the German rule and are willing to risk their lives to overthrow it. To some extent this has been going on ever since Hitler came to power. During the Spanish civil war, for instance, it sometimes happened that a shell landed in the Republican lines and failed to explode, and when it was opened, sand or sawdust was found inside it instead of the explosive charge. Some worker in the German or Italian arms factories had risked his life so that at least one shell should not kill his comrades.

But you cannot expect whole populations to risk their lives in this way, especially when they are being watched by the most efficient secret police in the world. The whole European working class, especially in the key industries, lives constantly under the eye of the Gestapo. Here, however, there comes in something which it is almost impossible for the Germans to prevent, and that is what is called passive sabotage. Even if you cannot or dare not wreck the machine, you can at least slow it down and prevent it from working smoothly. This is done by working as slowly and inefficiently as possible, by deliberately wasting time, by shamming illness, and by being as wasteful as possible with material. It is very difficult even for the Gestapo to fix responsibility for this kind of thing, and the effect is a constant friction which holds up the output of materials of war.

This brings out an essential fact: that anyone who consumes more material than he produces is in effect sabotaging the war machine. The worker who deliberately dawdles over his work is not only wasting his own time but other people's as well. For he has got to be watched and driven, which means that other potential workers have to be taken away from productive employment. One of the chief features, one might say the distinctive feature, of Fascist rule, is the enormous number of police that it employs. All over Europe, in Germany and in the occupied countries, there are huge armies of police, SS-men, ordinary uniformed police, plain-clothes police and spies and provocateurs of all kinds. They are extremely efficient, and so long as Germany is not defeated in the field they can probably prevent any open revolt, but they represent an enormous diversion of labour, and their mere existence shows the nature of the Germans' difficulties. At this moment, for instance, the Germans profess to be leading a European crusade against Soviet Russia. Yet they dare not raise large armies from the conquered European countries, because they could never trust them not to go over to the enemy. The entire number of the so-called allies of Germany now fighting in Russia is pitifully small. In the same way, they cannot really turn over the big business of armaments production to European countries outside Germany, because they are aware that the danger of sabotage exists everywhere. And even the danger can achieve a great deal. Every time a piece of machinery is wrecked or an ammunition dump mysteriously catches fire, precautions have to be redoubled lest the same thing should happen elsewhere. More investigations, more police, more spies are needed, and more people have to be diverted from productive work. If the Germans could really bring about the object they set themselves at the beginning – two hundred and fifty million Europeans, all united and working at full speed – it might perhaps be possible for them to outbuild Great Britain, the United States and Soviet Russia in munitions of war. But they cannot do so, because they cannot trust the conquered peoples and the danger of sabotage confronts them at every turn. When Hitler finally falls, the European workers who idled, shammed sickness, wasted material and damaged machinery in the factories, will have played an important part in his destruction.

4
Voice

A poetry magazine in six parts
edited by George Orwell

VOICE – No. 1

11th August 1942

ORWELL: This is the worst possible moment to be starting a magazine. While we sit here talking in a more or less highbrow manner – talking about art and literature and whatnot – tens of thousands of tanks are racing across the steppes of the Don and battleships upside down are searching for one another in the wastes of the Pacific. I suppose during every second that we sit here at least one human being will be dying a violent death. It may seem a little dilettante to be starting a magazine concerned primarily with poetry at a moment when, quite literally, the fate of the world is being decided by bombs and bullets. However, our magazine – 'Voice' we are calling it – isn't quite an ordinary magazine. To begin with it doesn't use up any paper or the labour of any printers or booksellers. All it needs is a little electrical power and half a dozen voices. It doesn't have to be delivered at your door, and you don't have to pay for it. It can't be described as a wasteful form of entertainment. Moreover there are some of us who feel that it is exactly at times like the present that literature ought not to be forgotten. As a matter of fact this business of pumping words into the ether, its potentialities and the actual uses it is put to, has its solemn side. According to some authorities wireless waves, or some wireless waves, don't merely circle our planet, but travel on endlessly through space at the speed of light, in which case what we are saying this afternoon should be audible in the great nebula in Orion nearly a million years hence. If there are intelligent beings there, as there well may be, though Sir James Jeans doesn't think it likely, it won't hurt them to pick up a few specimens of twentieth-century verse along with the swing music and the latest wad of lies from Berlin. But I'm not apologising for our magazine, merely introducing it. I ask you to note therefore that it will appear once monthly on a Tuesday, that it will contain prose but will make a speciality of contemporary poetry, and that it will make particular efforts to publish the work of the younger poets who have been handicapped by the paper shortage and whose work isn't so well known as it ought to be.

'Voice' has now been in existence nearly three minutes. I hope it already has a few readers, or I should say listeners. I hope as you sit there you are imagining the magazine in front of you. It's only a small volume, about twenty pages. One advantage of a magazine of this kind is that you can choose your own cover design. I should favour something in light blue or a nice light grey, but you can take your choice. Now turn to the first page. It's good quality paper, you notice, pre-war paper – you don't see paper like that in other magazines nowadays – and nice wide margins. Fortunately we have no advertisements, so on Page 1 is the Table of Contents. Here is the table of contents:

Page 2.   This editorial that you are listening to.
Page 4.   A poem by Herbert Read, 'The Contrary Experience', read by himself.
Page 6.   'Poor Relation', a monologue by Inez Holden, recited by Vida Hope.
Page 10.   A poem by Dylan Thomas, 'In Memory of Ann Jones', read by William Empson.
Page 11.   A short commentary on Dylan Thomas by several voices.
Page 12.   Three poems by Henry Treece, read by John Atkins.
Page 15.   Open Forum, a discussion of Henry Treece's poems by George Orwell, John Atkins, Mulk Raj Anand, William Empson, and others.
Page 16.   A sonnet by William Wordsworth, read by Herbert Read.

Also on Page 1, underneath the Table of Contents, are the Notes on Contributors. It is usual to put this at the end of a magazine, but we choose to put it at the beginning. It tells you about this month's contributors in the order in which they appear. Herbert Read hardly needs introducing to listeners in India, but he is the poet and critic, author of *In Retreat*, and *English Prose Style*. Inez Holden is a novelist, best known as the author of *Night Shift*. Vida Hope is the well-known character actress who has appeared at the Unity Theatre and had some brilliant successes in some of Herbert Farjeon's revues. Dylan Thomas, author of *The Map of Love, Portrait of the Author as a Young Dog* and other books, is probably the best known of the younger English poets. At this moment he is at work making documentary films. William Empson, also a poet, is author of *Seven Types of Ambiguity*. Henry Treece is one of the leading representatives of the Apocalyptic School, the most recent movement in English poetry, indeed the only new movement that can be said to have appeared since the war. He is serving in the RAF, which is why he is not here today, but his poems are being read by his personal friend John Atkins, who is on the staff of the *Tribune*, the Socialist weekly paper. George Orwell – who is apeaking to you now – is the novelist and journalist, best known as the author of *The Road to Wigan Pier*. Mulk Raj Anand is an Indian novelist, who writes in English. His most recent book is *The Sword and the Sickle*, just published, but he is also the author of *Untouchable, Two Leaves and a Bud*, and various others. He too ought not to need much introduction to the listeners on this service.

That brings us to the end of Page 3. Now please turn to Page 4. Here is

Herbert Read, reading his poem 'The Contrary Experience':

Herbert Read reads

Now please turn to Page 6. This is called 'Poor Relation'. It's a monologue by Inez Holden, recited by Vida Hope:

Vida Hope recites

Now please turn to Page 10. This is a poem by Dylan Thomas. It's called 'In Memory of Ann Jones':

William Empson reads

ORWELL: Has anybody any opinions on that? I suppose the obvious criticism is that it doesn't mean anything. But I also doubt whether it's meant to. After all, a bird's song doesn't mean anything except that the bird is happy.

EMPSON: Lazy people, when they are confronted with good poetry like Dylan Thomas's, which they can see is good, or have been told is good, but which they won't work at, are always saying it is Just Noise, or Purely Musical. This is nonsense, and it's very unfair to Dylan Thomas. That poem is full of exact meanings, and the sound would have no effect if it wasn't. I don't know any poet more packed with meaning than Dylan Thomas, and the use of the technique with sound is wholly to bring out and clarify the meaning.

ANAND: But it's also true that his poetry has become a good deal less obscure in an ordinary prose sense lately. This poem, for instance, is much more intelligible than most of his later work. Listen:

> Her fist of a face died clenched on a round pain;
> And sculptured Ann is seventy years of stone.

That has a meaning that you can grasp at first hearing, hasn't it?

ORWELL: Yes, I admit you grasp at a glance that this is a poem about an old woman, but just listen again to the last five lines:

> These cloud-sopped, marble hands, this monumental
> Argument of the hewn voice, gesture and psalm
> Storm me forever over her grave until
> The stuffed lung of the fox twitch and cry Love
> And the strutting fern lay seed on the black sill.

The last two lines in particular defy interpretation and even the syntax is a bit funny. But as sound, that seems to me very fine.

EMPSON: I think he takes for granted that she had a fern in a pot and a stuffed fox in her cottage parlour. The comparisons of woods and seas and so on are of course meant to tell you about the breadth of her own nature and its strength and kindness. It may be obscure, but it is obviously not meaningless.

ATKINS: There is one poet today who uses a lot of Dylan Thomas's methods, and has been influenced by him to a great extent, but consciously controls his material more than Dylan – I mean Henry Treece.

ORWELL: All right – will you read us something by Treece?

ATKINS: I'd like to read three of his poems. The first is called 'Walking at Night' ...

John Atkins reads

ORWELL: My criticism of the first of these three poems you read – 'Walking at Night' – is that there are too many adjectives in it, and what adjectives! 'Gentle' night, 'dainty' herbs, 'exquisite' thyme – it's almost like something out of Georgian poetry in 1913. I thought that when I first read the poem, but when I heard you read it aloud just now, another analogy struck me. It reminded me of bits out of *A Midsummer Night's Dream* – you know, that stuff about 'When you and I upon faint primrose beds were wont to lie'. It's too sugary altogether.

ATKINS: That's only a criticism of the first poem, isn't it? You don't mean it to apply to the other two?

ORWELL: No. The second poem is in quite a different category. It's more like a ballad.

EMPSON: Actually it's a savage attack on militaristic sentiment.

ORWELL: Possibly, but as I was saying, I should say the last one, 'In the Third Year of War', could be compared with the first, and it doesn't have the same faults. I'm only suggesting that by this very undisciplined manner of writing, you get a very uneven effect, sometimes to the point of absurdity.

EMPSON: Merely in passing, I should like to say that the first poem is very much better than the third.

HOLDEN: I rather like that eneven effect. Even the first poem isn't what you call sugary all the way through. 'The brush of blood paints not a ruined world' isn't a Georgian line. It's quite a different kind of imagery – a sort of surrealism.

ANAND: I should be inclined to say that the word which most exactly describes these poems is 'romantic'.

ATKINS: Yes, the poets of the Apocalyptic school – and I should say most of the younger poets writing now – definitely label themselves romantic. They are in revolt against the classical attitude. They are even more in revolt against the school which went immediately before them – the Auden-MacNeice school, which is classical by implication. It isn't the classical form they object to so much as the content and purpose of the Auden-MacNeice school. According to MacNeice's book on modern poetry, the emphasis of all his school is on 'information and statement'. In other words, they are didactic poets. At the back of their own minds is the idea of the poet as a citizen or even a member of a political party. That means discipline from the outside, which is the essence of classicism.

HOLDEN: The question is, what do you mean by classical and romantic?

EMPSON: These distinctions seem to me all nonsense. Treece is a perfectly good poet, and that means he is using the whole instrument, mind and passions and senses. These poems are no more all Romance than Dylan Thomas's poems are all Noise. Whether Treece has been irritated by a prose book by MacNeice is quite another thing; if he was, I daresay he was quite right. But his writing has plenty of intellectual toughness under it to carry it. And it's absurd for anybody to think that they're somehow pressing him by saying that he hasn't.

ANAND: Well, no one said so.

ATKINS: I don't suggest that Treece or anyone like that is less intellectual, which was what you seem to imply, but that they are less influenced by certain departments of the modern world, the political department – and are more open to other influences, such as nature – in fact, a definite return to the Georgian attitude. Their criticism of Auden and Co. would be that they are working only on one cylinder.

ORWELL: I think this is quite largely a sterile quarrel between generations. I think your choice of what is called classical and romantic is quite largely made for you by the time you live in. In a time like ours, you can't really remain unaffected by politics, and if there is a difference in this particular matter between the Auden school and the Treece school, I should say it was simply a difference between two kinds of politics.

ANAND: I should say that periods of classicism have alternated with periods of romanticism, and the distinction has lasted so long that there must be something in it.

ORWELL: Well, just for a change, let's go back to a period when the distinction between classical and romantic was probably clearer than it is now. Read, what about reading one of Wordsworth's sonnets. Read the one about 'the world is too much with us'. It won't spoil by repetition ...

Herbert Read reads

VOICE – No. 2

8th September 1942

ORWELL: This is the second number of 'Voice'. Here we all are in the editorial office as usual, putting the magazine together. 'Voice' is always chiefly concerned with poetry, especially modern poetry, and this time we are having a number specially devoted to war poetry. The trouble is that – according to some people at any rate – there isn't any war poetry this time. There was even an article about it in the *Times Literary Supplement* a little while back, headed 'Where are the War Poets?' Is that true, Empson, in your opinion? Are there no war poets this time?

EMPSON: Of course it isn't true. There's a whole string of war poets –

Henry Treece, J.F. Hendry, F.H. Scarfe, Keidrych Rhys, G.S. Fraser, Roy Fuller, Alan Rook, and I don't know how many more. A quite sizeable anthology of war poetry has just come out – edited by an Indian, by the way, J.M. Tambimuttu. I suppose what the *Times Literary Supplement* meant was that there are no Rupert Brookes this time. But neither were there last time after 1915.

ORWELL: Of course one might claim that any poem written in wartime is a war poem. But even if one doesn't ignore the war there is a difference between accepting war and rejecting it. I should say the poems being written now are mostly anti-war, are they not?

ANAND: There is very little that is jingoistic being written, and certainly we don't want anything jingoistic in 'Voice'. But I can think of poems written recently which do accept the war, though not quite in the same way as Rupert Brooke.

ORWELL: For example?

ANAND: Well, for example, Auden's poem, 'September 1941'.

ORWELL: Oh, yes, that's a very good one. I was forgetting that. That'll do to start the magazine with. Here it is, then. 'September 1941' by W.H. Auden. This is Herbert Read reading it:

Herbert Read reads

WOODCOCK: It sounds rather disillusioned. I should describe it as the poem of someone who had had his most intense war experience before the major war started and had grown rather sceptical of the whole value of war as a political instrument.

ANAND: But Auden is still a political poet. That poem has what you could describe as a direct political purpose.

EMPSON: I think the younger poets who are writing now are really unpolitical. They merely feel that the only way to deal with the war is to start from their personal situation in it. I've got a poem here which illustrates what I mean. It's called 'A Letter to Anne Ridler', by G.S. Fraser – who's fighting in Egypt, I believe.

ORWELL: Would you like to read it? That'll do for the second poem in the magazine.

EMPSON: All right. But it's too long. I'll start at the middle and go straight through to the end.

ORWELL: All right, go ahead. 'A Letter to Anne Ridler', by G.S. Fraser.

William Empson reads

ANAND: We ought to have something about the last war as well, oughtn't we?

[?]: And isn't it time we had a piece of prose? We can't fill a whole number of a magazine up with verse.

WOODCOCK: I think on the whole the best stuff written about the last war was in prose. But it was very passive, at least the later and better stuff was.

The great feature of the last war was its appalling slaughter, and, so far as the people mixed up in it could see, its meaninglessness. This time it isn't quite the same. It's difficult to think of any book about the last war which is still worth reading and which expresses any positive attitude.

ANAND: What about T.E. Lawrence's *Revolt in the Desert?*

EMPSON: Ah, that was a different war. Lawrence was engaged in a minor campaign, and it was fought for limited objects which the people fighting in it could understand. Besides, it was in the open, not in trenches. It wasn't machine warfare, and the individual counted for something.

ANAND: There is a very good description of Lawrence and his Arabs blowing up a Turkish troop train. Look, here it is. Lawrence and his party are lying beside the railway track, waiting to press the electric button which explodes the mine they have buried between the sleepers, and the train is approaching round the bend.

Extract from 'Revolt in the Desert'

EMPSON: That describes something which happened according to plan. I think it would be difficult to find its equivalent in war poetry. The characteristic poems of the last war were satire, and political pamphleteering at that. Sassoon's poems, for instance, were effective at the time but they don't wear well.

ANAND: But there was also Wilfred Owen. You remember the poem about 'What passing bells for those who die like cattle'?

ORWELL: It's a pity he isn't here to read it. He was killed. But we've got Edmund Blunden here today. He edited Owen's poems, by the way. How about getting him to read one or two of his poems?

ANAND: Ah yes, that will give just the right contrast between the last war and this one.

ORWELL: There is a very good one called 'Rural Economy'. I suppose Mr Blunden wrote it about 1917 – didn't you?

BLUNDEN: ...

ORWELL: Anyway, here it is. 'Rural Economy' – and this is Edmund Blunden reading it.

Edmund Blunden reads

ORWELL: That is a poem that goes into a certain amount of detail. Here's another that gives a more general statement. It's called 'Report on Experience'.

Edmund Blunden reads

ORWELL: I don't know if anybody has noticed one thing. We haven't yet had a poem *in favour* of war.

[?]: Is anyone in favour of war?

ANAND: Not as an end in itself. But there is such a thing as recognising that war may be necessary, just as a surgical operation may be necessary. Even an operation which may leave you mutilated for life.

EMPSON: Although there aren't any heroes in this war, I maintain that the attitude implied in the poem of Fraser's which I read is actually more heroic than the Rupert Brooke attitude. I think the key phrase is 'this just and necessary servitude'. It *is* just and necessary, and it *is* servitude. You see he's willing to do more than get himself killed. He's willing to cripple his own personality for the sake of a cause he believes in.

ORWELL: But there can be an actual enthusiasm for war when it's for some cause such as national liberation. I mean one can feel the war is not merely a disagreeable necessity, but that it is spiritually better than peace – the kind of peace you have in Vichy France, for instance.

ANAND: What about an example?

ORWELL: How about 'The Isles of Greece'?

ANAND: Of course! That comes very near home nowadays.

ORWELL: Here it is, then. 'The Isles of Greece', by Lord Byron.

Godfrey Kenton reads

VOICE – No. 3

6th October 1942

ORWELL: Good evening everybody. Much the same people are sitting around the table as last time, but we have two new contributors this month. One is Stephen Spender, whose poems are known to you, no doubt, and the other is Stevie Smith, author of *A Good Time Was Had By All* and other books.

We have found that this magazine goes better when all the contributions in it revolve round some central theme. Last month you may remember that we had a number devoted to war poetry, and war literature generally. This month we have decided to have a number devoted to childhood – not, of course, literature written *for* children, but *about* childhood. The trouble is that the volume of child literature is so enormous that one hardly knows where to start. Once again I think we shall have to narrow the field by only discussing childhood in two or three of its aspects. What is the outstanding characteristic of childhood, I wonder?

ANAND: Innocence, I suppose.

SMITH: We might start with something by Wordsworth. I suppose it's old fashioned to say so, but I'm very fond of 'Intimations of Immortality in Early Childhood'.

ORWELL: That's too long. What about starting with Blake's poem 'Holy Thursday'. That gives you the feeling of the innocence of children – not, perhaps, what they really possess, but what an adult sees in them when he looks at them from the outside. Here it is, 'Holy Thursday'. This is Herbert Read reading it.

Herbert Read reads

ORWELL: It's very nice, but Blake is looking at the child from the outside. He is seeing the child as a picture, representing innocence. There are many of his poems that succeed in doing that, but I don't remember one that tells you what the child itself actually feels.

ANAND: Has any writer succeeded in doing that?

READ: Yes, I think Blake himself does, because his own mind is childlike.

SPENDER: There's also cruelty in children. Nobody perhaps succeeds in conveying the actual feelings of the child, but there is a vast literature dealing with the adult's memories of childhood, and doing it accurately enough to raise the same feelings in a reader. Any programme dealing with childhood which left out the nostalgic element would be incomplete, I think.

[?] The trouble is there's so much to choose from. In a way all books of childhood reminiscence are alike. The incidents may be different but the essential atmosphere is the same.

ORWELL: It is the atmosphere of childhood. We must have at least one extract of that type. Read, will you read us a bit out of your autobiography, *The Innocent Eye*?

READ: All right.

ANAND: Might we have one of Tagore's poems on childhood first. For instance the one called 'First Jasmines'.

ORWELL: And there is a poem of D.H. Lawrence which I have in mind – 'The Piano' it's called. As those are both short poems, I suggest we do it like this. We'll read them straight through without any comment in between, and then the extract from Read's book to follow. Well, here they are. First of all Rabindranath Tagore's poem 'First Jasmines', read by Mulk Raj Anand, then D.H. Lawrence's 'The Piano', read by William Empson, and then an extract from *The Innocent Eye*, read by Herbert Read himself. Here they are, then:

Readings by Anand, Empson and Read

ORWELL: So far we've taken a rather romantic view of childhood. We've dealt with the innocence of childhood and the nostalgic feelings of the grown-up who looks back and remembers the time when he was a child. But childhood also has its pathetic side, and also its nightmare side. A child lives a lot of its time in a very terrifying world. And even seen from the outside a child is a very pathetic thing.

EMPSON: Once again there's an enormous literature in the pathos and helplessness of children. But if you want something that gives that effect in a few lines, there is a poem by W.H. Davies called 'The Two Children'.

ORWELL: I think that would go rather well with a short poem by Stevie Smith. Read, perhaps you would read that.

READ: And what about something from Dickens, for instance *David Copperfield*. Dickens knew that children in spite of all their innocence can suffer torments even when they are not physically maltreated.

ORWELL: Well, I suggest doing it the same way as we did before. First of all Stevie Smith's poem, read by Herbert Read. Then W.H. Davies's poem 'The Two Children', read by William Empson. And then an extract from *David Copperfield*, which I'll read myself. Here they are:

Readings by Read, Empson and Orwell

EMPSON: The extract from *David Copperfield* is very good, but it is about a very peculiar way of treating children, not about normal child life. Conditions have changed now.

ORWELL: Yes, I suppose so. The essential thing in that passage is education as an instrument of torture. It probably isn't quite the same nowadays.

ANAND: I doubt that very much, children still run away from school, don't they?

ORWELL: At any rate there isn't the Victorian theory that you have to 'break the child's spirit', as they used to call it.

READ: No, but there are more subtle ways of ill-treating children. In Victorian times, they at least had the advantage of being neglected.

ANAND: And there are still slums and malnutrition, not to mention bombs. Perhaps one can only say that the child's outlook is somewhat more hopeful nowadays.

ORWELL: I think that gives us the note to end on. I should like to end with Stephen Spender's poem 'An Elementary School Class in a Slum'. It tells the truth about actual conditions, and yet it's hopeful. Here it is. 'An Elementary School Class in a Slum', read by Stephen Spender himself:

Stephen Spender reads

VOICE – No. 4

3rd November 1942

ORWELL: Good evening everybody. This month we have decided that 'Voice' shall be devoted to American poetry and American literature generally. It's a big subject and we can only hope to cover it in an impressionistic way of picking out a characteristic fragment here and there. Thinking it over we came to the conclusion that the best way is to start at the end and work backwards. I mean, to start off with contemporary American writers and end up with the pioneering period. We shan't have time to go further back than that. Now, I wonder who is the most representative modern American writer?

ANAND: T.S. Eliot.

ORWELL: We'll have something of Eliot, of course, but I think we ought to start off with someone a bit more American. Eliot's an American by origin, but he's a British subject and rather Europeanised. Who else is there?

READ: Archibald McLeish, or Marianne Moore, or Hemingway, or John Steinbeck.

EMPSON: I think McLeish is the most representative. For instance there's that poem about the immigrant labourers who built the trans-American railway. It's called 'The Burying Ground by the Ties', I think.

ORWELL: All right, we'll start with that one. Here it is. 'The Burying Ground by the Ties', by Archibald McLeish. This is William Empson reading it.

William Empson reads

ORWELL: That speaks for the immigrants and for the American labourers generally. It's a pity we haven't time for a short story by Steinbeck or one of the I.W.W. [International Workers of the World] songs of the last war, or something from James Farrell. But now we've got to represent expatriate America. That's where Eliot comes in. I still think his earlier poems are his best.

ANAND: And surely the best of the early poems is 'The Love Song of J. Alfred Prufrock'?

ORWELL: All right, we'll have that one. Here it is. 'The Love Song of J. Alfred Prufrock'. This is Herbert Read reading it.

Herbert Read reads

ORWELL: Again, we ought to have a bit of prose from Henry James to balance that. But we haven't time. Before we go on to nineteenth-century writers we must have something to represent the Negro writers.

MARSON: Well, there are James Weldon Johnson, Countee Cullen, Paul Laurence Dunbar ...

ORWELL: But we'd like you to read something of your own. We're lucky in having a Negro writer with us in the studio today, Una Marson her name is. What do you think you could read us?

MARSON: Well, I've one here called 'The Banjo Boy'. That might do. It's only short, though.

ORWELL: All right, go ahead. Here it is. 'The Banjo Boy'. This is Una Marson, the West Indian writer, reading it.

Una Marson reads

ORWELL: Now we must start on the nineteenth-century writers. We'll have something from Walt Whitman presently. I think it's time now we had a bit of prose.

EMPSON: Well, there's Poe and Hawthorne and Emerson. But if we're sticking to the pioneering period and leaving the New England writers out, the best of all is Mark Twain's *Life on the Mississippi*. Or *Roughing It* and *The Innocents at Home*. These two books give you the disorderly side of the pioneering period, which Whitman rather leaves out. There's also a wonderful atmosphere in *Tom Sawyer* and *Huckleberry Finn*.

ORWELL: Unfortunately Mark Twain is difficult to quote from because he never talks about the same subject for more than half a page at a time.

READ: What about Hermann Melville? Something from *Moby Dick* for instance.

ANAND: Or *White Jacket*. That gives a picture of life aboard an American ship in the 'forties. It's about the time when Melville was a seaman in the American Navy.

EMPSON: The passage I like best in it is Melville's description of falling off the mast into the sea.

READ: Very well, let Orwell read that. Here it is. A passage from *White Jacket*, by Herman Melville.

George Orwell reads

EMPSON: It's a very ornate piece of prose, isn't it? And in a way very English. Quite unlike a modern American writer. I think you notice about the earlier American writers that they are much more deeply under European influence than the modern ones, even when they're very proud of not being Europeans.

ORWELL: Since we're trying to cover the pioneering period we ought to have something by Bret Harte. He's best known for his comic poems, but I should like something that brings in the Western mining camp motif.

READ: A very suitable piece from Bret Harte would be the poem he wrote after Dickens's death. That has the mining camp background and it illustrates what you were saying just now – the cultural dependence of America on Europe at that date.

ORWELL: All right, let's have that. Here we are then. 'Dickens in Camp', by Bret Harte. This is William Empson reading it.

William Empson reads

ORWELL: We're getting near the end of our time, and we must have something from Whitman. Which bit shall we have, I wonder?

READ: Again, the best are unfortunately the longest. Poems like 'Seadrift' and 'When Lilacs Last in the Dooryard Bloomed'.

ANAND: We haven't touched on the American Civil War yet. We ought to bring that in.

MARSON: Then why not have 'Oh, Captain, my Captain'? It'll bear repeating.

ORWELL: I tell you what. We'll have 'Oh, Captain, my Captain', and then to finish up with we'll have the poem about Ann Rutledge from the *Spoon River Anthology* by Edgar Lee Masters, which goes with it in a way. I suggest that as they're both short poems we read them straight off without a break between. Read, will you read the Whitman, and Empson, will you read the bit from the *Spoon River Anthology*? Here they are, then. 'Oh Captain, my Captain' by Walt Whitman, and 'Ann Rutledge' by Edgar Lee Masters.

Read and Empson read

[Voice – No. 5 has not been found]

VOICE – No. 6

29th December 1942

Fade up of 'Adeste Fideles'

ORWELL: This is a special Christmas number, and we are departing from our usual practice and having music in it. But as usual we want to start off by making sure what we are talking about. Christmas is something integral to the West and we all take its importance for granted, but we are talking to an audience to whom the festival of Christmas may not be so familiar. What is the essential thing about Christmas? What does it really stand for?

CHITALE: Well, first of all, I suppose, for the anniversary of the birth of Christ.

EMPSON: Not first in order of time. There was a pre-Christian festival at the same date, or about the same date. The ancient Saxon tribes that we are descended from used to celebrate something or other on Christmas day, for that [indecipherable]. The mistletoe hung up in English houses at Christmas time was a sacred plant when the aboriginal Britons were savages; it's green in winter. That's a natural thing in a cold northern climate. You must have a break somewhere in the long winter, and an excuse for a little feasting, this comes just after the days have started to get longer.

ORWELL: There seem to be three ideas mixed up in the Christmas festival. One is winter and snow, another is the Nativity of Christ, and the other is feasting and the giving of gifts. Of course some of it is a development of the last hundred years. I think the giving of Christmas presents is a modern custom, isn't it?

[?]: No. Christmas presents are supposed to have originated when the three kings from the East brought their gifts of gold and frankincense and myrrh to Bethlehem. In India the custom is that the child is given presents 12 days after birth.

ORWELL: Well, we'll try to cover those three aspects of Christmas. Let's start off with something about the snow and the characteristic winter plants, the holly and the ivy and the mistletoe.

EMPSON: You'll have difficulty in finding much about snow in English literature. It's never praised, at any rate until the last hundred years. That's natural. This is a cold country, and we don't write in praise of cold.

PEMBERTON: There's a poem by Robert Bridges, 'London Snow'. I've got it here. That's in praise of snow.

ORWELL: All right, let's have that one. I tell you how we'll do it. First of all we'll have the carol 'See amid the Winter's Snow', then we'll have the poem 'London Snow' by Robert Bridges – and then another carol, 'The Holly and the Ivy'. I think we'll go straight through with only pauses between.

Record

READ: It's time we had something dealing with the birth of Christ itself which is what our Christmas festival celebrates properly.

ORWELL: Let's start with a carol specially dealing with that time. For instance, 'The Seven Joys of Mary'.

Record

ORWELL: I think we ought to read the story itself before reading any poems about it. What is the absolutely essential thing about the story of the birth of Christ, I wonder?

READ: I think the essential thing – that is, the thing everyone remembers – is the idea of power and wisdom abasing themselves before innocence and poverty. Everyone who has ever heard of the birth of Christ remembers two picturesque details which don't, in fact, have anything to do with Christian doctrine. One is the child lying in the manger, and the other is the three Kings from the East coming with their gifts. The story is so perfectly right that it has become traditional, and it's acted every year in thousands of churches all over the world. But in fact not one of the versions in the Bible gives quite the full story.

ORWELL: I think we'll have the version from the Gospel according to St. Matthew. That's the fullest one. Perhaps Venu Chitale will read it for us. Here it is then – from the second chapter of the Gospel of St. Matthew.

Venu Chitale reads

ORWELL: And now what poems shall we have?

EMPSON: We ought to have Milton's 'Hymn on the Nativity'. I'm sure Herbert Read would read that very nicely.

[?]: And what about having T.S. Eliot's poem, 'The Journey of the Magi'? That would give a good contrast.

ORWELL: Yes, that's a good idea. We've got a recording of that which Eliot made himself. The 'Hymn on the Nativity' is rather long, so perhaps we should have another carol in between the two poems. Let's have 'In Excelsis Gloria'. First of all Milton, then the carol, the 'The Journey of the Magi'. Here they are then.

Herbert Read reads the 'Hymn on the Nativity'
Record of 'In Excelsis Gloria'
Record of 'The Journey of the Magi'

ORWELL: We've dealt with winter and the snow, and with the Nativity of Christ. We still haven't dealt with Christmas as it now is – the public holiday, the turkeys and plum puddings, Santa Claus and the reindeer, the Christmas parties and all the rest of it.

EMPSON: There's not so much about it in our literature, till the Victorian stress on it, and that seems to have come in from Northern Europe and America. Dickens is very good on it, especially the *Pickwick Papers*, but they're too long to quote.

READ: And perhaps they are hardly appropriate for a wartime Xmas. There's another poem of Robert Bridges which seems to me to give the feeling of the festival as it was celebrated this year, when after a long interval we heard the church bells again.

ORWELL: Yes, that's a good idea. Perhaps Empson will read it for us. We'll have the poem, and then straight after it another carol to end up with. We'll have *In Dulci Jubilo*, or as much of it as we've got time for.

William Empson reads 'Christmas Eve 1913' by Robert Bridges
Record of 'In Dulci Jubilo'

5

Story by Five Authors

PART I: by George Orwell

9th October 1942

It was a night in London in the late autumn of 1940. A bomb came whistling down, piercing the racket of the guns, and a man, a small shadowy figure, darted like a lizard into an already ruined house and flung himself down behind a pile of debris. He was none too soon, for the next instant the bomb exploded with a noise like the Day of Judgment less than a hundred yards away. He was quite unhurt, however, and it was only a few seconds before his ear drums began to work again and he realised that the objects which had spattered him all over were merely chips of brick and mortar.

Gilbert Moss, for that was his name, sat up and brushed some of the dust and plaster off his raincoat, after which he began mechanically feeling in his pockets for a cigarette. He noticed without surprise or even much interest that a dead man was lying face upwards a yard or two away from him. It did not seem to matter, either, that almost within touching distance some fallen beams or floor joists were burning fitfully. The whole house would be on fire before long, but in the mean time it gave a certain amount of protection.

Outside the barking of the guns rose and fell, sometimes bursting forth into an ear-splitting volley as a near-by battery came into action. This was the third time tonight that Gilbert had had to fling himself down to dodge a bomb, and on the second occasion he had had a small adventure, or what would have seemed an adventure in normal times. Caught by the blitz a long way from his own quarter of the town, he had struggled homewards through such a nightmare of gunfire, bomb flashes, falling shrapnel, burning houses and racing clanging fire engines as made him wonder whether the whole of humanity had not gone mad together. Under the rosy sky one had the impression that all London was burning. He had been passing down a side street he did not know when he heard a cry and saw a woman gesticulating to him from beside a demolished house. He hurried across to her. She was wearing blue overalls – curiously enough that was all he ever noticed about her – and a little boy of four or five, with a terrified face, was clutching at her leg. The woman cried out to him that there was a man under the wreckage and no rescue squad was near. With her help he had dug into the dusty pile of rubble, pushing and pulling at lumps of brick and mortar, splinters of glass,

95

panels of smashed doors and fragments of furniture, and sure enough, within five minutes they had uncovered the body of a man, whitened to the eyes with plaster but conscious and almost unhurt. Gilbert never discovered whether the man was the woman's husband or father, or merely a stranger. They had just helped him out on to the pavement when there was the whistle of another bomb. Immediately one thought had filled Gilbert's mind to the exclusion of all others – the child. He had swiftly grabbed the little boy, laid him flat on the pavement and covered him with his own body against the moment when the bomb would burst. However, it was a delayed-action bomb and no roar followed the whistle. As he got up the woman had suddenly flung her arms round his neck and given him a kiss that tasted of plaster. And then he had gone on, promising to inform the next warden he met about the injured man. But as it happened he had not met any warden, and there the incident ended.

That was half an hour ago and Gilbert had already almost forgotten it. On a night like this nothing seemed remarkable. Since entering his new refuge he had hardly given a second glance to the dead man lying beside him. The pile of smouldering beams sent out little spurts of flame which illumined Gilbert and the wreckage of various pieces of furniture. He was a thin smallish man in his middle thirties, with greying hair and a worn, sharp-featured, discoloured face. It had a sour expression which at most times was accentuated by a cigarette dangling from the lower lip. With his shabby raincoat and black felt hat he might have been an unsuccessful actor or journalist, a publisher's tout, a political agent or possibly some kind of hanger-on of a lawyer's office. He could find no matches in his pockets and was considering lighting his cigarette from one of the burning beams when an A.R.P. [Air Raid Precautions] warden in overalls and gumboots threaded his way through from the back of the ruined house, flashing his torch from side to side.

'You O.K., chum?'

'I'm O.K.,' said Gilbert.

The warden waited for the echo of a gun to die away before speaking again. He flashed his torch briefly onto the prostrate man but seemed too preoccupied to examine him.

'This poor devil's done for,' he said. 'We got a packet tonight, all right. I'd better report him. They'll pick him up in the morning, I s'pose.'

'No use wasting an ambulance,' agreed Gilbert.

The A.R.P. man had just disappeared when the burning beams burst into bright flame and the room was almost as bright as day. Gilbert glanced again at the dead man lying at his side, and as he did so his heart gave a violent, painful leap. It was the figure of a rather handsome man of his own age, the face calm and undamaged, the eyes closed. In the better light, however, Gilbert had noticed two things. In the first place it was not a stranger but a man he knew very well – or had once known very well, rather. In the second place the man was not dead, nor anywhere near it. He was merely unconscious, perhaps stunned by a falling beam.

A change had come over Gilbert's face the instant that the shock of recognition passed. It became very intent, with the ghost of a smile. The expression he wore was not a wicked expression, exactly – rather the expression of a man faced with an overwhelming temptation, an opportunity too good to be missed.

Suddenly he sprang to his feet and began looking for something which he knew he would have no difficulty in finding. In a moment he had got it. It was a heavy billet of wood, part of a broken floor joist, four feet long and tapering at one end to form a natural handle. He tested its weight and then, carefully measuring his distance from the unconscious man on the floor, gripped it with both hands and swung it aloft. Outside the guns were roaring again. Gilbert did not immediately deliver his blow. The man's head was not quite in the right position, and with the toe of his boot Gilbert pushed a few flakes of plaster under the head, raising it slightly. Then he took a fresh grip on his billet of wood and swung it aloft again. It was a heavy, formidable club. He had only to bring it down once and the skull would break like an egg.

At this moment he felt no fear, any more than he felt compunction. Curiously enough the racket of the guns upheld him. He was utterly alone in the burning town. He did not even need to reflect that on a night like this any death whatever would be attributed to the German bombs. He knew instinctively that in the middle of this nightmare you could do what you liked and nobody would have time to notice. Nevertheless the moment in which he had paused had temporarily saved the unconscious man's life. Gilbert lowered his club and leaned on it, as on a walking stick. He wanted, not exactly to think things over, but to recapture a certain memory, a certain feeling. It is not much use killing your enemy unless in the moment of striking him you remember just what he has done to you. It was not that he had faltered in his intention of killing this man. There was no question that he was going to kill him. But before doing so he wanted, in a sense, to remember *why* he was doing so. There was plenty of time, and complete safety. In the morning his enemy's body would only be one air-raid casualty among hundreds of others.

He leaned his club against a pile of wreckage and again took his unlighted cigarette from his pocket. He still could not find any matches. A thought striking him, he knelt down and felt in the unconscious man's pockets till he came on a slim gold cigarette-lighter. He lit his cigarette and put the lighter back, rather reluctantly. The initials on it were C.J.K.C., he noted. He had known this man as Charles Coburn, the Honourable Charles Coburn. Doubtless he was a lord by this time, though Gilbert could not remember the name of the title he was heir to. It was curious, but the excellent cloth of the man's waistcoat, and the expensive feel of the slender gold lighter, partly brought back the memory that he was looking for. They both felt like money. Gilbert had known Charles Coburn as a very rich young man, horribly elegant and superior, and rather cultured as they used to call it in the nineteen-twenties. With not many exceptions Gilbert hated all rich people – though that in itself was not a motive for killing anybody, of course.

He sat down again and drew the cigarette smoke deep into his lungs. The chorus of the guns stopped for nearly two minutes, then opened up again. It was so hard to remember – not the *fact*, of course, but the social atmosphere in which such things could happen. He remembered in great detail the outrageous, mean injury which this man had done him; what he did not remember so well were his own feelings at the time, the weakness and snobbishness which had made it possible for such a petty, humiliating disaster to happen to him. To remember that he had to remember the England of the nineteen-twenties, the old, snobbish, money-ruled England which was fast disappearing before the bombers and the income-tax came to finish it off. For a moment it eluded him, then suddenly it came back to him in a vision of a Mayfair street one summer morning – the flowers in the window boxes, a water cart laying the dust, a footman in a striped waistcoat opening a door. He could not remember when he had seen that particular street, or whether he had ever seen it. Perhaps it was only a symbolic street. But there it was, in the smell of pink geraniums and newly-drenched dust – fashionable London with its clubs and its gunsmiths and its footmen in striped waistcoats, the London of before the deluge, when money ruled the world and creatures like Charles Coburn were all-powerful because of their money.

Gilbert sprang to his feet again. He had no more doubts now. He did not merely know in an intellectual sense that he hated the man lying at his feet, he knew just why and how he hated him. Nor did it seem to him a barbarous thing to kill your enemy when you have him at your mercy; on the contrary, it seemed to him natural. As though encouraging him, the guns rose once again to an unbroken, rolling roar, like thunder. With an expression on his face much more purposeful than before he once more measured his distance, gripped his club firmly in both hands and swung it above his head, ready for a blow that would settle his enemy once and for all.

PART II: by L.A.G. Strong

16th October 1942

Gilbert Moss swung his club, and coldly eyed his enemy's head. Though with so heavy a weapon it did not matter where he struck – the sheer weight of the wood must smash in the skull – yet he chose a place with his eyes. He would strike exactly: the deliberate blow of an artist, certain of his aim, exacting vengeance: not a blind, clumsy, resentful smash.

His grip on the club was not right. He shifted his hands, until the balance was good and the great sullen mass of wood swung smoothly. Now! Now, Charles Coburn! Now you're going to get it. The only pity is, you'll never know who gave it to you. You'll never know it was Gilbert Moss – Mister Moss, as you were so careful to call him in public, in case any of your friends might for an instant suppose you knew him socially. The remembrance of the humiliations which had been put upon him rose in a red mist. He uttered a strangled cry of rage and pain, and swung the club up wildly, but his hands were shaking so much that it fell with a thud on one of the broken pieces of wood by the unconscious man's head, causing the head to jerk idiotically upwards and fall again. Gilbert could not tell whether it was his own eyes or a trick of the light from the burning beams, but for a moment he thought the eyelids flickered and the colour of the face changed. Steady, you idiot! Steady! You're imagining things.

Gilbert was sweating now, sweating and shaking all over. What a fool he had been to delay. A couple of minutes ago, his resolve was firm, he was cold and impersonal, an executor of absolute justice. Now he had let himself be worked up into a state. He'd always despised Hamlet for missing that chance of killing his uncle, by stopping to philosophise. Hamlet had been weak, and was only finding excuses for his weakness. Here was he now, Gilbert Moss, with his training as a scientist – yes: that had been another of Coburn's sneers, blast him, inferring by his tone that a laboratory assistant was not a scientist but just a menial, a bottle-washer: getting all that into the word scientist: how *did* they get those implications, those overtones of patronage, damn them, *damn* them! – here was he, Gilbert Moss, hesitating, dithering, telling himself that a vengeance was no vengeance if the victim never knew who struck him: that for all Coburn would know he might have been killed by the bomb that blew him where he lay.

A burning beam twenty feet away fell with a crash, making Gilbert jump. The flames flared up, lighting the unconscious face on the ground, and sent strange shadows chasing across it. In the new light, it seemed to wear a smile of disdain. 'Excellent', the Honourable Charles Coburn seemed to be saying, 'excellent. Hit a man when he can't defend himself. Splendid, Moss, splendid.' Not Mister Moss when they were alone – oh, dear no. Moss – as if he were a footman.

'Well,' Gilbert said, between his teeth. 'You've put it across me for the last time. Smile away. We'll see how you'll smile after this.'

Savagely he swung the club. So heavy was it, it swung too far, and all but jerked him off his feet. Panting, steadying himself, he made to raise it again, and stopped – just in time. In front of him, clear in the dancing light, a man stood, staring at him.

Gilbert let the end of the club fall, and stood, leaning on it, staring back. The man said nothing. He continued to look at Gilbert. His face was blank, but beneath its blankness Gilbert could see, even in this light, something calculating, nervous, alert: the face of one loitering with intent when a policeman suddenly walks round the corner. The hardships of the last few years had taught Gilbert a thing or two about the niceties of facial expression.

The man's eyes left Gilbert, almost casually, and looked past him. Then they came back again. He passed his tongue across his lower lip, and spoke.

'Ullo, mate.'

Gilbert cleared his throat. His voice, when it came, sounded to him stilted and pedantic.

'Hullo.'

The man moved a step nearer. He was looking around quickly now, but without moving his head.

'Wotcher doin'? Tryin' to bust something open?'

Gilbert thought in a flash – he hasn't seen. Coburn might be hidden from where he was standing. Then he realised that he wasn't answering the man's question, and that it was unpleasantly apt. His answer came before he had time to consider it.

'Well – yes, in a way.'

As he spoke, he looked on the ground, to see if there were any object he might conceivably have been trying to batter open.

'Can I give you a 'and?'

He had come closer. Shabby, clean-shaven, long upper lip, a muffler round his neck – still he wasn't looking at Gilbert. His little eyes were taking stock of everything round about – quick, accomplished eyes, the eyes of a pick-pocket or a tout, the predatory, hunted eyes of a man who lived by his wits, and didn't live well.

'I don't think so, thanks.'

'Please yourself. Sure? Two's better than one – sometimes.'

He was eyeing the club now – a slanting glance from under his eyelids. He edged closer. Before Gilbert could stop himself, he heard his voice cry out in nervous exasperation.

'Leave me alone. What are you doing here?'

The outcry produced no visible effect. The stranger, still glancing about him, came closer still.

'All right, mate. No offence. No bones broke. Come to that, wotcher doin' 'ere yourself?'

There was no threat in the words, and he did not look at Gilbert as he said them.

'I? I Just … found myself here.'

'Just dropped in, like, for a social call. To see an old pal, per'aps. 'E don't seem to know yer very well – does 'e?'

Gilbert drew himself up. 'As a matter of fact,' he said, 'he does. Too well.'

The newcomer raised his brows. The whites of his eyes showed alarmingly in the light of the flames.

'Like that, eh? Wot'd 'e give yer the sack for?'

Gilbert started as if he had been hit. This assumption on the part of the shabby stranger of the relationship between him and Coburn, this making of him into an inferior – he all but choked with fury. A wild impulse seized him to hit out with his club. Then the heat left his brain, and a swift flood of cunning rushed in. How much *had* the stranger seen? What gave him the confidence to be so familiar?

'I don't know what you mean,' he said, as steadily as he could. 'I've never been here before.'

'I see. Just club mates, you and 'im. Ascot – Royal Enclosure. I get yer.'

Gilbert's dry lips stretched in a grin. 'You won't believe me, of course. But I do know him. And he never employed me – much less gave me the sack. Still, it doesn't matter whether you believe me or not, does it?'

'No. And it don't matter whether you was usin' that little stick to pick yer teef wiv. Oh, all right, mate – don't look crooked. What you're doin' is no business o' mine. What I'm doin' is no business o' yours. I only thought, seeing we was both 'ere, we might' ave a look together, like.'

'What are you looking for?'

It was a silly question, but the stranger did not seem to mind.

'Well, you know – when a thing like this 'appens, yer might find a tin o' this layin' about, or a jar o' that. No good to the people wot lived 'ere; quite useful to the likes o' you and me. Pity to leave it layin' about, to be picked up by chaps as mightn't want it partic'lar.'

'I see.'

'Wot say – shall we 'ave a look round?'

'I don't think so. I'm not interested in – er – tins and jars. Don't let me stop you, though.'

'*I'm* not interested in wot's in blokes' pockets: but don't let me stop *you*.'

Gilbert opened his mouth to speak, and shut it again. He *had* taken a lighter from Coburn's pocket, even though he had put it back again. How much had the fellow seen?'

'All right. I'll help you, if you like.'

He hadn't intended to say that. It slipped out.

'Don't put yerself out.'

The stranger was exploring now, kicking at heaps of debris, testing piles of rubble, brushing dust aside with a sweeping motion of his sleeve.

'Now then. You two want anything?'

A Special. He'd loomed up from nowhere. The firelight leaped and danced, made him look bigger than he was. Gilbert coughed and stammered. Before he could find anything to say, the stranger had replied.

'Yes, Guv'ner. We're lookin' for a nice smooth plank. A bit o' floor-boardin' 'd do.'

'What d'ye want that for?'

''Orace.' He jerked his thumb at the figure on the ground. The constable started. He hadn't seen Coburn. Gilbert spoke.

'A warden was along here just now, and he thought the man was dead. So did I. But he isn't.'

'Oh.'

It was plain the constable did not believe them, but could not quite make up his mind what to do. He made a rumbling sound in his throat, as a preparation for speech, when suddenly Gilbert saw, passing close behind him in what remained of the street, the man he had pulled out of the wreckage – how long before? – he couldn't say: the man, with the woman holding the child's hand.

'Hullo!' he called. 'You all right now?'

The man turned, and stared vaguely. He couldn't see against the light. He seemed shocked still, and bewildered.

'Excuse me,' Gilbert said, and pushed past the Special. 'Is he all right?' he asked the woman loudly.

'Yes. Yes. We're all right now – thanks to you.' She saw the constable, and pointed to Gilbert. 'He's a brave chap, he is. Pulled Fred out from under all sorts. Ought to 'ave the George Medal.'

The constable was suddenly convinced. 'He's found another here,' he said.

'That's like 'im,' said the woman. 'Ought to 'ave the George Medal. Come on Fred. It ain't far now.'

'I'll see if I can find a stretcher-bearer.' The constable gave a nod, and moved off after the trio.

'Nice work.' Gilbert's associate in misdemeanour was bending over Coburn. 'Your college chum 'ere 'as opened 'is little eyes. Come and see if 'e reckonises yer.'

Gilbert came to where Coburn lay, and bent down. The handsome face was foolish with returning consciousness.

'Go on. Arsk 'im if 'e knows yer,' said the stranger, mockingly.

'Well, Coburn. Know me?'

'Can't say I – oh yes. Good Lord! Moss!'

'Yes. Moss.'

'Good. Nice to see a familiar face.'

'You think so, do you.'

'Decidedly. Come on – lend a hand, there's a good chap.'

'I don't think I will.' He turned to the stranger, who was watching with narrowed eyes. 'Do you know what this man did to me? Shall I tell him – Coburn? I will.'

PART III: by Inez Holden

23 October 1942

For those of you have not heard or will not remember the two earlier instalments of this serial, Part I by George Orwell and Part II by L.A.G. Strong – Gilbert Moss finds himself alone in a blitzed house during a London air raid. He sees an unconscious man lying near him. A reflected light from burning buildings shows him that it is his old enemy Coburn. He decides to take advantage of the circumstances to commit a murder which will be written off as the result of enemy action. The unconscious Coburn carries in his two pockets a gold cigarette lighter and a plain tinder-lighter. Moss takes the gold lighter and looks at it to revive bitter memories of how Coburn had wronged him, thereby justifying in his own mind the action he is about to commit. As he swings a club high to deal the death blow he suddenly sees that a sneak thief is calmly watching him. Coburn recovers consciousness. Moss threatens to tell the thief the reason for their enmity – there Mr Strong left off, and I go on …

Coburn came slowly to consciousness. He was not really aware of Moss or his henchman from the bombardment. Even his own identity eluded him – as if the various parts of his nature, his associations and memories were groping to join hands through a thick fog.

Coburn was aware only of wanting something to steady his nerves. Perhaps a cigarette could do this. He felt in the left-hand pocket of his trousers, and took out the tinder-lighter; he had left the gold lighter with his initials C.J.K.C. on it in his right-hand pocket. He took some Virginian cigarettes from his breast pocket and lit one. The tinder-lighter was very useful in the blackout, because it only gave out a spark, and on these cold nights the wind soon flicked it into a steady glow. Coburn could remember the time, during the Spanish war, when the Republicans had gone up to the front line with the ropes of these tinder-lighters tied round their waists. Once Coburn had worn his round his neck, like a halter. His cigarette wasn't really alight. He held the tinder in his hand and, with his thumb, turned the wheel back to make a spark.

It was this that set Coburn's memories on the move. It seemed as if his whole mind, with all its elaborate machinery, clocked into reverse, and then went ticking and somersaulting along, backwards.

Something of this sort had happened to Coburn once before. That was the day Mary came to see him in the hospital in Paris. He had a long conversation with her – or so she told him afterwards – yet he hadn't recognised her, and when he checked up on it, with her help, some weeks later, after he had got well, he realised that his speech had been automatic while his mind was elsewhere.

Now again his mind was working at a good speed, but in another direction.

He was lying in his bed in the slovenly French hospital again trying to recover from his wound, and watching the cockroaches crawling along the floor. They made dark smudges; the ceilings were smudged, too, but there was no movement on the ceiling, only small cells of accumulated dirt; and all around Coburn men were dying. Sometimes their comrades called out to the long-robed, funereal nuns: 'Numéro quinze' – or 'Numéro quatre là!' – pointing to the men who had got away early because their lives had gone from them.

The cockroaches were still moving slowly along the floor; Coburn had heard that there was cockroach-racing at the back of restaurants in Paris, and that the spectators would bet a few francs on their favourites. It might be so – he had never seen this himself. Anyhow, these cockroaches didn't hurry. Some of them had stopped moving altogether. He thought that if they could be enlarged they would be like crocodiles sleeping in the sun. Well – he was like them; powerless, unable to move. Suddenly the sun came into the hospital ward. There was a ray right across Coburn's bed. He was warmed by it and again there came to him the question, like an immense word shooting out in a caption from a film: '*Why?*'

He answered this in action. He was not weak any more, he wanted to get going and away from here. It didn't take him long to dress. His leg was not well, but he did not drag it after him as he limped out of the ward, instead he seemed to use his wounded leg to propel himself along at greater speed. No one tried to stop him.

He was back on the road to Spain. 'That's strange – I thought the war was over.' But he wasn't going back the way he had gone in. He was taking the route he had followed to come out, and with him the same refugees who had streamed over the frontier after the fall of Barcelona. They rose up all around him and travelled back.

He put his hand in his pocket for a cigarette, and remembered the gold lighter. He didn't really like that lighter – it reminded him too much of 1920 days. C.J.K.C. – those awful initials! Charles Joachim Kallahan Coburn.

Charles, after his blustering, fox-hunting uncle of whom he had said: 'He may be good to hounds, but he's not good to me!' But if he was honest, he had to admit that it had taken him some years to work up to this witticism. There had been a time when he had been quite proud of Uncle Charles, and boasted to the boys of his prep school that he came from this family of hard-riding land-owners. Of course the boys were all little snob-brats. 'I suppose it was the system of society that made them like this! Anyhow snobbishness was a harmful thing which boys absorbed like blotting paper.'

Joachim, the second name, was worse. That was after a Spanish Duke that used to come down to his father's place to play polo, an 'absentee-landlord' with a grandiose manner.

Kallahan, the third name, could pass all right. It was his mother's surname. There was really nothing much wrong with Kallahan.

Well, the gold lighter had gone. Coburn's brain cleared and suddenly, with piercing understanding, he knew where it was. A pick-pocket had taken it from him a few moments ago in a London air-raid. His thoughts were back now, pivoting themselves on to the moment of living.

He knew several things at once – that the cigarette he had lighted a little while ago was now burning his fingers; that the Spanish cause had been lost; that the German bombers were over London and the narrow-eyed, light-fingered fellow facing him at this second of existence, had got the gold lighter with the initials C.J.K.C. branded on it.

All the time in unconsciousness he had been living in reverse, like a film put on backwards. Sometimes they did this in the cinemas with the sports films, just to show you, the diver comes up right out of the swimming-pool into the air and back on the springboard; the fallen horse rises up and leaps backwards over the hedge unhurt again, the jockey goes from the ground over the horse's head, safe in the saddle once more. Just put the actions in reverse and the man you knocked down becomes the one you pick up, the refugees are drawn back into Spain; the pick-pocket presents you with a gold lighter with your own initials on it. Coburn thought: 'That's what we want in life. Some careful cutting as in a film, the sequence altered here and there –' He sighed, and said aloud: 'A New Order! Or a new "New Order"!'

The pick-pocket said: 'Cor, Mister, he's come to – he's speakin'. I never thought he wouldn't speak no more after I seen him pass clean out like that!'

There was a lull in the air-raid; the bombers had been driven off but soon another wave of them would be coming over. They usually kept it up until dawn.

The pick-pocket, taking advantage of this opportunity, ran out like a rat, he didn't want to be caught with the gold lighter on him.

Coburn said: 'You see, he doesn't want to hear the old story of rights and wrongs, Moss, but I do, – so why don't you tell me?' Why couldn't Moss get going on his story? He'd been so anxious to talk a little time ago. Of course, it must be a bit disconcerting for him, not to have an audience. It reminded Coburn of trying to talk to his father at home – it was always the same, after he'd got out a sentence or two, Father began shouting at the dogs under the sideboard: 'Lie down, Foozle! Stop scratching, Boozle!' Well, the sideboard was there still – or bits of it. But it was so splintered up that you had to have known it from childhood to be able to recognise it now. It wouldn't be worth much, so there need never be any trouble about who it should come to. Good-bye to inherited property – and not such a bad thing either!

'What did I do, Moss?'

A fire engine rushed through the streets, its bells clanging. Coburn saw the firemen standing up to attention on either side of a long ladder in the centre of the car.

'Speak up, Moss,' he said. 'I am waiting to hear!'

PART IV: by Martin Armstrong

30th October 1942

Gilbert Moss stood gazing incredulously at his old enemy. Coburn still lay in exactly the same position, still a dead man except that his eyes were now open and alive. But were they? Wasn't it simply the effect of the glare and flicker of the blazing rubbish? But he had spoken too. 'Come on, Moss,' he had said: 'I'm waiting to hear.' But no; that was impossible. It wasn't Coburn who had said that. Nobody had said it. The whole exhausting business was simply a dream. Moss felt suddenly as weak as a kitten and gave it up, stood there motionless and speechless, waiting. If he waited patiently, something would happen; a moment of confusion, then clearness, daylight, and the old alarm-clock rattling on the mantelpiece, telling him that it was time to get up and go to the lab. But what roused him at last was not the alarm-clock, but Coburn's voice again: 'I say, old man, do give me a hand. This isn't a bit comfortable. I can't move: some damned thing's wedging my shoulder.'

How amazingly familiar and attractive the voice was, recalling old times, happy times. Incredible that a few minutes ago he had been on the point of beating the fellow's brains out. And why? Why, because ... but no; his mind refused to focus itself. And then, for the first time, he noticed that the raid was over. All round him hung a blessed silence, broken only by the spasmodic crackle of burning beams. Not only that. Against a silvery-green background of luminous sky he could see clearly and steadily the jagged walls of the great hollow tooth in which he was standing. He clambered over to where Coburn lay. A joist, one of its ends buried in bricks and rubble, lay across his left arm and shoulder and in half a minute or so Moss had dragged it back.

With a sigh of relief Coburn sat up, then got on to his feet, steadying himself for a moment with a hand on Moss's shoulder. 'Come on,' he said, 'let's get out of this.' He glanced round him with an attempt at a smile. 'Sorry not to give you a better reception.'

Moss didn't understand. 'You mean to say ...?'

'Exactly; that this is our town house. In point of fact it was just through there that you and I ...'

Moss cut him short. 'You don't want to have a look round for the others?'

'The others? O, I see what you mean. No, there aren't any others. The house was empty. I was simply spending the night here. Come on.'

They scrambled out into the street. In the half-light of early morning it looked surprisingly unchanged. Coburn's house seemed to be the only one whose front had gone. The rest faced each other sedately across the roadway, though, here and there, pavements and road were littered with broken glass and splintered woodwork and here and there a gaping window betrayed that behind that respectable screen lay, not the gloom of domestic privacy, but the vacancy of open sky. Coburn slid his arm through Moss's and steered him across the street.

'Where are we off to?' Moss asked.

'To a seat in the Park, till there's a chance of breakfast somewhere. You're going to tell me, you know, what I did to you.'

Moss breathed out a long sigh. 'O damn all that,' he said. 'I don't know. I can't remember.' He had no energy left. When Coburn had taken his arm he had been aware of an immense relief. What a rest to give up all responsibility of thought and action and submit obediently to be led.

Coburn steered him across another road. 'But you must,' he said. 'Here's the Park. As soon as we can find a seat you must tell me all about it. You see, I've never understood.'

It was this fatuous assumption of innocence, that restored Moss's energies. With a sudden movement he shook his arm free and let fly. 'O no, of course you know nothing. You're as innocent as an unborn lamb, aren't you? Well, here's a seat for you. Sit down. If you want to have it, you shall have it.'

Coburn sat down. 'Yes,' he said, 'tell me what I did to you and, when you've done, I'll tell you what you did to me.'

Moss was too wrapped up in his old grievance to notice the final phrase. He sat down and turned to Coburn. 'And look here,' he said, 'if you want me to tell you, *let* me tell you. Don't butt in with excuses, or I stop and clear out.'

'I see,' said Coburn; 'as you did last time.'

'Exactly. Just as I did last time, and as I ought to have done the very first time I met you, if I'd had any sense, instead of letting you get round me. Yes, you're a wonderful chap for getting round people, aren't you, Coburn? Still, I was easy game in those days: any fool could have got round me. When Challenor asked me round and introduced me to his little set, I was simply delighted. I thought I'd got into the Kingdom of Heaven. And there were you, handsome, son of a lord, going to be a lord yourself some day, simply lousy with money, and yet interested in my views and treating me as your equal. Yes, you took me in properly. I believed you and I was enormously grateful, silly ass that I was. I danced round you and wagged my tail and let you put a collar around my neck and lead me on a string. Whenever you whistled I came galloping up, only too delighted to obey. I thought you the most wonderful chap I'd ever met. I simply adored you. Why, good lord, you transformed my whole life from top to bottom. Before I met you, I'd never had a soul to talk to about all the things that mattered. Nobody talked to me at the lab, where I did my bottle-washing as you politely called it one day. Lancaster, my boss, despised me and they all thought me a little worm not worth bothering about. And so I was. If I hadn't been a worm, I wouldn't have let *you* get round me. But you saw how useful I might be. You'd found out that I was methodical, and that I had a natural gift for organising and had read a devil of a lot of science and history, even though I was only a bottle-washer. Just the chap you wanted to do the jobs no one else could do on your precious new monthly magazine. Good God, how excited I was when you explained the scheme to me. A marvellous monthly review, dealing with art, literature, history, science, from a brand-new left-wing point of view. A sort of crusade. A six guineas a week salary for me. I shall never forget the evening we finally fixed it up. I'd been feeling rotten. Lancaster had given me a terrific ticking-off about some blessed experiment that somebody else had mucked up, and I'd taken it lying-down, because I was frightened of losing my job. You laughed when I told you about it. "Never mind about that," you said. "Tomorrow morning, when you go to work, ask to see Lancaster, tell him exactly what you think of him, and walk out. Then come round to our place for lunch and we'll fix up about moving into our office on Thursday. All's clear. My people are out of town."

'Yes, Coburn, that was very convenient, wasn't it? His lordship and her ladyship were out of town, so there was no fear of them running across the scruffy little worm you'd taken into your employment. That didn't strike me at the moment. It was the first time you'd asked me round to your place and I was so fatuously delighted that nothing else mattered. Well, there it was. Next morning I had a gorgeous row with Lancaster and cleared out. Then I went home and spruced myself up a bit and presented myself at your front door. I was a bit intimidated when that striped flunkey of yours opened the door and showed me into the library; but I was also pretty pleased with myself, dropping in for a bit of lunch at the house of a lord. However, I was kept waiting about twenty minutes in the library and that cooled me down a bit. Then you came in. How well I remember your face on that occasion, Coburn, all embarrassed and hesitating. I hardly knew you. You began to explain. Your people had turned up unexpectedly the previous evening and you and I couldn't lunch together after all. The flunkey would bring me *my* lunch, there in the library. Ha! You were in an awful hurry to get away from me. The lord and lady couldn't be kept waiting for their grub, still less be exposed to the company of the scruffy little worm. However, you were awfully nice about it; O awfully nice. You patted me on the shoulder and told me to come back at tea-time.

'At first I couldn't speak. Then I said I didn't want lunch; I had a lot of things to do; I preferred to go at once. That upset you a bit, and you mumbled something about being sure I wouldn't misunderstand you. Ha! you were right there, Coburn. I didn't misunderstand you any longer. I'd seen through you at last. Then you had a brain-wave. You got out a wallet, fished a bit of paper out of it and handed it to me. It was a ten-pound note. "What's that for?" I asked you. "Some cash in advance," you said. "Thought you might be needing it." Lovely, wasn't it? Ten pounds. More than enough to soothe the feelings of a worm. Well, *you* know the rest. I tore up your blasted ten-pound note and chucked it in your face, and told you I didn't want your dirty money, and then I told you one or two things about yourself and all the rest of your kind. And then I told you I was done with you. That made you sit up, didn't it, Coburn? Your face – I remember it still – turned suddenly white. But you didn't forget your manners. O dear me, no. You remained the perfect gentleman and your voice was perfectly calm. "I see," you said; "I see. Well, if you really feel like that, there's nothing more to be said."

'It was simple enough for you, wasn't it? But it wasn't quite so simple for me. I'd dished myself for good and all at the lab, and there was I, on the rocks. Still, that was a minor detail. O yes, I mean it; a minor detail compared with what you'd done to my ... well, to my mind, my self-respect, my ... my feelings. That's where you did me in. It was as good as murder. Worse, in fact; far worse. When a man's murdered, he thinks no more about it.

'Well, there you are. You're not going to deny all that, are you?'

PART V: by E.M. Forster

6th November 1942

This is a serial by five authors, and to-day I have to finish it. Here are a few reminders of what has been happening in previous instalments. The scene is London during the Blitz, and Gilbert Moss, a disgruntled intellectual, finds an unconscious man lying in a ruined house, and recognises his old enemy, Coburn. He decides to take advantage of the circumstances to commit a murder which will be written off as the results of enemy action. He swings a club high – then realises that a pick-pocket is watching him. Coburn recovers consciousness. Moss threatens to tell the thief the reason for their enmity. But the fellow makes off – taking with him Coburn's gold cigarette lighter, which Moss has been handling. Coburn, who, unknown to Moss, has fought in the Spanish Civil War, now takes him outside to talk things over, and they sit in the Park, waiting for the morning to come. Moss pours out his grievances in a passionate speech, showing that Coburn in the past has lost him his job and insulted his feelings. He ends up 'You're not going to deny all this, are you?' Now I start.

Stan – even pick-pockets and touts have names, and this one had been registered at birth as Stanley Barnes – Stan was creeping back across the Park in search of further booty. He had not done badly with the gold cigarette lighter, and his old Ma, to whom he had passed it, advised him to attempt no more until the Jerries were over again and breaking things up. The present raid was in control now, the police, the A.R.P., the A.F.S. [Auxiliary Fire Service] were all busy, and it really wasn't safe. But Stan, though cunning, was not always wise, nor could he ever keep still: he was always sliding and darting over the ruins, he was a creature of burning doorways, crashing beams, rubble heaps and spouting drains; he was half-lizard, half-rat; his sort haunted London ever since the foundation of the city, and 1940 seemed to be bringing it into its own. So he crept back across the park towards the ruins in Mayfair, and on his way he came to the bench where Coburn and Moss sat. He recognised Moss's voice. They were talking, talking, talking. What about? He dropped on the grass behind them, to find whether the talk would do him any good.

Moss – the one who called himself the poor one – talked most. Christ, 'ow he fancied the sound of his own voice, that Moss. Talking, talking about his feelings. Seemingly Coburn, the rich one, had once giv' Moss ten quid not to come to lunch, and did Moss take the money? No. He tear it up. He says 'my feelings is murdered'. He says 'You're not going to try to deny all that, are you?'

Then Coburn starts. Coburn's turn. Coburn says no, he's not going to deny it, still he did go to Spain. That seems to please and satisfy Moss no end. 'Spain! What, you fought in Spain?' he squawks. 'Spain! I never knew. 'Oo sent you there?' Coburn he says 'You did. You when you told me what you thought of me and made me see how worthless I was. You've changed my life.' And then they shook 'ands and started shouting and laughing like a pair of kids.

Stan made nothing out of this. To him both of them sounded completely crackers. If he was given money, he didn't give it away, and if there was a war he tried to dodge it. However he never criticised people – that is a pastime for the educated – he merely watched them in case they were any use. His big hope, when he crouched behind the seat, was to do a spot of blackmail. Moss had for sure been going to club Coburn in the burning house, they had for sure exchanged angry words, and where there are troubled waters Stan knew how to fish. But the hope faded. Blackmail was no use now that they were jabbering about Spain and what you did for me and what I did for you, and oh yes and oh no and wonderful.

Presently their voices dropped. Stan had to crawl nearer and he heard Coburn say, 'Moss, I should like you to meet my woman – Mary. She's wonderful. I suppose you'll refuse after the way I've treated you, still I should have liked it.'

Moss, he raised no objection. Moss's turn now. Moss, he say 'Coburn, I should like you – to meet a woman whom I shall never meet again perhaps myself, someone whose very name I don't know. She has kissed me, she has saved my life and more than life.'

There was nothing to be done now that they had started about their Judies. He had wasted his time, and it was now too light to work any more bombed houses. Out in the east, far behind Mayfair was a glow of fire – they had got the docks again – and in the direction of Westminster was another glow, faint, and dirty, which proceeded from the neglected sun. A new day was dawning on God's Earth, and Stan regretted it. Still one can't have everything, things being what they are, the night cannot last for ever, and a gold cigarette lighter is better than nothing.

'Well, what about breakfast? Let's see if my Club still exists,' said Coburn, stretching himself and suddenly rising. 'Brr ... it's good to be alive at the worst of times – Hallo, what's that?'

Moss, who felt happier than he had been for years, recognised the pick-pocket and pounced. 'It's the little worm I saw in your burning dining-room,' he cried.

'Oh, let him go!'

'He's got your lighter on him still. I can feel it.'

'I ain't, I never pinched it, I worn't there. Who was there? You was, I seed you,' spat Stan. The two educated men laughed: seemingly he had said the wrong things.

'I've got it – no I haven't – it's – whatever is it?' Moss extracted a flat metal object, fan-shaped, and pierced with four holes. It was a simple and inexpensive contraption for causing pain, it was a knuckle duster. Moss held it on the palm of his hand.

'Gimme that – that's mine.' Stan had acquired the knuckle duster while he was employed by the British Fascists. It had been a happy episode – plenty of food, a bed to sleep in at the local centre, and ten shillings a week. 'We will cleanse this city of London,' he had been told. 'We will hack our way through to power.' Well, and why not? And he had taken part in one or two party drives, and had hit one or two people whose noses were the wrong shape, upon the head. British Fascism had not come to a great lot, there hadn't been enough money behind it, it had never gone full steam ahead as in Germany. Still, it had been better than nothing, and the knuckle duster was a memento.

'Gimme that back.'

Moss tried it on, slipping his four fingers into the holes, and clasping the base in his palm. It fitted comfortably, and gave him a sense of power. The treacherous and primitive little gadget, made in some back alley, was a forerunner of the expensive bombs which had made a rubbish heap of Mayfair and a bonfire of the Docks. 'We'll keep this,' he told Coburn, who laughed cheerfully, and they turned to go. Chaos became visible: it looked as if civilization would never creep back, but Coburn, who had seen similar destruction in Spain, knew that this wasn't the case, and that a city can rise again and again to her knees. They spoke of matters pleasant to them: Moss realised that he had indeed been his friend's salvation, and had turned him from a dilettante aristocrat to a gay and selfless hero. The Coburn he had always longed for and loved was a reality – and then – then he got a blow on the back of the head.

It was a badly directed one, he staggered, turned round and swiped and caught Stan hard. Stan fell like a twig on to the grimy grass and lay motionless.

'My God, it's that pick-pocket again,' cried Coburn. 'Why won't he leave us alone. Come along Moss, don't wait about. If he's dead, we can't do anything, and if he's alive he'll get up.'

'Do you suppose I've killed him?' said Moss doubtfully, for the fallacy of Liberalism, that belief in the preciousness of human life, still vexed him at times.

'It can't matter either way. Poor lad, he has nothing to contribute. I have seen too many of his type.'

'And probably no one to care for him.'

Oh, one can't go in for that – it gets one all mixed. He may be greatly loved, who knows? Throw his knuckle duster away. It shows signs of use.'

'By Jove, you're right. I'm afraid you're always going to be right.' He dropped it into the trunk of a shattered elm. Then they turned down the Mall and up the steps by the Duke of York's column, looked at the closed German Embassy and the statue of Captain Scott, and reached Coburn's Club. It was in fair working order. A wash would be possible, even a bath, and presently they sat drinking coffee. Moss did not feel touchy or shy any more. They had helped each other, they had made good, and it seemed to be his club too. How decent Coburn was, and when he was exasperating again, as he would be, it would be bearable. They talked of their plans for the future, and of their hopes of helping to pull the world through; no doubt they would crash themselves, but they had seen what needed doing, and would help each other. Presently their voices dropped again, and Moss recurred to the woman – the woman in overalls who had kissed him, and as it were blessed him. There is something in a universe where such encounters can happen.

They gave no further thought to the mean-minded little pick-pocket, lying on his back in the dirt of the Park, nor to old Ma Barnes wondering where he was. They did not realise that the world might be his not theirs, that the future might be for the rat, the lizard, the night prowler who have patiently been awaiting their turn ever since civilization started, that the spirit of anarchy may be stealing out of the craters our science has made, and nesting in the ruins we have provided.

So that's how I've wound up this serial by five authors. I've shifted the interest from Coburn and Moss to the pick-pocket, and I've tried to show how their fine sentiments would appear to that sort of man. He doesn't care about snobbery or outraged feelings or moral redemption or heroism in Spain, or hopes for the world's future. He can't see either why the two mugs quarrelled or why they make it up. And when they punish him – which they do pretty thoroughly – they can't see that he too has a way of life, and a way which, in our present chaos, may possibly flourish. I expect that there are better endings to the story, and in particular that something more ought to have been done with that woman in overalls. But I could not work her in, and since the scenery prescribed was falling houses and the blitz, I turned to the character which best typifies destruction, and named him Stan Barnes. Did Stan's own knuckle duster kill him? I don't know, but I hope not, because I believe in the importance of individual life. Coburn and Moss don't know and don't care.

6

Jonathan Swift, an imaginary interview
by George Orwell

2nd November 1942

ORWELL: My edition of Swift's works was printed some time between 1730 and 1740. It's in twelve small volumes, with calf covers a bit the worse for wear. It's not too easy to read, the ink is faded and the long S's are a nuisance, but I prefer it to any modern edition I've seen. When I open it and smell the dusty smell of old paper – that's an intoxicating smell if you're fond of books – and see the woodcut illustrations and the crooked capital letters, I almost have the feeling that I can hear Swift speaking to me. I've a vivid picture of him in my mind's eye, with his knee-breeches and his three-cornered hat, though I don't believe I've ever seen a portrait of him. Sometimes I half expect that he'll step out of the printed page and answer me. There's something in his way of writing that seems to tell you what his voice was like. For instance, here's one of his 'Thoughts on Various Subjects': 'When a true genius appears in the world ...'

SWIFT: 'When a true genius appears in the world, you may know him by this infallible sign; that all the dunces are in confederacy against him.'

ORWELL: He's materialised after all! I knew it would happen sooner or later. So you *did* wear a wig, Dr Swift. I've often wondered.

SWIFT: Did you say that you possessed the first collected edition of my works?

ORWELL: Yes. I bought them for five shillings at a farmhouse auction.

SWIFT: You were lucky. I warn you to beware of all *modern* editions, even of my *Travels*. I have suffered from such damned dishonest editors as I believe no other writer ever had. It has been my especial misfortune to be edited usually by clergymen who thought me a disgrace to their cloth. They were tinkering at my writings long before Dr Bowdler was ever born or thought of.

ORWELL: You see, Dr Swift, you have put them in a difficulty. They know you are our greatest prose writer, and yet you used words and raised subjects that they couldn't approve of. In a way I don't approve of you myself.

SWIFT: I am desolated, sir.

ORWELL: I believe *Gulliver's Travels* has meant more to me than any other book ever written. I can't remember when I first read it, I must have been eight years old at the most, and it's lived with me ever since so that I suppose a

112

year has never passed without my re-reading at least part of it. And yet I can't help feeling that you laid it on a bit too thick. You were too hard on humanity, and on your own country. You even preferred Louis XV's France, which is almost like preferring Hitler's Germany today.

SWIFT: H'm!

ORWELL: For instance, here's a passage that has always stuck in my memory – also stuck in my gizzard, a little. It's at the end of Chapter VI in the Second Book of *Gulliver's Travels*. Gulliver has just given the King of Brobdingnag a long description of life in England. The King listens to him and then picks him up in his hand, strokes him gently and says – wait a moment, I've got the book here. But perhaps you remember the passage yourself.

SWIFT: Oh, ay. 'It does not appear, from all you have said, how any one virtue is required toward the procurement of any one station among you; much less that men were ennobled on account of their virtue; that priests were advanced for their piety or learning, soldiers, for their conduct or valour; judges, for their integrity; senators, for the love of their country; or counsellors for their wisdom. As for yourself (continued the king) who have spent the greatest part of your life in travelling I am well disposed to hope you may hitherto have escaped many vices of your country. But by what I have gathered from your own relation, and the answers I have with much pains wringed and extorted from you, I cannot but conclude the bulk of your natives to be the most pernicious race of little odious vermin that nature ever suffered to crawl upon the surface of the earth.'

ORWELL: I'd allow you 'pernicious' and 'odious' and 'vermin', Dr Swift, but I'm inclined to cavil at 'most'. 'The most pernicious.' Are we in this island really worse than the *rest* of the world?

SWIFT: Not at all. But I know you, better than I know the rest of the world. When I wrote, I went upon the principle that if a lower kind of animal than an Englishman existed, I could not imagine it.

ORWELL: That was two hundred years ago. Surely you must admit that we have made a certain amount of progress since then?

SWIFT: Progress in quantity, yes. The buildings are taller and the vehicles move faster. Human beings are more numerous and commit greater follies. A battle kills a million where it used to kill a thousand. And in the matter of great men, as you still call them, I must admit that your age outdoes mine. Whereas previously some petty tyrant was considered to have reached the highest point of human fame if he laid waste a single province and pillaged half a dozen towns, your great men nowadays can devastate whole continents and reduce entire races of men to the status of slaves.

ORWELL: I was coming to that. One thing I feel inclined to urge in favour of my country is that we don't produce great men and don't like war. Since your day something has appeared called totalitarianism.

SWIFT: A new thing?

ORWELL: It isn't strictly new, it's merely been made practicable owing to modern weapons and modern methods of communication. Hobbes and other seventeenth-century writers forecast it. You yourself wrote about it with extraordinary prescience. There are passages in Part III of *Gulliver's Travels* that give me the feeling that I'm reading an account of the Reichstag Fire trial. But I'm thinking particularly of a passage in Part V where the Houyhnhnm who is Gulliver's master is telling him about the habits and customs of the Yahoos. It appears that each tribe of Yahoos had a Dictator, or Fuehrer, and this Dictator liked to surround himself with yes-men. The Houyhnhnm says:

SWIFT: 'He had heard, indeed, some curious Houyhnhnms observe, that in most herds there was a sort of ruling Yahoo (as among us there is generally some leading or principal stag in a park), who was always more deformed in body, and mischievous in disposition, than any of the rest. That this leader had usually a favourite, as like himself as he could get, whose employment was to lick his master's feet and drive the female Yahoos to his kennel; for which he was now and then rewarded with a piece of ass's flesh. This favourite is hated by the whole herd, and therefore, to protect himself, keeps always near the person of his leader. He usually continues in office till a worse can be found; but the very moment he is discarded, his successor, at the head of all the Yahoos in that district, young and old, male and female, come in a body, and –'

ORWELL: We shall have to leave out that bit.

SWIFT: 'But how far this might be applicable to our courts' (continued Gulliver) 'and favourites, and ministers of state, my master said I could best determine.'

ORWELL: I remember that passage whenever I think of Goebbels or Ribbentrop, or for that matter Monsieur Laval. But looking at the world as a whole, do you find that the human being is *still* a Yahoo?

SWIFT: I had a good view of the people of London on my way here, and I assure you that I could remark very little difference. I saw all round me the same hideous faces, unshapely bodies and ill-fitting clothes that could be seen two hundred years ago in London, or in any other city, for that matter.

ORWELL: But the town had changed, even if the people had not?

SWIFT: Oh, it has grown prodigiously. Many a green field where Pope and I used to stroll after dinner on summer evenings is now a wilderness of bricks and mortar, for the kennelling of Yahoos.

ORWELL: But the town is also a great deal safer, and more orderly, than it was in your day. One can walk about nowadays without the fear of getting one's throat cut, even at night. You ought to admit some improvement there, though I suppose you won't. Besides, it's cleaner. In your day there were still lepers in London, not to mention the Plague. We have baths fairly frequently nowadays, and women don't keep their hair up for a month at a time and carry little silver goads to scratch their heads with. Do you remember writing a poem called 'A Description of a Lady's Bed-chamber'?

SWIFT: (*Reads*)

ORWELL: That's the one. But would you sign that poem nowadays? Tell me candidly, do we stink as we used to?

SWIFT: Certainly the smells are different. There was a new one I remarked as I came through the streets – (*sniffs*) –

ORWELL: It's called petrol. But don't you find that the mass of the people are more intelligent than they were, or at least better educated? How about the newspapers and the radio? Surely they have opened people's minds a little? There are very few people in England now who can't read.

SWIFT: That is why they are so easily deceived. Your ancestors two hundred years ago were full of barbarous superstitions, but they would not have been so credulous as to believe your daily newspapers. As you seem to know my works, perhaps you will remember another little thing I wrote, an 'Essay upon Genteel and Ingenious Conversation?'

ORWELL: Of course I remember it well. It's a description of fashionable ladies and gentlemen talking – an appalling stream of drivel which goes on and on for six hours without stopping.

SWIFT: On my way here I looked in at the Savoy Grill and at some of your fashionable clubs in Pall Mall, and listened to the conversation. I half believed that that little Essay of mine was being parodied. Even many of the cant phrases were still the same. If there was any change, it was only that the English tongue has lost something of the earthy natural quality it once had.

ORWELL: How about the scientific and technical achievements of the last two hundred years – railway trains, motor cars, aeroplanes and so forth? Doesn't that strike you as an advance?

SWIFT: I also passed through Cheapside on my way here. It has almost ceased to exist. Round St. Paul's there is only an acre of ruins. The Temple has been almost wiped out, and the little church outside it is only a shell. I am speaking only of the places I knew, but it is the same all over London, I believe. That is what your machines have done for you.

ORWELL: I am getting the worst of this argument, but I still feel, Dr Swift, that there is something deeply deficient in your outlook. You remember what the king of Brobdingnag said when Gulliver described cannons and gunpowder to him?

SWIFT: 'The king was struck with horror at the description I had given of those terrible engines, and the proposal I had made. He was amazed, how so impotent and grovelling an insect as I (these were his expressions) could entertain such inhuman ideas, and in so familiar a manner as to appear wholly unmoved at all the scenes of blood and desolation, which I had painted as the common effects of those destructive machines; whereof, he said, some evil genius, enemy to mankind, must have been the first contriver. As for himself, he protested, that although few things delighted him so much as new discoveries in art or in nature, yet he would rather lose half his kingdom than be privy to such a secret, which he commanded me, as I valued my life, never to mention any more.'

ORWELL: I suppose the king would have spoken even more forcibly about tanks or mustard gas. But I can't help feeling that his attitude, and yours, show a certain lack of curiosity. Perhaps the most brilliant thing you ever wrote was the description of the scientific academy in Part III of *Gulliver's Travels*. But after all you were wrong. You thought the whole process of scientific research was absurd, because you could not believe that any tangible result would ever come out of it. But after all the results have come.

Modern machine civilisation is there, for good or evil. And the poorest person nowadays is better off, so far as physical comfort goes, than a nobleman in Saxon times, or even in the reign of Queen Anne.

SWIFT: Has that added anything to true wisdom or true refinement? Let me remind you of another saying of mine: 'The greatest inventions were produced in the time of ignorance; as the use of the compass, gunpowder and printing; and by the dullest nations, as the Germans.'

ORWELL: I see now where it is that we part company, Dr Swift. I believe that human society, and therefore human nature, can change. You don't. Do you still hold to that, after the French Revolution, the Russian Revolution?

SWIFT: You know very well what is my final word. I wrote it on the last page of *Gulliver's Travels*, but I will speak it again. 'My reconcilement to the Yahoo kind in general might not be so difficult if they would be content with those vices and follies only, which nature has entitled them to. I am not in the least provoked at the sight of a lawyer, a pick-pocket, a colonel, a fool, a lord, a gamester, a politician, a whore-master, a physician, an evidencer, a suborner, an attorney, a traitor, or the like: this is all according to the due course of things: but when I behold a lump of deformity and diseases both in body and mind, smitten with pride, it immediately breaks all the measures of my patience; neither shall we ever be able to comprehend how such an animal ...' (*voice fading*)

ORWELL: Ah, he's fading out? Dr Swift! Dr Swift! Is that your last word?

SWIFT: (*Voice a little stronger then finally fading out*) 'Neither shall I ever be able to comprehend how such an animal and such a vice could tally together. And therefore I here entreat those who have any tincture of this absurd vice, that they will not presume to come in my sight.'

ORWELL: He's gone. I didn't get much change out of him. He was a great man, and yet he was partially blind. He could only see one thing at a time. His vision of human society is so penetrating, and yet in the last analysis it's false. He couldn't see what the simplest person sees, that life is worth living and human beings, even if they're dirty and ridiculous, are mostly decent. But after all, if he could have seen that I suppose he couldn't have written *Gulliver's Travels*.

7

Edmund Blunden, by George Orwell

8th January 1943

Today we are having a departure from the usual arrangement of these talks. The introducer of all the others has been Mr Edmund Blunden who has been chiefly responsible for arranging the whole series. Today, however, Mr Blunden is delivering the talk himself. So I am here to introduce him to you, as he has introduced so many others.

As a matter of fact, it ought not to be necessary to introduce Edmund Blunden to any audience interested in English literature for his name has been familiar to the reading public for not far short of thirty years. Although he is primarily a poet and would perhaps wish to be thought of as a poet, Edmund Blunden is best known for a prose work *Undertones of War*. The war of 1914 to 1918 produced a great spate of literature in England but it only produced some half-dozen books which seem worth reading after a lapse of years. Well, among these *Undertones of War* has an assured place. As its title implies, it is a restrained unemphatic book, it describes the reactions of a sensitive and intelligent human being when brought into contact with the horrors of modern mechanised war but it doesn't deal in any kind of sensationalism. Like Edmund Blunden's poems it expresses a quiet acceptance of the world as it is and a love of the surface of the earth – even nature worship if you prefer that name for it. It has never failed him even in the extremest hardship and danger. I believe nobody else who wrote about the war of 1914 to 1918 remained so aware of the procession of the seasons and the birds and wild flowers which somehow managed to survive even on the edges of the battle-field. Even if you had never read Edmund Blunden's poetry you could hardly glance into *Undertones of War* without realising that here was a man whose love of the countryside was his ruling passion. Today Edmund Blunden is speaking to you about Thomas Hardy's novel *Far from the Madding Crowd*. Few people could be more suitable, for perhaps Hardy's greatest quality is his power of invoking a picture of the English countryside which Edmund Blunden loves so well. Now here is Edmund Blunden to talk to you about Thomas Hardy.

8

Bernard Shaw, by George Orwell

22nd January 1943

Arms and the Man was performed for the first time in 1894, when Bernard Shaw was 38 years old and was at the height of his powers as a dramatist. It is probably the wittiest play he ever wrote, the most faultless technically, and, in spite of being a very light comedy, the most telling. But before discussing the play in general terms I must say something, as short as possible, about its theme and plot.

Briefly, *Arms and the Man* is a debunking of military glory and the romance of the warrior. The action takes place in the little Balkan state of Bulgaria – it doesn't, of course, matter whether the local colour is correct or not: the events might just as well have happened in England or Germany or America – at a time when a war between Bulgaria and Servia has just ended in a Bulgarian victory. The heroine, Raina she is called, a romantic young girl, has just heard at the beginning of the first act that her lover, Sergius Saranoff, has won the crucial battle of the war by charging at the head of his regiment of cavalry through the enemy's machine guns. Naturally she is wild with pride. She is standing at her window, gazing out on the mountains and dreaming of her lover, when the defeated Serbian army begins to stream through the town with the Bulgarians pursuing them. One hunted man climbs up the waterpipe and takes refuge in her bedroom. He is hardly there when Raina finds herself violating what she believes to be the code of true patriotism by helping him to hide, and even telling lies to protect him when the pursuers come to look for him. But the short conversation she has with him punctures her illusions much more completely than that. The hunted man turns out to be a Swiss professional soldier, Captain Bluntschli by name, and the most hopelessly prosaic person it is possible to imagine. He can hardly open his mouth without outraging the notions of military glory on which Raina has been brought up. He assures her that all soldiers are frightened of death, that a man who has been under fire for three days loses his nerve until he is ready to cry like a child, and that in battle food is far more important than ammunition. 'You can always tell an old soldier by the insides of his holsters and cartridge boxes,' he says. 'The young ones carry pistols and cartridges: the old ones, grub.' But then an even worse disillusionment occurs. It turns out that Captain Bluntschli was in command of the Serbian machine gun battery which was destroyed when Sergius, Raina's lover, made his heroic cavalry charge. And he is able to explain why it was that the charge succeeded – the machine gunners had been sent the wrong ammunition and were unable to fire. If the guns had gone off not a man would have survived; so Sergius has in fact won the battle by mistake. In the later acts some illusions are exploded. Sergius, a magnificent romantic figure with flashing eyes and sweeping moustaches, a character out of Byron's early poems, turns out to be an almost complete fraud. He tells Raina that he regards her as a saint and himself as her knight errant, but he begins making love to the maidservant the moment Raina's back is turned. Raina herself is exposed as a habitual liar and as laying claim to lofty emotions which she does not feel, and all the other characters are in their various ways impostors. The play ends by Raina marrying the prosaic Swiss soldier, the first man who has ever seen through her romantic pretensions to the real woman underneath.

Shaw is what is called a 'writer with a purpose', every one of his plays is designed to point some moral or other, and undoubtedly one reason why *Arms and the Man* has worn better than some of the other plays he wrote at about the same time, is that its moral, or 'message', still needs pointing. Shaw is saying, in effect, that war, though sometimes necessary, is not glorious, not romantic. Killing and being killed isn't the heroic, picturesque business that the propagandists make it out to be, and moreover, wars will usually be won by those who plan for them scientifically and not romantically. Nearly fifty years after the play was written this is still worth saying, because the romantic view of war dies very hard and tends to revive after every disillusionment. It so happens that I have seen *Arms and the Man* acted twice. The first time was in 1918, and the theatre was full of soldiers fresh from the front in France. They saw the point of it, because their experiences had taught them the same thing. There is a passage early in the play where Bluntschli is telling Raina what a cavalry charge is really like. 'It is,' he says, 'like slinging a handful of peas against a window pane: first one comes; then two or three close behind him; and then all the rest in a lump.' Raina, thinking of Sergius, her lover, charging at the head of his regiment, clasps her hands ecstatically and says: 'Yes, first comes One! The bravest of the brave!' 'Ah,' says Bluntschli, 'but you should see the poor devil pulling at his horse!' At this line the audience of simple soldiers burst into a laugh which almost lifted the roof off. The next time I saw the play acted was in 1935, at an experimental theatre before a much more highbrow audience. This time Bluntschli's line didn't get a laugh. War was far away and very few people in the audience knew what it was like to have to face bullets.

If you examine Shaw's other plays of the same period, you find that some of them, equally brilliant in execution – for every one of Shaw's early plays is a masterpiece of technique, with never a false note or a wasted word – don't have the same freshness today, because in them he is attacking illusions which no one any longer believes in. The play which caused a terrific scandal when it first appeared and did, perhaps, more than anything else to make Shaw famous is *Mrs Warren's Profession*. This play deals with prostitution, and its theme is that the causes of prostitution are largely economic. This idea was a novelty in the eighteen-nineties, but now, when everyone has read Marx, it seems a commonplace, hardly worth uttering. So also with *Widowers' Houses*, an attack on slum landlordism. Slums still exist and people still make a profit out of them, but at least no one thinks this normal and proper any longer. Or so again with a somewhat later play, *John Bull's Other Island*. The satire in this play depends largely on Ireland being under English rule, a state of affairs which has long ceased to exist. *Pygmalion*, one of the wittiest of Shaw's plays, revolves round class-distinctions which at this date are nothing like so strongly marked as they used to be, and even *Major Barbara* and *Androcles and the Lion* depended for their first impact on orthodox religious belief being very much more general then it is today. I don't, however, want to give the impression that Shaw is one of those writers, like the French dramatist Brieux or the English novelist Charles Reade, who squander their talents on 'showing up' some local and temporary abuse which will probably have disappeared of its own accord within a few years. Shaw deals in generalities, not in details. He is criticising society as a whole, and not merely its aberrations. Yet there is a reason why his early attack has lost something of its sting, and it raises certain questions about the whole position of satirists and political writers generally.

Briefly, Shaw is a debunking writer, what people used to call a 'shocker'. Now it is obvious that you can only play this part successfully when there is something to be debunked. For the background, the springboard as it were, of his witticisms, Shaw needed the solidity, the power and the self-righteousness of the late-Victorian society in which he first lived and worked. Shaw was born in 1856 and first came to England at the age of about 20, and quite apart from his natural talent he was especially fitted to satirise English society because he was an Irishman and able to look at it from the outside as a native Englishman could hardly do. The two great vices of England are hypocrisy and stupidity. But late-Victorian society differed from that of today in that it was far more self-confident, more Philistine, more frankly acquisitive. What we should call 'enlightened' people were relatively far fewer. Class privilege was more assured, there were no left-wing political parties worth bothering about, popular education and cheap newspapers had not yet had their full effect, art and literature had lost contact with Europe in the early part of the century and not yet regained it. The world of late-Victorian England was easy meat for a satirical writer. Indeed, Shaw was not the first of his kind. In the prefaces to some of his plays he has discussed his own literary ancestry, and though he admittedly owes much to Ibsen, the great Norwegian dramatist, he seems to feel that he owes even more to Samuel Butler, the English novelist, who a few decades earlier had criticised English society from somewhat the same angle as Shaw himself. Butler, it is worth noticing, utterly failed to reach the big public and only received recognition after his death: Shaw, born twenty years later, remained obscure till he was nearly forty but lived to be the best-known literary man of his age. The difference is partly one of time. Butler's great novel, *The Way of All Flesh*, was at once hailed as a masterpiece when it was published round about 1905, but it would probably have fallen flat if he had published it in the 'eighties, when he actually wrote it. Shaw happened upon the scene when the colossus of

Victorian society was still there, as imposing and self-satisfied as ever, but was actually due to fall to pieces within a few years. He was attacking something still strong enough to be worth attacking, and yet not so strong as to make the attack hopeless. People found it amusing to be shocked, but they were still capable of being shocked. These conditions existed to perfection in the years 1890-1910, the years when Shaw's best work was done, but they exist no longer. No one, nowadays, could make his reputation as a 'shocker'. What is there any longer to be shocked at? What conventions survive to be outraged? The self-satisfied, prudish, money-ruled world that Shaw made fun of has been washed away by the spread of scepticism and enlightenment; and for that scepticism and enlightenment Shaw himself, as much as any one writer of our time, is responsible.

In this short space I have necessarily dealt with only one aspect of Shaw's work, his debunking of current society and the consequent inevitable 'dating' of certain of his plays. But it would be an absurdity to regard Shaw as a pamphleteer and nothing more. The sense of purpose with which he always writes would get him nowhere if he were not also an artist. In illustration of this I point once again to *Arms and the Man*. Whoever examines this play in detail will notice that it is not only a witty satire on one of the abiding illusions of humanity, but a miracle of stage technique. There are only eight characters in it – two of them are small parts – and by the time any one of these eight has spoken half a dozen sentences you have the feeling that you would recognise him at a glance if you met him in the street. Nowhere is there a false emphasis or a clumsily contrived incident; the play gives the impression of having grown as naturally as a plant. There are not even any verbal fireworks; brilliant as the dialogue is, every word of it helps the action along. In this play, and in two or three others written about the same time, Shaw's genius reached its high water-mark. If I were asked to tabulate Shaw's plays in order of merit, I should bracket together at the top *Arms and the Man* and *The Devil's Disciple*, his play about the American War of Independence. In both of those there is a strong central theme that may grow familiar but never grows stale, and in both there is the most perfect mastery of character, dialogue and situation. A little way below those two I should put *Captain Brassbound's Conversion, Caesar and Cleopatra, Androcles and the Lion* and *The Man of Destiny*, all of them brilliantly witty comedies. The volume of Shaw's work that will survive on its own merits is much greater than that, and it includes not only plays but dramatic criticism and at least one of his early novels, *Cashel Byron's Profession*. But whoever has read or seen those six plays that I have named has skimmed the cream off Shaw. These are the works of his prime, done when he knew himself for what he really was, a dramatist, and before he had mistaken himself for a philosopher and begun to produce unwieldly plays like *Man and Superman* and *Back to Methuselah*, already unactable and unreadable.

9

Jack London, by George Orwell

5th March 1943

Jack London, like Edgar Allan Poe, is one of those writers who have a bigger reputation outside the English speaking world than inside it – but indeed, more so than Poe, who is at any rate taken seriously in England and America, whereas most people, if they remember Jack London at all, think of him as a writer of adventure stories not far removed from penny dreadfuls.

Now, I myself don't share the rather low opinion of Jack London which is held in this country and America, and I can claim to be in good company, for another admirer of Jack London's work was no less a person than Lenin, the central figure of the Russian Revolution. After Lenin's death his widow, Nadeshda Krupskaya, wrote a short biography of him, at the end of which she describes how she used to read stories to Lenin when he was paralysed and slowly dying. On the last day of all, she says, she began to read him Dickens' 'Christmas Carol', but she could see that he didn't like it; what she calls Dickens' 'bourgeois sentimentality' was too much for him. So she changed over to Jack London's story 'Love of Life', and that was almost the last thing that Lenin ever heard. Krupskaya adds that it is a very good story. It *is* a good story, and you will hear a passage from it read presently by Herbert Read. Here I want only to point to this rather queer conjunction between a writer of thrillers – stories about Pacific islands and the goldfields of the Klondike, and also about burglars, prizefighters and wild animals – and the greatest revolutionary of modern times. I don't know with certainty what first interested Lenin in Jack London's work, but I should expect that it was London's political or quasi-political writings. For London was among other things an ardent Socialist and probably one of the first American writers to pay any attention to Karl Marx. His reputation in continental Europe is largely founded on that, and in particular on a rather remarkable book of political prophecy, *The Iron Heel*. It is a curious fact that London's political writings have almost escaped attention in his own country and Britain. Ten or fifteen years ago when *The Iron Heel* was widely read and admired in France and Germany, it was out of print and almost unobtainable in Britain, and even now, though an English edition of it exists, few people have heard of it.

This has several reasons, and one of them is that Jack London was an extremely prolific writer. He was one of those writers who make a point of

122

producing a fixed amount every day – a thousand words in his case – and in his short life (he was born in 1876 and died in 1916) he produced an immense number of books, of very different types. If you examine Jack London's work as a whole, you find that there are three distinct strains in it, which don't at first sight appear to have any connection with one another. The first is a rather silly one about which I don't want to say much, and that is a worship of animals. This produced his best-known books, *White Fang* and *The Call of the Wild*. Sentimentality about animals is something almost peculiar to the English-speaking peoples, and it isn't altogether an admirable trait. Many thoughtful people in Britain and America are ashamed of it, and Jack London's short stories would probably have received more critical attention if he hadn't also written *White Fang* and *The Call of the Wild*. The next strain to notice in Jack London is his love of brutality and physical violence and, in general, what is known as 'adventure'. He is a sort of American version of Kipling, essentially an active, non-contemplative writer. By choice he wrote about such people as gold-miners, sea-captains, trappers and cowboys, and he wrote his best work of all about tramps, burglars, prizefighters and the other riff-raff of great American cities. To this side of him belongs that story I've already mentioned, 'Love of Life', and I shall have more to say about it, because it produced nearly all of his work that is still worth reading. But on top of this there is also that other strain, his interest in sociology and in economic theory, which led him in *The Iron Heel* to make a very remarkable prophecy of the rise of Fascism.

Well now, let me return to 'Love of Life' and the other short stories which are Jack London's greatest achievement. He is essentially a short-story writer, and though he did produce one interesting novel, *The Valley of the Moon*, his especial gift is his power of describing isolated, brutal incidents. I use the word 'brutal' advisedly. The impression one brings away from Jack London's best and most characteristic stories is an impression of terrible cruelty. Not that Jack London himself was a cruel man or enjoyed the thought of pain – on the contrary he was even too much of a humanitarian, as his animal stories show – but his vision of life is a cruel one. He sees the world as a place of suffering, a place of struggle against a blind, cruel destiny. That is why he likes writing about the frozen polar regions, where Nature is an enemy against which man has to fight for his life. The story 'Love of Life' describes an incident which is typical of Jack London's peculiar vision. A gold-prospector who has missed the trail somewhere in the frozen wastes of Canada is struggling desperately towards the sea, slowly dying of starvation but kept going simply by the force of his will. A wolf, also dying of hunger and disease, is creeping after the man, hoping that sooner or later he will grow weak enough for it to attack him. They go on and on, day after day, till when they come within sight of the sea each is crawling on his belly, too weak to stand up. But the man's will is the stronger, and the story ends not by the wolf eating the man but the man eating the wolf. That is a typical Jack London incident, except that it has in some sense a happy ending. And if you analyse the subject-matter of any of his best stories you find the same kind of picture. The best story he ever wrote is called 'Just Meat'. It describes two burglars who have just got away with a big haul of jewellery. As soon as they get home with the swag it occurs to each of them that if he killed the other he would have the whole lot. As it happens they each poison one another at the same meal, and with the same poison – strychnine. They have a little mustard which might save one or other of them if used as an emetic; and the story ends with the two men writhing in agonies on the floor and feebly struggling with one another for the last cup of mustard. Another very good story describes the execution of a Chinese convict in one of the French islands in the Pacific. He is to be executed for a murder committed in the prison. It happens that the prison governor, by a slip of the pen, has written down the wrong name, and consequently it is the wrong prisoner who is taken out of his cell. His guards do not discover this till they have got him to the place of execution, which is twenty miles from the prison. The guards are uncertain what to do, but it hardly seems worth the trouble of going all the way back, so they solve the question by guillotining the wrong man. I could give further instances, but all I am anxious to establish is that Jack London's most characteristic work always deals with cruelty and disaster; Nature and Destiny are inherently evil things against which man has to struggle with nothing to back him up except his own courage and strength.

Now it is against this background that Jack London's political and sociological writings have to be seen. As I have said, Jack London's reputation in Europe depends on *The Iron Heel*, in which – in the year 1910 or thereabouts – he foretold the rise of Fascism. It's no use pretending that *The Iron Heel* is a good book, as a book. It's a very poor book, much below Jack London's average, and the developments it foretells aren't even particularly close to what had actually happened in Europe. But Jack London did foresee one thing, and that was that when the working-class movements took on formidable dimensions and looked like dominating the world, the capitalist class *would hit back*. They wouldn't simply lie down and let themselves be expropriated, and as so many Socialists had imagined. Karl Marx, indeed, had never suggested that the change-over from Capitalism to Socialism would happen without a struggle, but he did proclaim that this change was *inevitable*, which his followers, in most cases, took as meaning that it would be *automatic*. Till Hitler was firmly in the saddle it was generally taken for granted that Capitalism could not defend itself, because of what are generally called its internal contradictions. Most Socialists not only did not foresee the rise of Fascism but did not even grasp that Hitler was dangerous till he had been about two years in power. Now Jack London would not have made this mistake. In his book he describes the growth of powerful working-class movements, and then the boss class organising itself, hitting back, winning the victory and proceeding to set up an atrocious despotism, with the institution of actual slavery, which lasts for hundreds of years. Who now will dare to say that something like this hasn't happened over great areas of the world, and may not continue to happen unless the Axis is defeated? There is more in *The Iron Heel* than this. In particular there is Jack London's perception that hedonistic societies cannot endure, a perception which isn't common among what are called progressive thinkers. Outside Soviet Russia left-wing thought has generally been hedonistic, and the weaknesses of the Socialist movement spring partly from this. But Jack London's main achievement was to foresee, some twenty years before the event, that the menaced capitalist class would counter-attack and not quietly die because the writers of Marxist text-books told it to die.

Why could a mere story-teller like Jack London foresee this when so many learned sociologists could not? I think I have answered that question in what I said just now about the subject-matter of Jack London's stories. He could foresee the rise of Fascism, and the cruel struggles which would have to be gone through, because of the streak of brutality which he had in himself. If you like to exaggerate a little, you might say that he could understand Fascism because he had a Fascist strain himself. Unlike the ordinary run of Marxist thinkers, who had neatly worked it out on paper that the capitalist class was bound to die of its own contradictions, he knew that the capitalist class was tough, and would hit back; he knew that because he himself was tough. That is why the subject-matter of Jack London's stories is relevant to his political theories. The best of them deal with prison, the prize-ring, the sea and the frozen wastes of Canada – that is, with situations where toughness is everything. That is an unusual background for a Socialist writer. Socialist thought has suffered greatly from having grown up almost entirely in urban industrialised societies and leaving some of the more primitive sides of human nature out of account. It was Jack London's understanding of the primitive that made him a better prophet than any better-informed and more logical thinkers.

I haven't time to speak at length about Jack London's other political and sociological writings, some of which are better, as books, than *The Iron Heel*. I will only shortly mention *The Road*, his reminiscences of the time when he was a tramp in America, one of the best books of its kind ever written, and *The People of the Abyss*, which deals with the London slums – its facts are out of date now, but various later books of the same kind were inspired by it. There is also *The Jacket*, which is a book of stories but contains at the beginning a remarkable description of life in an American prison. But it is as a story-writer that Jack London best deserves to be remembered, and if you can get hold of a copy I earnestly beg you to read the collection of short stories published under the title *When God Laughs*. The best of Jack London is there, and from some half-dozen of those stories you can get an adequate idea of this gifted writer who has been, in a way, so popular and influential but has never in my opinion had the literary reputation that was due to him.

10

English Poetry since 1900
by George Orwell

13th June 1943

The six talks that follow this one are intended to give a survey of modern English poetry from about the year 1900 until the present. The speakers in the series are Desmond McCarthy, who is well known as a literary and dramatic critic and is literary editor of the *Sunday Times*; L.A.G. Strong, the novelist; Alan Rook, who is one of the most promising of the very young poets who have made their appearance in England since the outbreak of war; Lord David Cecil, who is well known for his life of the poet Cowper, his recent book on Thomas Hardy and other critical works; John Lehmann, who from 1936 onwards has been editing the periodical *New Writing*, which apart from publishing the less-known English and American writers has done a lot to introduce contemporary European and Asiatic literature to the English public; and Desmond Hawkins, the critic, whose voice is pretty well known to listeners on the Eastern Service. Each of these six talks will include one poem belonging to the period, and we hope where possible to broadcast the poem in the author's own voice. After they have been broadcast, these talks, like various others of the series we do in this service, will be printed and sold in India in pamphlet form for a few annas.

I don't want to anticipate what the other speakers will say, merely to give a sort of background sketch of the period they will be covering. Poetry is of all arts the most national, or I should rather say local, the most difficult to export or import. Whereas prose can always be adequately translated, and in some cases may actually be better in translation than in the original, poetry is almost untranslatable. And just as a poem belongs, more than a piece of music or perhaps even a picture, to a particular place, so it belongs to a particular time. It is much easier to appreciate a foreign poem, and perhaps even one in your own language, if you know something about the social, moral and religious background from which it springs. For the music of poetry depends on word-associations, and in order to appreciate it you have to share those associations to some extent, or at any rate to be able to imagine them. It isn't therefore irrelevant to try to supply a sort of historical background to the talks that will follow. The period that they will cover is only 43 years, but during that time enormous changes have happened and the

126

prevailing mental climate has altered out of recognition. To some of the English poets who were writing in 1900, the Great Exhibition of 1851 would have been a vivid memory; those who are now beginning to publish their work don't even remember the war of 1914-18. They live in a different world, though a short lifetime would span the two dates. I am trying to indicate here the differences that have come over British society in that time.

If you put yourself into the mind of a man who was mature in 1900, you find that several pieces of mental furniture that we are very much accustomed to are missing. The first of these is what I might call the concept of the machine. We live in an age in which everyone who thinks at all, everyone who ever reads a book or newspaper or listens to the radio, is very much aware of the power of machinery and technology to raise our standard of living. Films, textbooks, posters, pamphlets, the speeches of political leaders, rub this into us all the time. Every educated person knows that given a reasonable amount of international co-operation, the world's wealth could be increased, health and nutrition improved, drudgery abolished, to an extent unthinkable a few decades ago. Now this fact was not in the consciousness of most of the writers who were mature in 1900, although the essential technological changes had already happened. If you look at a writer like Thomas Hardy, or Robert Bridges, or Gerard Manley Hopkins, or A.E. Housman, a thing that strikes you is that they still think of England as an agricultural country – which as a matter of fact it wasn't even in 1900. They haven't much conception of the new sort of world, now obviously possible though it hasn't arrived, in which the brute labour is done by machinery and the peasant or workman is better off than a king would have been in the Middle Ages. They still think in terms of the harsh peasant world where it is normal to work hard, to till the ground with primitive implements, to do without foreign luxuries, and to die rather young.

On the other hand, what you are not likely to find in the mind of anyone in the year 1900, is a doubt about the continuity of civilization. If the world as people then saw it was rather harsh, simple and slow-moving, it was also secure. Things would continue in a more or less recognizable pattern; life might not get appreciably more pleasant, but at any rate barbarism wouldn't return. Now here again is a great change that has occurred in these four decades. We have seen an enormous technological advance, and with it a reversion to barbarism that our grandfathers would not have believed possible. We have invented machines that would have seemed magical only a hundred years ago, and we have used them almost solely for making war. The world has grown into an economic unit, so that if you merely look round the room you are sitting in you'll see products that come from every corner of the earth; and at the same time nationalism has been erected into a sort of evil religion and the races of mankind are shut off from one another by insane hatreds. All that is in the consciousness of anyone who is writing now. All the younger writers, people like Auden or Spender, or the still younger ones like Henry Treece and Alex Comfort who have appeared more recently, have it as the background of their thoughts that the basis for a decent society is already there, and on the other hand that the very existence of civilization is menaced. If you had told the average person, and that would include most of the poets, in 1900 that it would soon be easy to fly from London to Calcutta he wouldn't have believed you; and if you had told him that before long Jews would be persecuted more fiercely than they ever were in the Middle Ages, he wouldn't have believed that either. Anyone born within this century takes both facts for granted, and that establishes a valid distinction.

However, other things have happened between 1900 and today besides scientific invention and the rise of the new kind of barbarism that we call Fascism. There was also the period of exceptional prosperity between the opening of the century and the war of 1914, there was the war itself, there was the period of exhaustion and recovery that followed the war, and there was the economic depression of 1930. Those, with the two periods I've just been speaking of, make up the background of the six talks you will hear. It's worth saying a little about each of them.

The period between about 1905 and 1914, generally referred to when one's speaking of literature as the 'Georgian' period, was a very good time to be alive, at any rate in England. There was great prosperity, much of the dullness and prejudice of Victorian society had been broken down, and there was a growth of what appeared to be enlightenment and internationalism. The great nations of the world were in fact getting ready for war, but the ordinary man didn't believe that war was coming. A carefree attitude towards life was more possible then than it has been since, and also a rather shallow pantheism summed up in the then popular phrase, 'Nature worship'.

The war of 1914 butted into this comfortable period more unexpectedly than the present war has done. Whether it caused more or less suffering than the present war is hard to say. It killed more people than have been killed hitherto, but it probably impinged less on the lives of non-combatants. But what is unmistakeable in the characteristic literature of the 1914 war is the sense of something unprecedented and something meaningless. Whereas all the best writing of the nineteen-thirties is heavy with the sense of approaching disaster, so that it is almost a relief when the expected happens and the guns begin to shoot, the characteristic reaction in the other war is surprise and resentment. The war is thought of as a horror that has come as it were from nowhere, and for no reason, like an earthquake. It is just a purposeless slaughter – nearly all the best writing of that time expresses that feeling, which may have been mistaken but was at least subjectively true.

The war of 1914–18 left Britain much exhausted, but after it ended there was still another decade when life was well worth living, at any rate in the victorious countries. There was a worldwide revulsion from war, another seeming growth of internationalist feeling, and better contacts between the writers and artists of different countries than there had ever been before. That was the period in which for the first time the great Russian writers were fully popularised in England, and when the French writers of the past few decades had their greatest influence. It is perhaps significant that the best writers of this particular period were most of them either Americans or Irishmen. For a while it could almost be said that the headquarters of the English literary world were in Paris. In that emancipated, fairly prosperous period of the nineteen-twenties there was room for a culture and refinement that English literature had not seen since the eighteenth century. But the mental climate changed very suddenly at the beginning of the next decade, with the onset of the economic depression and the beginning of something that Britain had not experienced before – middle-class unemployment. Inevitably, after 1930, there was a far geater preoccupation with politics, with sociology, with economics than had seemed necessary in the decade before. The younger writers almost all of them turned to Karl Marx because the basis of their own existence had been shaken and Marx was the prophet who had foretold that this would happen. And then a little later came the rise of Fascism, the undisguisable drift towards world war, and the new orientation of the younger writers who find themselves in a world which has all the potentialities of peace and plenty combined with the *fact* of destruction and hatred.

11

'Crainquebille' by Anatole France adapted by George Orwell

11th August 1943

NARRATOR: Jerome Crainquebille, 60 years of age, was a vegetable-seller in the Rue Montmartre in Paris. Every day of his life he went up and down the street, pushing his barrow in front of him and crying: 'Cabbages! Turnips! Carrots!' When he had leeks he cried: 'Asparagus!' because leeks are the asparagus of the poor. Now it happened that one day, just about noon, he was going down the Rue Montmartre when Madame Bayard, the shoemaker's wife, came out of her shop. She went up to Crainquebille's barrow, and picked up a bundle of leeks with a disdainful air:

MDE. MAYARD: These leeks aren't much good, are they? How much are they a bundle?

CRAIN: 15 sous, Ma'am. Best leeks on the market!

MDE. BAYARD: What! 15 sous for three miserable leeks?

NARRATOR: And she flung the bundle of leeks back on to the barrow with a gesture of disgust. It was just at this moment that a policeman, Constable No. 64, arrived on the scene and said to Crainquebille:

C.64: Move on, there. Keep moving.

NARRATOR: Now Crainquebille had been moving on from morning till night for the last 50 years. To be told to move on didn't seem in the least unnatural to him. He was quite ready to obey, but he did stop and urge Madame Bayard to take whatever vegetables she wanted. Madame Bayard said sharply that she must have time to choose, and with great care she felt all the bundles of leeks over again. Finally, she picked out the one she thought best, and held it clasped against her bosom, rather as the saints in sacred pictures hold the palm of victory.

MDE. B: I'll give you 14 sous. That's plenty. But I'll have to fetch the money out of the shop, because I haven't got anything on me.

NARRATOR: Still clasping the leeks, she went back into the cobbler's shop. At this moment Constable 64 spoke to Crainquebille for the second time:

C.64: Move on, there. Didn't you hear me tell you to keep moving?

CRAIN: But I'm waiting for my money!

C.64: Never mind about waiting for your money. I'm not telling you to wait for your money. I'm telling you to move on.

NARRATOR: Meanwhile in the cobbler's shop Madame Bayard had thrown the leeks onto the counter and was busy fitting a pair of slippers onto a child whose mother was in a hurry. Crainquebille had a profound respect for authority. He had acquired it during the 50 years in which he had been pushing his barrow through the streets. But at this moment he was in a peculiar position, and his mind was not adapted to complex problems. Perhaps he attached too great an importance to the 14 sous that Madame Bayard owed him, and too little to his duty of moving on when a policeman told him to. At any rate, instead of moving on as he had been told to do, he simply stood still. Constable 64 quietly and calmly spoke to him again.

C.64: For the third time, move on, will you?

NARRATOR: Crainquebille merely shrugged his shoulders and looked sadly at the police constable. Now it happened that at this moment the block of traffic in the Rue Montmartre was just at its worst. (*Crowd noises.*) Carriages, drays, carts, buses and trucks were jammed one against another in such a tangle that it looked as though they would never be sorted out again. There was an uproar of shouting and swearing. (*Crowd noises.*) Cabmen and butcher boys exchanged insults at long range and the bus conductors, who considered Crainquebille to be the cause of the traffic jam, called him 'silly turnip'. The crowd on the pavement were pressing round to listen to the dispute. Constable 64, finding himself the centre of attention, felt that it was time to display his authority. With a solemn air he took a stump of pencil and a greasy notebook out of his pocket. Crainquebille wasn't moving; all he could think of were those 14 sous. Besides, he couldn't move. The wheel of his barrow had got jammed with that of a milkman's cart. At the sight of the notebook he tore his hair under his cap and cried:

CRAIN: But didn't I tell you that I'm waiting for my money? How can I go away without getting my money? It's a bloody shame!

NARRATOR: These words expressed despair rather than rebellion; but Constable 64 felt that he had been insulted. Now, according to Constable 64's ideas, every insult inevitably took the form of a shout of 'Down with the police!' In his experience all rioters, demonstrators, anarchists, in general, all enemies of society invariably shouted 'Down with the police!' 'Down with the police!' was the regular, traditional, classical insult. Consequently it was in this time-honoured form that he heard what Crainquebille said.

C.64: Ah! that's enough! 'Down with the police!', you said. Very well, then. Come along with me.

NARRATOR: Crainquebille was stupefied:

CRAIN: What! me? I said, 'Down with the police'? Why should I say that?

C.64: That'll do! D'you think I didn't hear you? Come along with me.

NARRATOR: It was no use. Constable 64 had it firmly in his head that 'Down with the police' was what Crainquebille had said. He began to lead him away. Even as he was doing so Madame Bayard, the shoemaker's wife, came out of the shop with the 14 sous in her hand.

MDE. B: Mon Dieu! ...

NARRATOR: But Constable 64 already had Crainquebille by the collar. Madame Bayard promptly decided that one does not need to pay money to a man who is being taken to the police station and put her 14 sous back in her apron pocket. Crainquebille was taken before the Commissioner of the Police, and spent the night in the lock-up. Next morning he was taken to the police court in a prison van.

Being in prison did not seem to Crainquebille particularly painful or humiliating.

CRAIN: It's a queer place, this. I've never been in jug before. I wonder what they did with my barrow? Doesn't seem much sense to shut a man up in a stone cell all by himself. And doesn't the time go slowly! Of course they have to do it. There's some people that have to be locked up, otherwise nobody'd be safe. But it's not what I'd call home-like. It's all so clean! They must swab these walls down every morning. And fancy chaining that stool to the wall! It isn't as if you could take it away with you. And it's so quiet! Makes every minute seem like an hour. I wonder what they did with my barrow?

NARRATOR: On the third day he received a visit from his lawyer, Maître Lemerle, one of the youngest members of the Paris bar. Crainquebille endeavoured to tell his story. But this wasn't easy. Crainquebille was no conversationalist, and the lawyer didn't give him much help, but merely twiddled his fair moustache in a bored manner while he listened.

CRAIN: You see, Monsieur, it was like this – I didn't insult him, you understand that? He just took it into his head that I'd said it. Besides he was in a bad temper because of the way the bus drivers were carrying on. But I couldn't go away without my 14 sous, could I? You couldn't expect a man to go away without his money?

LEMERLE: You say definitely that you did not insult this man? Are you perfectly certain that you did not say, 'Down with the police?'

CRAIN: Of course I didn't, Monsieur. That is to say I did say it, but –

LEMERLE: You did say it?

CRAIN: In a manner of speaking I said it, Monsieur. But not the way he meant. And what about my 14 sous? Madame Bayard had taken the bunch of leeks. Besides, how could I move on when my barrow was jammed against the milk cart?

LEMERLE: This is a complicated business, Crainquebille. I don't find anything about a milk-cart in my brief; nor about a bunch of leeks.

CRAIN: You see Monsieur, it's all a little difficult to explain.

LEMERLE: Crainquebille, let me give you a piece of advice. It would be in your own interest to plead guilty. If you persist in denying it, it will create a bad impression. If I were you I should confess.

CRAIN: Very well, Monsieur. But just tell me. What is it that I have to confess?

NARRATOR: Next morning Crainquebille was taken before the magistrates. Monsieur Bourriche, the president of the court, devoted six whole minutes to examining him. The examination would have been more useful if Crainquebille had answered the questions that were asked of him. But he was not used to discussions, and he was too much overawed by the ceremonious atmosphere of the court to be able to speak freely. So he was silent. The president solved the problem by answering his own questions himself. He concluded solemnly:

PRESIDENT: And, so, prisoner at the bar, you admit to having said, 'Down with the police.'

CRAIN: Monsieur, I did say, 'Down with the police', but only after he said it, if you understand me. He said, 'Down with the police', and so than *I* said, 'Down with the police', don't you see?

PRESIDENT: Are you seriously trying to maintain that this policeman shouted, 'Down with the police' himself?

NARRATOR: Crainquebille gave up trying to explain. It was too difficult. The President took this as a sign of guilt.

PRESIDENT: So you do not persist in your statement. Quite right. That is the wisest course you can take.

NARRATOR: The President then had witnesses called. Constable 64, by name Bastien Matra, was called and gave evidence in the following terms:

C.64: I promise that what I say shall be the truth, the whole truth and nothing but the truth. On the 20th of October at noon, I was on my beat when I noticed in the Rue Montmartre a person who appeared to be a coster-monger unduly blocking the traffic with his barrow opposite No. 328. On three occasions I gave him the order to move on, but he refused to comply. I then gave him warnings that I was about to charge him. He retorted by shouting, 'Down with the police!' I saw that this was intended as an insult, and took him in custody.

NARRATOR: Constable 64's evidence was delivered in a firm and moderate tone. It made an excellent impression on the magistrates. After the calling of other witnesses Maître Lemerle, Crainquebille's lawyer, made a speech in which he endeavoured to show on the one hand that Crainquebille had not shouted 'Down with the police', and on the other that he had shouted it, but had not meant it seriously.

LEMERLE: Your worship, my client is accused of having shouted 'Down with the police'. Now we all know that this expression is frequently shouted in the streets by a certain class of people. So the question resolves itself into this: in what spirit did Crainquebille say it? And on the other hand did he say it at all? Permit me to doubt it, gentlemen.

Gentlemen, I will say no word against the police force. A finer body of men does not exist. I would be far from suspecting Constable 64 of any evil intention. But we know that a police officer's profession is an arduous one. He is often tired, harassed, overworked. Is it not possible, gentlemen, that in such circumstances Constable 64 may have suffered from some kind of aural hallucination and merely imagined that my client uttered the words attributed to him? And on the other hand, let us suppose that Crainquebille did shout 'Down with the police'. It still remains to be proved whether, on his lips, such words can be regarded as contempt. Crainquebille is the natural child of a coster-monger, ruined by years of drinking and other evil courses. Crainquebille was born alcoholic. You have only to look at him to see how completely he has been brutalised by 60 years of poverty. Gentlemen, you must conclude that he is not responsible for his actions.

NARRATOR: Maître Lemerle sat down. His speech had accomplished nothing. Monsieur Bourriche, the president of the court, immediately pronounced a sentence condemning Crainquebille to pay 50 francs fine and to go to prison for a fortnight. The evidence of Constable 64 had been too strong. Crainquebille was led away to prison.

When he had got back to his cell Crainquebille sat down with a feeling of wonder and admiration on the stool which was chained to the wall.

CRAIN: There's something gone wrong somewhere. Or is it me that's wrong? I *didn't* shout 'Down with the police', that's certain. Or did I? The funny thing is, you couldn't imagine these gentlemen on the bench making a mistake. They were all of them clever men, they understood all about the law and all that, you could see that with half an eye. And they were very fair, I must say that. They didn't try to stop you speaking up for yourself. How could they make a mistake? Maybe I *did* shout 'Down with the police'? Could you shout out a thing like that without knowing you'd done it? Or maybe I just forgot about it afterwards. I don't believe that magistrate would make a mistake. A regular learned man he looked, with his spectacles and his black gown. He had a way of holding his head down and looking at you over his spectacles – it kind of made you feel that he was looking right through you and knew all about you. And yet I *didn't* shout 'Down with the police', I could swear to that. It's all a puzzle.

NARRATOR: On the next day his lawyer came to visit him:

LEMERLE: Well, Crainquebille, things didn't turn out so badly after all, did they? Don't be discouraged, a fortnight is soon over. We haven't much to complain of.

CRAIN: I must say, Monsieur, that the gentlemen were very kind, very polite. Nobody called me any names. It was quite different from what I expected. Did you see the white gloves the officers were wearing?

LEMERLE: All things considered, Crainquebille, I think we did well to plead guilty.

CRAIN: Perhaps, Monsieur. You know best.

LEMERLE: Now, I have some good news for you, Crainquebille. A charitable person whom I managed to interest in your case has sent me fifty francs for you. That will just do to pay your fine, you see.

CRAIN: And when do I get the fifty francs?

LEMERLE: It will be paid into the clerk's office, don't bother about that.

CRAIN: Thank you, Monsieur. I'm very grateful to this person. This is a queer business that's happened to me, isn't it Monsieur?

LEMERLE: Not so queer, really. Things like this are happening every day, you know.

CRAIN: There's one other thing, Monsieur. I suppose you couldn't tell me where they put my barrow?

NARRATOR: A fortnight later Crainquebille was discharged from prison. Once again he was back in the Rue Montmartre, pushing his barrow and shouting 'Cabbages! Turnips! Carrots!' He was neither ashamed nor proud of his adventure. The memory of it was not even painful. It was merely a mysterious interval like a dream. But above all he was glad to be once again tramping over the mud and the cobbles and to see overhead the rainy sky as dirty as the water in the gutter, the familiar sky of Paris where he had been born. At every corner he stopped for a glass of red wine, and then with an invigorated feeling he would spit on his horny hands, seize the shafts and push his barrow on again. Meanwhile the flocks of sparrows flew away at the sound of his familiar cry: 'Cabbages, turnips and carrots!' Like Crainquebille the sparrows were poor and got up early, and like him they sought their living in the streets. When he met his customers:

WOMEN: Where have you been all this time, Crainquebille? We haven't seen you for three weeks.

CRAIN: Oh, I've been in prison.

NARRATOR: There appeared to be no change in his life except that he went oftener to the pub, because coming out of prison had given him the feeling of being on holiday. He came back to the garret where he slept a little bit the worse for drink. Stretching himself on his mattress, he drew over him the sacks which he had borrowed from the chestnut-seller at the corner, and which served him as blankets; and he thought to himself:

CRAIN: Well, really, prison isn't so bad. You've got everything you want there. It's clean, there's enough to eat and they keep you warm. They give you clothes to wear, and you don't have to worry about the rent either. But all the same, there's no place like home.

NARRATOR: However, Crainquebille did not remain long in this contented frame of mind. Very soon he noticed that his old customers were looking askance at him. All kinds of people who had previously flocked round his barrow when it was piled with fresh green vegetables, now turned away when they saw him coming. He went round to Madame Bayard, the cobbler's wife, who owed him the 15 sous which had started the whole trouble. But when he reminded her about the 15 sous Madame Bayard, who was sitting at her counter, did not even deign to turn her head.

The fact was that the whole of the Rue Montmartre knew that Crainquebille had been in prison. As a result the whole quarter gave him the cold shoulder. It ended with Crainquebille having a disgraceful wrangle in the street with Madame Laure, an old customer of his, whom he found buying vegetables from somebody else's barrow. The two of them stood there shouting insults at one another in the street, while a group of idlers looked on. It might even have come to something worse if a policeman had not suddenly appeared on the scene. The policeman did not do anything, but by his mere appearance he reduced both of them to silence. So they separated. But this quarrel was the final touch and had the effect of discrediting Crainquebille once and for all in the eyes of everyone in the Rue Montmartre.

It was the same with all of them. They all avoided him as though he had the plague. Even his old friend the chestnut-seller would no longer have anything to do with him. Crainquebille felt himself an outcast. He used to mutter to himself about the injustice of it all.

CRAIN: It isn't fair, that's what I say, it isn't fair! I get put away for a fortnight and after that I'm not even thought good enough to sell leeks. Do they call that justice? Where's the sense of making a fellow die of starvation just because he once got into a bit of trouble with the police? What's to become of me if I'm not allowed to sell vegetables? I'd like to give a few of the people in this quarter a bit of my mind, the hypocrites!

NARRATOR: In fact, he did give several people a bit of his mind, and in no uncertain terms. He got into a number of quarrels at the wine shop. People said that old Crainquebille was turning into a regular porcupine, and they were right; he was becoming disagreeable, foul-mouthed and abusive. The fact was that for the first time in his life he was discovering the imperfections of society; but not having the equipment of a philosopher he expressed his thoughts in hasty and ill-judged words. Misfortune made him unjust. He took his revenge on people who wished him no evil and sometimes on people weaker than himself. One day Alphonse, the wine-seller's little boy, innocently asked him what it was like in jail. Crainquebille smacked him on the ear and said:

CRAIN: You dirty little brat! It's your father who ought to be in jail instead of filling his pockets by selling poison.

NARRATOR: It was an unworthy action, for as the chestnut-seller rightly pointed out, a child does not choose his own parents and ought not to be blamed for them. Crainquebille was also beginning to drink too much. The less money he earned the more brandy he drunk. This was a great change in his habits, for before he went to prison he had always been thrifty and sober. He himself noticed these changes. Often he blamed himself severely for his bad habits and his laziness.

CRAIN: It's funny. I never used to be one for the drink. The fact is you don't get any better as you get older. Nowadays it seems I'm no good for anything except boozing. But then I just have to have a pint or two now and then to put a bit of strength into me. It's like as if I had a fire burning in my inside and there's nothing except drink will put it out. I can't do without it, that's the trouble.

NARRATOR: Nowadays Crainquebille often missed the auction at the vegetable market in the morning, and had to pick up inferior fruit and vegetables on credit. One day, with discouragement at his heart and a tired feeling in his legs, he left his barrow in the shed and spent the whole day hanging round the tripe stall and lounging in and out of the wine shops near the vegetable market. In the evening, sitting on a basket, he meditated on the deterioration which had overtaken him. He remembered how strong he had been in his early years, how hard he used to work all day, and how happy he had been in the evenings. He remembered the innumerable days, swiftly passing, all alike and all full of labour. He remembered the darkness of the early mornings, when he waited in the cobbled yard for the auction to begin; he remembered how he used to carry the vegetables in armfuls and arrange them artistically on his barrow; and then the little cup of black coffee swallowed standing at one gulp, and then the shafts grasped vigorously and then his own loud cry of 'Cabbages! Turnips! Carrots!', piercing as a cock-crow, rending the morning air as he passed through the crowded streets. The rough, innocent, useful life, like that of a human pack horse, which he had led for fifty years – it all came before his eyes. He sighed:

CRAIN: No, I can't go on any longer. I'm done for. Nobody lasts for ever. Besides ever since that time I was had up by the police it seems as if I haven't the same character any longer. No, I'm not the man I used to be.

NARRATOR: The fact is Crainquebille had given up hope, and when a man reaches that state he might as well be lying on his back in the mud. Every passer by treads him under foot.

Poverty came to him, black, grinding poverty. The old coster-monger who used once to come back from Montmartre with a bag full of five-franc pieces now had not a single copper to his name. It was winter now. Driven out of his garret, Crainquebille slept under some carts in a shed. It had been raining for days, the gutters were overflowing, and the shed was flooded.

As he squatted in his barrow to get away from the filthy water, amid spiders, rats and half starved cats, he meditated. He had had nothing to eat all day and he no longer had the chestnut-seller's sacks for a covering. At this moment he remembered that fortnight in prison when the government had provided him with food and shelter. He found himself actually envying the prisoners' fate:

CRAIN: After all, it isn't so bad in jail. At any rate you aren't cold and you aren't hungry. They're better off in there than I am out here. And it's easy enough to get inside. It didn't take much to make them lock me up last time. I'll do it! Why didn't I ever think of it before?

NARRATOR: Crainquebille got up and went out into the street. It was a little past eleven on a cold dark night. A drizzling mist was falling, colder and more penetrating than rain. The few passers by crept along under cover of the houses.

Crainquebille turned into the Rue Montmartre. It was deserted. A solitary policeman was standing under a street lamp outside a church, while all around him fell a fine rain which looked reddish in the gas light. The policeman was standing so still that he looked scarcely human. The reflection of his boots on the wet pavement prolonged his shape downwards and gave him, from a little distance, the appearance of some amphibious monster half out of the water. Seen closer to, with the hood of his water-proof cape covering his head, he had more the appearance of a monk. The coarse features of his face, magnified under the shadow of the hood, were sad and by no means aggressive. He was an old policeman, with a thick grey moustache. Crainquebille went up to him, halted and summoned up his courage. Then in a weak, quavering voice he cried out:

CRAIN: Down with the police!

NARRATOR: Nothing happened. Crainquebille waited for the terrible words to take their effect. Still nothing happened. The policeman remained motionless and silent, his arms folded beneath his short cloak. His eyes were wide open, they glistened in the darkness and regarded Crainquebille with a mixture of sorrow, watchfulness and scorn. Crainquebille was astonished, but he was still resolute. He tried again:

CRAIN: Down with the police! Didn't you hear me? Down with the police!

NARRATOR: There was a long silence in the chill darkness and the fine penetrating rain. At last the policeman spoke:

POLICEMAN: You mustn't say things like that. Don't you know better at your age? You'd better get along home.

CRAIN: Why don't you arrest me! Didn't you hear me shout 'Down with the police'? They arrested me last time.

POLICEMAN: Listen, if we were to take up all the fools who say things they oughtn't to, we'd have our work cut out. Besides what would be the use of it?

NARRATOR: Crainquebille was defeated. The policeman's magnanimous attitude was something he had never bargained for. For a long time he stood stupefied and silent, with his foot in the gutter. He was about to make off, but before going he tried to explain:

CRAIN: Listen, I didn't mean any harm. I wasn't saying 'Down with the police' to you, you understand. Not you more than anyone else. It was only an idea, if you understand me.

POLICEMAN: Maybe it was an idea, maybe it wasn't, but it's not a thing you ought to say. Because when a man does his duty and has a lot to put up with there's no sense in calling him names. Now, you go home to bed.

CRAIN: And you're not going to arrest me?

POLICEMAN: No. Why should I? What is there to arrest you for? Go home.

NARRATOR: So Crainquebille, with his head bowed and his arms hanging limply from his body, slouched away into the rain and the darkness.

12

'The Fox' by Ignazio Silone
adapted by George Orwell

9th September 1943

(*Pig effects*)

NARRATOR: Daniele was a peasant of the Ticino, in Switzerland, just over the border from Italy. One morning when he was busy in the pig-sty helping the sow to litter, his daughter Silvia came a little way down the path from the house and called to him:

SILVIA: Father! there's someone here that says she wants to speak to you.

DANIELE: Go away, child. I can't see anyone now. Didn't I say I wasn't to be disturbed? I'm too busy looking after the sow.

(*Pig effects*)

NARRATOR: Daniele had taken every care to see that the birth should go off successfully, but with a sow you can never be absolutely certain. He had put her on a strict diet the day before and as an extra precaution had given her a stiff dose of castor oil. Agostino, a young Italian who had been living in the Ticino for some years, was helping him. Agostino was a builder by trade but he did odd jobs of all kinds in the off season.

The birth started well and three little pigs hardly bigger than rats had already come into the world. There was practically nothing for Agostino to do except to find a suitable name for each little pig as it appeared. There was some trouble with the fourth one, but after that it went well and there were seven altogether. Agostino held up the fourth pig, the one which had not wanted to be born.

AGOSTINO: That's a very poor pig. We'll call this one Benito Mussolini.

DANIELE: Impossible. I'm going to sell these pigs in Italy.

SILVIA: Father! Didn't you hear me calling you? There's somebody here who wants to talk to you.

DANIELE: Go away, child. I'm busy. (*To Agostino*) Now we must wrap these young pigs up warmly. You can't be too careful with them their first day. Help me put them in this box. Agostino. The straw will keep them warm. Now, this blanket on top ... There, they ought to be all right now. We'll have to take care that the fox doesn't get hold of them, though.

139

AGOSTINO: Do you get many foxes round here?

DANIELE: Lots of them. And they're cunning brutes, too. It takes a lot of catching, a fox does. A farmer's life is just one trouble after another. When it isn't bad weather it's birds, or weeds, or plant disease, or vermin. But a fox is the worst of all.

AGOSTINO: Here's Silvia coming down the path with someone.

DANIELE: Who is it?

AGOSTINO: Looks like Caterina.

DANIELE: Caterina! That dried-up old chatter box, she'll go on for hours if she once starts talking. Quick. Come down to the orchard, Agostino.

SILVIA (*calling*): Father!

CATERINA: Signor Daniele!

AGOSTINO: Too late, Daniele – you're cornered.

CATERINA: Signor Daniele, I want your advice about something. An Italian gentleman came to see me yesterday afternoon.

DANIELE: Well, what about it?

CATERINA: You'll hardly believe it. He asked me to become a spy!

DANIELE: A spy!

CATERINA: Yes. He wants me to spy on the Italian workers who go to and fro between Italy and Switzerland. He said to me, 'You're a dressmaker. With your work you must go into hundreds of houses and hear all kinds of conversations. And besides, you're an old maid and nobody takes any notice of you. You could pick up all kinds of information if you cared to.' Well, he went on talking like this for some time, and then he said straight out: 'If you're prepared to gather information about the activities of certain Italian anti-Fascists living in the Ticino, we can make it worth your while. In fact, you could look forward to making something to lay aside for your old age.' That's what he said to me, Signor Daniele.

DANIELE: Why do you come to me with this story? I'm not Italian. I'm not interested in your Italian affairs.

CATERINA: But I want your advice.

DANIELE: What kind of advice? Advice about what?

CATERINA: Why, whether to accept the gentleman's offer or not. I don't know what to do. I've never been so upset and worried in all my life. If I do accept I shall earn a lot of money, but only by doing harm to people who've never done any harm to me. But it's dangerous to refuse too. If I refuse they'll put me down as an anti-Fascist and then I shall be persecuted in all kinds of ways. You know me, you know I'm neither a Fascist nor an anti-Fascist. I don't know anything about politics, all I want is to be able to earn my living and be left alone. I'm so upset about it.

DANIELE: You know I don't meddle in politics either. But don't be afraid, it'll be all right. Tell Agostino what you've just told me and then do what he tells you.

CATERINA: Are you working against the Fascists too, Signor Daniele?

DANIELE: If I was, I shouldn't talk about it. The trouble with all you Italians is that you talk too much. Now you go along and tell Agostino all about it, and remember to do exactly what he tells you. I must get back to my pigs.

NARRATOR: Some days later Daniele was at work in the orchard with Silvia. He had a free morning and was using it to disinfect his vines against disease. He was going over the affected places with a small metal brush and Silvia was following him with a can of boiling water, when Agostino appeared driving a lorry loaded with bricks.

(Lorry slows down and stops)

AGOSTINO: Daniele! Hi! That business of ours is going ahead.

DANIELE: What business?

AGOSTINO: You know well enough what I mean.

DANIELE: I know nothing about it.

SILVIA: Father, I *know* you're really working against the Fascists, aren't you? Although you don't talk about it. I would like so much to help you!

DANIELE: Then take these rotten twigs up to the house and burn them, that's the only way you can help me at the moment. All you people talk too much.

AGOSTINO: Did you hear that there's another fox at work in the neighbourbood? It got into a chicken-run the night before last and nearly fifty chickens were found with their necks broken.

DANIELE: We'll have to be careful with our chickens. We'll set the trap tonight. But it's a difficult job trapping a fox. The brutes are so sly that they won't touch the bait even when they're starving.

AGOSTINO: A bit of poisoned meat is better than a trap.

DANIELE: Even that doesn't always work. No one knows just the right amount of strychnine to kill a fox. If you put too little the fox only gets a belly-ache, and if you put too much he merely vomits it up again.

AGOSTINO: Listen, Daniele. Now that Silvia's gone, I'll tell you about the other fox we are trying to catch, the fox on two legs, I mean. Caterina's doing just as I told her. The Italian spy went to see her again yesterday, and after a lot of sobbing and sighing she agreed to do the work. You see the idea. Caterina's the bait. We'll make use of her to bring the spy here, and then we've got him. He's told her to find out the names of all the Italian workers who cross the frontier every day and come in contact with political refugees in this country. He also told her that it would be worth a big sum of money to her if she could help him to find out who are the people who are smuggling revolutionary books and pamphlets into Italy.

DANIELE: Did he tell her that they suspected anyone in particular?

AGOSTINO: No. She herself doesn't know anything in any case.

DANIELE: Does Caterina know that I have anything to do with the Italian revolutionaries?

AGOSTINO: No, she thinks you have nothing to do with politics. Here's Silvia coming back ...

DANIELE: It's rain we need, the land's cooked as dry as a bone.

NARRATOR: Every evening Daniele set the steel trap outside the hen house and scattered poisoned scraps of food. But the fox did not put in an appearance. And Agostino's fox, the two-legged one, the spy – he didn't seem in any hurry to be caught either. At any rate Daniele heard no more of the matter for some days. Then one morning Agostino arrived.

AGOSTINO: The trap is set, Daniele. The fox will be caught tonight.

DANIELE: How are you going to set about it?

AGOSTINO: Caterina has written to the spy and told him that she has some important information for him. She has arranged to meet him at nine o'clock tonight near the lake, outside the old San Quirico chapel. Only, you see, Caterina won't be alone. I and two others are going to keep the appointment too.

DANIELE: Don't you think it would be better to tell the police and have the man arrested? After all, he is an Italian spy.

AGOSTINO: No, that would be stupid. The consulate would hear about it and the fox wouldn't turn up. You leave it to us. We'll make the man sorry he was ever born.

NARRATOR: That evening Daniele took a train to Locarno and strolled along the lake to the place where he had arranged to wait for Agostino. However, at about half past ten it was not Agostino who turned up but Luca, another Italian who worked in Switzerland, a carpenter by trade. He explained why Agostino had not appeared.

LUCA: Agostino has hurt his hand a bit. He didn't want people to notice his bandage.

DANIELE: But what about the spy?

LUCA: Oh, we left him lying there. He turned up at the meeting place and met Caterina, while we stayed in hiding behind the chapel. Caterina began sobbing and sighing as usual and then told the spy a lot of absolute rubbish. Among other things she told him that the revolutionary books which are being smuggled into Italy came from the Franciscan monastery at Locarno.

DANIELE: That was a good idea!

LUCA: Well, Agostino went across to the spy and left us behind the church. We had agreed that Agostino should only draw his revolver if the man showed any sign of using his own revolver first. Agostino walked up to him as though he was passing that way by chance. Then he lit a cigarette and recognised him by the light of the match. 'Ah, I think I've seen you before! You're the Italian spy!' And then the fight started. We came out of our hiding place and Caterina took to her heels.

DANIELE: Did you join in too?

LUCA: There was no need to. We only kept a look-out to make sure no one was coming. Agostino had got the spy down in a moment and then he punched his head so hard it would have broken a stone. It quite surprised me. I always knew Agostino was strong, but I didn't know he hated the Fascists so much as all that.

DANIELE: They killed his brother, don't forget. But how did he hurt his hand?

LUCA: The spy bit it. He got Agostino's left hand between his teeth. Agostino punched his jaw like a madman with the other hand, but he wouldn't let go. So Agostino took him by the throat and throttled him.

DANIELE: You don't mean to say he finished him off?

LUCA: It looked like it. At any rate we left the man for dead.

DANIELE: That's a bad business! Agostino must disappear at once. He'll have to get out of the country – to France perhaps. I'd better stay the night at Locarno and see what arrangements I can make.

NARRATOR: As Daniele was going to spend the night away from home he thought he had better let his family know where he was, so he went into the nearest café and telephoned. Silvia answered the telephone.

SILVIA: Hallo, oh it's you, father. It's a good thing you rang up. I've been trying everywhere to find you for the last hour.

DANIELE: What's the matter?

SILVIA: There's been a bad motor accident; two cars collided near here on the road to Gordola. A man has been badly hurt. The doctor said he was too bad to be moved far so they made enquiries and all the neighbours said that ours was the only house where there would be room for him. Mother didn't want to take a stranger into the house while you were away, but I knew you'd agree.

DANIELE: Of course. Where have you put him?

SILVIA: On the first floor, in my room. I'll sleep with Luisa. The doctor is sending a nurse along tonight. We don't know who the man is or where he comes from. He's still unconscious. But we think he must belong to a rich family because the doctor wanted to give mother money in advance.

DANIELE: Now listen, I can't come home tonight. But take good care of this man, and do everything the doctor tells you. Tell him to make quite free with my house till the man gets better. I wouldn't like to feel we hadn't done our best for him.

NARRATOR: Next morning Daniele learned that the injured man was an Italian engineer named Umberto Stella, who had come to Switzerland to study electric power production. Meanwhile, Daniele was trying to find out how far the police had got with their enquiries into the attempted murder the night before. He was far too clever to start talking about it himself, but he waited for others to begin, and bought several morning papers. However, he could hear nothing about it, not even when he made an excuse to go and see his lawyer and settle some formalities. In the end he decided that Luca must have exaggerated the whole business. These Italians, he said to himself, are fine people but they all talk too much. But he was glad that the spy had not been killed after all, otherwise Agostino and Caterina might have had to leave Switzerland.

As soon as he got home Daniele went up to the first floor to see the injured man. At the door of the room he found Silvia barring the way. She put her fingers to her lips.

SILVIA: Sh! You mustn't make such a noise. He's got to be kept absolutely quiet. He must have no visitors, and there must be no talking. The doctor said that there must be nothing that would excite him in any way.

DANIELE: So there's nothing I can do, then?

SILVIA: Yes. You can take off your boots before you go downstairs, so as not to make any noise.

NARRATOR: Daniele took his boots off and went downstairs and out into the garden. Even then, when he started chopping some wood, Silvia came running out to tell him not to make so much noise. Daniele kept as quiet as possible, and then presently, when he saw Silvia leave the house, he went indoors again, took off his boots and crept upstairs. The nurse let him peep into the sickroom. All he could see in the bed was an enormous head completely covered in bandages. Although it was nothing to laugh at he could not help being reminded of a snowman. It was nothing but a great big white ball with a little hole for one eye and slightly bigger one for the mouth. Nothing else of the man's face was visible.

For a long time after this Silvia was completely wrapped up in looking after the patient, especially when he began to get a little better and the regular nurse was discharged. For days together Silvia hardly went out of doors, except now and then to gather a few flowers for the sickroom. Daniele went in to see the patient once or twice, but only for a few moments. He seemed a decent fellow enough, but there was always something to attend to on the farm. Even so Daniele could not help noticing the change in his daughter, and he was worried about it. The fact was he suspected that Silvia had fallen in love with the Italian engineer. Daniele took her out for a long walk and tried to talk to her, but she would not say anything. At last the engineer was well enough to leave his room and lie in a chair in the orchard. It happened that that morning Caterina and Daniele were coming back together from Gordola. They were just getting near the orchard when on the other side of the hedge they heard someone calling out.

ENGINEER: Signorina Silvia!

CATERINA: Who's that?

DANIELE: That's Umberto Stella, the Italian engineer. The doctor said he could come and sit out of doors this morning.

CATERINA: Wait ... let me have a look at him through the hedge ... Yes, I thought so. Do you know who that is? It's the spy! That man in the orchard there is the Italian spy I told you about.

DANIELE: You're mad! That man is an engineer. He was hurt in a motor accident while I was away and they brought him into my house.

CATERINA: I know it's the man! I'd know him anywhere. I must get away before he sees me.

DANIELE: My God. Well listen, tell Agostino to come here tomorrow at the same time. Yes yes, I'll take care the man doesn't see him.

NARRATOR: Daniele said nothing to the others. The patient was now so much better that Silvia suggested that they should all have their midday dinner together. At dinner the situation was almost intolerable. They talked uncomfortably about this and that. In order to make conversation Daniele started telling them about a railway accident that had just been reported in the newspapers.

DANIELE: And they say hundreds of people have been killed.

SILVIA: How terrible.

ENGINEER: Ah, Signor Daniele. Just consider the hundreds of people who were killed in that accident yesterday. They were all kinds of people, students, peasants, commercial travellers, officers, doctors, lawyers – everything. They were in the same train and yet they were not in the same train. The peasants were thinking about market prices, the lawyers were thinking about the cross of the Legion of Honour, the officers were thinking about finding themselves rich brides, the students were daydreaming about the new ties they had just bought. It was as if they were all travelling in different trains. And then suddenly all of them were put into the same train, the train of death. They were just a lot of corpses mixed up together. They were all in the same train without knowing it. Death is the only unity.

DANIELE: Still, the railway authorities took care to destroy that unity. They had the corpses in fur coats laid out separately from the others.

SILVIA: Then people must continue to be enemies even after death?

DANIELE: Present-day society is based entirely on the antagonism of man to man. The great majority of mankind are separated from the results of their labour. The product of their labour has hardly left their hands when it no longer belongs to them, but to their enemies. Some day it will be different.

ENGINEER: I see that you're an idealist. I also used to look forward to a better society than the one we live in. Nowadays I've grown more realistic in my views.

NARRATOR: Daniele went outside again and continued digging in the orchard. Spring was near and there was a great deal of work to do. It troubled him to have this man in the house – a spy and an enemy, and yet a human being with whom it was possible to talk. That evening they had another long conversation. They started talking about Tolstoy's *War and Peace* and ended by talking about the moon. The trouble was that Daniele could not bring himself to hate the spy as bitterly as he ought to have done. Next day Agostino arrived as had been arranged. When Daniele saw him coming he went out to meet him and took him into the house through the door on the side away from the orchard, where the so-called engineer was lying in the sun. From behind a curtain Agostino had a good look at the spy without any danger of being seen.

AGOSTINO: That's him! That's the man right enough.

DANIELE: You're sure?

AGOSTINO: Perfectly. And now we've got him. He won't get away alive this time!

DANIELE: You don't mean that seriously, do you?

AGOSTINO: I do mean it. The fox is in the trap, and I'm not going to let him out of it.

DANIELE: But you can't murder a man in cold blood!

AGOSTINO: You know who that man is, don't you? He's one of those dirty Fascists who murder our comrades in Italy and shut them up in prison and on the islands. Now he's in our power. Do you think we're going to let him go?

DANIELE: But he's lived in my house for weeks. He's my guest.

AGOSTINO: He's a spy!

DANIELE: He *was* a spy, but now he's my guest. He was brought in here half dead and we've nursed him back to life. He's eaten my salt.

AGOSTINO: Don't you under*stand* that we can't afford these scruples when we're fighting against Fascists? *They* don't have scruples.

DANIELE: I know. That's why I'm not a Fascist.

AGOSTINO: Daniele, you're old-fashioned. It was just because *we* had scruples that the Fascists beat us in the first place. When your enemy is down, smash him. Do you remember that bit in the Bible where King Agag was captured by the Israelites? Saul wanted to let him off but the prophet Samuel knew better. I've always remembered the words: 'And Samuel said, As *thy* sword hath made women childless, so shall *thy* mother be childless among women. And Samuel hewed Agag in pieces before the Lord.'

DANIELE: That was five thousand years ago. Don't be so bloody-minded.

AGOSTINO: You have to be. Anything else isn't fair to your own side. But you'll change your mind before long. Tell me, how much longer is this man staying here?

DANIELE: I should think he'll be here another week. He's still very feeble.

AGOSTINO: Oh, that's all right, then. There'll be time enough to talk this over before he gives us the slip.

NARRATOR: Daniele decided to say nothing about all this to the family. He did not want to worry them. And he took care to see that his guest noticed nothing either. It happened that one of his wife's sisters had recently had a baby and Daniele decided to go over and see her with his wife and Silvia. So Luisa, his younger daughter, was left alone with the invalid. Luisa was only a young girl and very anxious to entertain him. She took a childish pride in showing him all over the house and garden. She even showed him the store-room where the potatoes, onions, fruit and gardening tools were kept. Then she showed him the room on the first floor in which she and Silvia now slept. When they got there something immediately attracted the engineer's attention. It was a framed picture on the wall decorated with two red paper carnations. In reality it was a picture of Matteotti, the Italian socialist deputy who was murdered by the Fascists in 1927.

ENGINEER: Whose picture is that?

LUISA: That's Matteotti.

ENGINEER: And who is Matteotti?

LUISA: He was a man who stood up for the poor and so he was murdered by Mussolini.

ENGINEER: Do you hate Mussolini? Are you an anti-Fascist?

LUISA: Of course.

ENGINEER: And Silvia?

LUISA: She's even more anti-Fascist than I am.

ENGINEER: And how about your Father?

LUISA: He's more anti-Fascist than any of us. But Father doesn't talk about it. He never talks about anything. He just acts.

ENGINEER: This is a very nice house that you live in. You've showed me all of it except for one room. What is that room on the second floor next to your parents' room?

LUISA: Oh, nobody's allowed in there. Father forbids it. It's his private room. All I know is that there are lots and lots of papers in there.

ENGINEER: Papers?

LUISA: Yes, and Father's ever so careful of them. He won't let any of us touch them. I suppose he doesn't want them untidied.

ENGINEER: Those must be his business papers – bills and receipts and so on.

LUISA: I expect so.

NARRATOR: Luisa and the engineer went back to the garden. The engineer paced up and down the garden path for some time and seemed to be thinking. Then he asked Luisa to send off a telegram for him, and having given her the message and the money he said he was tired and was going straight to bed.

Next morning Silvia took up the engineer's breakfast. There was no answer when she knocked at his door. She knocked again, more loudly. There was still no answer. Immediately Silvia was certain that something was wrong. She cried out for the others:

SILVIA: Father! Father! I think there's something the matter here. He doesn't answer, and the door's locked.

DANIELE: One moment. I'll get the door open for you.

(Sound of door being forced)

SILVIA: He's gone!

LUISA: He's gone without even saying good-bye.

SILVIA: And the bed hasn't been slept in.

NARRATOR: In fact, the room was empty, and what was more, the engineer's luggage had disappeared. A sudden thought struck Daniele, and in two bounds he was on the second floor.

DANIELE: Thief! Spy! Traitor! He's taken all my papers. Come up here! Look at this!

LUISA: What is it?

DANIELE: Look, all the drawers have been emptied on to the floor. It's that Italian.

AGOSTINO: *(calling)*: Anyone at home?

SILVIA: Agostino, is that you? Come on up here quick.

AGOSTINO: What is it?

DANIELE: Look at this! Look what that dirty spy has done! He cleared off last night and he's taken nearly all my secret papers with him. He's taken all the papers dealing with the traffic across the frontier. We've got to warn the men involved at once. There's not a moment to lose.

AGOSTINO: So that explains it. Do you know that twenty workers were arrested at Luino station early this morning? They were all men who come into Switzerland to work for the day and go home to Italy at night.

SILVIA: No! no! no! It isn't true. It can't be true. I can't believe it of a man like that. Not after he'd lived in this house for weeks!

DANIELE: What we've got to think of is the ones who haven't been caught yet.

AGOSTINO: Come on. There'll be time to warn a few of them, anyway.

NARRATOR: Daniele and Agostino hurried away. Daniele did not return until late that evening. His wife Filomena and Luisa were sitting by the stove. Silvia was sitting on a box at the back of the dark kitchen.

DANIELE: Well, it's all up. The people who smuggle our pamphlets for us were arrested early this morning. A book depot was raided at mid-day. The police have been to Caterina's place and Agostino seems to have been arrested. If he has, he'll probably be expelled from Switzerland. Haven't the police been here yet?

SILVIA: No.

DANIELE: They soon will, then.

NARRATOR: Daniele sat down on the door-step. The night came and the stars appeared. The cock crowed for the first time, but no one thought of going to bed. No one wanted to set foot on the first floor, where until yesterday the spy who called himself an engineer had slept. The cock crowed a second time. Filomena and Luisa remained sitting by the stove, Silvia remained sitting on the box at the back of the dark kitchen and Daniele sat at the threshold. It was like a death-watch, as though somebody had died. The cock crowed a third time.

Just then an animal cry broke the silence.

(Fox howling followed by a cackle of chickens)

SILVIA: Listen, what's that? It's like a dog that's been hurt.

LUISA: And listen to the noise the chickens are making.

DANIELE: It's the fox! He's in the trap.

NARRATOR: Daniele sprang to his feet and dashed down the garden towards the hen house. Sure enough, there was a fox with its paw caught in the trap. The animal was pulling with its three legs trying to loose the captured limb. When it saw Daniele approaching it started jumping frantically from side to side, though it was hampered by the chain which held the trap.

DANIELE: At last I've got him!

NARRATOR: He seized an axe which was lying near the hen house and struck at the fox as though he were felling an oak tree. He struck at its head, its back, its belly and its legs, and went on striking long after he had hacked the carcase to pieces and reduced it to a bloody pulp.

13

'A Slip Under the Microscope'
by H.G. Wells
adapted by George Orwell

6th October 1943

NARRATOR: It was an autumn morning, forty years ago. The grey London fogged against the windows of the College of Science, but inside the laboratory there was a close warmth and the yellow light of gas lamps. On the tables were glass jars containing the mangled remains of the crayfish, frogs and guinea-pigs on which the students had been working, and a litter of handbags, boxes of instruments and anatomical drawings. And on one table there lay – looking rather incongruous in its surroundings – a prettily-bound copy of William Morris's *News from Nowhere*. The clock had struck eleven and the lecture in the adjoining theatre had just come to an end. The students were arriving in the laboratory by ones and twos and getting their dissecting instruments ready amid casual conversation.

(Feet – voices)

GIRL STUDENT: Have you been reading *News from Nowhere*?

MISS HAYSMAN: Yes. I borrowed it from Mr Hill. I brought it to give back to him.

GIRL STUDENT: It's about Socialism, isn't it? It must be terribly dull.

MISS HAYSMAN: It's a wonderful book. Only there's so much in it that I don't understand.

GIRL STUDENT: There's Mr Hill over there. He's having an argument as usual. He's a terribly self-assertive young man, isn't he? I think Mr Wedderburn is really much cleverer in a quiet way. Of course he inherits it. His father is the famous eye-specialist, you know. These classes are terribly mixed, aren't they, with all these scholarship people? Do you see that tall man with the beard? They say he actually used to be a tailor! Now I think Mr Wedderburn is really nice-looking.

MISS HAYSMAN: Mr Hill has an interesting face, too.

GIRL STUDENT: But you couldn't call him good-looking, could you? And he's so badly dressed. Just look at his collar! It's all frayed along the top.

NARRATOR: Hill was a sturdily-built young man of twenty, with a white

149

face, dark grey eyes, hair of an indeterminate colour, and prominent, irregular features. His clothes were obviously ready-made and there was a patch on the side of his boot near the toe. At the moment he was standing beside the laboratory sink with two other students, a tall fair-haired youth and a little hunchback, and arguing – a little more loudly than was necessary – about the lecture they had just been listening to.

HILL: You heard what he said: 'From ovum to ovum is the goal of the higher vertebrate.' I agree with him entirely. There is no world except this world – no life except bodily life.

FAIR-HAIRED STUDENT: I admit that science can't demonstrate the existence of any other kind. But there are things above science.

HILL: I deny that. Science is systematic knowledge. An idea has no value unless it can be scientifically tested.

HUNCHBACK: The thing I can't understand is whether Hill is a materialist or not.

HILL: Of course I am. There is only one thing above matter, and that is the delusion that there is something above matter.

F/HAIRED STUDENT: So we have your gospel at last. It s all a delusion, is it? All our aspirations to lead something more than dogs' lives, all our work for anything beyond ourselves – just a delusion. But look how inconsistent you are. Your socialism, for instance. Why do you trouble about the interests of the race? Why do you concern yourself about the beggar in the gutter? Why are you bothering to lend William Morris's *News from Nowhere* to everyone in this laboratory?

HILL: Why not? Materialism isn't the same thing as selfishness. There's no reason why a man should live like a brute because he knows of nothing beyond matter, and doesn't expect to exist a hundred years hence.

F/HAIRED STUDENT: But why shouldn't he?

HILL: Why *should* he?

F/HAIRED STUDENT: What inducement is there to live decently if death ends everything?

HILL: Oh, inducements! You religious people are always talking about inducements. Can't a man seek after righteousness for its own sake?

F/HAIRED STUDENT: And what would be your definition of righteousness?

NARRATOR: The question disconcerted Hill. The fact was that he could not have said exactly what he meant by righteousness. At this moment, however, the laboratory attendant came in, carrying a batch of freshly-killed guinea-pigs by their hind legs. He slapped down a couple of guinea-pigs on each table, and the students took their instruments out of the lockers and got ready for work.

Hill was the son of a cobbler. He had entered the College of Science by means of a scholarship and was living in London on an allowance of a guinea a week, which paid not only for his board and lodging but also for ink and paper. It even covered his clothing allowance – an occasional water-proof collar, that is. He had learned to read at the age of seven, and had read omnivorously ever since, in spite of the fact that he had gone to work in a boot factory immediately after passing the seventh standard at the Board School.

He had a considerable gift of speech – indeed he was a leading light in the College Debating Society – a serene contempt for clergy of all denominations, and a fine ambition to reconstruct the world. He regarded his scholarship as a brilliant opportunity. As for his limitations, except that he knew that he knew neither Latin nor French, he was completely unaware of them.

He was in his first year at the College of Science. So far his interest had been divided pretty equally between his biological work and those vague rambling arguments on generalities which are so dear to students everywhere. At night, when the museum library was shut, he would sit on the bed in his Chelsea room, with his coat and muffler on, writing out his lecture notes and revising his dissection memoranda; and then presently his friend Thorpe, the physics student, would call him by a whistle from the pavement, and the two of them would go prowling through the gaslit streets, talking endlessly about God and Righteousness and Carlyle and the Reorganisation of Society. It was only recently that he had become aware of a competing interest – Miss Haysman, the girl with brown eyes, who worked at the next table to him and to whom he had lent the copy of *News from Nowhere*.

She was a paying student. Socially, she and Hill belonged in totally different worlds. Hill could never forget this, he could never feel at ease with her, indeed it was not often that he had an opportunity of speaking to her. But he found himself thinking of her more and more.

HILL: I'm not much good at talking to girls. I suppose that young Wedderburn would be more her style. He's got the proper clothes and manners – he's good-looking too. His father's the famous eye-specialist, she told me. I must say, though, she didn't seem surprised when I told her that *my* father was a cobbler. I oughtn't to have said that; it almost looked as though I was jealous. Of course she knows all sorts of things that I don't, poetry and music and so forth. She must have learnt French and German at school, perhaps Latin too. But when it comes to Science I'm ahead of her. She had to come and ask me about the alisphenoid of the rabbit's skull. And she'd hardly heard of Socialism until I told her about it.

NARRATOR: Miss Haysman has also thought about Hill – more frequently, perhaps, than he imagined.

MISS HAYSMAN: He told me he went to work in a factory at fourteen and won his scholarship years afterwards. I do admire him for that. But it's terrible to think of all the things he's missed. He seemed almost suspicious when I offered to lend him that book of Browning's poems. I remember he told me that he'd never 'wasted time' on poetry. What an idea! But what I do admire about him is that he doesn't seem to care about money or success in the ordinary sense. He seems quite ready to live all his life on less than a hundred a year. But he does want to be famous, and he does want to make the world a better place to live in. The people he admires, people like Bradlaugh and John Burns, all seem to have been poor. Somehow a life like that seems so terribly bare. But I've started him reading poetry. That's something.

NARRATOR: In fact, Hill spent much of the Christmas holiday in reading poetry. The examinations were over and the results would be anounced at the beginning of the next term. There were no scientific textbooks in the public library of the little town where his father lived, but there was plenty of poetry, and Hill read everything he could lay hands on – except Browning, because he hoped that Miss Haysman might lend him further volumes later on. On the day that the term opened he walked to the College with the volume of Browning in his bag, turning over in his mind various neat little speeches with which he might return it. In the entrance hall, however, a crowd of students was pressing round the notice board. The results of the biology examination had just been posted up. For a moment Hill forgot all about Browning and Miss Haysman and pushed his way to the front. There on the board was the list:

Class 1: 1st H.J. Somers Wedderburn
2nd William Hill

There were no other names in the first class. Hill backed out of the crowd amid the congratulations of his friends.

F/HAIRED STUDENT: Well done, Hill!

GIRL STUDENT: Congratulations on your first class, Mr Hill.

HILL: It's nothing.

GIRL STUDENT: We poor folks in the second class don't think so.

F/HAIRED STUDENT: You'd think he'd be more pleased at being in the first class, wouldn't you?

HUNCHBACK: He wants to be top of it.

GIRL STUDENT: Of course he's terribly jealous of Mr Wedderburn, you know.

NARRATOR: In fact, Hill was jealous, a little. A moment earlier he had felt generously enough towards Wedderburn. He had been ready to shake him by the hand and congratulate him on his victory. But when he entered the laboratory the first thing he saw was Wedderburn leaning gracefully against the window, playing with the tassel of the blind, and talking to no less than five girls at once. This was too much for Hill. He could talk confidently and even overbearingly to one girl, and he could have made a speech to a roomful of girls, but to exchange light conversation with five of them simultaneously was beyond him. Moreover, one of the girls in question was Miss Haysman. Hill decided to put off returning the volume of Browning. He sat down at his table and took up his notebooks, just as a stout heavy man with a white face and pale grey eyes passed down the laboratory, rubbing his hands together and smiling.

F/HAIRED STUDENT: Who's that old fellow?

GIRL STUDENT: That's professor Bindon, the professor of botany. He comes up from Kew Gardens for January and February. He's going to take the botany course this term.

NARRATOR: In the term that was now beginning Hill worked harder than ever. But he was in a curious emotional state. Wedderburn, whom he had hardly noticed a term ago, was more and more in his consciousness. He was growing less shy of Miss Haysman. They talked a great deal about poetry and socialism and life in general, over mangled guinea-pigs in the laboratory, or at lunchtime in the comparative privacy of the museum. One day, however, she told him casually that she had met Wedderburn socially, 'at the house of some people she knew'. She hardly realised what a pang of jealousy that sent through Hill. It infuriated him to think of that remote upper-class world to which she and Wedderburn both belonged, and from which he himself was excluded.

HILL: He meets her in a drawing-room, and they talk the same language: I can only meet her here in the laboratory among a crowd of people. And I suppose she notices when my collars are frayed. He's always so well dressed. I hate these snobs! He beat me in the last exam, but look at his background and look at mine! He has a comfortable study to work in, all the books he wants, good food, servants and tailors and barbers to look after him, and a famous man for his father. I have to work in a bedroom and wear my overcoat to keep warm. But I'll beat him next time, I swear that.

NARRATOR: It seemed to Hill absolutely necessary that he should beat Wedderburn in the forthcoming examination. And Wedderburn, in his quieter way, obviously returned his rivalry. As the time of the examination drew nearer Hill worked night and day. Even in the teashop where he went for lunch he would break his bun and sip his milk with his eyes intent on a closely-written sheet of memoranda. In his bedroom there were notes on buds and stems pinned round his looking-glass, and over his washing basin there was a diagram to catch his eye, in case the soap should chance to spare it. Everyone knew about the rivalry between the two men – the Hill-Wedderburn quarrel, it was called. Miss Haysman was perhaps not altogether sorry to feel that she was the cause of it. Wedderburn had been paying her much more attention to Hill* – indeed, he made rather a point of joining in conversation in which Hill was taking part. He had an irritating trick of intervening when Hill was in the middle of a speech, and uttering some neat little sneer about Socialism or atheism which Hill found difficulty in answering.

HILL: I tell you Socialism is the only hope of the human race. As I was saying at the Debating Society last night –

WEDDERBURN: Still talking about Socialism, Hill? I'm afraid I find your belief in it rather hard to share. My impression is that if you divided the money up on Tuesday it would all be back in the same places on Wednesday.

HILL: Who's talking about dividing the money up? Have you ever made a serious study of Socialism?

WEDDERBURN: I've made a serious study of Socialists, my dear fellow. That's equally enlightening.

(Laughter)

HILL: Anybody can make cheap jokes. Why don't you come down to the Debating Society one evening and have it out?

WEDDERBURN: What time does this debating society of yours meet?

HILL: Half past seven.

* So reads the typescript.

WEDDERBURN: Impossible. I always dine at eight.

HILL: Socialism means common ownership of the means of production. If you'd read Karl Marx –

WEDDERBURN: Nobody has read Karl Marx, my dear fellow. He is unreadable.

(*Laughter*)

NARRATOR: Hill was no good at this kind of conversation, and he knew it. It seemed to him cheap, unfair and connected in some subtle way with Wedderburn's well-cut clothes, manicured hands and generally sleek and monied exterior.

HILL: He's got such a mean, sneering way of talking. He never really argues, only tries to raise a laugh. How I wish he'd come to the Debating Society one night! Then I'd smash him. Of course that class are all the same. Millionaires, cabinet ministers, generals, bishops, professors – they're all the same. Just hiding behind their money and their little social tricks. He's not a man, he's only a type. Wait till the exam, though. This time I'll wipe the floor with him.

NARRATOR: At last the day of the examination arrived. The professor of botany, a fussy, conscientious man, had rearranged all the tables in the long narrow laboratory to make quite sure that there should be no cheating. All the morning from ten till one Wedderburn's quill pen shrieked defiance at Hill's, and the quills of the others chased their leaders in a tireless pack, and so it was also in the afternoon. Wedderburn was a little quieter than usual, and Hill's face was hot all day, and his overcoat bulged with textbooks and notebooks against the last moment's revision. And the next day, in the morning and in the afternoon was the practical examination, when sections had to be cut and slides identified. It was in this part of the examination that the mysterious slip occurred.

The professor of botany had placed on the table a microscope holding a glass slide, in which there was a preparation from some portion of a plant. The test for the students was to identify the preparation. The professor explained clearly that the slide was not to be moved.

PROF. BINDON: Will you please make quite sure, all of you, not to move the slide under that microscope. I want each of you in turn to go to the table, make a sketch of the preparation, and write down in your answer book what you consider it to be. And once again, *do not* move the slide. I want you to identify the preparation in that position, and no other.

NARRATOR: The professor's reason, of course, was that the preparation – actually it was a lenticel from the elder tree – was difficult to recognise in this particular position, but easy enough in certain others. But it was a foolish stipulation to make, because it offered opportunities to a cheat. To move the slide under a microscope takes only a second and can be done accidentally; and besides, it would be quite easy for anyone to move the slide and then move it back. When it came to Hill's turn to go to the table, he was already a little distraught. He had just had a struggle with some re-agents for staining microscopic preparations. He sat down, turned the mirror of the microscope to get the best light, and then –

HILL: My God! I've moved the slide!

NARRATOR: In fact, he had moved it from sheer force of habit. And even as he did so he remembered the prohibition, and with almost the same movement of his fingers he moved it back again. All the same, he had had time to see what the preparation was. Slowly he turned his head. Nobody had seen – nobody was looking. The professor was out of the room and the demonstrator was reading a scientific journal. Hill's eyes roved over his fellow-students, and Wedderburn suddenly glanced over his shoulder at him with a queer expression in his eyes. Hill sketched the preparation under the microscope, but he did not as yet write down the answer. He went back to his seat and tried to think it over.

HILL: I *did* move the slide. It was cheating, I suppose. No, because I didn't do it intentionally. Of course, when I moved the slide I recognised the thing at once. It was a bit of elder. But then I'd probably have recognised it in any case. What ought I to do? Own up at once? No! Why should I? Of course, I don't have to write down the answer. I could leave a blank and get no more marks for that question, and then if I did cheat I shan't have profited by it. But if I do that Wedderburn will probably beat me again. I *must* beat him! After all, it was only a chance. I didn't move it on purpose. I don't see why I should throw those marks away. It's no more unfair than a lot of other things.

NARRATOR: Hill watched the clock until only two minutes remained. Then he opened his book of answers, and with hot ears and an affectation of ease, he wrote down the answer. When the results of the examination were announced, the previous positions of Hill and Wedderburn were reversed. Hill was now top of the first class, Wedderburn second. Everyone congratulated him warmly.

F/HAIRED STUDENT: Well done, Hill. Jolly good!

GIRL STUDENT: Congratulations, Mr Hill. Do you know that you're just one mark ahead of Mr Wedderburn on the two exams. You've got 167 marks out of 200, and he's got 166. The demonstrator told me so.

MISS HAYSMAN: I *am* so glad you were top this time, Mr Hill.

HUNCHBACK: Well done Hill! We were all hoping you'd take him down a peg or two.

NARRATOR: But unfortunately Hill did not get much pleasure from their congratulations, not even from Miss Haysman's. The feeling of triumph that he had at first soon wore off. Once again he was working very hard, he made brilliant speeches at the Debating Society in the evenings, he borrowed yet more books of poetry from Miss Haysman. But there was a memory that kept coming into his mind, and curiously enough it was a memory that grew more and not less vivid as time went on: it was a picture of a sneakish person manipulating a microscope slide.

HILL: I *did* move that slide, I can't get away from that. And I suppose it was unfair to take advantage of it, even though I hadn't done it on purpose. But why should I worry about it? Nobody will ever know. But a lie is a lie, whether it's found out or not. The trouble is that it's no satisfaction now to have beaten Wedderburn. Perhaps he'd have beaten me again if we'd both started fair. Why *did* I move that slide? Perhaps it was partly because I was so keen to beat him. The queer thing is that I'm not even certain any longer that it *was* an accident. Could you intend to do something without knowing that you intended it, I wonder.

NARRATOR: Perhaps Hill's state of mind was becoming morbid. He was overworked, and unquestionably he was also underfed. The memory of what he had done even poisoned his relations with Miss Haysman. He knew now that she preferred him to Wedderburn, and in his clumsy way he tried to reciprocate her attentions. Once he even bought a bunch of violets and carried them about in his pocket all day before finally presenting them to her when they were dead and withered. But most of all he was tormented by the feeling that he had not beaten Wedderburn fairly. To feel himself superior to Wedderburn – that, really, was what he wanted most of all. And at last – moved, curiously enough, by the very same motive force that had resulted in his dishonesty – he went to Professor Bindon to make a clean breast of the whole affair.

HILL: I want to speak to you, sir. I've been wanting to for some weeks. I – well, there's something I feel it's my duty to say. You remember that slide under the microscope in the botany examination?

BINDON: Yes?

HILL: Well – I moved it.

BINDON: You moved it!

NARRATOR: And then out came the whole story, just as it had happened. As Hill was only a scholarship student, Professor Bindon did not ask him to sit down. Hill made his confession standing before the professor's desk.

BINDON: It's a curious story – a most remarkable story. I can't understand your doing it, and I can't understand this confession. Why did you cheat?

HILL: I didn't *cheat.*

BINDON: But you have just been telling me you did.

HILL: I thought I explained –

BINDON: Either you cheated or you did not cheat.

HILL: But my movement was involuntary!

BINDON: I am not a metaphysician. I am a servant of science – of fact. You were told not to move the slide, and you did move it. If that is not cheating –

HILL: If I was a cheat, should I come here and tell you about it?

BINDON: Of course your repentance does you credit, but it doesn't alter the facts. Even now you have caused an enormous amount of trouble. The examination list will have to be revised.

HILL: I suppose so, sir.

BINDON: Suppose so? Of course it must be revised. And I don't see how I can conscientiously pass you.

HILL: Not pass me? Fail me?

BINDON: Of course. What else did you expect?

HILL: I never thought you would fail me. I thought you would simply deduct the marks for that question.

BINDON: Impossible! Besides, it would still leave you above Wedderburn. I have no choice. The Departmental Regulations distinctly say –

HILL: But this is my own admission, sir.

BINDON: The Regulations say nothing whatever of the manner in which the matter comes to light. I must fail you, and there is an end of it.

HILL: But it will ruin me, sir. If I fail this examination they won't renew my scholarship. It's the end of my career.

BINDON: You should have thought of that before. The Professors in this College are machines. Possibly the Regulations are hard, but I must follow them.

HILL: If I'm to be failed in the examination I might as well go home at once.

BINDON: That is for you to decide. As a private person, I think this confession of yours goes far to mitigate your offence. But – well, you have set the machinery in motion. I am really very sorry that this has happened – very.

NARRATOR: For a moment a wave of emotion prevented Hill from answering. Suddenly, very vividly, he saw the heavily-lined face of his father, the cobbler. His father had been so proud of his success and of the brilliant career which seemed to be opening before him. Already in many a public house he had made himself unpopular by boasting about 'my son, the professor'. And now Hill would have to go home, confessing that he was a failure and his scientific career was at an end.

HILL: My God! What a fool I have been!

BINDON: You have certainly been very foolish. I hope it will be a lesson to you.

NARRATOR: But, curiously enough, they were not thinking of quite the same indiscretion. Next day Hill's place was vacant and the laboratory was buzzing with the news.

GIRL STUDENT: Have you heard?

WEDDERBURN: Heard what?

GIRL STUDENT: There was cheating in the examination.

F/HAIRED STUDENT: Cheating!

HUNCHBACK: Who cheated?

MISS HAYSMAN: Cheating? Surely not!

WEDDERBURN: Cheating! But I – how?

GIRL STUDENT: That slide –

WEDDERBURN: Moved? Never!

GIRL STUDENT: It was. The slide we weren't to move –

WEDDERBURN: Nonsense! How could they possibly find out? They can't prove it. Who do they say –?

GIRL STUDENT: It was Mr Hill.

F/HAIRED STUDENT: Hill!

MISS HAYSMAN: Not *Mr Hill*!

WEDDERBURN: Not – surely not the immaculate Hill?

MISS HAYSMAN: I just don't believe it! How do you know?

GIRL STUDENT: *I* didn't believe it. But I know it now for a fact. Mr Hill went and confessed to Professor Bindon himself.

WEDDERBURN: By Jove! Hill of all people. But I must say I always was inclined to distrust these high-minded atheists.

MISS HAYSMAN: Are you quite sure?

GIRL STUDENT: Quite. It's dreadful, isn't it? But what else can you expect? His father is a cobbler.

MISS HAYSMAN: I don't care. I just don't believe it. I will not believe it until he has told me so himself – face to face. I would scarcely believe it even then.

GIRL STUDENT: It's true all the same.

MISS HAYSMAN: I just don't believe it. I'm going to find him and ask him myself.

NARRATOR: But she never did ask him, because Hill had packed up his textbooks and boxes of instruments on the previous day, and had already left London.

14

'Macbeth', a commentary
by George Orwell

17th October 1943

Macbeth is probably the most perfect of Shakespeare's plays. I mean by that that in my opinion Shakespeare's qualities as a poet and as a dramatist are combined in it more successfully than in any other. Especially towards the end it is full of poetry of the very highest order, but it is also a perfectly constructed play – indeed it would still be a good play if it were quite clumsily translated into some foreign language. I don't want here to say anything about the verse in *Macbeth*. You will hear some of the best passages from it acted in a few minutes' time. I am concerned simply with *Macbeth* as a tragedy, and I had better give a short outline of the plot.

Macbeth is a Scottish nobleman of the early Middle Ages. One day he is returning from a battle in which he has particularly distinguished himself and won the King's favour, when he meets three witches who prophesy to him that he will become king himself. Two other prophecies which the witches have made are fulfilled almost immediately, and it is inevitable that Macbeth should find himself wondering how the third is to be fulfilled, since the King, Duncan, is still alive and has two sons. It is clear that almost from the moment of hearing the prophecy he has contemplated murdering Duncan, and though at first he shrinks from doing it, his wife, whose will appears to be stronger than his own, talks him over. Macbeth murders Duncan, contriving that suspicion shall fall on Duncan's two sons. They fly the country, and as Macbeth is the next heir he becomes king. But this first crime leads inexorably to a chain of others, ending in Macbeth's ruin and death. The witches have told him that though he himself will become king, no child of his will succeed to the throne, which will fall to the descendants of his friend Banquo. Macbeth has Banquo murdered, but Banquo's son escapes. They have also warned him to beware of Macduff, the Thane of Fife, and half-consciously Macbeth knows that it is Macduff who will finally destroy him. He tries to have Macduff murdered, but once again, Macduff escapes, though his wife and family are murdered, in a peculiarly atrocious way. By an inevitable chain of circumstances Macbeth, who has started out as a brave and by no means bad man, ends up as the typical figure of the terror-haunted tyrant, hated and feared by everyone, surrounded by spies, murderers and

159

sycophants, and living in constant dread of treachery and rebellion. He is in fact a sort of primitive medieval version of the modern Fascist dictator. His situation forces him to become more cruel as time goes on. Whereas at the beginning it is Macbeth who shrinks from murder and Lady Macbeth who jeers at him for his squeamishness, in the end it is Macbeth who massacres women and children without a qualm and Lady Macbeth who loses her nerve and dies partially insane. And yet – and this is the greatest psychological achievement of the play – Macbeth is quite recognizably the same man throughout and speaks the same kind of language; he is pushed on from crime to crime not by native wickedness but by what seems to him inescapable necessity. In the end rebellion breaks out and Macduff and Duncan's son Malcolm invade Scotland at the head of an English army. The witches have made another prophecy which seems to promise Macbeth immunity. How that prophecy is fulfilled, and how, without being falsified, it ends in Macbeth's death, you will hear in the acted extract from the play. In the end he is killed by Macduff, as he has known all along that he would be. When the full meaning of the prophecy becomes clear to him he gives up hope and dies fighting from the mere instinct of a warrior to die on his feet and never surrender.

In all of Shakespeare's major tragedies the theme has some recognizable connection with everyday life. In *Antony and Cleopatra*, for instance, the theme is the power which a worthless woman can establish over a brave and gifted man. In *Hamlet* it is the divorce between intelligence and practical ability. In *King Lear* it is a rather subtler theme – the difficulty of distinguishing between generosity and weakness. This reappears in a cruder form in *Timon of Athens*. In *Macbeth* the theme is simply ambition. And though all of Shakespeare's tragedies can be translated into terms of ordinary contemporary life, the story of Macbeth seems to me the nearest of all to normal experience. In a small and relatively harmless way, everyone has at some time done something rather like Macbeth, and with comparable consequences. If you like, *Macbeth* is the story of Hitler or Napoleon. But it is also the story of any bank clerk who forges a cheque, any official who takes a bribe, any human being in fact who grabs at some mean advantage which will make him feel a little bigger and get a little ahead of his fellows. It centres on the illusory human belief that an action can be isolated – that you can say to yourself, 'I will commit just this one crime which will get me where I want to be, and after that I will turn respectable.' But in practice, as Macbeth discovers, one crime grows out of another, even without any increase of wickedness in yourself. His first murder is committed for self-advancement; the even worse ones which follow from it are committed in self-defence. Unlike most of Shakespeare's tragedies, *Macbeth* resembles the Greek tragedies in that its end can be foreseen. From the beginning one knows in general terms what is going to happen. This makes the last act all the more moving, but I still think the essential commonplaceness of the story is its chief appeal. *Hamlet* is the tragedy of a man who does not know how to commit a murder: *Macbeth* is the tragedy of a man who does. And though most of us do not actually commit murders, Macbeth's predicament is nearer to everyday life.

It is worth noticing that the introduction of magic and witchcraft does not give the play an air of unreality. Actually – although the climax of the last act depends on the exact working-out of the prophecy – the witches are not absolutely necessary to the play. They could be cut out without altering the essential story. Probably they were put in to attract the attention of King James I, who had just come to the throne and who was a firm believer in witchcraft. There is one scene which was quite certainly put in with the idea of flattering the King – this scene, or part of a scene, is the only flaw in the play and should be cut out of any acting version. But the witches, even as they stand, do not offend one's sense of probability. They do not alter anything or upset the course of nature, they merely foretell the future, a future which the spectator can in any case partly foresee. One has the feeling that in one sense Macbeth foresees it too. The witches are there, in fact, simply to increase the sense of doom. A modern writer telling this story, instead of talking about witchcraft, would probably talk about Macbeth's subconscious mind. What is essential is the gradually unfolding consequences of that first crime, and Macbeth's half-knowledge, even as he does it, that it *must* lead to disaster. *Macbeth* is the only one of Shakespeare's plays in which the villain and the hero are the same character. Nearly always, in Shakespeare, you have the spectacle of a good man, like Othello or King Lear, suffering misfortune; or of a bad man, like Edgar or Iago, doing evil out of sheer malice. In *Macbeth* the crime and the misfortune are one; a man whom one cannot feel to be wholly evil is doing evil things. It is very difficult not to be moved by this spectacle. And since the play is so well put together that even the most incompetent production can hardly spoil it on the stage, and since it also contains some of the best verse that Shakespeare ever wrote, I think I am justified in giving it the description I gave it at the beginning – that is, Shakespeare's most perfect play.

15

'The Emperor's New Clothes'
by Hans Andersen
adapted by George Orwell

18th November 1943

(Trumpet fanfare)

NARRATOR: The Emperor of Bithynia cared for nothing except his clothes. He spent so much time in adorning himself that just as in other countries people will say, 'The King is in the Council Chamber', in Bithynia they used to say, 'The Emperor is in his dressing-room'. More than half of the public revenues was spent on the Emperor's clothes. But the people did not mind. They were rather proud of being ruled over by the best-dressed monarch in Christendom; and they were always ready to leave their work in order to watch the Emperor march through the streets in velvet and cloth-of-gold, with his jewels flashing, and a dozen courtiers following him to hold up his train.

One day two weavers from a foreign country arrived in the capital. These men claimed to be able to make a kind of cloth more beautiful than any in existence – and a cloth, moreover, that had some mysterious or magical quality, though nobody quite knew what. I need hardly say that the Emperor was one of the first to hear of their arrival; and the very next day, in obedience to his command, they presented themselves at the palace. The Chancellor was rather perturbed to hear of their arrival.

CHANCELLOR: Your Majesty, those two foreigners who arrived here yesterday ...

EMPEROR: Oh, the weavers. Yes, I sent for them. Are they here?

CHANCELLOR: They are, your majesty. But –

EMPEROR: Well?

CHANCELLOR: Common swindlers, I have no doubt, your majesty.

EMPEROR: Ah, well, we shall see about that. I understand that they are able to make a very remarkable kind of cloth. I feel that I have been dressing myself too plainly lately. I should like something a little more magnificent for a change.

CHANCELLOR: If I might make so bold, your majesty – the peasants have been rather slow with their taxes this year. It might be better to avoid extravagance.

EMPEROR: I am never extravagant. If you want money, make a cut in the Civil Service estimates. Bring these men before me.

CHANCELLOR: Yes, your majesty ... Bring in the two weavers!

MAJOR-DOMO: (*distant*) Bring in the two weavers! ... (*Door opens*) The two weavers!

CHANCELLOR: Your majesty, here are the two weavers.

WEAVER: Your majesty ...

EMPEROR: Ha! Now what is this wonderful cloth of yours that I have heard about? I should like to see a sample of it.

WEAVER: The most beautiful cloth in the world, your majesty. Nothing like it has ever been seen. But we shall have to weave it before you can see it. And we are tailors as well, your majesty. After weaving the cloth we will cut it and fit it for you. But we make no charge for that – only for the cloth itself. The price – to *you*, your majesty – is a hundred crowns a yard.

CHANCELLOR: (*coughs*)

EMPEROR: A hundred crowns a yard. Let me see, suppose we said fifty yards – oh, yes, I think we can manage that.

WEAVER: And we shall be requiring raw silk as well, your majesty, and also ten pounds of golf leaf. We use it in the embroidery, you see.

EMPEROR: Ten pounds of gold leaf? Very well, my Chancellor will give you anything you need.

CHANCELLOR: (*coughs*) Your majesty! In the present state of the Treasury –

EMPEROR: Nonsense! Give them whatever they ask for. Now, the sooner you two men get to work, the better.

WEAVER: There is just one other point, your majesty. Naturally we are very anxious that your majesty shall not be disappointed. Your majesty's royal neighbour, the King of Pontus –

EMPEROR: That wretched impostor!

WEAVER: He suffered a disappointment, your majesty. At his command we made seventy-five yards of cloth, but when it was made he was unable to see it.

EMPEROR: Couldn't see it!

WEAVER: Our cloth is no ordinary cloth, your majesty. To those who can see it, it is the most magnificent cloth in the world. But not everyone can see it. Its peculiar quality is that it can only be seen by the good and the wise. To any foolish man, or to any man who is unfitted for the position he holds, this cloth is quite invisible. If you hold up a piece of this cloth, a wise man can see it as clearly as I see your majesty; while to a fool or an impostor there appears to be nothing there.

EMPEROR: Invisible to fools, eh! Ha, ha! No wonder poor old Pontus couldn't see it. Just what I should have expected. And invisible, you say, to anyone who is unfitted for his position? I shall be able to try it on some of my ministers. (*Sycophantic laughter of courtiers*) How much did you say the King of Pontus ordered?

WEAVER: Seventy-five yards, your majesty.

EMPEROR: Make me eighty yards. (*Cough from Lord Chancellor*) You shall start work today.

NARRATOR: A large room in the palace was set aside for the two weavers, and nothing was seen of them for three days. Servants who peeped through the keyhole reported only that the weavers had set up a great loom at the far end of the room and seemed to be very busy upon it. The Emperor could hardly contain his curiosity. On the fourth day he sent the Lord Chancellor with orders to visit the two workmen and find out what this wonderful cloth was like. The Lord Chancellor came back with a solemn and rather curious expression on his face.

EMPEROR: Have you seen it? You *could* see the cloth, of course?

CHANCELLOR: Oh, yes, your majesty! I could see it clearly.

EMPEROR: Good! I should be sorry to have to change my Chancellor. And what is it like?

CHANCELLOR: Well, your majesty, I should say – an *unusual* cloth; that would be my description of it. Like – er, like velvet, and yet, on the other hand, *not* like velvet, if your majesty understands me.

EMPEROR: And the colour?

CHANCELLOR: I should describe it as green, your majesty. Or perhaps it was nearer to blue, or even to red. It was decidedly an *unusual* colour.

EMPEROR: I must see it at once. I can't wait any longer. Warn them that I am coming.

NARRATOR: The Emperor made his way to the room where the two weavers were working. He entered. Sure enough, there at the other end was the great loom and the weavers busily at work upon it, moving the shuttles up and down, reaching out for fresh threads and calling out instructions to one another.

(*Sound of hand-loom*)

NARRATOR: But a terrible shock awaited the Emperor.

EMPEROR: (*whispering*) I can't see the cloth! There's nothing there!

WEAVER: It is a magnificent cloth, is it not, your majesty? Does your majesty observe the pattern we are weaving into it?

EMPEROR: What? Yes, of course, of course. (*Whispering*) This is terrible. To my eye there appears to be nothing on that loom whatever. And even that old fool of a Chancellor could see it. This will never do. I shall have to – (*aloud*) Excellent! Excellent! The finest cloth I have ever had. Well worth the money. When do you expect that it will be ready?

WEAVER: Only a few days now, your majesty.

EMPEROR: Good. If you want any more gold leaf, apply to the Lord Chancellor.

NARRATOR: Three days later the weavers announced that the cloth was finished. They were bidden to bring it to the audience room, and all the court assembled to see it. No one had any doubts that he would be able to see the cloth, since no one had any doubts about his own wisdom. The weavers entered, staggering under a vast wicker-work basket which they set down and opened in front of the throne. Then they made the motions of taking out a bale of cloth, unrolling it, and holding it up for the Emperor's inspection. The whole court burst out into cries of admiration.

(*Loud ah-ah-ah*)

EMPEROR: Very fine. Very fine indeed.
1st LADY: Isn't it *lovely*!
COURTIER: That gold leaf is magnificent.
1st LADY: And the colour!
2nd LADY: Can *you* see it, my dear?
1st LADY: Of course I can see it!
2nd LADY: How funny! Because you're looking in the wrong direction.
CHANCELLOR: A very superior cloth. A little expensive, perhaps.
EMPEROR: Make the train twenty yards long. As soon as my new clothes are ready I shall make a royal progress through the capital. My people will enjoy seeing me, I am sure. I will wear my small crown – the one with the pearls.
NARRATOR: Now that the cloth was woven the next thing was to make the clothes. The two weavers were busy for a whole day taking measurements and cutting out the cloth. They snipped their scissors through the empty air, ran their tape-measures round the Emperor's chest, and with their mouths full of pins made the movements of fitting the pieces of cloth about his body. Then they sat up all night, sewing – so they said; at least they had needles in their hands and went through the motions of sewing. The clothes were to be ready in the morning. It had already been proclaimed that the Emperor intended to make a progress through the capital in his new clothes. Everyone was full of curiosity; no one doubted his ability to see the clothes. In the morning the weavers entered the Emperor's chamber, appearing to carry something over their arms. The Emperor took off the clothes he was wearing, and the weavers helped him on with the new ones.
WEAVER: Permit me, your majesty. The girdle should be a little tighter. Now the cloak – just so. You will notice that we have made this a little full in the shoulders. It suits your majesty's style. Now the shoes – there. The great thing about this cloth of ours, your majesty, is that it is so light. It is like a spider's web. Your majesty might almost think you had nothing on. Yes ... Quite, quite perfect!
EMPEROR: Good ... Major-Domo!
MAJOR-DOMO: Your majesty!
EMPEROR: You may admit the members of the court.
MAJOR-DOMO: Yes, your majesty ...

(*Door opens: chorus of exclamation*).

1st LADY: Oh, what *lovely* clothes!
COURTIER: They fit your majesty like a glove.
2nd LADY: What it must have cost! It will take twelve men at least to hold up that train.
EMPEROR: The procession will start in half an hour. Chancellor, warn the

heralds to be ready. I do not intend to distribute any largess today. I think the people will be quite satisfied with the spectacle of my (*modest cough*) new clothes.

NARRATOR: In fact, the people had been lining the streets since early morning. At last the procession came into sight, with the heralds riding ahead of it on their white chargers.

(Fade up distant trumpeters: cheering)

1st MAN: Look, here they come!
1st WOMAN: There they are!
2nd MAN: That's the Emperor – him under the umbrella. Hurray!
3rd MAN: Long live the Emperor! Three cheers for the Emperor!

(Trumpeters and cheering nearer)

2nd WOMAN: Don't he look fine?
1st MAN: Glorious! It's worth paying taxes for, that is.
CHILD: Mummy!
1st WOMAN: Drat the child! Long live the Emperor!
CHILD: Mummy! The Emperor's got no clothes on!
3rd MAN: What did the child say?
CHILD: He's got no clothes on! Look at him! He's got nothing on 'cept his crown!
3rd MAN: Why, so he hasn't! The child's right!
1st WOMAN: Nothing on! Well, now!

(Cheering dies down)

1st MAN: Got no clothes on.
2nd WOMAN: Disgraceful I call it.
2nd MAN: No business to come out like that.
1st WOMAN: Wouldn't have noticed it if it hadn't been for the child.
3rd MAN: He'll catch his death of cold, too.
2nd WOMAN: Disgraceful.
1st MAN: Go home.
2nd WOMAN: Ought to be ashamed of yourself! At your age, too!
VOICES: Boo! Down with the Emperor! Boo!

(Fade up booing above trumpeters: fade out)

NARRATOR: At last the Emperor realised what had happened. But it did not seem to him that he could do anything about it now. There was nothing for it but to walk majestically onward, pretending not to notice that there was anything wrong.

(Trumpeters: booing in background)

EMPEROR: (*Whispering*) This is terrible! And I made sure they could all see the clothes except me. No matter, I must put a good face on it. After all, I *am* the Emperor. (*Aloud*) Chancellor!
CHANCELLOR: Sire?

EMPEROR: Tell these courtiers to hold my train up more carefully. They're letting it trail in the mud.

NARRATOR: So the procession moved stiffly onwards, with the heralds blowing their trumpets, and the twelve courtiers pretending to hold up a train which was not there, and all the people booing.

(*Fade up booing above trumpeters: fade out*)

NARRATOR: As soon as they got back to the palace the Emperor put his clothes on, real ones this time, and then –

EMPEROR: Chancellor!

CHANCELLOR: Sire?

EMPEROR: Those two abominable scoundrels – those two men who called themselves weavers –

CHANCELLOR: Yes, your majesty?

EMPEROR: Cast them into the lowest dungeons immediately.

CHANCELLOR: Certainly, your majesty.

EMPEROR: And tell the executioner to sharpen his sword up.

CHANCELLOR: With pleasure, your majesty.

NARRATOR: But as it turned out, it was too late. The two weavers were sought for, but they were never found. Indeed the servants reported that they had left the palace as soon as the procession started out. And after that – taking with them the eight thousand crowns for the cloth, as well as the silk and the ten pounds of gold leaf – they had vanished for a distant country; and they were never seen again.

16

'Lady Windermere's Fan'
a commentary by George Orwell

21st November 1943

Lady Windermere's Fan was first acted in 1892, more than half a century ago. It has been seen on the stage less often than *The Importance of Being Earnest*, but it has worn well, and by and large it is probably Wilde's most successful play.

Wilde is a difficult writer to judge, because it is very hard to disentangle his artistic achievement from the events of his life: also because he himself was never fully certain of what he wanted to say. Like many others of his time, Wilde professed to be a devotee of 'Art for Art's sake' – that is, of the idea that Art has nothing to do with religion, morals or politics. He set it down as one of the tenets of his creed that 'Every work of Art is completely useless'. But in practice he contradicts this by making nearly everything that he writes turn upon some point of morals. And there is a further contradiction in the fact that he is never certain whether he is attacking current morality or defending it. The dialogue of his plays and stories consists almost entirely of elegant witticisms in which the notions of right and wrong which ruled Victorian society are torn to pieces; but their central theme, curiously enough, often points some quite old-fashioned moral. His novel *Dorian Gray*, for instance, is a deeply moral book. Although it was denounced as cynical, frivolous and so forth at the time when it was published, it is in essence a religious parable. Quite a lot of the time Wilde is uttering the maxims of the copybook in the language of light comedy; he wants at all costs to be clever, without being quite certain what he is to be clever *about*, and at the same time he is never fully able to escape from the effects of a mid-Victorian upbringing. The thing that saves him from the results of this intellectual chaos is that he is, after all, a genuinely gifted dramatist: he can construct a play neatly, and he has the light touch that Irish writers more often possess than English ones – for Wilde, like most of the best British dramatists, was an Irishman. These faults and these qualities are well displayed in *Lady Windermere's Fan*. But to get a full understanding of the play one ought to see it against the background of its time.

When *Lady Windermere's Fan* was first acted, what is now called 'British hypocrisy' was still immensely powerful. To defy accepted beliefs, particularly religious or moral beliefs, needed more courage than it does now. Notions of

168

right and wrong do not change so suddenly or completely as some people like to think, but it is a fact that certain things which seemed immensely important in the 'nineties now seem comparatively trivial. One of the subjects about which this play turns is divorce. Now, nobody thinks that divorce is desirable in itself or that it is not an immensely painful event in anyone's life: but still it is not the case in our own time that a divorced woman is ruined for life. When *Lady Windermere's Fan* was written it was an accepted fact that a divorced woman must become almost an outcast; she was practically debarred from decent society for the rest of her life. This should be kept in mind, because it gives point both to certain episodes in the play, and to Wilde's incidental attacks upon current morality.

The plot of the play, as briefly as I can outline it, is this. Lady Windermere, an affectionate but rather puritanical young woman, believes that her husband is unfaithful to her with a woman of very doubtful antecedents called Mrs Erlynne. In reality she is quite mistaken. Her husband has indeed been associated with Mrs Erlynne, but not for the reason that she imagines. Mrs Erlynne is Lady Windermere's own mother. But she is also a divorced woman, and the knowledge – as it would then have seemed, the almost unbearable knowledge – that she is the daughter of a divorced woman has been kept from Lady Windermere, who imagines her mother to be dead. Mrs Erlynne has been blackmailing Lord Windermere, holding over him the threat that she will reveal her identity to her daughter. What she wants from him is partly money, but still more, a reintroduction into fashionable society. Lady Windermere has an admirer, Lord Darlington, who is trying to persuade her to leave her husband and elope with him. (Parenthetically I must point out that the very great prevalence of lords, dukes and what-not in Wilde's plays is a period touch. The British public of those days liked to see titled people on the stage, and the majority of dramatists were quite ready to humour them.) In normal circumstances Lady Windermere would be very unlikely to listen to Lord Darlington, but finally her jealousy brings her to the point of deciding to leave her husband. She goes to Lord Darlington's rooms, intending to leave England with him. Mrs Erlynne finds out what is happening, and when she sees her daughter, as she thinks, going the same road as she has gone herself, her maternal instincts revive. She follows her to Lord Darlington's rooms, intending to dissuade her. It is this scene that you will hear acted in a few minutes' time, and I won't describe in detail what happens. The point is that Mrs Erlynne, still acting the repentant mother, saves her daughter from ruin by taking all the blame upon herself. Lady Windermere goes back to her husband, and – since this is a comedy and has to end happily all round – Mrs Erlynne also manages to find her way back into respectable society by marrying a foolish but good-natured old man.

You can see that this play, as I have outlined it, is a harmless and even edifying story by the standards current at the time. The situation in which somebody is the child of somebody else, the parent being aware of it and the child not, was a favourite on the Victorian stage. The mother sacrificing herself for her child was another favourite. And the unjustly suspected person who has to suffer in silence rather than reveal some deadly secret – the part played here by Lord Windermere – was yet another. Mrs Erlynne's behaviour involves one of those sudden and drastic changes of character which were a regular occurrence in Victorian fiction though they are unknown in real life. She is shown first of all as taking no interest in her daughter for twenty years and as having no aim in life except to get back into so-called 'good' society, and as being willing to make use of blackmail in the most cynical way in order to achieve this. Then, in the moment of crisis, she is shown throwing away the very thing she has been scheming for, and all for the sake of a daughter whom she has hitherto used simply as a pawn in her game. Psychologically this is an absurdity, though by skilful writing Wilde is able to make it seem credible. In its plot and its main action the play is a sentimental romance with a touch of melodrama. Yet that is not the impression it gives when one reads it or sees it acted, and we may guess that that was even less the impression it gave at the time. So far from seeming sentimental and edifying, the play appears frivolous and what used to be called 'daring'. Why? Because in addition to the central characters there is a kind of chorus of worldly 'sophisticated' people who keep up a ceaseless running attack upon all the beliefs current in Wilde's day – and in our own day, to a great extent. In the contradiction between the action of the play and its language one can see Wilde's own uncertainty as to what he is after.

Wilde's greatest gift was his power of producing those rather cheap witticisms which used to be called epigrams. These are stuck all over his writings as arbitrarily as the decorations on top of a cake. Nearly always they take the form of a debunking of something that his contemporaries believed in, such as religion, patriotism, honour, morality, family loyalty, public spirit, and so on and so forth. Remarks like, 'I can resist anything except temptation', or 'Men become cold, but they never become good', or 'When her third husband died her hair turned quite gold from grief', occur on almost every page that Wilde ever wrote. The essence of this kind of witticism is to disagree with the majority at all costs. Clearly, this kind of thing is more effective when there is a really strong and vocal majority opinion to be reckoned with. Remarks like, 'There's nothing in the world like the devotion of a married woman. That's a thing no married man knows anything about', are less likely to shock anyone in 1943 than in 1892, and to that extent they are less amusing. But Wilde does this kind of thing so well, so naturally one might even say, that his dialogue is still charming even when it has ceased to seem wicked or iconoclastic. So long as no serious emotion enters he has also a fairly good grasp of character and situation. But his great charm is his neat rapid dialogue, which is freer from padding, and conceals its machinery more successfully, than anything that has since been seen on the English stage.

Wilde lived at the moment when the literate public was just becoming emancipated enough to enjoy seeing the Victorian conventions attacked. It was therefore natural for him to make a name by laughing at the society he lived in; though that society avenged itself in the end, when Wilde was sent to prison for a sexual offence. If he had lived earlier the sentimental and melodramatic strain in him, which is clear in all his work except for *The Importance of Being Earnest* and a few short stories, would probably have predominated. It is quite possible to imagine him as a sensational novelist, for instance. If he had lived in our own day, when debunking no longer seems worth while as an end in itself, it is harder to say what he would have done. It is uncertain whether he had anything in him except his native wit and his intense desire to be famous. Coming just when he did, he won an easy fame by pushing over an idol that was toppling already. In its fall the idol killed him, for Wilde never recovered from the shock of his trial and imprisonment, and died soon after he was released. He left behind, as his essential contribution to literature, a large repertoire of jokes which survive because of their sheer neatness, and because of a certain intriguing uncertainty – which extends to Wilde himself – as to whether they really mean anything.

Part Two

Letters

The range of Orwell's commissions for the Indian Section of the Eastern Service was very wide. To each contributor he wrote himself, and often he followed up his initial approach with a letter commenting on the text presented and shorter notes relating to technical matters of recording or live presentation. In the course of two years he wrote many hundreds of such letters. We print here the main ones to his principal contributors. The only author with whom he corresponded continuously over the whole period was E.M. Forster; the extant correspondence is reproduced complete, telegrams and all.[1] As Forster's letters and postcards are all in his autograph they have been transcribed exactly. Orwell's own letters and memoranda are usually in typescript, sometimes from dictation. For the convenience of the reader they have been reproduced with literal errors and inconsistencies tacitly corrected.

P[ortland] P[lace]/E[ric] B[lair]   25th November 1941

Dear Tambimuttu,

   The Facilities Unit have arranged for you to go to see the offices of the *Daily Express* on December 4th – Thursday – at 9.p.m. I gather that this is a special favour, as they have given up showing people round in the ordinary way.

   You should ask for the Commissionaire and tell him what you have come for, and he will know all about it.

J.M. Tambimuttu Esq.,	Yours sincerely,
18, Oakley Gardens,	Eric Blair
S.W.3.	Empire Talks Assistant

---

[1] A number of Forster's talks for Orwell were published later in *Two Cheers for Democracy* (1952), edited by Oliver Stallybrass (1972). Their titles were: 'Why *Julius Caesar* lives', 'Edward Gibbon', 'Three stories by Tolstoy', 'Webb and Webb', 'Our Second Greatest Novel – a comment on Marcel Proust's *A la recherche du temps perdu*' and 'Gide and George'. Full bibliographical details in Stallybrass.

PP/EB   26th November 1941
Dear Mr. Singh,[2]
   With reference to our conversation yesterday, I am sending you three
specimen scripts of our series 'The Debate Continues'. None of these is
altogether satisfactory, but they will give you some idea of what to do, as well
as what to avoid, and I have written some comments in red ink in the margin.
If you could let us have a specimen of your own any time within the next three
or four weeks, I should be much obliged.
   I would also like it very much if you could do us a Christmas Day
broadcast of 10 minutes. Christmas in Wartime would be the sort of line,
though we will think of some more striking title later. Please let me know as
soon as possible whether you can undertake this, as we are now only five
weeks from Christmas. The talk can be recorded some days beforehand, so
that you will not have to broadcast on Christmas Day.

Bahadur Singh Esq.,   Yours sincerely,
44, Wellington Square,   Eric Blair
Oxford.   Empire Talks Assistant

PP/EB   22nd December 1941

Dear Anand,
   You will no doubt remember our conversation on the subject of
broadcasting. You told me that your time was very full at the moment, but
that you might perhaps have time to do some talks after the New Year. We
have an idea for a series of talks which I think would just suit you. Do you
think you could be kind enough to come and see me some day during the
early part of the week beginning December 28th, in my office, at 55, Portland
Place, W.1.
   You might ring me up in advance and let me know just when you are
coming.

Mulk Raj Anand Esq.,   Yours sincerely,
8, St. George's Mews,   Eric Blair
Regent's Park Road, N.W.1   Empire Talks Assistant

PP/EB   14th January 1942

Dear Mr. Hsiao Ch'ien,
   Very many thanks for your script, which I like very much. I shall have to

   [2] Bahadur Singh (1915–   ), an Oxford undergraduate who had come from Queen's Royal
College, Trinidad. He was successively Librarian, Secretary and President (1941) of the Oxford
Union Society.

make some small alterations but they are only verbal ones. Before we broadcast this one, I should like it if you could do me another to go with this one and to be broadcast before it. The reason is that in this script you deal, as I asked you to, with the more subtle ways in which the Japanese tried to get the Chinese population over to their side. I also want one talk on the ordinary atrocity lines, and I think it better that that one should go first, and this one second. I have not been able yet to meet another Chinese who has been in occupied territory, and from what you said to me and from what you have said in the script, I have no doubt you are able to do it. I want something about the extortions of the Japanese, looting, raping, and the opium traffic etc. Possibly you could make an appointment to come and see me about this. Then perhaps we could broadcast both your scripts next week and the week after.

Hsiao Ch'ien Esq.,   Yours sincerely,
13, South Hill Park Gardens, N.W.3.   Eric Blair
                            Empire Talks Assistant

PP/EB   19th January 1942

Dear Anand,
    I don't know how things are progressing about your appointment,[3] but meanwhile would you care to do one or two talks in the ordinary way? You know something, I think, about our new series. Would you like, for instance, to do a talk on H.G. Wells, Bernard Shaw, or some other well-known literary man, on Tuesday 10th February? You know the kind of talk I want. I should also like another of the same type on Tuesday, February 24th. Please let me know about this as soon as possible, as if you decide to do the talks we shall want your first one in about a week before the date of the broadcast.

Mulk Raj Anand Esq.,   Yours sincerely,
8, St. George's Mews,   Eric Blair
Regent's Park Road, N.W.3.   Talks Assistant
                            Indian Section

PP/EB   24th January 1942

Dear Mr. Hsiao Ch'ien,
    Very many thanks for your second talk. I should be very glad to make use of both of these, which are exactly the kind of thing I wanted. I am not quite

---

[3] Presumably Anand was being considered for a full-time post; but he was not appointed to one and no record has been found relating to the matter.

certain, however, when to fit them in to my programme and I think the best arrangement will be for you to record them. Do you think you could come here for the recording some day next week? The whole process, rehearsal and recording, will probably take about an hour and a half. The best days for me would be Tuesday, Wednesday or Thursday, but I cannot say in advance what time of day, because it is a question of getting the studio for the recording. Will you ring me up as soon as possible and tell me which day will suit you, and I will then fix things up as rapidly as possible.

Hsiao Ch'ien Esq.,   Yours sincerely,
13, South Hill Park Gardens, N.W.3.   Eric Blair
                                          Talks Assistant
                                          Indian Section

PP/EB   2nd February 1942

Dear Mr. Eliot,
    Bokhari tells me that you have kindly consented to do us a series of six talks on the philosophy of the East and the West.[4] I wonder if you would be able to do these on Mondays, and to start with the first talk on Monday, 16th February (this would mean our having the script some days previously)?
    Perhaps you could let me know whether you can manage this. If 16th February is too early we can postpone the date.

T.S. Eliot Esq.,   Yours sincerely,
c/o Messrs. Faber & Faber   Eric Blair
    Ltd., (Publishers),   Talks Assistant
24, Russell Square, W.C.1.   Indian Section

PP/EB   3rd February 1942

Dear Horrabin,
    Very many thanks for the synopses you sent me. I like them very well, my only criticism is that I would like the talks to be a little more definitely about geography, with less direct reference to the war situation. Of course, one must mention the war at every turn, but what I am chiefly after is to try to give people an interest in geography which may lead them to look at an atlas occasionally. I am trying to arrange with one or two Indian papers that at the time of your first talk they shall publish a map of the world and mention your forthcoming talks in connection with it. I should not actually refer to this in anything you say, but I think you can talk with the assumption that some of

---

4 Eliot does not appear to have done these talks. No record of them can be found in WAC.

your hearers will be looking at the map as they listen.

Each of these four talks should take about 12 minutes. I think if you allow 1500 words for each that will be about right. It is very difficult to be sure what audience you are speaking to, but the one I am aiming at is the University students and the better educated Indians generally. I think you can assume, therefore, that you are talking to people who are intelligent and well educated, but have a continental outlook, and very little grasp of world geography. I don't think it would hurt to mention even quite elementary facts, such as the lack of friction in water which makes water communications important.

Could you do these four talks on February 18th, 25th and March 11th and 18th? They will go out at approximately 3.45 p.m. We can arrange about rehearsals and so forth later. If you could manage these dates I want the first talk by February 12th.

J.F. Horrabin Esq.,	Yours sincerely,
16, Endersleigh Gardens,	Eric Blair
Hendon, N.W.4	Talks Assistant
	Indian Section

PP/EB   13th February 1942

Dear Cyril,

Confirming our talk yesterday, I want your broadcast to take place on Friday, 13th March, which means that we should have the script not later than 6th March.

The talk should be a half-hour one, i.e. should take not less than 25 minutes and not more than 28. You can do it alone, or in the form of a discussion with somebody else, just as you please, and of course use your discretion about putting in readings from other people's work etc. In a talk of that length it is best to break it up in some way.

You suggested 'the thirties'[5] as a subject, and that would do very well. But if you want to choose some other approach, you might let me know fairly soon. I want this series of six talks to more or less cover the literary period 1918-1940.

Cyril Connolly Esq.,	Yours,
6, Selwyn House,	Eric Blair
Lansdowne Terrace, W.C.1	Talks Assistant
	Indian Section

[5] The title had been used by Malcolm Muggeridge in a book published in 1940.

PP/EB   27th February 1942

Dear Connolly,
    I want your talk to be delivered on March 31st, which means that I should
have the script *not later than March 21st*. You might let me know if you intend to
modify the scope of it in any way, but I think we might as well stick to The
Thirties for the title, as it is a good catch title, and we have already publicised
it.

Cyril Connolly Esq.,   Yours,
c/o Horizon,   Eric Blair
6, Selwyn House,   Talks Assistant
Lansdowne Terrace, W.C.1   Indian Section

PP/EB   28th February 1942

Dear Dr. Waddington,[6]
    I wonder whether you would be interested in doing a talk for us in a series
which is beginning shortly, and is aimed chiefly at the English-speaking
Indian population. These are a series of talks on contemporary literature, and
we want the third in the series to be about the influence of science on
literature during recent times. You could take very much your own line, and
say whatever you thought about it, provided that it is more or less within the
scope of the series, i.e. provided that it deals mainly with the English
literature of the last twenty years. These are half-hour talks, that is, making
not more than 28 minutes; and with a talk of that length it is better to break it
up in some way, either by fairly frequent quotations, or, if you preferred, you
could do it in the form of a discussion with somebody else. Do you think you
could be kind enough to let me know fairly soon whether this would interest
you?

Dr. C.H. Waddington,   Yours sincerely,
Christ's College,   George Orwell
Cambridge   Talks Assistant
                                        Indian Section

    [6] C.H. Waddington (1905-1975), Buchanan Professor of Animal Genetics in the University of
Edinburgh from 1947. In 1964 he contributed to a series of predictive articles, *The World in 1984*,
which appeared in the *New Scientist*. He was the only contributor to that series who had also
contributed to this one of Orwell's.

PP/EB   5th March 1942

Dear Stephen,

This is to confirm my telephone conversation with you. The talk is to be called 'Poetry and Traditionalism', and to take anything up to 28 minutes. It is due to be delivered on March 17th, which means that I want this script by the 14th at the latest. I don't, of course, want to dictate what you will say, but I will just give you a line on the scope of the whole series. These talks are supposed to cover English literature in the period between the two wars, and I want you to discuss the movement which started with Eliot and others about the middle of the last war. I have [given] the talk that title because it seems to me that poetry from Eliot onwards has been actually more in touch with the poetry of the past and with European literature than English poetry from the Romantic Revival up to 1914 had been. Of course, you must say whatever you feel about it. No doubt you will have to mention the younger poets who have come up in the last three or four years, some of whom you were discussing in your last essay in *Horizon*;[7] but I don't want you to give much space to them because I am getting Herbert Read to do a talk specifically on the literature subsequent to the Auden group, perhaps to be called Surrealism or something like that.

Stephen Spender Esq.,   Yours,
2, Maresfield Gardens, N.W.3   Eric Blair
                                   Talks Assistant
                                   Indian Section

PP/EB   5th March 1942

Dear Princess Indira,

I wonder whether you would care to do me another talk, as well as 'The Debate Continues'? The talk I should very much like you to do, if you have time, is one in our series 'Changing Britain', on Clothes. This series deals with the social changes brought about by the war, and a variety of subjects have already been dealt with – from Taxation to Popular Literature.

Perhaps you will let me know, when we meet on Monday, whether you will undertake this talk for me, and if there is anything more that you want to know we can discuss it then. The date of the talk is March 25th, and the script should reach me before March 18th.

Princess Indira of Kapurthala,   Yours sincerely,
512A Nell Gwynn House,   Eric Blair
Sloane Avenue, S.W.3   Talks Assistant
                                   Indian Section

[7] 'Poetry in 1941', February 1942.

PP/EB   19th March 1942

Dear Mr. Hsiao Ch'ien,

Many thanks for your letter of March 17th. I am afraid it would be very difficult, in fact impossible, to alter the dates of these talks. It might possibly be more convenient for you to do them a little earlier, in which case it will be quite easy for us to have them recorded. The actual dates of the broadcasts are May 19th and 26th, which means I would want the first talk not later than May 15th.

As to the scope of the talks, I want you to cover shortly much the same ground as you did in your book. I don't think it will do to talk on the literature of the last 2,000 years and merely end up with modern literature, because the whole idea of this series is that it should deal with what is contemporary, that is, in general, the literature of the last twenty or thirty years. We are having six talks on English literature, four on Russian literature, and are ending up with the two on Chinese literature.

What you said in your book opened up to me a completely new world which I had hitherto known nothing about, and I think it will be the same with our listeners. I want to bring home to them that there is a vigorous modern Chinese literature which is most likely to be accessible to them through English translations. But, of course, you would have to put in just a little background stuff about earlier Chinese literature, in order to show in what way contemporary writing is a new departure.

Yes, I have seen certain Chinese stories in *New Writing*,[8] and they were what first gave me the idea for these talks. Could you be kind enough to let me know whether you could manage the dates named?

Hsiao Ch'ien Esq.,   Yours sincerely,
c/o The School of Oriental Studies,   Eric Blair
University of London, W.C.1   Talks Assistant
                                      Indian Section

PP/EB   25th March 1942

Dear Hsiao Ch'ien,

(I think we might drop the 'Mr.', might we not?) I want your two talks to be on two consecutive weeks, i.e. the second script to be delivered on May 26th and to reach me by about May 22nd (not later than that). I hope you will be able to manage this.

These literary talks seem to go best when they run for about 20 minutes, that is to say, 2500-3000 words. I wouldn't go much over 3000.

[8] Two stories by Chinese writers had appeared in *Penguin New Writing*: 'Hatred' by Tchang T'ien-Yih in no. 1, and 'Along the Yunnan-Burma road' by Pai Ping-Chei in no. 5.

I look forward to seeing your article on modern Chinese culture.

Hsiao Ch'ien Esq.,   Yours sincerely,
School of Oriental Studies,   Geo. Orwell
University of London, W.C.1

PP/EB   26th March 1942

Dear Sir,

I am arranging a series of talks on the development of Science for the Eastern Services of the B.B.C. Professor Bernal, with whom I have discussed the series, suggests that you might care to undertake the fourth talk, which I have called provisionally 'The Economic Bases of Science'. We can think of a better title later.

Roughly what I want is a discussion of the position of Science in different economic systems with particular reference to its position in capitalist societies and under Fascism.

I can give you fuller particulars if you are interested in doing the talk. These talks take 15 or 20 minutes, which means something over 2,000 words. The approximate date would be about 12 weeks from now.

Perhaps you could be kind enough to let me know whether this interests you.

Professor Joseph Needham   Yours truly,
  M.A., Ph.D.,[9]   Eric Blair
1 Owlstone Road,   Talks Assistant
Cambridge   Indian Section

PP/EB   27th March 1942

Dear Lady Grigg,

I am enclosing herewith your Pass for April.

I wonder how full up your schedule now is. Mrs. Amabel Williams-Ellis[10] was here yesterday, and is anxious to do some talks, not necessarily in the very near future, on popularised Science, Dietetics, Progress of Medicine, and that kind of subject. I think she had in mind a series of two, three or four talks.

---

[9] Joseph Needham (1900-), FRS, FBA, author of *Science and Civilisation in China* (7 vols, 1954-). Work by him recently published at this time included *The Nazi Attack on International Science* (1941) and *Science in Soviet Russia* (1942), edited with Jane Sykes Davies, which contained a contribution by J.D. Bernal.

[10] Author of *Women in War Factories* (1943), with a Foreword by Isobel, Lady Cripps, and later of many children's books. She was married to the architect Clough Williams-Ellis and died in 1984.

I wonder if you could let me know whether you are likely to have any dates open, for instance some time in May or June.

Lady Grigg,   Yours sincerely,
3 Whitehall Court,   Eric Blair
Westminster, S.W.1   Talks Assistant
                                      Indian Section

From: Eric Blair, Indian Section, 200 Oxford Street   [n.d.]
Subject: Lady Grigg's[11] broadcasts ('Women Generally Speaking')
To: Eastern Services Director

I wonder if it would be possible for us to get Lady Grigg's broadcasts somewhat more under our own control, as we have to bear the responsibility for them.

This morning everything went wrong that could have gone wrong. The talk had not been properly timed and was far too long. When I pointed out that it was too long and had better be cut I was told this had been timed to $12\frac{1}{2}$ minutes. I then said that I would signal if it were going to over-run and had to be cut. After about two pages I saw that it must over-run considerably and prepared a cut and went in with this to Lady Grigg. She offered it to Sir James who refused to take it and cut it himself in transit, with the result that Lady Grigg's closing announcement was cut out and there was a lot of rustling and whispering. In addition, Sir James referred to the sinking of H.M.S. 'Renown' (instead of the Repulse) at Singapore. This was in his own script and it had been copied from that into the censored script. He read from his own however.

I don't, in most cases, see Lady Grigg's scripts before transmission, as Tuesday is supposed to be my day off, and they are not usually in before then; I think it would be better if it were made a rule that Lady Grigg's scripts were always in not later than Monday, and also that the Talks Producer could have some control over the way they're put on.

We had trouble only a week or two ago as can be seen from the attached memo. On another occasion, when Miss Ellen Wilkinson[12] was broadcasting she did not follow her script at all but almost composed a fresh talk on the spot. I know, of course, that eminent speakers have to be given more latitude but it is difficult for us to bear the responsibility when the speaker is practically not under our control.

[11] See above, Introduction p. 27 and n.49.
[12] Ellen Cicely Wilkinson (1891-1947). Labour MP for Jarrow, appointed Minister of Education in 1945. She had been a Communist but left the party in 1924.

PP/EB   27th March 1942

Dear Professor Bernal,
   I am just writing to confirm the details of the two talks we agreed at our conversation. You are doing the first and sixth talk in the series. The first, 'The Birth of Modern Science', will be on 2nd May, and the other, 'The Future of Science', will be 4 weeks later. These talks should be 15-20 minutes, which means something over 2,000 words.
   I wonder if you could let me know the exact title and address of Mr. J.G. Crowther (I am not certain whether these initials are correct), who, you told me, is Scientific Adviser to the British Council.

Professor J.D. Bernal,   Yours sincerely,
60 Clifton Hill, N.W.8   Eric Blair
                                         Talks Assistant
                                         Indian Section

PP/EB   31st March 1942

Dear Professor Needham,[12]
   Many thanks for your letter of March 29th. The talks in the series are arranged as follows:

   1. The Birth of Science (Prof. Gordon Childe)[13]
   2. The Beginnings of Modern Science (Prof. Bernal)
   3. Experimental & Applied Science (Prof. A.C.G. Egerton)[14]
   4. The Economic Bases of Science (Prof. J. Needham)
   5. Science in the USSR (Prof. J.G. Crowther)
   6. The Future of Science (Prof. Bernal)

I would have liked to have had two talks on the economic bases of science, i.e. two other than the talk on science in a Socialist economy, but we had to compress them into one if we were to have two talks about the origins of science. What I should like you to do is a talk about the effects of capitalism on science, the extent to which it has stimulated its development, and the point at which it becomes a retarding influence, followed by a discussion of

[13] Gordon Childe (1892-1959), Marxist prehistorian, author of *What Happened in History* (1942).
[14] Alfred Charles Egerton (1886-1959), Professor of Chemical Technology at Imperial College, London, and a brother-in-law of Sir Stafford Cripps. He was a member of the War Cabinet Scientific advisory committee, and was responsible for the reorganisation of the British Central Scientific Office in Washington in 1942. He was knighted in 1943.

the position of 'pure' science under Fascism. Fascism evidently doesn't prevent the application of scientific discoveries to practical ends, e.g. war, but it is difficult to see how freedom of research can survive under any totalitarian system.[15]

This roughly is what I want discussed – in something under twenty minutes, if you can manage it.

Professor Joseph Needham M.A.,	Yours sincerely,
Ph.D.,	Eric Blair
1, Owlstone Road,	Talks Assistant
Cambridge	Indian Section

PP/EB   31st March 1942

Dear Hsiao Ch'ien,
    Many thanks for your letter of March 29th. I am glad you can manage the two dates. As for China's political history, you can say anything you like, because so far as we are concerned there are no complications, and nothing that is likely to cause offence. As to India, it is a more prickly subject, but as you say, there is no particular reason to bring it in here.

Hsiao Ch'ien, Esq.,	Yours,
c/o School of Oriental Studies,	
University of London, W.C.1	

PP/EB   31st March 1942

Dear Mrs. Williams-Ellis,
    Lady Grigg writes to say that her schedule is full up until about June 10th, and she is rather nervous about arranging talks too far ahead because of possible changes in the political situation etc. Perhaps you might care to write to her directly suggesting the subjects you wanted to talk about. Lady Grigg arranges the talks for this series more or less independently.

Mrs. Amabel Williams-Ellis,	Yours sincerely,
Plas Brondanw,	George Orwell
Llanfrothen,	Talks Assistant
Merioneth, North Wales	Indian Section

---

[15] After the war Orwell commented on the persecution of scientists in the Soviet Union: *CE* IV, p. 520. He is seen already making the point here to Needham.

PP/EB   10th April 1942

Dear Mr. Forster,

Mr. Bokhari has asked me to let you know the dates of your next three book talks. We should like you to give them on Wednesdays, 29th April, 27th May, and 24th June. As from April 19th we are changing the times of our programmes, and your talks will now go out at 1.30 p.m., D[ouble] B[ritish] S[ummer] T[ime]. I have asked our Contracts Department to get in touch with you.

I understand that you have some books which were sent to you for your last book talk; these were taken out in Mr. Bokhari's name, so that he is responsible for returning them to the BBC Library. They are beginning to ask for some of the books back, so he would be very grateful if you would return them to him, and he will pass them on to the Library.

E.M. Forster Esq.,   Yours sincerely,
West Hackhurst,   George Orwell
Abinger Hammer,   Talks Assistant
Dorking   Indian Section

West Hackhurst Abinger Hammer
Dorking   13-4-42

Dear Mr. Orwell,

Thank you for your letter and I have noted the dates. Have you any suggestions for the 29th? I thought of mentioning the Indian number of Life & Letters and the new novel of Anand,[16] for which I will write direct to the publishers. I don't suppose that, by this time, Indians will be very attentive to Western culture. I believe that the B.B.C., some time ago, instituted an inquiry in India to find out what interested them: if this bore any fruits, I should be most grateful for them.

I returned the books in two batches on March 31st and April 1st, I think, and gave them in at the Reception in Bokhari's name and asked that they should be sent straight to the library. I think they must be there – will you please tell the library to have a hunt: the first batch I saw [?] departing in the hands of a messenger.

Yours sincerely,
E.M. Forster

---

[16] *The Sword and the Sickle* (1942). It was Orwell who gave Anand the title for his book from Blake's poem, during a walk across Primrose Hill in the blackout (personal communication from Dr Anand).

EB/NP   14th April 1942

Dear Mr. Forster,

Many thanks for your letter. As to the questionnaire of the BBC which you mention, I don't think it ever bore much fruit, but I am finding out what replies did come in and will let you have any material which looks as if it might be useful.

I think it would be a good idea to more or less wrap your talk around Anand's novel and the Indian number of *Life & Letters*. *Indian Writing* could be mentioned in the same connection, and perhaps also the recent selection of Kipling's poems with Eliot's introduction.[17] A book which is more or less a propos but unfortunately must *not* be mentioned is K.S. Shelvankar's *The Problem of India*.[18] This has been banned in India and if we refer to it the censorship will cut it out. If you could delicately hint that people here are very interested in English-language Indian writers such as Ahmed Ali, etc. it would be a good propaganda point. It might even be worth mentioning that people are becoming more interested in Indian painting, and *Horizon* are shortly publishing an article by an Indian on Bengali folk painting.[19] One minor cause of trouble with the Indian intelligentsia is that English magazines won't print their stuff.

E.M. Forster,   Yours,
West Hackhurst,   George Orwell
Abinger Hammer,
Nr. Dorking

W.H.   15-4-42

Dear Mr. Orwell,

Thank you for your letter. I had as a matter of fact carried out most of those suggestions in an earlier broadcast, but I suppose I might as well repeat myself: there seems little else to do. It would help me if I could have a few minutes' talk with you. I expect to be up Monday: if I am, could we meet at about 4.00?

Does Indian Writing still appear? I have not received my copy for months.

Please will you send me the Eliot Kipling which I suppose is in the library. By the way, have the missing poetry books been tracked?

                                        Yours sincerely
                                        E.M. Forster

[17] *A Choice of Kipling's Verse* (1941).
[18] Khrishnarao Shivarao Shelvankar (1906-   ). *The Problem of India*, a 'Penguin Special', had been published in 1940.
[19] Ajit Mookerjee, 'Kalighat Folk Painters'. *Horizon*, June 1942.

1. George Orwell at the microphone. Photo: BBC

2. Two recording sessions for the poetry magazine 'Voice'.
(a) *(sitting)* Venu Chitale, J.M. Tambimuttu, T.S. Eliot,
Una Marson, Mulk Raj Anand, C. Pemberton, Narayana
Menon; *(standing)* George Orwell, Nancy Barratt, William
Empson. (b) *(sitting)* Herbert Read, Edmund Blunden; *(standing)*
George Woodcock, Mulk Raj Anand, George Orwell, William
Empson. Photos: BBC

3. Princess Indira of Kapurthala, Orwell's political correspondent. Photo: BBC

4. Venu Chitale, Orwell' assistant. Photo: BBC

5. Lady Grigg, Z.A.
Bokhari and another.
Photo: BBC

6. Z.A. Bokhari with
T.S. Eliot. Photo: BBC

7. E.M. Forster reading his weekly programme 'Some Books'.
Photo: BBC

8. George Bishop and Mulk Raj Anand. Photo: BBC

9. Stephen Spender in his Auxiliary Fire Service uniform. Photo: BBC

10. Ignazio Silone at a post-war reception with Gwenda David and her husband, Eric Mosbacher, translators of 'The Fox'. Photo: Hulton Picture Library

11. Hugh 'Humphrey' Slater, taken at Osterley Park. Photo: Hulton Picture Library

12. Brendan Bracken ('B.B.') proposing a toast, in water, to the
BBC in 1943. Clement Atlee is at the extreme left. Photo: BBC

13. 'Landscape with figures', Osbert Lancaster's cartoon of the
Café Royal. Sir Osbert identifies some of the figures as follows: 1.
Arthur Calder-Marshall, 2. Tom Driberg, 3. Stephen Spender, 4.
Kingsley Martin, 5. Cyril Connolly, 6. Osbert Lancaster, 7.
Brian Howard, 8. Jack Beddington.

Rec. March 1st St.6.   Friday, March 5th 1115-1145 ~~BST~~ GMT
2.30 to 4. BST.

For censorship, please. (To be recorded 1.3.43)

B.B.C. ~~JACK LONDON~~
PASSED FOR SECURITY

LANDMARKS IN
AMERICAN LITERATURE. No.5.

Talk on JACK LONDON. by
George Orwell

~~n~~ Jack London, like ~~Edgar~~ Allan Poe, is one of those writers
who have a bigger reputation ~~outside the English speaking world~~

B.B.C.
PASSED FOR POLICY
DATE................. SIGNATURE.............

than inside it - but indeed, more so than ~~Poe, who~~ is at any rate
taken seriously in England and America, whereas most people, ~~if they~~
remember Jack London at all, ~~think of him as a writer of adventure~~
stories not far removed from penny dreadfuls.

Now, I myself don't share the rather low opinion of Jack London which is held in this country and America, and I can claim to
be in good company, for another admirer of Jack London's work was
no less a person than Lenin, the ~~author of~~ *central figure of* the Russian Revolution.
After Lenin's death his widow, Nadeshda Krupskaya, wrote a short
biography of him, at the end of which she describes how she used to
read stories to Lenin when he was paralysed and slowly dying. On the
last day of all, she says, she began to read him Dickens's "Christmas Carol", but she could see that he didn't like it; what she calls
Dickens's "bourgeois sentimentality" was too much for him. So she
changed over ~~xxx~~/ *to* Jack London's story "Love of Life", and that was
almost the last thing that Lenin ever heard. Krupskaya adds that it
is a very good story. It **is** a good story, and ~~I will return and say~~ *In will hear a [?]*
~~from it~~ *read presently & Herbert* ~~some moral about it in a moment.~~ *read.* Here I want only to point to this
rather queer conjunction between a writer of thrillers - stories
about Pacific islands and the goldfields of the Klondike, and also
about burglars, prizefighters and wild animals - and the greatest
revolutionary of modern times. I don't know with certainty what

14. The final script for Orwell's talk on Jack London, showing
the two censor's stamps. The note at the top – 'For censorship,
please' – and the editorial corrections are in Orwell's hand.
Photo: BBC

"The Deserts & the Poles".

Q.1. Is the earth already populated up to capacity? Are there areas which are now empty but could be ~~utilised~~ colonised?

Q.2. What abt areas now ~~empty~~ seemingly uninhabitable.

a. Deserts. Where are the principle desert areas. & could anytg be due to reclaim them? ~~Is it true~~ what produces deserts? Does desert reclamation have any adverse effects elsewhere?

b. Polar regions. Are these inhabitable to any extent? Have any of the ~~at~~ artic or antartic areas a summer during which cultivation could be practiced? Is anytg being ~~done~~ Are/ in this line now? ~~Are the~~ the polar regions fully explored? What abt the northern polar area as a means of communication between the new & old worlds? Is anytg being due in this line? How is arctic transport affected by aviation & meteorology?

15. An autograph note from Orwell to J.F. Horrabin suggesting lines of enquiry for a talk on world geography. Photo: BBC

TALKS BOOKING REQUISITION

1 TO A.A.
Mr. Boswell.
Talks Bkg.Mgr.

FROM Eric Blair
Indian Section

DATE OF
APPLICATION: 11/5/43

Please book the following for .... Eastern (Red) ~~English~~ .... transmission

in the **English** language. PHONE No.

New G4

NAME AND ADDRESS (George Strauss) Esq., M.P.

1 Kensington Palace Gardens, W.8

SERIES .... THE DEBATE CONTINUES

TITLE OR SUBJECT .... A talk of approx. ~~18~~ 6 minutes
to come within the period THE DEBATE CONTINUES.
which he will write and broadcast.

SCRIPT AND READING/~~READING ONLY~~ (Please cross out whichever does not apply)

PRE-RECORDING DATE(S) ....

TIME .... PLACE ....

FIRST BROADCAST DATE(S) Monday, May 17th 1943

TIME 1115-1130 GMT PLACE 200 O.S.

REMARKS The title of this talk is JOINT
PRODUCTION COMMITTEES IN THE FACTORIES. *Dunstan*
.... (For I.P.O.)

2

FROM A.A.

TO TALKS BOOKING MANAGER

DATE OF APPLICATION

Please book above, fee not to exceed 5gs.

REMARKS ....

FORM .... DIARY .... INDEXED 14/5/43 A.A.

3

FROM TALKS BOOKING MANAGER

TO A.A.

DATE ....

Please note booking as above, fee ....

REMARKS ....

.... TALKS BOOKING MANAGER

P/81/P. 10M K. 100 Pads. 8.3.43.

16. A typical specimen of the Talks booking requisition forms
used in the Indian Section. Photo: BBC

17. Commemoration plaque at 200 Oxford Street recording the building's use by the BBC.
Photo: W.J. West

18. Dorset Chambers, Orwell's first London wartime home.
Photo: W.J. West

LANGFORD COURT

19. Langford Court, St John's Wood, where Orwell lived after he joined the BBC. Photo: W.J. West

20. The Barcelona Restaurant today, then a haunt of Spanish
Civil War veterans and one of Orwell's favourite meeting places.
Photo: W.J. West

21. Senate House, Malet Street, wartime headquarters of the Ministry of Information and model for the 'Ministry of Truth' in *Nineteen Eighty-Four*. It was visible to Orwell from Langford Court. Photo: W.J. West

22. A wartime Home Guard exercise of the kind Orwell strongly supported. The figure fifth from the right looks remarkably like Orwell. Photo: Hulton Picture Library

23. Letter from Forster to Orwell (see p.272).

W.H.

24-9-43

Dear Orwell,

I rang you yesterday, but no answer.
I hope you had a good holiday.
I suggest recording for the Friends
broadcast on Friday afternoon, it is at
about 3.0, and for the record book till
on Friday it is f.

Mrs. Blackham did not know about
the Stanley broadcast. It is to be on Queen
Victoria's birth — with Mrs. Lily Vesper...
to the rest of his work on to his personality?
As for the book till I have John
Morris on Japan. I'm keen to fix the
investigation: J. R. Dean was bringing on
... Sanger and Huckleberry Finn. By an...
Mail in Evryman. Could you get that
this is a way for me? I like the Sanger
very much, and Huckleberry Finn will
have never gone on will, is said to be better
still. Any two of would make a nice
extravagant change.

Please with you that both ...
his letters, and as Mr. Thing Nov. 4th
will suit. Mr. right for the change has ...
Live. I had intended to write to him, by ...
stay I am writing to you with be obliged?
you will transmit this message?

Yours,
E.M. Forster.

Can you for me nice on Roof end
Mary Krishna, artists who have
seen from their sunreclift. They it's for
Lahore? Their book must be
mentioned sooner than they! it be going
to slip me.

[Postcard]
9 Arlington Park Mansions, W.4. (Chiswick 2407)   17-4-42

I shall be at the above address tomorrow (Monday) until Wednesday, and should like to see you. – Tuesday morning not later than 11.0. would be suitable. I will try to ring you; did ring yesterday. I have no ideas except to lead off with an account of the Nat[ional] Gall[ery] as a cultural centre,[20] and music, art, and coffee are scarcely books. – Please get me Rebecca West's book on Yugoslavia.[21] I think they should be told of it. Will probably ring you about 4.0. on Monday.

E.M. Forster

W.H.   Saturday

Dear Mr Orwell,
    I enclose script. I come up on Monday address 9 Arlington Park Mansions. Chiswick. W.4. Tel: CHI 2407. I suggest that you keep the typescript and that I come round and see you Wednesday not later than 12.0. and go through it, or take it away to study. Will you kindly let me know whether this suits, and whether I come to Broadcasting House.
    Ajit Mookerjee did not send the Horizon proof.

Yours sincerely
E.M. Forster

PP/EB   27th April 1942

Dear Professor Bernal,
    I think that my letter to you of March 27th must have gone astray, but in any case I am sorry that I gave you the wrong date for the first talk. You will be doing the second and sixth talk in the series. The second, 'The Birth of Modern Science', will be on Tuesday, 9th June, at 1.15 p.m. DBST from Broadcasting House, and the sixth talk – 'The Future of Science' will be on July 7th, at the same time, from Broadcasting House.
    I have got Professor Crowther's address, and have written to ask him if he will do the fifth talk, and am waiting for his reply.

---

[20] The National Gallery had become a place for lunch-time concerts and other cultural activities. Its pictures were stored in Wales for safekeeping.
[21] *Black Lamb and Grey Falcon* (1942).

I think I told you when we had lunch together that these talks should be between 15 and 20 minutes, which means something over 2,000 words.

Professor Bernal,	Yours sincerely,
R. & E. Branch,	Eric Blair
Forest Products Research Station,	Talks Assistant
Princes Risborough, Bucks.	Indian Section

PP/EB   27th April 1942

Dear Mr. Forster,

Many thanks for your script. I don't think there is anything in it that needs altering. I don't suppose that Ajit Mukerjee's article is in type yet, as I believe it is going to be published in *Horizon* for June or July.

It would do very well if you came round to 55 Portland Place at 12 o'clock on Wednesday, as you suggest. You will be going on the air at 1.30, so that will give us time to run through it once and then you can take it away with you.

E.M. Forster Esq.,	Yours sincerely,
c/o 9, Arlington Park Mansions,	George Orwell
Chiswick, W.4	Talks Assistant
	Indian Section

PP/EB   5th May 1942

Dear Professor Bernal,

I am very sorry indeed that you will not be able to give the two talks in our series on Science. We made out the schedule of talks as follows:

1. The Birth of Science (Prof. Gordon Childe)
2. The Beginnings of Modern Science (Prof. Bernal)
3. Experimental and Applied Science (Prof. A.C.G. Egerton)
4. The Economic Bases of Science (Prof. Joseph Needham)
5. Science in the USSR (Mr. J.G. Crowther)
6. The Future of Science (Prof. Bernal)

We have now heard from all the other speakers, and they are all willing to give the talks. I shall be most grateful if you can suggest someone to take your place in this series, because I want to be able to have a complete list of speakers cabled to India, as soon as possible, for publicity purposes.

Professor J.D. Bernal,	Yours sincerely,
R. & E. Branch,	George Orwell
Forest Products Research Station,	Talks Assistant
Princes Risborough, Bucks.	Indian Section

PP/EB   5th May 1942

Dear Reg,[22]

When Dover[23] told me about your talk, I wrote saying that it was the sort of thing we wanted to use later, but could not at this moment. However, after seeing your script, I am not sure it isn't possible from a censorship point of view even now. I am going to get it typed out and then do my best to get it past the censor. This might possibly mean excision of a few phrases, and I could discuss that with you. But we shan't in any case be able to put it on the air till about July, because of my schedule being so full. Of course, by that time the political situation may have altered, and we may be able to speak rather more freely. The line you have taken in your script is one which I am particularly anxious to put across to India in so far as it is possible.

R. Reynolds Esq.,	Yours,
St. Mark's College,	
King's Road, S.W.10	

PP/EB   7th May 1942

Dear Mr. Haldane,

We have had sent on to us a script on A.R.P.,[24] which you wrote for transmission in Hindustani. It has been suggested that you might like to

---

[22] Reginald Reynolds (1905-1958), author of *Gandhi's Fast: its causes and significance* (1932) and joint editor with Orwell of *British Pamphleteers* (vol. 1, 1948; vol. 2, 1951). In 1942 he wrote a pamphlet, *Why India?*, for the War Resisters International. Like Mulk Raj Anand Reynolds had lived at Gandhi's ashram. Anand met him again in wartime London and introduced him to Orwell (personal communication from Dr Anand).

[23] Cedric Dover (d.1951), an Anglo-Indian writer whom Orwell knew and from whom he commissioned several talks. His best-known book was the novel *Half Caste* (1937). Unfortunately there is no Contributors File for him at WAC, and none of his letters to Orwell or of Orwell's to him have survived there.

[24] J.B.S. Haldane (1892-1964), the geneticist, had published *A.R.P. [Air Raid Precautions]* in 1938, forecasting the likely effects of air raids, and wrote and spoke extensively on the subject during the early years of the war. During the Spanish Civil War he had advised the Spanish government about defence against air raids and gas attacks. Haldane had been a Communist sympathiser in the 1930s. He joined the Party in 1942, but resigned in 1950 because he could not accept Soviet interference with scientific research, particularly in the matter of the controversial theories of the Russian geneticist Lysenko. In 1961 he and his wife became Indian citizens. Haldane died in Orissa, where he had become head of the Laboratory of Genetics and Biometry.

broadcast it in English as well. If so, I think the best arrangement would be for you to record it at some time in the near future convenient to yourself, and we can keep it for use at a suitable moment. As your script was written in order to be translated, you might care to change certain phrases. I presume you have got a copy by you. Perhaps you could let me know about this.

Professor J.B.S. Haldane,	Yours sincerely,
Rothamsted Experimental Station,	George Orwell
Harpenden, Herts.	Talks Producer
	Indian Section

PP/EB   8th May 1942

Dear Mulk,
    I have arranged with our Bookings Department that contracts should be sent to you – for the first six talks – and to George Bishop. I should be very grateful if you would let me have the names and addresses of the other speakers as soon as you possibly can, so that we can give you some publicity. When you let me have the names of the speakers I should also like to have a few personal notes about them – their job, anything interesting they have done, and so on. And if there is anything you would like us to say about the series as a whole, do let me know, and we will include it in our publicity notes next week, which is the latest date to send anything in about the first talk, on May 27th.
    I think the idea was that you should record the first one, so would you be able to do it on Monday, May 25th? This would mean that I should have a script by May 18th, if you can let me have it by then.

Mulk Raj Anand Esq.,	Yours,
8, St George's Mews,	
Regent's Park Road, N.W.1	

PP/EB   11th May 1942

Dear Horrabin,
    We have just received two comments on the talks on Geography you did for me – as the comments only cover the second half of February, they had only heard your first two talks. The report from Delhi says –

    'On February 25th J.F. Horrabin's talk on Geography – Sea Lanes – was a very informative comparative study of the strategic importance of the different seas of the present war. The talker had an extremely interesting manner of explaining the background of war in terms of geography.'

The report from Trichinopoly says –

'Horrabin's talk "The World is Round" was of outstanding interest.'

We don't get many comments at the moment, but I think these are encouraging, and I hope you will be able to do some more talks for us.

J.F. Horrabin Esq.,   Yours sincerely,
16, Endersleigh Gardens, N.W.4   George Orwell
                                Talks Producer
                                Indian Section

PP/EB   11th May 1942

Dear Hsiao Ch'ien,
   We have just received reports from India on our broadcasts during the last half of February. I thought you would be interested in the following, which came from Dacca –

'Talk by Chinese talker on occupied China and Japan's New Order on 26th February very interesting.'

   We don't receive very many comments from India, so I think this is all the more encouraging! I am very much looking forward to seeing your first talk on Chinese contemporary literature.

Hsiao Ch'ien Esq.,   Yours sincerely,
c/o School of Oriental Studies,   George Orwell
Malet Street, W.C.1   Talks Producer
                                Indian Section

                                          11.5.42

Dear George,

   I am putting down on a separate page a few particulars about the 'friends' I am going to bring to the microphone.
   Generally I am a little vague about the character their talks will take. I think of them as dialogues held in London in war time such as may make the English less the collective 'they' and more individual human beings to the

Indian listeners. Perhaps you could help to redefine the talks if necessary.

Yours M.R.A.

P.S. The last two names on my list are tentative, as I have not yet received confirmation of their agreement to take part in the talks.

'Meet my friend'

1. George Bishop: Actor, at present a civil servant lecturing on anti-gas decontamination etc. Widely travelled, ex-engineer in Nigeria. A friend of India. 37 Blenheim Terrace, W.9.
2. Albert Edward Manderson: Chimney sweep, named after the Prince of Wales. Iconoclast. Anti-humbug. Man of strong character. Natural philosopher. 1 Eglon Mews, Berkeley Rd, N.W.1.
3. Ian Jay Bell: fire-watcher. Sometime on the *Moscow Daily News*. Scholar of Russian Literature. Interviewed Stalin, [?] etc. Playwright. 37 Frederick Street, Gray's Inn Rd, W.C.1.
4. Inez Holden: Factory worker. Writer. 37 Glebe Place, Chelsea, S.W.3.
5. Sergeant Frederick Collett: Army Educational Corps. [?]. Of exceptionally sincere views about the role of the Anglo-Indian people in India. 36 Rutland Gate, S.W.7.
6. Dr. L. Haden Guest M.C., M.P. Labour member for Islington. Widely travelled. Has vigorous views about post-war reconstruction etc.

EB/PP   14th May 1942

Dear Mulk,

Thanks very much for letting me have the list of your first six speakers. We have asked for contracts to be sent to them. There is just one point, and that is, has Sergeant Collett got his Commanding Officer's permission to do the broadcast? If not, would you ask him to get it in writing, or if he can let me have the name and address of his C.O., we can do it from this end. We shall also need the script of that particular discussion in fairly well ahead, because it has to go to our War Office liaison, just as a matter of form.

Mulk Raj Anand Esq.,   Yours
8, St. George's Mews
Regent's Park Road, N.W.1

PP/EB   15th May 1942

Dear Dr. Darlington,

I am writing to ask whether you could do a talk for us on July 7th. This is the sixth and last of a series of talks on the history of science which we are broadcasting to India. To give you an idea of the scope of the series, I had better give you a list of the titles of the six talks.

1. 'The Birth of Science' by Professor V.G. Childe.
   (Science among the ancients)
2. 'The Beginnings of Modern Science' by Mr. J.A. Lauwerys[25]
   (From the early Middle Ages to the Industrial Revolution)
3. 'Experimental & Applied Science' by Professor Egerton
   (The subsequent history of science).
4. 'The Economic Bases of Science' by Professor Needham
   (Science under capitalism, Fascism and Socialism)
5. 'Science in the USSR' by Mr J.G. Crowther.

The sixth, which we want you to do, is to be called 'The Future of Science'.

These talks are supposed to take from 15 to 20 minutes, which means something in the neighbourhood of 2,000 words or perhaps a little over. I should like to have the script by about July 1st. If it is not convenient for you to broadcast on that particular date we can easily record the talk beforehand.

Could you be kind enough to let me know as early as possible whether you can undertake this?

Dr. C.D. Darlington, FRS.,	Yours truly,
[Director]	George Orwell
John Innes Horticultural Institute,	Talks Producer
Mostyn Road,	Indian Section
Merton Park, S.W.19	

[Postcard]

I had better talk about New Books next month, and want to write the script now since I may be occupied later. Please will you send me as soon as possible Carr,[26] *Conditions of Peace* and A.L. Rowse's *Cornish Childhood*, together with anything which you recommend. I have got Ron [?] *Social Life in England* and the anthologies of Tambimuttu and L.A.G. Strong. – Anand tells me that Gangulee (Tagore's nephew) has brought out a Russian anthology,[27] and I should like this too if you can track it down. – Would like to keep in touch with all books written over here by Indians.

E.M. Forster

24-5-42   W. Hackhurst

[25] Joseph Albert Lauwerys(1902-1981), author of *Film and Radio as Educational Media* (1939). His *The Roots of Science in Basic English* (1951) indicates an interest he had in common with Orwell.

[26] E.H. Carr (1892-1984), pro-Stalinist historian of Russia.

[27] The anthologies referred to here were: *Poetry in Wartime*, edited by J.M. Tambimuttu (1942), *A New Anthology of Modern Verse*, edited by L.A.G. Strong and Cecil Day-Lewis (1941), and *The Russian Horizon* compiled by Nagendranath Gangulee with a preface by H.G. Wells (1942?).

PP/EB   19th May 1942

Dear Mr. Titmuss,[28]

I wonder whether you would consider doing a talk for us in a series which we shall be broadcasting to India during June and July. This is a series dealing with the future of India, and is called A.D. 2000 – the idea being that it is an attempt to forecast what is likely to be happening fifty or sixty years hence. We want the second talk in the series, which I have called provisionally '400 Millions', to be on the Indian population problem. You seem to me to be much the most suitable person to do it, and you could approach it from whatever angle you liked; i.e. you could discuss whether the Indian population is likely to go on growing at its present rate, how it will be affected by industrialisation, at what point you think the saturation level of India will be reached, and so on.

These talks are supposed to take between fifteen and twenty minutes, which means something over 2,000 words. I should want the talk to be delivered on July 3rd, at 1.15 p.m., which means that I should like the script by about June 25th. In the case of your not being able actually to broadcast on that day, it is quite easy to record beforehand.

Could you please let me know as soon as possible whether you would like to undertake this?

Yours truly,
George Orwell
Talks Producer
Indian Section

as from W.H.   5-6-42

Dear George Orwell

How about an American talk? If you agree please get me that recent book on Walt Whitman. Also information about American magazines – weekly, monthly, quarterly. I am just reading the Virginia Quarterly.

I have asked Hilton Brown[29] to get me in connection with my home broadcast books by Dos Passos, Davies, and Steinbeck,[30] which would work in.

Yours
E.M. Forster

[28] Richard Morris Titmuss (1907-1973) had written *Poverty and Population* (1938) and *Our Food Problem* (with F. Le Gros Clark, 1939). In 1950 he became Professor of Social Administration at the London School of Economics.

[29] A Home Talks Producer.

[30] Dos Passos' book here referred to is probably *The Ground We Stand On: some examples from the history of a political creed* (1942). Dos Passos also wrote *Nineteen Nineteen* (1932) (the title written out in words, as Orwell was to insist on for *Nineteen Eighty-Four*) and *The Villages are the Heart of Spain* (1937). The other two books are *Mission to Moscow* by Joseph Davies (1942) and Steinbeck's *The Moon is Down* (1942).

PP/EB   June 10th 1942

Dear Mr. Forster,

I am sending herewith the book on Whitman which you wanted. As to American magazines, the BBC Library seems very poorly provided with them, and I can only tell you of the ones I personally know about – I am referring to the more serious magazines, of course. These are:

Weekly: The Nation; the New Republic; and I think New Masses still exists.
Monthly: The Atlantic Monthly; Harpers; Scribner's; Decision; Poetry.
Bi-monthly: The Partisan Review.
Quarterly: I don't know, but I think there is a Virginia Quarterly.

I am sorry to be so unhelpful about this.

E.M. Forster Esq.,   Yours,
West Hackhurst,   George Orwell
Abinger Hammer,   Talks Producer
Nr Dorking, Surrey   Indian Section

[Postcard]
Thank you for your postcard, I should be glad of the Whitman as soon as possible.

Hilton Brown, for whom I am broadcasting on July 3rd has sent me some of the books I wanted, but none of them are the American ones which I want for our broadcast also. Perhaps you could get in touch with him, and he or you would send me at once the Dos Passos and the Davies (ambassador to Moscow). Both these are out, and I want them urgently for India. I should also like the Steinbeck novel – I don't know whether this is out yet.

EMF   10-6-42

PP/EB   10th June 1942

Dear Princess Indira,

We are considering having a regular rotation of speakers to broadcast our weekly News Review on Saturday afternoons. This is a summing-up of the world situation during the current week, and is written by myself.[31] It goes out at 1.15 p.m. DBST. Would you care to be put on the list, and to do the broadcasting of these reviews either once every four or once every five weeks? It would be possible to arrange the dates a good long time ahead. There will,

[31] This is one of a number of statements that confirm Orwell's authorship of the news broadcasts put out weekly by the Indian Section (to be published shortly as *Through Eastern Eyes: Orwell's War Commentaries*).

of course, be a fee for the reading, but as it does not entail any actual composition, it would not be a large one.

Princess Indira of Kapurthala,	Yours sincerely,
512A, Nell Gwynn House,	Eric Blair
Sloane Avenue, S.W.3	Talks Producer
	Indian Section

Sunday   W.H.

Dear Mr. Orwell,

Have managed to get this off today after all, and will come to 55 P[ortland] P[lace] on Wednesday at about 12.0. for rehearsal etc.

I think the length is right, but I will bring up Hsiao Ch'ien's book so that I can add a few words on it if necessary. But I should prefer to leave it over for another talk.

Two points. How to pronounce Herzgovina. A[nd] does the story *The Salt of the Earth* occur, in fact, in the volume called *The Harsh Voice*? (see my first remarks). I think MacMillans [sic] published it – would you kindly ring up, or otherwise discover, since I have no means of verifying here.

Yours E.M. Forster

PP/EB   June 11th 1942

Dear Mulk,

I wonder if you've arranged any more speakers for your series yet? You gave us the names of the first six, ending with Dr. Haden Guest, but now our Publicity Department is beginning to ask for more. I should be glad if you will let me have at least three names, as soon as you can, – that is of course, if you haven't fixed up all six yet.

I will meet you and Inez Holden on Monday at 2 p.m. at 200, Oxford Street.

Mulk Raj Anand Esq.,	Yours,
8 St. George's Mews,	
Regent's Park Road, N.W.1	

PP/EB   13th June 1942

Dear Dr. Darlington,

You are already doing a talk for us in the series 'Science and Politics', and I am wondering whether you would like to do another, of approximately the same length, in a series called 'A.D. 2000'. The idea of this series is to give some kind of picture of what will probably be happening in 50 or 60 years time. The one I would like you to undertake is the third in the series, to be called 'India in the Steel Age', and to deal with the industrialisation of India. You could have an entirely free hand, and could talk about how far India is likely to become industrialised, whether you think it ought to do so, how the industrialisation is to be brought about, or whatever other aspect of the subject you prefer. To give you an idea of the general scope of these talks, here are the subjects dealt with in the other five –

1. Agriculture
2. The population problem
4. Education
6. India's cultural future.

The date of the talk would be on July 10th, which would mean that I should want the script by about the beginning of July. Perhaps you would be kind enough to let me know whether you would like to undertake this. As this is in the same week as your other talk, if it is inconvenient to you to make two visits, you could record the second talk on the same day as you deliver the first.

Dr. C.D. Darlington, F.R.S.,	Yours sincerely,
John Innes Horticultural Institution,	George Orwell
Mostyn Road,	Talks Producer
Merton Park, S.W.19	Indian Section

16.6.42

Dear Blair

I am going to put down on paper three further names for the 'Meet my friend' series for winter. These are:

1. George Downes, painter. Has exhibited with various young artists during the last ten years. Was at one time a waiter, also had a stall in Caledonian Market. His work is marked by an extraordinary love for colouring and a sense of musical pattern.
2. Dr Mac Fisher, scientist: zoologist. Sometime assistant to Julian Huxley at the Zoo and collaborator with him on various papers. Fellow of [?]

College, Oxford. Author of a book on bird watching in the Penguins. At present engaged in supervision of rat-catching in the [?].

3. André Van Gyseghem, theatrical producer and actor. Associated with the production of various pageants during the last few years. Actor-Manager. Has studied the Soviet Theatre.

Of them the first two have already been contacted while the third is in the process of being contacted.

I shall supply you a further list of three names by the end of next week.

I enclose a tentative draft of three numbers of 'Voice'.

> Yours
> MRA

PP/EB   17th June 1942

Dear Mr. Needham,

Thank you very much for your script, which reached me just after my secretary rang you up. I am sending you copies of the scripts that we have had in this series up to date. Your talk is just the kind of thing I wanted.

Can you come to my office at 200, Oxford Street, at about 12.30 on Tuesday? We want you to broadcast the talk direct, at 1.15 p.m., and that will give you time to run through it once for timing. 200, Oxford Street, is on the corner of Great Portland Street and Oxford Street, and the entrance is opposite Studio One Cinema. Thank you for correcting me about your description, I will see that it is given correctly in the announcements preceding your talk. I shall look forward to seeing you on Tuesday.

Professor Joseph Needham   Yours sincerely,
                                  Eric Blair
                                  Talks Producer
                                  Indian Section

PP/EB   23rd June 1942

Dear Sir,

I am writing to you because it has been suggested to me that you might be able to advise us about selecting a speaker for a forthcoming talk.

We are looking for a speaker on the Future of Education in India. We have a series of talks called 'A.D. 2000', which deal with the probable condition of India about 50 or 60 years from now. We want one on education and we naturally are looking for a speaker with some experience of India, though not necessarily very prolonged experience. The date of the talk is July 17th, which means that we want to make sure of engaging our speaker within the next week or so. Could you be kind enough to give me your advice? If you could reply by telephone, it might save time. My telephone number is Euston 3400, and the extension 180.

I am sorry to trouble you, but I am anxious to have the advice of somebody with expert knowledge of this matter.

Sir Frank Brown, C.I.E.,[32]	Yours truly,
Dilkusha,	Eric Blair
Westbourne Drive,	Talks Producer
Forest Hill	Indian Section

PP/EB   23rd June 1942

Dear Tambimuttu,

I am writing to ask whether you would care to do us another talk in a forthcoming series. This series is called 'Open Letters': the idea is to discuss the origins and political meaning of the war and to put this in a simple popular form we are going to do it in the form of open letters to imaginary people representing the most important trends of modern thought. The one I should like you to do is the Letter to a Marxist, the date of which will be September 10th at 12.45 p.m. BST, and I should want the script *not later than September 3rd*. No doubt you will understand that though I want the talks to be of a popular intelligible type, I also hope they will provide a serious discussion of modern political problems. As far as possible your talk should have a direct bearing on India. Could you please let me know as early as possible whether you would like to undertake this?

J.M. Tambimuttu Esq.,	Yours sincerely,
18, Oakley Gardens,	Eric Blair
S.W.3	Talks Producer
	Indian Section

PP/EB   23rd June 1942

Dear Mr. Foot,

I am writing to ask whether it would interest you to do a talk in one of our forthcoming series in the Eastern Service. These talks are in the form of short discussions between people with special knowledge of subjects of current interest. The one I hope you will undertake is on the Press, and the speaker with whom I suggest you should hold your discussion is J.L. Garvin. These broadcasts take about 13½ minutes, which means probably that your contribution would be in the neighbourhood of 750 words. The date of this broadcast would be August 7th, at 1.45 p.m. DBST. This means that I should

---

[32] Sir Frank Brown (d.1949), previously editor of the *Indian Daily Telegraph*, was at this time on the editorial staff of *The Times* and Hon. Sec. of the East India Association.

like to have the script by July 31st if possible. If you agree, I will make all the arrangements for the necessary meeting and discussion. Could you be kind enough to let me know as soon as possible whether this interests you?[33]

Michael Foot Esq.,   Yours sincerely,
c/o The Evening Standard,   George Orwell
47, Shoe Lane, E.C.4   Talks Producer
                                             Indian Section

PP/EB   23rd June 1942

Dear Mr. Worsley,[34]

I am writing to ask whether it would interest you to do a talk in one of our forthcoming series in the Eastern Service. These talks are in the form of short discussions between people with special knowledge of subjects of current interest. The one I hope you will undertake is on Education.[35] I haven't yet selected the other speaker, but obviously we shall choose someone who is more disposed to defend the current educational system than you are. These broadcasts take about $13\frac{1}{2}$ minutes, which means probably that your contribution would be in the neighbourhood of 750 words. The date of this broadcast would be September 11th, at 12.45 p.m. BST. This means that I should like to have the script by September 4th if possible. If you agree, I will make all the arrangements for the necessary meeting and discussion. Could you be kind enough to let me know as soon as possible whether this interests you?

T.C. Worsley Esq.,   Yours sincerely,
c/o The New Statesman & Nation,   George Orwell
10, Great Turnstile, W.C.1   Talks Producer
                                             Indian Section

PP/EB   25th June 1942

Dear Mulk,

I'm afraid I didn't tell you when you were here the other day that the last

[33] Foot, who occupied the highly paid post of Editor on Beaverbrook's *Evening Standard*, declined to contribute a talk.

[34] T.C. Worsley, who had been a schoolmaster at Wellington, was author of *Barbarians and Philistines: Democracy and the Public Schools* (1940) and (with W.H. Auden) *Education Today and Tomorrow* (1939).

[35] Orwell had serious views about education, which he developed with reference to his own schooldays in 'Such, such were the joys' (*CE* IV, p. 379-422). Though not published until after the war, this may well have been written as early as 1938. See Bernard Crick, *George Orwell: a life*, Appendix B, and the introduction to Peter Davison (ed.) *Nineteen Eighty-Four the Facsimile of the Extant Manuscript*, p. ix.

date for the Meet My Friend talks will be 22nd July, which means, I am afraid, that the talk by André Van Gyseghem will have to be the last in the series.

I am getting in touch with the Contracts Department about the last three speakers, and they will receive their contracts in due course.

Mulk Raj Anand Esq., Yours sincerely,
8, St. George's Mews, George Orwell
Regent's Park Road, N.W.1 Talks Producer
Indian Section

P.S. I find now that you haven't given me the address of any of these people, so I can't issue the contract slips. If you will let me know before I go away, or else tell Mr. Bokhari's secretary, then we can get on with the contracts.

EB/PP 13th July 1942

Dear Cyril,
Did Anand ask you about reading a poem on our forthcoming magazine programme 'Voice'?
You might let me know as we want to get the programme all sewn up as soon as possible.

Cyril Connolly Esq., Yours,
Eric Blair
Talks Producer
Indian Section

PP/EB 14th July 1942

Dear Mr. Easterbrook,[36]
I am sending herewith Sir John Russell's draft for his part in the forthcoming dialogue with you. His suggestion was that you should write what you wanted to say, after which we will work it up into a proper discussion. You will notice, however, that Sir John Russell has talked almost entirely about Indian agriculture. It is not altogether suitable for us from this end to talk to Indians exclusively about conditions in their country, and I really wanted the talk to deal with modern developments in agriculture generally. Do you think, therefore, that you could cast your talk in a more general vein, but particularly with reference to agricultural development in

---

[36] Laurence F. Easterbrook, author of *Machines on the Farm* (1943) and *Achievement in British Farming* (1943). (There are no detectable allusions to Easterbrook's work in Orwell's own *Animal Farm*!)

temperate countries. If we have something of that sort from you, I think we can work the two up into a balanced discussion.

Could you let me have the script within four or five days from now; we have arranged the recording for July 22nd, and I should be glad if you could come to 200, Oxford Street at 10.15 a.m. on that day. The recording will finish at about 11.45 a.m.

> Yours sincerely,
> George Orwell
> Talks Producer
> Indian Section

PP/EB   16th July 1942

Dear Mr. Young,[37]

I am writing to ask whether it would interest you to do a talk in one of our forthcoming series in the Eastern Service. These talks are in the form of short discussions between people with special knowledge of subjects of current interest. The one I hope you will undertake is on the Press, and the speaker with whom I suggest you should hold your discussion is H.N. Brailsford.[38] These broadcasts take about $13\frac{1}{2}$ minutes, which means probably that your contribution would be in the neighbourhood of 750 words. The date of this broadcast would be August 7th, at 1.45 p.m. DBST. This means that I should like to have the script by July 31st if possible. If you agree, I will make all the arrangements for the necessary meeting and discussion. Could you be kind enough to let me know as soon as possible whether this interests you?

G.M. Young Esq.,   Yours sincerely,
Old Oxyard,   George Orwell
Oare,   Talks Producer
Nr. Marlborough, Wilts   Indian Section

PP/EB   18th July 1942

Dear Miss Hope,

I am writing to ask you whether you would be interested in taking part in a

---

[37] G.M. Young (1882-1959), Tory historian and educationalist. He joined the Board of Education in 1908 and became the first Secretary of what was to become the University Grants Committee.

[38] H.N. Brailsford (1873-1958), one of the first Western journalists to visit Russia after the First World War. He later became a severe critic of Soviet Communism. A close friend of Gandhi and Nehru, he believed passionately in Indian independence. At this time he was the chief leader-writer of the *New Statesman* under Kingsley Martin. His books on India were: *Rebel India* (1931), *India in Chains* (1936), *Democracy for India* (1939) and *Subject India* (1943).

somewhat experimental programme which we are producing for the first time on 11th August. This programme is called 'Voice', and is a kind of spoken magazine, with poems, short stories and so forth. We have for the first number a monologue by Inez Holden, which could make a very good item, if read by a suitable actress. It was written for print, and therefore will need a certain amount of alteration, but we can manage that. It would take about 6 minutes, possibly even less. I think it would be a case of two rehearsals besides the actual recording of the programme.

As this programme is something in the nature of an experiment, the fees involved will not be very large – I don't want to be handicapped in advance by incurring great expenses. Would you be interested to hear more of this? If so, could you be kind enough to let me know as early as possible?

Miss Vida Hope,   Yours truly,
21, Belsize Crescent, N.W.3   George Orwell
     Talks Producer
     Indian Section

PP/EB   23rd July 1942

Dear Mr. Young,

I am sorry you do not feel equal to broadcasting on the Press, but I quite see your objection. How would you like to take part in a similar discussion on the subject of Education? This talk is fixed for September 11th, and we have already fixed on T.C. Worsley, whose work you probably know, as one speaker. We should like it very much if you could be the other, and you may perhaps find this subject more congenial. Worsley will doubtless attack the current educational system very violently, and you may feel more inclined to defend it, so the basis of a real discussion is probably there.

Could you let me know as soon as possible whether you are interested, and in that case I will give you a more detailed directive. I may say, however, that by the method we usually adopt in these discussions, it is possible to get the whole thing over with only one visit to London.

As to copies of the *Gem* and *Magnet*,[39] I am sorry to say I have been unable to procure you any. My surviving copies are all in the country where I cannot get at them, and as they discontinued publishing them more than a year ago, I cannot procure any copies here. But I will see that you get some sooner or later.

G.M. Young Esq.,   Yours sincerely,
The Old Oxyard,   George Orwell
Oare,   Talks Producer
Nr. Marlborough, Wilts.   Indian Section

[39] Two boys' magazines mentioned by Orwell in his article 'Boys' Weeklies' published in *Horizon*, March 1940 (*CE* I, p. 505-31).

PP/EB   23rd July 1942

Dear Eliot,
Very many thanks for your kind letter. I believe Bokhari is arranging with you to read your three latest long poems during the latter part of October. I wonder if I can also interest you in a rather experimental programme which we are starting shortly? This is a spoken magazine, which we are calling 'Voice', and it will be devoted mainly to poetry, and as far as possible we are getting people to read their own poems. We are bringing out the first number on August 11th, and if it is not a failure we are likely to continue with at any rate three more numbers, at monthly intervals. I will tell you how the first one goes off, and you might find it interesting to take part in a later number.

T.S. Eliot Esq.,   Yours sincerely,
c/o Faber & Faber Ltd., Publishers,   George Orwell
24, Russell Square,   Talks Producer
London, W.C.1   Indian Section

PP/EB   25th July 1942

Dear Mr. Treece,[40]
Very many thanks for sending along a selection of poems, which Mulk Raj Anand has brought to me. I have been through them and provisionally picked out three, which I think suitable for broadcasting. We have to consider two things, the first is that we can only broadcast something fairly short, and second we have to broadcast what is fairly easily intelligible because, although we are aiming at making this programme highbrow, we are speaking to people whose English is not necessarily perfect, and also because something which is merely heard and not read needs to be comparatively simple. However, we may change the selection when you come here. I wonder whether you could come to London next Friday afternoon, about 2.30 (July 31st), and I will try to get as many of the other people taking part in the programme as possible together, so that we can do something towards putting the whole programme together. I should be very glad to put you up for the night so that you don't need to be troubled about times for getting back. Could you please let me know as soon as possible whether you can manage this?

                                          Yours sincerely,
                                          George Orwell
                                          Talks Producer
                                          Indian Section

[40] Henry Treece (1911-1966), poet and co-editor of *Kingdom Come*, one of the few wartime poetry magazines.

PP/EB 25th July 1942

Dear Read,
   About our magazine programme 'Voice', in which we hope you are going to take part. Can you by any chance come in here next Friday afternoon about 2.30 p.m.? Even if you can't manage that particular time, it would no doubt do if you could come at some time in the afternoon. I am making efforts on that day to get hold of Henry Treece, who presents the biggest difficulty as he lives out of London. It will probably be easy enough to get hold of the others. Please let me know as soon as possible.
   It may interest you to know that I am having a row with your publishers,[41] who, however, tell me that it is not their fault, but that of the Fabian Society. I will let you know developments later.

Herbert Read Esq.,	Yours,
Broom House,	George Orwell
Seer Green,	Talks Producer
Beaconsfield, Bucks.	Indian Section

PP/EB 25th July 1942

Dear Inez,
   We still have not contacted the actress we want to do your monologue, and therefore I have not yet attempted the changes which are needed to put it into spoken form. We were trying to get Vida Hope, but she has not yet replied to my letter. So I am now trying to get Joan Sterndale-Bennett. Can you by any chance come in here (200 Oxford Street) on Friday afternoon, July 31st, at about 2.30 p.m.? I am trying to get all the contributors together then. It may not be possible before that time. Please let me know as soon as possible whether you can manage this.

Miss Inez Holden,	Yours,
37, Glebe Place, S.W.3	George Orwell
	Talks Producer
	Indian Section

[41] George Routledge and Sons, publishers of *Victory or Vested Interest* (1942) which included an essay by Orwell, 'Culture and Democracy'. Orwell was annoyed to discover that his text had been drastically altered without his knowledge, and wrote a stern letter on BBC writing paper demanding an explanation. The original text of the essay seems not to have survived. The letter is in the Orwell Archive.

PP/EB   27th July 1942

Dear Worsley,

About the discussion on Education that you are doing for us. I am sorry for the delay, but we hesitated some time about the other speaker before fixing on G.M. Young, who I think will do very well. The procedure I suggest is as follows: you let me have your piece, about 750 words, saying what you think about the subject, I send it on to Young to criticise and then, having received his remarks, work it up into a dialogue which can be emended and rehearsed by both of you before being recorded. I think that method should work out reasonably well.

As to the manner of treatment. We are dealing with the Indian (Student) public which can't be depended on to know all about conditions here. Therefore, although the Public Schools and what they stand for ought to be mentioned, they should not be the exclusive subject. The real point at issue (and here is where Young is likely to disagree, making a real discussion) is whether education should aim at fostering aristocratic or democratic values; and incidentally whether current English educational methods are suited to the modern world. I fancy you will not find it very difficult to produce something along these lines.

I hope things are going well with you. Looking forward to seeing you.

T.C. Worsley Esq.,   Yours,
The Elms,   George Orwell
Bathmore Road, Torquay   Talks Producer
                                Indian Section

PP/EB   30th July 1942

Dear Mr. Treece,

Many thanks for your letter. I am so sorry you can't come this time, but I think I shall still use some of your poems. I selected three provisionally and will let you know which we actually do use, and get someone else to read them. Perhaps another time, when you are actually in London, you could come in and record a poem which we could stick into a later programme. That particular operation does not take long, perhaps half an hour, but we have to arrange the recording beforehand which means about a day's notice.

Hoping to meet you some time.

Henry Treece Esq.,   Yours sincerely,
Course 13,   George Orwell
School of Flying Control,   Talks Producer
Watchfield, Near Swindon.   Indian Section

PP/EB   6th August 1942

Dear Mr. Menon,[42]

We are shortly starting a new series of talks called 'Books that Changed the World', and are wondering if you would like to take part in it.

This series is supposed to deal with outstanding books in the European literature of the last 200 years which have a direct effect on public opinion and caused people to see some major problem in a new light. The one we should like you to undertake is *Gulliver's Travels*, on September 17th, at 12.15 p.m. I think you should start with the assumption that your audience has heard of the book but is not necessarily well acquainted with it. The talk should not therefore be a mere critique of the book but should give a clear account of what it is about and show just how, why and to what extent it influenced public opinion. You should give the date of the book's publication and say at any rate a few words about the social background of the time. It may also be of interest to say a word or two about the author, but the main emphasis should be on the book itself. The talk will be of $13\frac{1}{2}$ minutes duration. Could you be kind enough to let me know whether you can undertake this?

                            Yours sincerely,
                            Eric Blair

PP/EB   10th August 1942

Dear Mr. Forster,

Owing to the change in the hour, your talk on 'Some Books', on August 19th will be at 12.30 p.m. BST, instead of 1.30 p.m.

I am also looking after your introductory talk in the series 'My Debt to India', on Friday next. This goes on the air at 12.15 p.m. BST. I think the best thing would be for you to come in at about 11.30 a.m., and we can run through it once for timing. Sir Malcolm Darling has passed the script on to me,[43] and it will be ready for you to broadcast from on Friday.

E.M. Forster Esq.,   Yours sincerely,
West Hackhurst,   George Orwell
Abinger Hammer,   Talks Producer
Nr. Dorking, Surrey.   Indian Section

---

[42] Vatake Kurnpath Narayana Menon (1911-   ), author of *The Development of William Butler Yeats* (1942), with a preface by Sir Herbert J.C. Grierson.
[43] i.e. from the censor.

PP/EB   10th August 1942

Dear Lord Winterton,
   Many thanks for your letter of 6th August. I think perhaps the best way of
doing this particular discussion will be to let Professor Laski write what he
thinks about the future of Parliament, and then send his draft on to you to
criticise, and on the basis of the two statements we can work up a discussion.
I am communicating with him to this effect, and will send you on his stuff as
soon as I can get hold of it.

The Right Hon.   Yours sincerely
   The Earl Winterton,M.P.,   George Orwell
61, Eccleston Square, S.W.1   Talks Producer
                                        Indian Section

PP/EB   11th August 1942

Dear Miss Hope,
   I am sorry about this morning, and hope we did not make some kind of
fresh mistake. I had arranged to meet you at the Barcelona Restaurant in
order to listen to our programme at 1.15, having forgotten that by that time
the clocks would be back, so that the programme actually went out at 12.15.
My secretary rang up both the theatre and your private address, and
explained the change of time to your friend, asking you to come here at about
ten past 12, in time for the programme. When you did not appear we were
afraid you must be waiting at the Barcelona Restaurant, so we rang up there,
but you were not there either, so we left a message. I hope very much that you
have not been inconvenienced in any way. You did not, I may say, lose much
by missing the programme, as it was spoilt in transmission, but your
particular contribution went out quite satisfactorily.

Miss Vida Hope,   Yours sincerely,
21, Belsize Crescent, N.W.3   George Orwell
                                        Talks Producer
                                        Indian Section

PP/EB   11th August 1942

Dear Treece,
   I delayed answering your letter of August 6th until the programme in
which your poems appear should have gone out. I am very sorry to say it was a
complete muck-up, owing to some technical hitch, and consisted largely of
scratching noises and so forth. However, you will be glad to hear that your

poems went out quite O.K., read by John Atkins, who I think delivered them reasonably well. I trust that this kind of thing won't happen again. Next time we have the programme we may think it safer to broadcast it live, in which case this sort of accident does not happen. But still, if you are in town some time, you might ring me up and arrange about recording one or two of your poems, which I can always use somewhere or other, if not in the Voice programme. I am sending back the manuscripts which you kindly sent. The three poems which were used were 'Walking at Night', 'In the Third Year of War', and the one beginning 'Oh come my joy, my soldier boy'.

Henry Treece Esq.,   Yours sincerely,
R.A.F. Officer's Mess,   George Orwell
Waddington, Lincs.   Talks Producer
            Indian Section

PP/EB   18th August 1942

Dear Miss Freeman,
 Your letter has been passed on to me by Balraj Sahni. We would like to have a short obituary notice of Ram Nahum in the Indian Service, if we can arrange someone to do it.[44] It seems hardly worth while anyone coming up from Cambridge to do a five minute broadcast, but meanwhile I am communicating with Narayana Menon to see whether he can either do the broadcast for us, or tell us somebody else who is now in London who can do it. In the case of our being able to arrange this, I will send you a copy of the script.

Miss Freeman,   Yours sincerely,
University Labour Federation, Eric Blair
22, King Street,   Talks Producer
Cambridge.   Indian Section

as from West Hackhurst   19-8-42

Dear George
 Thank you for letting me know about Elton's broadcast. I daresay it was effective as a broadcast, but it was, from my point of view, too soft and literary to be of any use. Any suggestions I could have offered would have been fundamental ones, so I didn't send them along.
 I wish you could organise a dispute between (say) Unwin and an official from the Ministry of Supply.[45]

---

[44] Ram Nahum was an Egyptian student leader at Cambridge killed in a bombing raid.
[45] An allusion to the difficulty of publishers, such as Stanley Unwin, in getting paper for their books.

The Stopes is charmed with your kind reception of her. I hope it was not much bother.

Yours
Morgan

PP/EB   24th August 1942

Dear Miss Freeman,
    Enclosed is a copy of the talk Narayana Menon is doing on Ram Nahum. As you see it is only a short thing, about five minutes, which is all we had space for. It will go out at about 12.30 p.m. BST tomorrow – Tuesday 25th – on wave-lengths of 16, 19, 25 and 31 metres.
    I am afraid it is too late to inform anyone abroad, but I did not receive your letter asking about this till this morning.

Miss Freeman,   Yours sincerely,
University Labour Federation,   Eric Blair
22, King Street,   Talks Producer
Cambridge   Indian Section

PP/EB   24th August 1942

Dear Mr. Young,
    I am sending herewith a copy of Worsley's remarks. He apologises for its coming so late, but his time has been rather full in the R.A.F. He says that he will be in London from August 26th to September 2nd. I suggest therefore that if you could let me have *your* criticisms of Worsley (about 750 words) by Friday of this week (28th) or Saturday morning (29th) at latest, we could all meet on Tuesday afternoon (September 1st) and have the discussion recorded. I am sorry to give such short notice. Please let me know at once if you can do Tuesday afternoon.

G.M. Young Esq.,   Yours sincerely,
The Old Oxyard,   George Orwell
Oare,   Talks Producer
Nr. Marlborough, Wilts.   Indian Section

PP/EB   28th August 1942

Dear Waddington,
    We want a speaker to say something to the Indian audience about Ersatz

and raw materials. Could you suggest somebody to do an interesting popular talk on these lines? The problems raised by interruption of communications and so forth are now just about beginning to touch India, I should think we could find an audience for a fairly advanced talk of this kind. These talks are usually done in the form of dialogues between two people, but in this case, I fancy we shall do it simply as an interview. I should be very glad to know of any suggestions you can make.

Dr. C.H. Waddington,	Yours,
Christ's College,	George Orwell
Cambridge.	Talks Producer
	Indian Section

[Postcard]
I have no ideas about the next broadcast so far: perhaps one is due on new books. I shall ring you up on Tuesday or Wednesday this week, and shall be glad of any suggestions.
  E.M. Forster

W.H.   Sunday

PP/EB   9th September 1942

Dear Inez,
  We did arrange, didn't we, for you to take part in a broadcast called Story by Five Authors? You might just let me know whether this is O.K., and I will let you have further particulars. Your broadcast will be on October 23rd.

Miss Inez Holden,	Yours,
37, Glebe Place, S.W.3	George Orwell
	Talks Producer
	Indian Section

PP/EB   9th September 1942

Dear Mr. Strong,
  I wonder if you would care to take part in a broadcast of an experimental and slightly unusual type which we are projecting in October. This is called Story by Five Authors and the idea is to have a serial story in five parts each written by a different author, who can carry on the story just as he chooses

from the last instalment. The instalment we want you to do is the second. I am doing the first, the third will be done probably by Inez Holden, the fourth by Martin Armstrong, and we hope the concluding one by E.M. Forster. I cannot yet give further details because the first instalment which I am doing is only in process of being written. This idea may be a failure but on the other hand it might be rather interesting. Could you let me know whether you will at any rate provisionally accept this, and in that case I can let you have the first instalment from which yours would follow at about the end of this month. Each instalment should take $13\frac{1}{2}$ minutes which means about 1500 words. The date of yours would be October 16th. If you are not able to come on that day we can always record it.

L.A.G. Strong Esq.,	Yours sincerely,
Salterns,	George Orwell
Eashing,	Talks Producer
Godalming, Surrey	Indian Section

PP/EB   9th September 1942

Dear Mr. Armstrong,
    I believe Gerald Bullett[46] asked you whether you would like to take part in a broadcast called Story by Five Authors, and that you said you would. Could you just let me know for certain whether this is so, and if so, I will let you have all the necessary further particulars.

Martin Armstrong Esq.,	Yours sincerely,
Farrs,	George Orwell
Sutton,	Talks Producer
Nr. Pulborough, Sussex	Indian Section

[Postcard]
    Friday
Please will you find out whether *Death of Ivan Ilyitch* is in a cheap edition. Perhaps it is with 'World's classics' volumes called *The Cossacks* or in the one called *The Kreutzer Sonata*. Anyhow please bring both these vols. along if you can. – Am reading the stuff in Library editions.
    EMF
Will deposit MS. on Tuesday.

---

[46] Gerald Bullett (1893-1958), novelist and critic. He was a Talks Producer in the BBC and took over Orwell's job for brief periods in 1942-3 when Orwell was ill.

PP/EB   15th September 1942

Dear Mr. Lauwerys,
I am writing to ask whether you can advise me about some speakers in a new scientific series we are going to broadcast to India. I want to have a series on what one might call popular science, dealing with new inventions and processes which alter the way of life of ordinary people. I would like to have the first talk, which is on October 20th, on dehydrated food, which is obviously a very important development and makes, for example, the maintenance of big armies in foreign countries a great deal easier than it would be otherwise. I want to have the second talk, four weeks later, on microfilms, which again may, I think, have very important effects. Unfortunately I don't know who are the experts or competent speakers on these subjects.
I also want to have a talk of a slightly different style on ersatz and raw materials, on October 9th. The only person I know who has expert knowledge of this is the German writer, Oswald Deutsch, whose English is not good enough for India. I should be very much obliged if you could let me have as soon as possible your advice about speakers for these three talks.

J.A. Lauwerys Esq.,   Yours sincerely,
Three Ashes,   George Orwell
Burton Joyce, Notts.   Talks Producer
                               Indian Section

PP/EB   22nd September 1942

Dear Calder,[47]
With reference to that talk I phoned you about the date is November 17th, which means I would like to have the script by November 10th. These talks are $13\frac{1}{2}$ minutes in length, which means about 1600 words. I would like something rather like the *New Statesman* article you did,[48] but one has to be careful not to be too technical and to establish in the first few minutes just what microfilms are, as it is certain that some of your listeners will have never heard of them. I should like the important part that these things are likely to play in preventing libraries from being destroyed by bombs or by the police of totalitarian regimes to be emphasised.

Ritchie Calder Esq.,   Yours,
6th Floor,   George Orwell
Bush House, (Centre Block)   Talks Producer
Aldwych, W.C.2   Indian Section

---

[47] Ritchie Calder (1906-1982), scientific journalist and broadcaster. His *Lesson of London* (1941) appeared in Orwell and Fyvel's 'Searchlight Books' series. He was elevated to the peerage in 1966 and subsequently became chairman of the Metrication Board.
[48] 'Science on the Screen', *New Statesman*, 22 August 1943.

PP/EB   28th September 1942

Dear Read,
   We are having another number of Voice on Tuesday, October 6th, and
would like you to take part, if you will. We want to use a piece of about two
pages out of *The Innocent Eye*[49] and of course it would be nice if you could read
it yourself. Also a poem by D.H. Lawrence. This is a number devoted to
childhood, and the poem we want you to read is 'The Piano', which you
doubtless know. As before it means giving up most of the morning, but I
believe you are in town on Tuesdays normally. Could you let me know as
soon as possible whether this will be all right.

Herbert Read Esq.,   Yours,
Broom House,   George Orwell
Seer Green,   Talks Producer
Beaconsfield, Bucks.   Indian Section

PP/EB   1st October 1942

Dear Mulk,
   You know you are scheduled to do another series of interviews rather like
the ones you did before, starting on 6th November. I think I talked this over
with you. This series is called 'A Day in My Life' and you are down to
interview various types of ordinary people who are playing a part in the war
effort. The first three are – a munitions worker, a soldier, and a merchant
seaman. I have no doubt that you have the necessary contacts. As far as
possible, however, we would like to know well in advance who is actually
taking part, so that we can do some advance publicity about them. We want
the speakers in these talks to give a picture of their day to day life and explain
just what they are doing to help the war effort. Do you think you could see me
about this within the next few days?

Mulk Raj Anand Esq.,   Yours,
8, St. George's Mews,   George Orwell
Regent's Park Road, N.W.1   Talks Producer
                                      Indian Section

PP/EB   1st October 1942

Dear Princess Indira,
   We are just working out our schedule of talks until the end of the year, and

---

[49] Herbert Read's autobiography (1933), which had recently been republished by Wrey
Gardiner's Grey Walls Press.

we hope very much that you will go on with your talks in the series 'The Debate Continues' each week. I understand from Mr. Lockspeiser that he is anxious for you to go on with the music programme on Saturdays as well. I hope you will agree to continue with both these programmes.

Princess Indira of Kapurthala,   Yours sincerely,
512A, Nell Gwynn House,   Eric Blair
Sloane Avenue, S.W.3   Talks Producer
                                          Indian Section

PP/EB   1st October 1942

Dear Forster,
   I believe your contract for 'Some Books' expires on October 14th. We of course want you to continue, and I hope you will want to do so as well. It is just necessary to have this in writing, but if you confirm this verbally when you come next Wednesday that will be all right.

E.M. Forster Esq.,   Yours,
West Hackhurst,   George Orwell
Abinger Hammer,   Talks Producer
Nr. Dorking, Surrey   Indian Section

PP/EB   7th October 1942

Dear Mulk,
   We are starting shortly a series of talks giving the History of Fascism in seven parts. I am wondering whether you would like to take part, and to deal with the talk covering the Spanish Civil War. Please let me know whether you would like to undertake this, and I will let you have more detailed particulars. I should like an answer fairly soon, as the first talk is to be on November 5th.
   The date of your talk – the fifth in the series – would be December 3rd, which means that we should want the script not later than November 26th.

Mulk Raj Anand Esq.,   Yours,
8, St. George's Mews,   Eric Blair
Regent's Park Road, N.W.1   Talks Producer
                                          Indian Section

PP/EB   7th October 1942

Dear Mulk,

I am sending back your script on *War and Peace* because I wish you would rewrite the later part, roughly speaking from page 4 onwards in order to deal more with the sociological aspect of *War and Peace*. I think it is quite true that Tolstoy marked the beginning of a new attitude towards the novel, but that in itself is not big enough to justify the title 'Books that Changed the World'. What I wanted was a talk on *War and Peace* as exemplifying the new attitude towards war. If not the first, it is certainly one of the first books that tried to describe war realistically and many modern currents of thought, probably including pacifism, derive from it to some extent. I do not of course want pacifist propaganda, but I think we might make valuable use of a comparison between Tolstoy's description of the battle of Austerlitz and for instance Tennyson's 'Charge of the Light Brigade'.

Gollancz has expressed interest in your idea for a book about India. He says it would have to be done quickly, which however would be quite easy by the method we were projecting of doing it. He wants you, or failing you, me to go and see him today week, October 14th, at 11 a.m. at his office. Do you think you could see me between now and then so that we can draw up a synopsis of the book?[50]

Mulk Raj Anand Esq.,   Yours sincerely,
8, St. George's Mews,   George Orwell[51]
Regent's Park Road, N.W.1

PP/EB   7th October 1942

Dear Mr. Strong,

I am sending herewith the first instalment of our serial. Your instalment goes on the air on Friday week, October 16th, at 12.15 by the clock, from 200, Oxford Street. If possible, I would like to have your script by the end of this week, or at any rate not later than Tuesday, the 13th. There is not likely to be any difficulty over the censorship, but your instalment must go on as soon as possible to the next contributor, so as to leave at any rate five or six days for her to write her contribution. I hope you do not find this opening chapter too hard to follow on from. I have left plenty of possibilities. I don't want to lay down conditions, but as the thing has to run for five instalments, I think we ought to say at any rate that neither of the two principal characters who have been introduced ought to die off in the second instalment. You can follow up

---

[50] Anand recalls that this book was an account of India written jointly to give a Briton's and an Indian's point of view. It was never published.

[51] Note two letters written by Orwell to the same person on the same day, one signed 'George Orwell' and the other 'Eric Blair' – a neat reflection of Orwell's view of his two personae at the time (see above, p. 23).

the story in any way you choose, and I hope you will be able to leave a fairly good jumping off place for your successor.

L.A.G. Strong Esq.,   Yours sincerely,
Salterns,   George Orwell
Eashing   Talks Producer
                                        Indian Section
                                        (Dictated by Mr. Orwell and
                                            despatched in his absence)

W.H.   8-10-42

Dear Orwell,
    Here is the script in good time, so may I have a typescript of it here by next Tuesday. Then I can make any necessary cuts – the Rose Macaulay could go entirely, and the Strong too. I do not think Ha[rry] Roberts good enough to mention – all his stuff is in such a muddle. But I am very glad you sent me Richard Hillary.[52]
    I should be glad of my full time at the mike if I want it. I got the idea last month that Lady Grigg was trying to steal.
    Thank you for your letter; yes I shall be pleased to renew the contract if all concerned are agreeable. I should like to see you before the dates are fixed, in case they clash with existing engagements.
    Perhaps when I have the typescript I could have the one of my last talk, on Tolstoy, which I didn't take away.

    Yours
    E.M. Forster

PP/EB   10th October 1942

Dear Forster,
    Many thanks for your script – I thoroughly enjoyed reading it. It has now been typed, and I enclose a copy together with a copy of last month's talk.
    The dates that have been fixed in our new schedule for your next talks are November 11th and December 9th – we haven't yet planned any further ahead, but your talks will follow on, every fourth Wednesday, as usual. If these dates don't happen to suit you, we can always record the talks beforehand, at any time you happen to be in London, although of course it's much nicer to have it direct.

---

[52] Richard Hope Hillary's posthumous *The Last Enemy* (1942) was a cult book of the day. Hillary, a fighter pilot, had been severely wounded and disfigured. He recovered to fly again, but was later shot down and killed.

You can certainly have your full time at the mike, there is no question of Lady Grigg's programme encroaching on your time, unless, of course, you under-run, and then Lady Grigg follows straight on in the usual way.

E.M. Forster Esq.,   Yours,
West Hackhurst,   George Orwell
Abinger Hammer,   Talks Producer
Nr. Dorking, Surrey   Indian Section

PP/EB   16th October 1942

Dear Eliot,
   I wonder if you would like to take part in a programme on Tuesday November 3rd. We have a magazine number once a month which is called 'Voice' and pretends to be a magazine in broadcast form. Where it is possible we try to get poets to read their own work. We usually arrange each number round a central theme and we think next time of having an American number. You are I think the only American poet at present in England, though there may perhaps be others, in which case I should be glad to hear about them. In any case we would like it very much if you would take part and read something of your own, either one or two poems taking anything up to five minutes in all. The other people who will probably be taking part are Herbert Read, William Empson, myself, and Mulk Raj Anand, though we will try to dig up some American writers if we can. Please do this if the date is at all possible for you. It will only mean giving up the morning of that particular day.

T.S. Eliot Esq.,   Yours sincerely,
c/o Faber & Faber Ltd.   George Orwell
   (Publishers),   Talks Producer
24, Russell Square, W.C.1   Indian Section

PP/EB   17th October 1942

Dear Mr. Armstrong,
   I send you herewith the three previous instalments of the story. I [would] have sent them a day or two earlier, but I was hesitating about the third one, which does not seem to be very good, and it does not carry on the story or rather gives it a twist in another direction. However, as you say you work slowly I thought it better to send them along at once, rather than get this instalment rewritten. Your instalment is the fourth and should therefore bring the story within sight of a climax. You will see that both the second and the third contributors have passed on the baby by not explaining what was

the cause of the quarrel between the two men introduced in the first chapter. I don't want of course to dictate what you are to say, but I think your contribution should certainly make this clear and then end in some way that will make a climax possible. You are on the [air] on October 30th, so if I can have yours by the 25th at the very latest, I should be obliged. The time is 13½ minutes, which generally means about 15 hundred words. On the day of the broadcast will you come to 200, Oxford Street at 11.40 which will give us time for rehearsal before the broadcast which is at 12.15.

Martin Armstrong Esq.,   Yours sincerely,
Farrs,   George Orwell
Sutton   Talks Producer
                                  Indian Section

PP/EB   19th October 1942

Dear Hawkins,

This is to confirm that you are doing our Anniversaries feature for us. I think we arranged this verbally. The broadcast this time is on Tuesday November 3rd, so it should be the anniversary of something occurring in November. We have looked through the list and the two which seem to me most promising are the opening of the Suez Canal in 1869 and Stanley finding Livingstone in 1871. These are the 16th and 10th respectively. Will you let me know your ideas about this pretty soon, and we should want the script not later than October 30th. We did agree, I think, that it would be better to do a programme of this type on one event rather than on a number.

Desmond Hawkins Esq.,   Yours,
Todds Farm,   George Orwell
Saxtead,   Talks Producer
Framlingham, Suffolk   Indian Section

PP/EB   20th October 1942

Dear Mulk,

I have written to the first four speakers in your series 'A Day in My Life', confirming that they will be giving the talks, and telling them that if they can't come on the day, they can record the talk beforehand. I have also asked them to send me some publicity about themselves. You will probably be able to supplement this.

I imagine that you will write the scripts with them, and let me have a copy.

In each case, we shall want the script *not later* than a week before the broadcast – in the case of Keidrych Rhys[53] and Bill Balcome, we'd like the scripts earlier, because they have to be sent to the War Office and the Ministry of Transport respectively.

When are you going to let me have the names of the other speakers? I should like some of them at least as soon as you can let me have them.

Mulk Raj Anand Esq.,	Yours,
8, St. George's Mews,	George Orwell
Regents Park Road, N.W.1	Talks Producer
	Indian Section

PP/EB   20th October 1942

Dear Read,

We are having another number of 'Voice' on Tuesday, November 3rd, and would like you to take part as usual, if you will. We want to make this a number devoted to American poetry. I have written to Eliot, suggesting that he might like to take part, but he has not answered yet. I have not yet decided what we shall use, but will let you know as soon as I do. If you are able to take part, I am afraid it will mean giving up most of the morning again – we should like you to be here at about 10.30 as usual.

Herbert Read Esq.,	Yours sincerely,
Broom House,	George Orwell
Seer Green,	Talks Producer
Beaconsfield, Bucks.	Indian Section

PP/EB   24th October 1942

Dear Forster,

You remember my asking whether you would like to wind up the 'Story by Five Authors', each instalment of which was written by a separate person. I am sending you herewith the first four instalments. I am afraid it was an unsuccessful experiment, the second and third writers having failed to carry on the story as it should have been. The fourth instalment, which is quite good, really does what the second instalment ought to have done. Nevertheless the germ of a story is there and it might amuse you to wind it up in some way or even if you like simply to comment on it, saying it might end this way or it might end that way and in my opinion the following would be

[53] Keidrych Rhys, poet. He was editor of *Poems from the Forces: a collection of verses by serving members of the navy, army and air force* (1941) and author of *The Van Pool and other poems* (1942).

the best ending. It would, however, be necessary to manufacture *some* kind of denouement. The only thing is I would like to know pretty promptly whether you can do this, because if not, we shall have to arrange for somebody else. But I would of course like you to do it if you feel equal to it. The date of the broadcast is November 6th, at 12.15.

E.M. Forster Esq.,   Yours,
West Hackhurst,   George Orwell
Abinger Hammer,   Talks Producer
Nr. Dorking   Indian Section

W.H.   Tuesday

Dear Orwell,
    This is scarcely my cup of beer, but I should like to have a try. Yes – the theme has been badly messed about, especially by the Spanish expedition,[54] and I am afraid that any denouement will seem unreal, and can only be handled 'cleverly'. I have an idea and will do my best with it.
    Thanks for your p.c. I had already been to the Indian Dancing – not much of a show I am sorry to say, but I will make brief friendly reference to it, also to Gangulee's book and the strange novel which Firoshar Noon has sent me from India.[55] – The rest of the talk I thought of devoting to The Managerial Revolution,[56] which I have, and to Carr's book if you can borrow it for me again and give me when I come up to [say(?)] the story on Nov 6th.
    I enclose the voucher for my Indian Dancing ticket. I don't see why the B.B.C. shouldn't refund the money if they would like to, but do not put yourself to trouble over this.

    Yours ever
    E.M. Forster.

PP/EB   27th October 1942

Dear Treece,
    Many thanks for your telegram. I will arrange a recording time for you on Tuesday afternoon, if this will suit you. I think we can arrange for you to record between 3 and 4 that afternoon, but I'll let you know definitely before Tuesday.
    As it happens, we are doing the fourth number of 'Voice' on that day – it is

[54] i.e. Inez Holden's contribution.
[55] Sir Firoz Khan Noon (1893-1970). The strange novel referred to here was almost certainly *Scented Dust* (Lahore, 1941).
[56] *The Managerial Revolution* (1942) by James Burnham. See above, Introduction p. 27.

a number devoted to American poetry. If you'd care to come along and listen
we'd be very pleased to see you – it goes on the air at 12.15.

We should be glad if you would get permission from your Commanding
Officer to record some of your poems – this is just a formality, of course. It is
best to have it in writing.

You should come to 200, Oxford Street, on the corner of Great Portland
Street – Mr. Schimanski[57] knows where it is.

> Yours sincerely,
> George Orwell
> Talks Producer
> Indian Section

PP/EB   27th October 1942

Dear Rhys,

I think Mulk Raj Anand has approached you about a broadcast we would
like you to do in the Eastern Service (to India) on 13th November. This series
is called 'A Day in My Life' and is done in the form of interviews with
war-workers of various descriptions who describe how they spend their time
and what work they are doing. We should like you to speak in the capacity of
a soldier. Mulk will ask the necessary questions and you give the answers.
You can be reasonably honest in broadcasts in this service. I hope you will
undertake this. Please let me know as soon as possible, and then if you are
willing I will get Mulk to come and do his stuff. You must get the permission
of your Commanding Officer in writing to do this, but that is only a formality
and there is never any difficulty as a rule. The time of the broadcast is 12.45,
which means coming to 200 Oxford Street at 12 o'clock to rehearse, but if you
can't manage that we can record it some time beforehand.

I am sorry we haven't yet been able to arrange for you to take part in our
monthly poetry programme 'Voice', but we shall have other numbers coming
on later and perhaps you will contribute some time.

> Yours sincerely,
> George Orwell
> Talks Producer

---

[57] Stefan Schimanski, co-editor with Henry Treece of *Kingdom Come*. Treece and Schimanski
also edited anthologies together, such as *A Map of Hearts* (n.d.).

From: Eric Blair, Indian Section, 200 Oxford Street   28th October 1942
Subject: 'Story by Five Authors' – Serial for Eastern Service
To: Miss Alexander, Prog. Copyright.

Thank you for your memo. of 27th October.

We have heard from E.M. Forster that he will do the final instalment in this series. The date of the broadcast is November 6th, at 1115 GMT (1215 BST), and the length of the broadcast is 13½ minutes. I should be glad if you would kindly arrange terms with Forster.

I am sending a booking slip to Talks Bookings, so that they may book Forster for the reading of the material.

EB/NP   Eric Blair

29th October, 1942

Dear Mr. Young,

I am so sorry that I have forgotten until now to let you know about Ezra Pound.[58] Apparently he only broadcasts irregularly, but he was heard about a week ago, speaking from Rome in English, for Europe at 10 p.m. on the following wavelengths:

25.1	shortwave	221	medium
29.04	shortwave	263	medium
41.45	shortwave		
47.62	shortwave		

He also broadcasts in English to North America at 3 o'clock in the morning, and was heard about a fortnight ago on the following shortwave bands:

25.1
25.4
31.15

I am sorry I cannot give you any more details, but I hope from this information you will be able to find him without much difficulty.

I enclose copies of the last two Forums.

G.M. Young Esq.,   Yours sincerely,
The Old Oxyard,
Oare, Wilts.

---

[58] Orwell read the monitor's reports of Ezra Pound's radio talks and spoke vehemently against Pound after the war (*Partisan Review*, May 1949: *CE* IV, p. 552). By contrast he defended P.G. Wodehouse for his relatively minor transgression in the same vein ('In defence of P.G. Wodehouse', *Windmill* no. 2: *CE* III, p. 388).

PP/EB   30th October 1942

Dear Forster,

Many thanks for agreeing to do the final instalment of the serial story. I'm afraid it didn't turn out quite as I had hoped.

Thanks very much for sending the voucher for your ticket for the Indian ballet. We have sent in a claim for the money, and I shall let you have it next week when you come.

I wonder if you could write a sort of résumé of 'the story so far', to preface your instalment? We have done this as a rule, and I think it helps people who may have missed an instalment, or who haven't been listening to it before. It only needs to be a few lines.

I am enclosing a letter from Gangulee which was sent to you from this address.

E.M. Forster Esq.,   Yours,
West Hackhurst,   George Orwell
Abinger Hammer   Talks Producer
                                      Indian Section
                                      (Dictated by George Orwell
                                         and despatched in his absence)

West Hackhurst. Abinger Hammer. Dorking.   1-11-42

Dear Orwell

Thanks for your letter. I think it's best to use the same words in résumés, so would you send me the text used by Armstrong, and I will repeat it – with the necessary addition.

I am here till Wednesday. On Thursday I should rather like to show my script to a man who may be helpful over the dialogue. Would it be all right if I brought it to you at about 10.0. on the Friday and read from the MS. at 11.15.? Or must it be sent earlier, to be typed?

Charles Coburn is a G.O.M. of Variety and wrote The Man who Broke the Bank at Monte Carlo, I believe. He is still alive. I don't think the scripts are libellous, but perhaps you should ring up the B.B.C. legal adviser if you don't feel sure. (It's the 'Artemus Jones' trouble.)

    Yours ever
    E.M. Forster

PP/EB   2nd November 1942

Dear Forster,

Thanks for your letter of November 1st. I am sending you the résumé to the third instalment, because Armstrong's script was rather on the long side, and we didn't have time for him to give a résumé.

We should like to have your script some time on Thursday, if possible. It would be quite all right if you brought it here in the afternoon or early evening, as long as you can let us know when it will be coming. I'm sorry about this, but it has to be censored first thing on Friday morning.

E.M. Forster Esq.,   Yours sincerely,
West Hackhurst,   George Orwell
Abinger Hammer,   Talks Producer
Dorking   Indian Section

PP/EB   4th November 1942

Dear Eliot,

We were sorry you could not take part in yesterday's production of 'Voice', so we are giving you plenty of notice about the next one. It will be on December 1st, which is a Tuesday. We will let you have further details later, but if you are free on that morning, roughly speaking between eleven and one (we usually begin rehearsing at 10.30) we should like it very much if you would take part.

T.S. Eliot Esq.,   Yours sincerely,
c/o Faber & Faber Ltd.   George Orwell
  (Publishers)   Talks Producer
24, Russell Square, W.C.1   Indian Section

PP/EB   5th November 1942

Dear Treece,

I forgot to ask you for a copy of the two poems which you read from manuscript. They are called 'Love Song' and 'Through Seven Days and Seven Nights'. We have got them on the record of course, but we had better have a written copy as well. Can you let me know, at the same time, whether these two have been published yet, or not, as I want to get the Copyright covered.

You will get the written authorisation from your Commanding Officer, won't you? There is no immediate hurry, because I don't expect to be able to use these till about January.

Henry Treece Esq.,   Yours,
55, Ferriby Road,   George Orwell
Barton-on-Humber, Lincs.   Talks Producer
                                           Indian Section

W.H.   9-11-42

Dear Orwell
    Herewith script. Please supply information about Noon's present job – [?].[59]
Will come along Wednesday for usual timing etc. at 11.45.
    Carr only just arrived – too late for inclusion.
    Thank you for your kind remarks about my instalment of the story. It represented my first attempt at fiction for many years, and I enjoyed doing it.[60]

    Yours
    E.M. Forster

EB/NP   11th November 1942

Dear Sir,
    I am sending you herewith a copy of a talk to be broadcast in the Eastern Service of the BBC on Friday November 13th. The writer, Gunner Keidrych Rhys, was previously serving in your battery but has now been discharged from the Army. As he is no longer a soldier it is not technically necessary for him to get your permission for the broadcast, but we thought that you might like to see a copy of the talk. It has already been passed for censorship in the normal way. Should you wish to make any changes, could you be kind enough to ring me up at Euston 3400, Ext. 208. If we do not hear from you we will assume that you have no alterations to suggest.

The Officer Commanding,   Yours truly,
E Battery,   Eric Blair
R.M.A.,   Talks Producer
Woolwich, S.E.18   Indian Section

[59] Noon was Labour Member of the Governor-General's Executive Council, India.
[60] Forster made no reference to it in the preface to his *Collected Short Stories* (1947), which of course did not include it.

PP/EB   16th November 1942

Dear Eliot,

Many thanks for your letter of the 11th. There would not be any need for you to come up to London on Monday, 30th November, and on Tuesday morning it would really do if you could come in any time before 12. The programme goes on the air actually at 12.15, and we are rehearsing from 10.30 onwards, but if you are only reading something, there is not much rehearsal needed. We have not yet picked the stuff for this programme, but the idea of this number is to be the influence of Oriental literature on English literature. I suppose we shall make use of some direct translations, but we shall also use poems where it is only a case of direct or indirect influence. I don't know whether you have anything which you feel comes under this heading in your own work. We should certainly like you to read something of your own if possible. Perhaps 'What the Thunder Said' from *The Waste Land*? But we will let you know more about the make-up of the programme later. I certainly hope you will be there, in any case, and as you say you come up to town on Tuesday mornings, perhaps it won't mean wasting very much of your time.

T.S. Eliot Esq.,   Yours sincerely,
c/o Faber & Faber Ltd.   George Orwell
    (Publishers),   Talks Producer
24, Russell Square, W.C.1   Indian Section

EB/NP   17th November 1942

Dear Hawkins,

The anniversaries for December seem somewhat thin. I suggest one of the following:

Sir Isaac Newton, born December 25; Milton, born December 9; Nostradamus, born December 14; Kepler, born December 27; Tycho Brahe, born December 14; Karel Čapek, died December 25; Sibelius, born December 8; Richelieu, died December 4;

That seems to be about all, unless one puts in war things, which I rather want to avoid in this programme. The Aswan Dam was completed on December 10th 1902, but as we have just had one dealing with Egypt, it might be better to select one from the others I have given you. There seems to be rather a preponderance of astronomers this month, but there is one astrologer if you prefer that. Let me know which of them you choose.

We shall want the script by November 26th if possible. The broadcast is on

December 1st, at 1145 GMT, and we hope to get Malcolm Baker-Smith to produce it again.

Desmond Hawkins Esq.,   Yours,
Todds Farm,   George Orwell
Saxtead,   Talks Producer
Framlingham, Suffolk   Indian Section

PP/EB   November 18th 1942

Dear Forster,
    I don't know if you have heard about Narayana Menon's book[61] on W.B. Yeats? It will, I think, be suitable to mention in your next talk. It is also being published in India. He tells me he is going to send you a copy. If he doesn't, we can get one for you.
    Have you finished with *Conditions of Peace*? We don't want to hurry you, but there seems to be a considerable demand for it, so perhaps you could post it, when you have finished with it.

E.M. Forster Esq.,   Yours,
West Hackhurst,   George Orwell
Abinger Hammer,   Talks Producer
Near Dorking, Surrey   Indian Section

W.H.   21-11-42

Dear Orwell,
    I am so sorry to have been such a nuisance over this book, and I have again tried to get through it and have failed.
    I shall be glad of the Yeats book, and of the book by an Indian published by Gollancz[62] as soon as possible. The quickest plan really seems that I should write to the publishers direct, but I won't do so as regards these two books since I assume that the BBC has already got going.

    Yours ever
    E.M. Forster

---

[61] See above, n.42.
[62] *My India, My West* by K. Shridharani (1942).

PP/EB   21st November 1942

Dear Eliot,
   Thank you for your letter of the 18th. I should like it very much if you
would read 'What the Thunder Said', on December 1st. It will be quite all
right if you are at 200 Oxford Street by 11.30 on that day.
   I am rather anxious to arrange for the speakers in that particular
programme, who will include Mulk Raj Anand and Narayana Menon, to be
photographed. I hope you will have no objection to this.

T.S. Eliot Esq.,   Yours sincerely,
Shamley Wood,   George Orwell
Shamley Green,   Talks Producer
Guildford, Surrey   Indian Section

PP/EB   26th November 1942

Dear Bahadur Singh,
   Thanks for your letter. I am sorry, but I don't think I can arrange to do
anything on Christmas Day itself, as we have more or less Christmas items
on the 23rd and also the 29th. We have a new series coming on in January in
which I think you could take a hand occasionally. This is a series called 'In
the Public Eye' which will be short character sketches of prominent
personalities of the week, and probably in most cases adapted from the
Profiles in the *Observer*, which you may have seen. This will be a weekly item,
done by different people, and there is no reason why you would not cover this
item from time to time.

J.J. Bahadur Singh Esq.,   Yours sincerely,
44, Wellington Square,   Eric Blair
Oxford   Talks Producer
                                          Indian Section

PP/EB   30th November 1942

Dear Mr. Marshall,[63]
   I am enclosing herewith the questions provided by Mr. and Mrs. Sahni.
Mr. Sahni asked me to emphasise that, although he has divided the questions
into two sets, it rests entirely with you which lot you take first, and so on. He

---

[63] Norman Marshall (1901-1980) was a well-known enthusiast of the amateur theatre, author
of *The Other Theatre* (1948).

also says that if you don't like the questions and would prefer to make your own, please do![64]

As you know, you will be recording the 5th discussion on Saturday, 6th December, from 5.45 to 6.45 p.m. at 200 Oxford Street. We shall expect you on Thursday next, at about 6 o'clock, as usual.

Norman Marshall Esq.,   Yours sincerely,
9, Arundel Court,   George Orwell
Jubilee Place, S.W.3   Talks Producer
                                      Indian Section

PP/EB   4th December 1942

Dear Read,

About the talks on American literature. It isn't after all, so urgent as I thought when I spoke to you, as we have decided to postpone this series for six weeks so that the first will be on February 6th. The authors I suggested having the talks on (subject to your revision are):

1. Hawthorne
2. Poe
3. Melville
4. Mark Twain
5. Jack London
6. O. Henry
7. Hemingway

These, I think are a representative selection, though not in all cases necessarily the *best* authors. They also all, except perhaps Mark Twain, have the advantage of being quotable in fairly short extracts.

The way we have decided to do the programmes is this. First, perhaps, two minutes (at most) from you, introducing the speaker. Then 11-12 minutes talk on the chosen author, then a 7 minutes interlude of music which will be selected by Narayana Menon, and then a 5 minutes reading from the chosen author. In the case of Poe, London and Hemingway, at any rate, this should be easy enough. I shall have to leave most of the work to you as I'm very busy.

Please let me know what you think about this.

Herbert Read Esq.,   Yours
Broom House   George Orwell
Seer Green   Talks Producer
Beaconsfield, Bucks   Indian Section

[64] Mr and Mrs Sahni, who worked for the Indian Section at 200 Oxford Street, were interested in reviving amateur theatre in Indian towns and villages where the cinema was making inroads into traditional Indian performances. They had given Marshall a set of questions designed to clarify the situation of the amateur player in England.

PP/EB   4th December 1942

Dear Eliot,

Thanks for your letter of December 3rd. All right, let's make it lunch on
Friday the 18th. You will hear from Read about the American talks, but we
are, I think, postponing this series for six weeks, so the matter is not so urgent
as it seemed when I wrote.

If you would like, I should like you to do one talk in the series preceding the
American ones. Do you think you could do a talk on the Book of Job? This
series is probably being looked after by Edmund Blunden, and I have already
suggested your name to him as the speaker for this particular talk. Blunden
will get in touch with you about this, but I should warn you that this script is
wanted by about 25th December, because we propose to publish all the talks
in the form of a pamphlet in Calcutta[65] – the talks cover some of the set books
in the B.A. course in English literature at Calcutta University.

T.S. Eliot Esq.,   Yours sincerely,
c/o Faber & Faber Ltd. Publishers,   George Orwell
24, Russell Square, W.C.1   Talks Producer
                                       Indian Section

PP/EB   5th December 1942

Dear Mr. Blunden,

Brander tells me that he has spoken to you on the phone and that though
very much occupied you have kindly agreed to undertake our special series of
talks to students. You have a list of the subjects and suggested speakers. Of
course you can arrange with whatever speakers you like, but I have already
written to Eliot asking him to do the talk on Job and I would like that
arrangement to stand if Eliot is willing.

The way we thought of doing the talks was this. First you do about two
minutes introducing the speaker, then the speaker does his stuff for 15
minutes or thereabouts – say not more than 1700 words – then there is an
interlude of music which we will be responsible for choosing, and then five
minutes reading from the works of the author who is the subject of the talk.
In some cases this can be done by the speaker. Where it is a case of a play, we
shall have to act a scene of it, but that will be quite easily arranged.

The idea, as I have already explained to you, is to have these six talks
making about 10,000 words published in book form in India in time to appear
before the Calcutta University examinations. That is the reason for the haste
with which the manuscripts are needed.

The talks will be actually going on the air between December 25th and
January 29th inclusive. I am afraid I shall have to leave most of the dirty

---

[65] Some of these pamphlets were published; examples are to be found in the Orwell Archive.

work to you, including making the speakers produce their stuff on time. Please let me know any further particulars you want. I should be glad if you would also let me know the names of the speakers you choose if you depart from the list I suggested, as we have to do publicity about them. If anyone cannot do his talk on the day appointed, they can always be recorded beforehand.

> Yours sincerely,
> George Orwell
> Talks Producer
> Indian Section

W.H.   7-12-42

Dear Orwell

I will be round on Wednesday as usual at about 11.30. for timing etc.

Yeats' The Second Coming is quoted in its entirety (22 lines) from The Collected Poems, p. 210,: published by MacMillans [sic]. – This in case you have to arrange copyright.

I am leaving My East-My West over till next month, but can bring the volume up with me Wednesday if you send a p.c. by return. – It's the only library book I have.

> Yours
> E.M. Forster

If it's too long the first page can go, or nearly so.

07/ES/EB   10th December 1942

Dear Mr. Blunden,

Eliot says he cannot do the talk on the Book of Job as he is too busy. This is a pity but no doubt you could think of someone else. Forster says he can do the first one on Shakespeare and I think it would be a good idea to stick to him for this talk as his name carries weight in India.

I hope all is going well with the series and that we shall not be behind time.

I shall make arrangements to record the whole of the first talk so that no one need be here on Christmas Day.

Edmund Blunden Esq.,	Yours sincerely,
Merton College,	George Orwell
Oxford	Talks Producer
	Indian Section

P.S. The dates of the talks are December 25th, January 1st, 8th, 15th, 22nd and 29th, at 12.15 to 12.30 BST.

07/ES/EB   14th December 1942

Dear Forster,

I have just sent you a telegram, to the effect that I have been able to arrange a recording session on Tuesday December 22nd, from 12 to 12.45, at 200, Oxford Street, and I suggest that you rehearse from 11.30-12.00 approximately. I do hope this arrangement will suit you, because it is extremely difficult to fix up recordings so close to Christmas. I hope that Blunden will be able to come at the same time, but if he can't manage it, we can record his introduction to your talk separately.

We really arranged Tuesday because I thought you might like to bring your script in on Monday for typing, or on Tuesday morning first thing, at the latest.

E.M. Forster Esq.,   Yours,
West Hackhurst,   George Orwell
Abinger Hammer,   Talks Producer
Near Dorking, Surrey   Indian Section

07/ES/EB   14th December 1942

Dear Blunden,

I am glad our series of talks seems to be going ahead. We have asked Forster to come here and record his talk on Tuesday December 22nd. This is about as late as we can safely leave it and also we have to take what recording dates we can get, owing to the Christmas rush. If so be that you can't yourself come on that day to do your introduction of Forster, it would be possible to record it separately, but it is simpler to do it all in one go. Forster is to record at 12 o'clock. He is supposed to bring his script on Monday to be typed but probably won't bring it till Tuesday morning. With the other five speakers it is not quite equally urgent, but I would like to have all their scripts during Christmas week.

When you send us the list of your speakers, could you let me have their addresses at the same time, so that we can have their contracts sent on?

Edmund Blunden Esq.,   Yours sincerely,
Merton College,   George Orwell
Oxford   Talks Producer
                                       Indian Section

[Telegram]
Abinger Hammer 5.47 pm 14 December 42
Orwell Broadcasts London
   22nd impossible but could record morning 23rd
   Forster

[Telegram]
Abinger Hammer 7.10 pm 14 December 1942
Orwell Broadcasts London
   Yes Forster

W.H.   15-12-42

Dear Orwell,
   Thanks for your letter and wire. I am coming up for a night on Friday the
18th, and will meet you Saturday morning if there is anything to discuss –
But I hope that my suggestion (recording on the 23rd) is workable. I can't
manage 21st or 22nd.
   Nothing from Blunden so far. I understand that the *Julius Caesar* is the first
of a series for students of Calcutta University, and [?] *The Return of the Native*
which I gave some time ago. If there are any further instructions I should like
them at once. – Have undertaken to contribute to the *War & Peace* pamphlet,[66]
and am a bit rushed. – Am never available Tuesdays as I have a class in a
Search Light Unit down here.

   Yours ever
   E.M. Forster

07/ES/EB   30th December 1942

Dear Blunden,
   I suppose it is O.K. for Friday and George Sampson[67] will be here in good
time to do his Milton talk. As to the reading afterwards, I thought the best
thing to have would be a passage from Lycidas, taking about five minutes,
and the intervening music will be chosen by Menon, as before. I don't know
whether Professor Sampson wants to read Lycidas himself. If he specially
wants to do so, well and good, but we often find it better to have a change of
voice, and we have a young man here who would do the reading very nicely.

<hr>

[66] A BBC publication – *Tolstoy's War and Peace: an introduction to the broadcast series* (1943).
[67] George Sampson (1873-1950), scholar and pioneering teacher, who had just published the
Concise Cambridge History of English Literature (1941).

You will be glad to hear that the Shakespeare talk went off very well. I couldn't listen to all of it as I was on the air most part of the time, but others listened and said it was very good. I believe the *Listener* is going to print this series of talks en bloc, but we, unfortunately, don't get any rake-off from them.

I have passed the business about your fees on to the right quarter and I think it will be all right. Will let you know on Friday.

Edmund Blunden Esq.,   Yours sincerely,
Merton College,   George Orwell
Oxford   Talks Producer
                                        Indian Section

07/ES/EB   30th December 1942

Dear Hawkins,

I am sorry to say that as I suggested might be the case there's [been] trouble about the speeches on pages 7 and 8 of your script. The ones objected to are (a) [the] Shopkeeper, who describes himself as behaving like shopkeepers everywhere, (b) the Jolly Chap who does ditto, and (c) the Oppressed, who ask for death when it is thought better propaganda that they should ask for revenge.[68]

I don't think one can alter those passages in the sense required, while keeping those characters. It might be possible to simply cut out that passage, but we don't want to cut the feature if we can help it because it is on the short side already. However, Douglas Cleverdon wishes to produce it and he, no doubt, will know how to fill up with music and so forth. I understand you are seeing him on Friday next, so we might leave the matter open until then.

Desmond Hawkins Esq.,   Yours sincerely,
Todds Farm   George Orwell
Saxtead,   Talks Producer
Woodbridge, Suffolk

07/ES/EB   30th December 1942

Dear Beavan,

You will remember my ringing you up last week and suggesting the

[68] The trouble referred to here was, of course, from the Policy Censor. In a BBC radio programme, 'Orwell at the BBC' (Radio 4, October 1984), Hawkins related an even more amusing example of the Censor's work: the banning of an old sailor's reminiscences of fishing in the North Sea during the Boer War, on the grounds that naval information could not be broadcast.

importance of giving prominence not only to the persecution of the Jews but to any proposed relief scheme in order to forestall the Axis claims that this is some sort of Jewish invasion of Palestine and other countries. I enclose an extract from the Japanese radio of three days ago aimed at India.[69] This is the sort of thing that will be said and it seems to me important to forestall it, especially if the British Government really intends any relief measures.

John Beavan Esq.,	Yours sincerely,
News Editor	George Orwell
The Observer	Talks Producer
22 Tudor Street, E.C.4	Indian Section

07/ES/EB   30th December 1942

Dear Eliot,
   Herewith copy of the photograph of which I spoke to you.
   I wonder if you could come to my place for dinner on Tuesday, the 12th January. The address is 10A Mortimer Crescent, N.W.6.[70] You can get there on the 53 bus, stopping at Alexandra Road or from Kilburn Park tube station. It would be much better if you stayed the night and we can make you quite comfortable. Perhaps you could let me know about this.

T.S. Eliot Esq.,	Yours sincerely,
c/o Faber & Faber Ltd.,	George Orwell
24 Russell Square, W.C.1	Talks Producer
	Indian Section

[Postcard]
Will return *My India My West*: it is very wordy. Am gravelled for subject matter for Wednesday. Will you please on getting this have an obituary list for 1943 made out (writers and cultured generally.) I will ring up on *Saturday morning*, and it can be read to me over the phone. – Will ring about 11.30.
   E.M. Forster.
   Thursday

[69] This is probably a news commentary, 'More Jews to oust the Arabs from Palestine', monitored from an English-language radio station broadcasting from Batavia (Java) on 28 December 1942. It was published in the *Daily Digest of World Broadcasting*, no. 1260 on 29 December 1942, and is reprinted below in Appendix C as an example of the great amount of enemy propaganda Orwell had to read as part of his day-to-day duties.
[70] Orwell's last home during his time in the BBC and the only one not to survive the blitz.

From: Mr. L. Brander, Eastern Intelligence Officer   6th January 1943
Subject: Reactions to 'The Debate Continues'
To: Eastern Services Director
A member of the Delhi office reports on 21.12.43:

'A friend from Poona writes: "I listened last week to one of the weekly talks by
Princess Indira of Kapurthala. It was about the reaction to Mosley's release in
the House of Commons. It was very interesting and the speaker seemed to have
a very good command of English." '

'The head of an aristocratic family in Simla writes: "We enjoy the discourses
given by Princess Indira of Kapurthala. She has done and is doing extra-
ordinarily well in all her broadcasts and I have been given to understand that
all such discourses are prepared by herself – which is most creditable." '

LB/HC   L. Brander

07/ES/EB   6th January 1943

Dear Hawkins,
    Our next 'Anniversaries of the Month' feature programme is scheduled for
Tuesday, February 2nd, the usual time, 1145 to 1200 GMT. Do you again feel
like writing the script for this programme? I shall be glad if you will do it.
    I am enclosing a list of the Anniversaries for February. Will you be kind
enough to return this to us, without fail, as soon as possible.

Desmond Hawkins Esq.,	Yours sincerely,
Todds Farm,	George Orwell
Saxtead,	Talks Producer
Woodbridge, Suffolk	Indian Section

07/ES/EB   18th January 1943

Dear Read,
    I think it is a very good idea to have Rayner Heppenstall for the last talk as he
has an excellent voice. If he cannot get away from his unit we can quite easily
record the talk at Leeds or somewhere. I think, however, that –

    a) His subject should be the one you have indicated, i.e. The American
Short Story, dealing with a number of contemporary writers, and not merely
concentrating on one rather obscure one like Saroyan, and

    b) He would need a lot of prodding to make him deliver his stuff on time.

Could you get in touch with him and tell him that we are putting his name down in the publicity and that I am really keen for him to do this talk. I did not know he was free to do talks or I would have approached him before this.

I will send out contracts for all the others.

Herbert Read Esq.,   Yours,
Broom House,   George Orwell
Seer Green,   Talks Producer
Beaconsfield   Indian Section

08/CN/ALCB   25th January 1943

Dear Mr. Bullock,
    Thank you for your letter of the 22nd January. I will do the suggested talk with pleasure, if I can be reasonably frank. I am not going to say anything I regard as untruthful.[71]

A.L.C. Bullock Esq.,   Yours sincerely,
European Talks Director   George Orwell
The BBC   Talks Producer
Broadcasting House, W.1   Indian Section

W.H.   26-1-43

Dear Orwell,
    I am very sorry you are ill again. I hope you will take a good rest now. – This letter will probably be dealt with by your secretary, and is to recapitulate what I said not very clearly over the phone.
    I cannot find Lord Ponsonby's life of his father.[72] I think I left it behind to be posted here direct, together with the book about Max Plowman which we agreed you should procure for me. – If I took it away and lost it, I must replace of course. But we will wait a bit. I am coming up on Monday, and shall ring to find out how things are, and there should be some sort of script on Tuesday. – At present I have two C.S. Lewis books and my own copies of Gerald Heard and Anand. Not much of a bag.

    Yours ever
    E.M. Forster

[71] An echo here of the remark in Orwell's resignation letter (see above, p. 57). Clearly Orwell was suspicious; he did not do the talk.
[72] *Henry Ponsonby: his life from his letters* (1943), a biography of Queen Victoria's private secretary by his son Arthur Ponsonby, First Baron Ponsonby. It won the James Tait Black Memorial Prize. Arthur Ponsonby's pre-war *Falsehood in War-time* (1928) went through several editions during the war.

07/ES/EB   4th February 1943

Dear Mr. Forster,
 I am sorry to have to worry you but our library is making enquiries about the
books we lent you. I think they are *The Screwtape Letters*, *The Problem of Pain*, and
Man, The Master[73] – also Lord Ponsonby's life of his father. Would you kindly
return them so that I may hand them over.
 Your broadcast was a very good one indeed and I enjoyed listening to it.
 Your next broadcast 'Some Books' will be on Wednesday, March 3rd, but I
will send our usual card of reminder beforehand.

E.M. Forster Esq.,   Yours sincerely,
West Hackhurst,   for Eric Blair
Abinger Hammer,   Talks Producer
Dorking   Indian Section

07/ES/EB   10th February 1943

Dear Mr. Todd,
 Many thanks for your letter of the 30th January. I am sorry about the delay
in answering but as you perhaps know I have been ill and have been away. We
had to discontinue the film talks because there was so much uncertainty as to
what films were being produced in India that we were no longer able to give any
useful information about forthcoming films. If the position improves again, as I
fancy it will, so that it will be possible to know in advance exactly what films are
coming, then I shall be very glad to take up your suggestion about giving special
publicity to shorts and documentaries produced by the British Council, but, at
the moment, I do not care to broadcast on these alone while we are unable to
say anything about ordinary commercial films.

Harry W. Todd Esq.,   Yours truly,
The British Council,   Eric Blair
Film Department,   Talks Producer
3 Hanover Street, W.1   Indian Section

From: Eric Blair, Indian Section, 200 Oxford St.   13th Feb. 1943
Subject: Approaching distinguished or well-known
   people in regard to broadcast talks.
To: Mr. Norman Collins   [WAC: R51/257/2]

We are going to approach the following MPs, to do five minute talks on subjects

[73] The first two by C.S. Lewis, the third by Gerald Heard.

of current interest, to be included in 'The Debate Continues' period on Mondays at 1115 to 1130 GMT.

> Dr. Edith Summerskill
> Cyril Lakin
> Will Lawson

EB/WMB   Eric Blair

07/ES/EB   16th February, 1943

Dear Sir,
  Mr. Rushbrook-Williams, the Eastern Service Director, has asked me to send you the enclosed script for approval, before we go ahead with the broadcast on the 12th March, 1943. I shall be glad to hear from you in due course that it will be in order for us to broadcast the talk.

Graves Law, Esq.,	Yours faithfully,
Middle East Section,	Eric Blair
Ministry of Information.	Talks Producer

07/ES/EB   22nd February 1943

Dear Mr. Forster,
  Mr. Blair has asked me to send you the enclosed book *Mr. Bowling Buys a Newspaper*[74] – about which I understand he has already spoken to you.
  I hope it reaches you safely, and in time.

E.M. Forster Esq.,	Yours sincerely,
West Hackhurst,	for Eric Blair
Abinger Hammer,	Talks Producer
Dorking	

07/ES/EB   24th February 1943

Dear Mr. Stephens,[75]
  I wonder if you would care to do a 10 minutes talk in a forthcoming series

---

[74] *Mr Bowling Buys a Newspaper* (1942) by Donald Landels Henderson. A 'Mr Bowling' was the hero of Orwell's novel *Coming Up For Air*.
  [75] James Stephens (1880?-1950), Irish writer, author of *The Crock of Gold* (1912). In later life he was well known as a broadcaster of stories and verse.

which we are calling 'Great Dramatists'. I will explain the purpose and lay-out of these programmes, each of which will take half-an-hour in all.

The programme consists of a 10 minutes talk on the chosen author, a scene from one of his plays acted by the BBC Repertory Company, and taking 8 or 10 minutes, and about 8 minutes of music. The lay-out will be as follows:

1. Opening announcement
2. About a minute taken from the scene to be acted.
3. Talk
4. Music
5. Scene from chosen dramatist

You can see, therefore, that the speaker's opening words should refer to the fragment of the scene which has just been heard. He should start off – 'Those lines you have just heard were written by John Dryden' – (or whoever it may be).

The one we want you to undertake is W.B. Yeats, and the play from which we propose chosing a scene is *The Hour Glass*. The date of your talk would be Thursday, May 27th, at 12.30 to 1 p.m. (British Summer Time). If this date is not convenient to you we can easily record the talk beforehand. Would you be kind enough to let me know, as early as possible, whether you can undertake this.

James Stephens Esq.,   Yours sincerely
Woodside Chapel   George Orwell
Tunley   Talks Producer
Sapperton   Indian Section
Near Cirencester, Glos.

P.S. The plays we shall choose are not absolutely fixed yet and I am open to suggestions.

From: Eric Blair, Indian Section, 200 Oxford St.   24th Feb. 1943
Subject: Indian Programme – Eastern Service
   Contract for Dr. Narayana Menon
To: Mr. Wynn, Music Bookings Manager, Eagle House.

As the point has been queried, we are asking Dr. Menon to choose the 15 minute musical programmes in weeks 12, 14, etc., because he has shown himself competent in selecting programmes of this type, and he has the advantage of being a student both of European and Indian music. He is therefore probably a good judge of the types of European music likely to appeal to Indian listeners.

To arrange his contract on a weekly basis would no doubt be a better arrangement and we will do so.

This is being sent through Eastern Services Director for his approval.

EB/WMB   Eric Blair

07/ES/EB   24th February 1943

Dear Eliot,
I wonder if you would like to do us a ten minutes talk on Christopher
Marlowe on Thursday, the 18th March. If that date is not itself convenient to
you we can always record beforehand. I should explain the purpose of this
series of talks and the way we intend doing them.

This is a series called 'Great Dramatists' and each talk will consist of a ten
minutes talk, a scene from the chosen dramatist taking 8 or 10 minutes and
about 8 minutes of music. We propose, at the opening of each programme, to
trail about a minute of the scene which is to be acted in full at the end of the
programme and the talk will come immediately after this. The speaker's
opening words should therefore refer to the fragment of a scene which has just
been heard. In this case we're going to have a scene from *Dr. Faustus*, though
I haven't yet decided which. You could perhaps start off therefore – 'Those
lines you have just heard come from a scene in Marlowe's *Dr. Faustus* which
you will be hearing acted in a few minutes time', or words to that effect. I
should be glad if you would let me know as early as possible whether you can
undertake this. I hope you will as this ought to be an interesting series and we
want to start it with a good talk.

T.S. Eliot Esq.,   Yours sincerely,
c/o Messrs. Faber & Faber Ltd.,   George Orwell
24 Russell Square, W.C.1   Talks Producer
                                         Indian Section

07/ES/EB   27th February 1943

Dear Hawkins,
Thanks for the script of the 'Feature' which is now being roneoed.
Miss Blackburn[76] tells me you would like to take a part yourself. I think
this would be O.K. but I don't think you ought to take the part of Donne
himself because I don't think your voice is suited to this. Would you like to
take one of the other parts?

---

[76] Mary Blackburn, Orwell's Programme Assistant.

The rehearsal is at 10.30 a.m. Tuesday morning, in Studio 6, Oxford Street. Don't be late will you.

Desmond Hawkins Esq.,	Yours sincerely,
Todds Farm,	George Orwell
Saxtead,	Talks Producer
Woodbridge, Suffolk	Indian Section

07/ES/EB   4th March 1943

Dear Eliot,

Thanks for your letter. I was very sorry to hear you were ill and as soon as I heard this from your Secretary I abandoned the idea of your doing the first talk, which would have given you very little notice.

I wonder whether you would, by any chance, care to do the second in the series, which is two weeks later, that is to say, on Thursday, April 1st, at the same time. This talk is on Dryden, the play being the *Indian Empress*, and the plan of the programme would be the same as I gave you. You might let me know whether you could do this, as otherwise I must approach someone else. I am hoping to get George Sampson to do the one on Marlowe.

I quite agree about this stuff in the *Listener* and I will try and get this regulated for the future. In theory the BBC holds the copyright of all broadcast material for 28 days after transmission but I have no doubt we could come to an agreement with them.

T.S. Eliot Esq.,	Yours sincerely,
Messrs. Faber & Faber Ltd.,	George Orwell
24 Russell Sq., W.C.1.	Talks Producer
	Indian Section

W.H.   7-3-43

Dear Orwell,

Here are the three books for which you asked and one for which you didn't.

Thinking it over, I had better not venture on Ibsen – I am not sufficiently equipped socially. I hope you will get Shaw.

I might manage Dryden (i) if you can't get a scholar (ii) if I'm given a bit of notice (iii) if I'm given some instructions (iv) if you decide to include this difficult writer.

Difficult because he's the only big writer of whom we've formed no image. How, in ten minutes, is the broadcaster to create one? I think he was all to pieces and yet strong: but one would need a good hour to put such a thesis across.

If your actors want, as they probably will, to do some All for Love, your broadcaster had better circle round them. But this won't be presenting Dryden.

Yours ever
E.M. Forster.

07/ES/EB   11th March 1943

Dear Eliot,

Following on our telephone conversation – here are the particulars about the talk on Dryden, just in case you haven't seen the other letter.

This talk is the second in a series called 'Great Dramatists' and each programme will deal with one dramatist, with special reference to one of his plays. The play chosen for Dryden is *The Indian Empress*. The programme consists of a ten-minutes' talk, a scene from the chosen play, acted by the BBC Repertory and taking about ten minutes, and about eight minutes of music. The layout is like this:

1. There is about a couple of minutes of music, and then – cutting into this – a few lines from the acted scene, which will have been recorded beforehand, as a sort of trailer.
2. The speaker then gives his talk.
3. After this, the recorded scene is acted right through, and then there is more music.

You will see therefore that the speaker's opening words should have some reference to the fragment of the scene which has just been heard. If you start off – 'Those lines you have just heard come from John Dryden's play *The Indian Empress*' – or words to that effect, that would be the kind of thing. If you liked you might also refer to the forthcoming scene at the end of your talk.

A ten-minutes' talk means about 1200 words. This is to be broadcast on April 1st at 12.30 p.m., so if you were here on that day at a quarter-to-twelve it would be all right. Of course you can record beforehand if that date is not convenient. I should like to have the script in by March 25th if possible. In case you would like to know, the other people taking part in the series are: George Sampson, Sherard Vines,[77] James Stephens and I hope Bernard Shaw.

T.S. Eliot Esq.   Yours sincerely,
c/o Faber & Faber   Eric Blair
24 Russell Sq., W.C.1   Talks Producer

[77] Sherard Vines, Professor of English in University College, Hull, and author of *A Hundred Years of English Literature* (Duckworth, 1950).

07/ES/EB   15th March 1943

Dear Eliot,

I suppose you've had my wire. I am sorry I made the mistake of calling the play you are to talk on *The Indian Empress*. It should have been *The Indian Emperor*. As I believe there is another one called *The Indian Queen* it would have been rather a puzzle to know just which play was intended.

Although *The Indian Emperor* refers to the Mexican Indians I wonder whether you could tie your talk on to India by just mentioning even if only in one sentence that Dryden wrote a play about Aurungzib, or however it is spelt.[78] We shall expect your script round about the 25th.

T.S. Eliot Esq.,	Yours sincerely,
Messrs. Faber & Faber Ltd.,	George Orwell
24 Russell Square, W.C.1	Talks Producer
	Indian Section

07/ES/EB   18th March 1943

Dear Mr. Stephens,

Thank you for your letter of the 27th February.

We are looking forward to receiving your script and would like to have it about May 15th, not later.

We shall be acting a bit from the *Hour Glass*, and a few lines from this will be trailed immediately before your talk, so could you start off – 'Those lines you have just heard came from W.B. Yeats' play the *Hour Glass* – or words to that effect.

The broadcast will take place at 200 Oxford Street.

James Stephens Esq.,	Yours sincerely,
Woodside Chapel,	George Orwell
Tunley, Sapperton,	Talks Producer
Near Cirencester, Glos.	Indian Section

07/ES/EB   29th March 1943

Dear Reg,

Thanks for your letter of the 27th. I am glad it is O.K. about the contribution to the book. Re your query. I signed that letter 'Orwell' because it was a circular letter and some of the contributors only knew me as that.

I would like, very much, to have a talk on the Russian discovery of Alaska.

---

[78] *Aurengzebe* (1675). The eponymous hero of Dryden's play was the last effective Mogul emperor. He died in 1707 at the age of 88.

Russia is always news, more or less. But I would like to have this talk to keep in what is called 'The Ice-box' to be broadcast at any odd moment when something or other falls through. So could you do it so that nothing is tied down to a particular date, e.g. don't say 'last week there was a paragraph in the paper which said', etc., etc. Although we might keep the talk for months before using it you will get paid when it is recorded.

I would like, very much, also to have something about Elizabethan literature, but I can't have it yet because of changes in our programme. During the summer months they are shoving us on to a time of day which means that our broadcasts will reach India at half-past four in the afternoon. It is no use broadcasting literary stuff at that hour but I shall be going back to our old programmes in September and perhaps we can fix something then. Let me have the talk on Alaska whenever convenient to you. 13½ minutes, which means about 1500 words. Perhaps you could mention in the talk that the United States acquired Alaska from Russia by the peaceful method of buying it. I think that is good propaganda.

I have just heard from Cedric Dover, who is in the Army, apparently in Nottinghamshire. He doesn't seem to be enjoying it but then who does.

Reginald Reynolds Esq.,   Yours,
St. Mark's College   Eric Blair
King's Road, S.W.10   Talks Producer
                                         Indian Section

07/ES/EB   1st April 1943

Dear Mr. Sitwell,
    I wonder whether you would like to do a ten minutes talk on Oscar Wilde for the Indian Service of the BBC. I had better explain about the series of which this talk will be part.

We have a series of half-hour programmes called 'Great Dramatists'. Each programme consists of a ten-minutes talk on the dramatist in question, with special reference to one of his plays; a scene or extract from the play acted by the BBC Repertory, and some music. The play of Wilde's which we should like you to tackle is *The Importance of Being Earnest*, but of course your talk should also give some sort of account of Wilde's work as a whole. The way we introduce these programmes is to record the scene which is acted and start the programme by trailing a few lines from the scene. The speaker's talk follows immediately after this, without any announcement. So your talk should start off – 'Those lines you've just heard come from Oscar Wilde's play, *The Importance of Being Earnest*', or words to that effect.

I hope very much you will undertake this talk. I may mention that the other playwrights dealt with in the series are Marlowe, Dryden, Sheridan, Ibsen and Yeats. The date of the Wilde talk will be Thursday, May 13th, and the time, 1.30 p.m. If this date is not convenient to you we can easily record beforehand. Could you let me know whether you will do this.[79]

Osbert Sitwell Esq.,   Yours sincerely,
2 Carlyle Square, S.W.3   George Orwell
                                       Talks Producer
                                       Indian Section

W.H.   3-4-43

Dear Orwell,
    Thank you for your letter. If the idea is a pamphlet all by me it will want a little thought and I'm afraid I can't answer right off. I am asking the Society of Authors what they think about terms, and I am coming up Thursday or Friday next and could perhaps have a talk with you over the other details – am free Friday lunch, by the way.
    I don't much like other people's reprinted talks – they read so chatty and scrappy – and I don't recall six presentable ones of my own. And, my mentality not being official, I should want to control the text and prevent any softening of it, by omissions, in the direction of official propaganda.

    Yours ever
    E.M. Forster

07/ES/EB   5th April 1943

Dear Forster,
    Thanks for your letter. I am going to go through all the scripts of yours which we have and pick out the ones which I think would make a suitable pamphlet. You can then have a look at them. I can guarantee that they will not be messed about in any propagandist manner as they have already passed the censorship and that is all that is required. You could make any alterations of a literary kind that you felt they needed. However, I don't want to press you into this against your will. Perhaps we could talk it over? Would you like to have lunch with me on Friday, the 9th? Owing to summer time I shan't be free for lunch until 2 o'clock, but I could make it 2 o'clock sharp at the Ariston, where we had lunch before, if you could manage it.
    Perhaps you could let me know?

E.M. Forster Esq.,   Yours,
West Hackhurst,   George Orwell
Abinger Hammer,   Talks Producer
Dorking, Surrey   Indian Section

[79] Sitwell declined Orwell's invitation.

07/ES/EB   6th April 1943

Dear Forster,
    I am sorry to ask such a thing, but I wonder if you would be kind enough to re-fund the cost of the book you lost – *Arthur Ponsonby* by Henry Ponsonby. It was 12/6d. Apparently The Times Book Club[80] hold us responsible and expect us to pay the price of the new copy.

E.M. Forster Esq.   Yours,
West Hackhurst,   George Orwell
Abinger Hammer,   Talks Producer
Dorking, Surrey

07/ES/EB   7th April 1943

Dear Lord Winterton,
    I understand from Princess Indira that you have kindly agreed to broadcast a short talk, of about ten minutes' duration, in our Eastern Service directed to India, 1.15-1.30 p.m. on Monday, 3rd May, 1943.
    I should be glad if you could let us have a copy of your script not later than Friday 30th April, and at the same time perhaps you will let us know at what time we may expect you at 200 Oxford Street on the 3rd May, to rehearse your script before transmission.

Lord Winterton,   Yours sincerely,
61 Eccleston Square, S.W.1   Eric Blair
                                         Talks Producer

07/ES/EB   9th April 1943

Dear Lord Winterton,
    Many thanks for your letter dated April 8th. A ten minutes talk would probably be 12 or 1300 words. It does not matter if you do rather more because we have no other speaker on that day and Princess Indira will merely be introducing you.
    It will be quite all right for you to rehearse your India talk on the same day

---

[80] One of the last of the great private lending libraries, now closed, but at the time still patronised by the BBC.
[81] This is the only record I have found of collaboration on a programme by Orwell and Burgess.

as your talk for the Home Service. As soon as I hear from Guy Burgess I will fix it up.[81]

The Rt. Hon. The Earl Winterton	Yours sincerely,
61, Eccleston Place, S.W.1	Eric Blair
	Talks Producer
	Indian Section

07/ES/EB   13th April 1943

Dear Mr. Lehmann,

I wonder whether you would like to do another talk for the Indian Section during June. I should want the script by the middle of May. I will explain about the series of which this is part.

From time to time, we do a series of talks which are afterwards printed in India as pamphlets, six talks making one pamphlet. This particular series is to deal with English poetry, since 1900, the title to be 'Modern English Verse', or something of that kind. As there are to be six talks we have to divide it up into six periods, somewhat arbitrarily you may feel, but it would be difficult to do it in any other way. I enclose a copy of the schedule I have drawn up.

I would like you to deal with the fifth talk on what one might call the political poets. I have put Simpson, Campbell[82] and Plomer in brackets because we are bound to stick to a chronological arrangement in these talks and these three obviously don't belong, in a political sense, with the others.

With each period there is a list of 'Poets to be mentioned'. This does not mean that you have to mention all those in the body of your talk, and, on the other hand, you can bring in any other poets of the period whom you choose to mention. I append these names merely because, when the pamphlet is printed, we shall print at the end of each talk, a list of the best known poets of the period.

I hope very much that you will undertake this. Can you please let me know, as soon as possible, whether you would like to do so? These talks are $13\frac{1}{2}$ minutes, which means 15 or 1600 words. I will let you know the exact date later, and if it is inconvenient we can easily record the talks beforehand. But, in any case, I must have the script by the middle of May, so that I can despatch all six to India simultaneously.

John Lehmann Esq.,	Yours sincerely,
601 Carrington House	George Orwell
Hertford Street, W.1	Talks Producer
	Indian Section

[82] Roy Campbell, South African poet (1901-1957), editor with William Plomer and Laurens van der Post of the periodical *Voorslag (Whiplash)* and author of many books including the pro-Franco *Flowering Rifle* (1939). He was a BBC Talks Producer from 1946 to 1949. He died in a car accident.

07/ES/EB   15th April 1943

Dear Lehmann,
Many thanks for your letter. I am glad you will do the talk. Perhaps you
could come round and have tea one day here and we could settle the
outstanding points. Any day of the week, except Thursdays or Saturdays,
would suit me.
The classification of poets to be printed after each talk isn't hard and fast,
and I only made it out in order to give speakers a general idea. In any case, as
soon as I had made it out, I found that there were a lot I had forgotten. As to
the ones you queried; I have put them into those classifications because it is
difficult to avoid doing this on a chronological basis, but we can fix all that
when we talk it over. I have no wish to dictate what speakers shall say, but I
do want to avoid overlapping.
As to what you will be paid, I have no power over that, and am not supposed
to know anything about it, but I should imagine that you will be paid £8.8.0.
for a talk of about 1500 words. I think I told you that we proposed
broadcasting one poem in each talk, where possible, spoken by the writer
himself. You might think over what poem, from your period, you would like to
broadcast, and I will see whether we have a recording of it.
Can you ring me up, and let me know when you're coming. My telephone
number is Euston 3400, Extension 208.

John Lehmann Esq.,   Yours sincerely,
601, Carrington House,   George Orwell
Hertford Street, W.1   Talks Producer
                                       Indian Section

[Postcard]
Thanks for [?]. It will have to be a job lot I'm afraid, if you can't send more
Orientalia send me Mark Benney[83] again. I have got Cecil's *Thomas Hardy*.
E.M.F.

07/ES/EB   20th April 1943

Dear Forster,
Herewith the book *Over to Bombers* by Mark Benney. Do you mind sending
it back when it is finished with?

[83] Mark Benney, *pseud.* Henry Ernest Degras (1910-   ). His *Over to Bombers* (1943) was a
fictional story of the transformation of a pre-war luxury car factory into an aeroplane factory.

Your broadcast is next week, the 28th, at 1.15 to 1.30 pm (DBST).

E.M. Forster Esq.,   Yours,
West Hackhurst,   George Orwell
Abinger Hammer,   Talks Producer
Near Dorking, Surrey   Indian Section

07/ES/EB   22nd April 1943

Dear Hawkins,
      Thanks for yours. I am glad you will do the talk. As I said before, you don't
have to mention the poets I listed, and you can bring in any others you like,
provided they're not chronologically wrong. I forgot about Gascoyne, but he
certainly belongs in that lot. The list which I made out is only there because
in the pamphlet we intend to put a comprehensive list of poets of the period at
the end of each talk. The next thing to fix is which poem of the period you
think should be broadcast in the body of your talk. Of course, it is an
advantage to have the poet broadcast it himself, which should be possible with
these younger ones. We have got a very nice poem by Henry Treece, but we
have broadcast it once already. How about getting Alex Comfort[84] to do
something? If he has a good voice something of his might be suitable. It
should be not more than 30 lines, I should say. Or what about Alan Rook?[85]
You might let me know about this. I would like the poem to be fitted in
somewhere in the middle of your talk, so that you can say – 'Now here is an
example of what I mean' or words to that effect.

                        Yours,
                        George Orwell

      [84] Alexander Comfort (1920-   ), medical biologist, poet and novelist. He refused military
service and did a degree at London Hospital instead. Under the pseudonym 'Obadiah
Hornbrooke', he published a pacifist poem, 'Letter to an American Visitor', in *Tribune*, 4 June
1943, to which Orwell wrote a vigorous answer 'As one non-combatant to another: a letter to
Obadiah Hornbrooke', 18 June 1943. The letter here shows that Orwell was not totally
antagonistic to Comfort, even considering him for a programme, a possible explanation of his
strong response to Comfort's poem two months later.
      [85] Alan Rook, poet. His wartime publications included *Soldiers, this Solitude* (1942) and *These are
my Comrades* (1943).

West Hackhurst. Abinger Hammer.

Dear Orwell,

Will you get me Beatrice Webb's My Apprenticeship[86] as soon as you can? I should like to give the talk on her next time – I assume I do talk, though I have not had the formal invitation or a contract form to do so yet. – I knew her a little and one or two reminiscences will come in suitably.

Yours ever
E.M. Forster   [Received 4-5-43]

07/ES/EB   18th May 1943

Dear Miss Rathbone,[87]

I understand from Princess Indira of Kapurthala that you are willing and will be able to take part, with Princess Indira, in our weekly broadcast of 'The Debate Continues' on Monday, 7th June. The actual time of this broadcast is from 1.15 to 1.30 p.m. DBST., and we should very much like you to be at 200 Oxford Street, W.1. for rehearsal with Princess Indira in the Studio at 12.45 p.m.

Princess Indira would like her broadcast to fit in with yours – either in the form of a discussion, or so that her preliminary few minutes of speech may lead up to your broadcast. With regard to subject, you will probably have some definite ideas of what you would like to talk about in your six to eight minutes talk, but it would be helpful if you could discuss the subject matter with me on the 'phone, in the course of the next week.

We should like it if your script can be ready some time on Thursday, 3rd June, and if it is any help to you, we can send someone to collect it from you.

Miss Eleanor Rathbone, M.P.   Yours sincerely,
5 Tufton Court, S.W.1   Eric Blair
                                                      Talks Producer

[86] Beatrice Webb had just died. Forster's talk is among those published in *Two Cheers for Democracy* (see above, n.1).

[87] Eleanor Florence Rathbone (1872-1946), elected to Parliament in 1929 as an Independent Member for the Combined English Universities, was a leading proponent of family allowances in Britain, which made the statute book in 1945. She was also a tireless advocate of extended franchise for women in India.

07/ES/EB   18th May 1943

Dear Mr. Roberts,[88]

I understand from Princess Indira that you have kindly agreed to do a talk for us on the refugee problem on Monday next, 24th May, and we shall be glad if you could be here (at 200 Oxford Street) at 12.45 p.m. on that day.

I will arrange for a messenger to collect a copy of your script at 10.30 on Friday morning, and Princess Indira will phone you later in the day, after she has seen it.

I have instructed our Contracts Department to get into touch with you, and you will be hearing from them shortly.

Wilfrid Roberts Esq.,   Yours sincerely,
22 Gayfere Street, S.W.1   Eric Blair
                                         Talks Producer

07/ES/EB   19th May 1943

Dear Darlington,

I am writing to you on the advice of Professor Haldane. I wonder if you would like to do a talk for us in a forthcoming series to India. I should want the script in about a fortnight's time.

We nowadays do a series of talks which are designed after being broadcast, to be printed as pamphlets in India. Usually there are *six* talks in a series, making a pamphlet of about 10,000 words. In most cases these talks are literary, but I want for the next one, to have a series of Scientific ones. The subjects are: Malnutrition, Soil Erosion, Plant or Animal Breeding, Malaria, House-flies and Drinking Water. This sounds a very heterogeneous collection, but each touches on problems important to India, and if put together, they should make a readable popular pamphlet. I wonder whether you would like to do the one on 'Plant and Animal Breeding'. You could concentrate on Plants or Animals, whichever you prefer, but I suppose that in a talk of $13\frac{1}{2}$ minutes – that is about 1500 words, it would be better to stick to one or the other. The main thing we want emphasized is the great differences that can be made in Agricultural production by breeding only from good strains.

---

[88] Wilfrid Roberts (1900-   ), M.P. for North Cumberland 1935-50. In 1943 he was Parliamentary Private Secretary to Sir Archibald Sinclair, Secretary of State for Air.

Could you let me know as soon as possible whether you will undertake this? The date of the broadcast would be June 30th. Of course, you can always record beforehand if the date is inconvenient, but my main concern is to have the scripts in early, so that I can send them to India to be printed.

Dr. C.D. Darlington   Yours sincerely,
John Innes Horticultural Institution,   George Orwell
Mostyn Road,   Talks Producer
Merton Park, S.W.19   Indian Section

Dear Orwell

Here is the script. I will come along on Wednesday about 12.30 as usual. I will return the book, and if the script is too short I can read something from it.

Yours ever
E.M. Forster
W.H.   24-5-43

Dear Orwell,   2-6-43

Thanks for Queen Victoria, but I can't get going unless I receive the Max lecture,[89] which is the topical excuse for a talk on Strachey. I have written to the publishers and asked them to lend me proofs.

Failing them the broadcast on June 20th must be on something else. Would you like another on plays [?] running in London? I have seen *Heartbreak House* and the *Ballet* and heard a concert performance of *Smetana; the Kiss*, and next Wednesday shall see *Love for Love*. Thursday, if you like this plan, I will go to *Molière* at the Westminster or to the *Priestley* play.[90] – But I'll wait to hear about the Max lecture first.

Will try to ring you Saturday morning.

Will also arrange when I can record the broadcast for the 20th. What a damned nuisance it is being shifted to Sunday. I like talking live much better because it keeps me alive. I suppose there is no chance of my being fitted back into a week day.

Yours ever,
E.M. Forster

[89] 'Lytton Strachey: The Rede Lecture' (1943) by Max Beerbohm.
[90] Priestley published *Three Plays* (1943), and presumably it was one of these – *Music at Night*, *The Long Mirror* and *They Came to a City* – that is referred to here.

07/ES/EB 4th June 1943

Dear Forster,

I cannot get a copy of Max Beerbohm's lecture, partly, perhaps, because I don't know to what Society he delivered it. You said that you had written to his publishers. I don't know whether that has borne fruit yet?

If the Strachey project falls through, then I think it would be quite a good idea to do the one about Plays, particularly as most of them are of a kind which might be read, if not seen, in India. We could, after all, return to the Strachey talk another month.

I am sorry about this change to Sunday but it doesn't seem to be avoidable. The simplest way would be for you to arrange to record always on one day of the week – any day which is convenient to you, but preferably not Saturday. Could you let me have a suitable date for your recording for the 20th? It might be better to give two alternative dates and I would like the script the day before you come to record, because we have to get it censored.

I am sorry for all this change-about, but once we get into the new arrangement it will no doubt be as simple as before.

E.M. Forster Esq., Yours sincerely,
Abinger Hammer, George Orwell
Dorking, Surrey Talks Producer
Indian Section

[Postcard]
Thank you for letter and p.c. Friday the 18th, 3.0., O.K. for recording, and script should reach you on the 17th. The Cambridge University Press has sent me proofs of Max's lecture, but I think I will keep this time to theatres as I have started on them. Bokhari has sent me 3 books on the Indian situation, and I should like to do these one time if I am allowed sufficient freedom of reference: otherwise it doesn't seem worth while. Will discuss with you when next we meet what 'sufficient' is.
    E.M. Forster
    W.H. 7-6-43

07/ES/EB 17th June 1943

Dear Eliot,

Following on our telephone conversation I want to ask whether you would do one talk in the new literary series we're starting towards the end of August. We're going to have a series dealing with English prose literature of the present century, and are calling it 'Modern Masterpieces'. I want each talk to deal ostensibly with a single book, but in doing so to give some account of the author's work as a whole. The projected list of talks is attached. Would you like to tackle the talk on James Joyce, with special reference to *Ulysses*. I can't give you the exact date of the talk because I haven't yet fixed the order in which they will appear, but it will not be earlier than the 21st August. This would be a talk of the usual length, that is, 15/1600 words. I must also ask whether, in the event of your doing the talk, you will object to its being printed in India as part of a pamphlet. We now have a number of our programmes printed in pamphlet form.

T.S. Eliot Esq.,   Yours sincerely,
c/o Messrs. Faber & Faber Ltd.,   George Orwell
24 Russell Square, W.C.1   Talks Producer
                                           Indian Section

07/ES/EB   18th June 1943

Dear Eliot,
    With reference to my letter yesterday I very much regret the list of projected talks was omitted but am sending you one herein.
    I hope very much you will be able to do the talk on James Joyce.

T.S. Eliot Esq.,   Yours sincerely,
c/o Messrs. Faber & Faber Ltd.,   George Orwell
24 Russell Square, W.C.1   Talks Producer
                                           Indian Section

07/ES/EB   18th June 1943

Dear Plomer,
    I wonder whether you would like to do a talk for the Indian Section. I can't give you an exact date but it would be some time in September.
    We're going to start a series called 'Modern Masterpieces', dealing with English prose works of this century. We want each talk to deal ostensibly with a single book but in doing so to give some account of the author's work as a whole. I attach a list of the projected talks. If you would like to do E.M. Forster, I think it might be better to concentrate on *Howard's End*, because any Indian audience likely to listen in to a talk of this type would know about *A Passage to India* already.[91]
    These are talks of 13½ minutes, that is, 15/1600 words. I assume that you would not object to your talk being afterwards printed as part of a pamphlet in

---

[91] Moreover it had already been broadcast by the German radio as anti-British propaganda (see above, Introduction, p. 14, n.4).

India. We do this with some of our literary talks. In theory you get a royalty but in practice the profits are negligible. Could you let me know whether you will undertake this?

William Plomer Esq.,   Yours sincerely,
29 Linden Gardens,   George Orwell
Nottinghill Gate, W.8   Talks Producer
                                 Indian Section

From: Controller (Home)   19th June, 1943
Subject: 'He Died Younger than he was Born':
   James Stephens on W.B. Yeats (see 'Listener' of 17/6, p. 728)
To: Director of Talks

We may, I think, expect the Board to echo the question suggested by Laws in the 'News Chronicle' – why was Stephens' talk not given in the Home Service? – and should be prepared with a reply.

RRM/EMB   Sir Richard Maconachie

07/ES/EB   25th June 1943

Dear Eliot,
   It doesn't matter greatly which order these talks are done in, so how about Sunday the 19th September for you? (As it is a Sunday there is no need to do it live – you could record any time beforehand.) We should want the script by about the 10th September. If that doesn't suit you could have September 5th or 26th. Please let me know.

T.S. Eliot Esq.,   Yours sincerely,
Messrs. Faber & Faber Ltd.,   George Orwell
24 Russell Square, W.C.1   Talks Producer
                                 Indian Section

07/ES/EB   25th June 1943

Dear Desmond,
   I am writing to ask whether you would like to undertake a weekly programme which Bokhari proposes starting at the beginning of August? The projected title is 'Remember this?' (incidentally this is a rotten title and you might be able to think of a better one). The idea is to make a sort of re-hash

programme out of our programmes of the preceding week. For example, one can re-play bits of the music that have been put out or from other works of the same composer, and similarly, where we have talks on literary subjects, as we do every week, you could put in readings from the works of the authors dealt with. The idea is to try to make the listener guess the context of each passage of literature or music before being told. This is a half-hour programme but ought not to entail a great deal of work. Miss Chitale would help you with compiling the stuff, i.e. by giving you details of the programme but you would have to jazz it up and make it into an attractive programme. What is aimed at is a sort of mosaic of words and music. Could you let me know, at once, whether you would like to do this because we have only got about a month in which to start it going?

Desmond Hawkins,	Yours,
Todds Farm,	George Orwell
Saxtead,	Talks Producer
Woodbridge, Suffolk	Indian Section

07/ES/EB　　　　　　　　　　　　　　　　　　　　　　25th June 1943

Dear Stephen,

Would you like to do another talk for the Indian section? We have a series starting about the end of August on 'Modern English Prose Writers'. The way we intend to do it is to make each talk deal ostensibly with one particular book, but in doing so, to give, if possible, some idea of the writer's work as a whole. I thought you might like to do the talk on E.M. Forster.[92] The book I would like you to drape it round is *Howard's End*, as *A Passage to India* will be already well-known to our audience. These talks are of $13\frac{1}{2}$ minutes, which means 15/1600 words. I can't yet give you an exact date, but it would probably be a Sunday about the beginning of October. You could record it any time beforehand. Could you let me know whether you would like to do this?

Stephen Spender Esq.,	Yours,
Flat 4,	Eric Blair
2, Maresfield Gardens, N.W.3	Talks Producer
	Indian Section

[Postcard]

Thanks for p.c. Yes – Friday the 16th for recording, I suppose at 3.0. – The talk, as planned, may be difficult, and I want to start on it in good time.

---

[92] William Plomer had been unable to do it.

Please will you send me Brogan's *England* for I am told there is an Indian chapter in it of the type I require. – Also any book on India from the imperialist standpoint, if there's a recent one.

E.M. Forster

If not a bother, might I have copies of my two last broadcasts.

W.H.   26-6-43

07/ES/EB   28th June 1943

Dear Forster,

We have fixed a recording for you for Friday, the 16th July, at 3 to 3.30 p.m. In Studio 6.

We are sending you *The English People* by D.W. Brogan. I have another book at home, (a Penguin) by a man called Hancock, an Australian.[93] It is written from a more or less Imperialistic standpoint, but I will send it along to you later this week.

E.M. Forster Esq.,   Yours,
West Hackhurst   George Orwell
Abinger Hammer,   Talks Producer
Nr. Dorking, Surrey   Indian Section

07/ES/EB   1st July 1943

Dear Forster,

I have seen Mr. Rushbrook-Williams about Brailsford's book.[94] He says that it is not officially banned in India and that it will be all right to talk about it on the air but that to balance it one should have some book giving the opposite viewpoint. He suggests Professor Coupland's book called, I think, *Indian Constitutional Problems*, and issued by the Nuffield Trust. I will endeavour to get it for you, as quickly as possible. I am afraid all this is rather short notice as you are due to record your talk on the 16th, but if I can produce the book within the next day or two that will give you, at any rate, ten days to consider it. I think it will be safe to go ahead now with, of course, the normal precautions.

E.M. Forster Esq.,   Yours,
West Hackhurst,   George Orwell
Abinger Hammer,   Talks Producer
Nr. Dorking, Surrey   Indian Section

[93] William Keith Hancock, born in Melbourne in 1898, had been Professor of History at Birmingham University since 1933. The book referred to is probably his *Survey of British Commonwealth Affairs* (1940).

[94] Presumably *Subject India* (1943).

Dear Orwell,

Not banned! Well I'm blowed. I assume Fielden & Dover[95] can also be mentioned by name now, but if you are doubtful perhaps you will ring Rushbrook Williams up.

A short Coupland is always more welcome than a long one, and Fielden's Bibliography[96] includes 'Britain & India 1600-1941. R. Coupland. Longmans Green. 6d.' If this exists you might send it me with the larger volume.

Yours
E.M. Forster
W.H.   2-7-43

07/ES/EB   2nd July 1943

Dear Forster,
I understand that the library have sent you off Volume 1 of Professor Coupland's book, which, I imagine, is no use in itself. The one I intended them to send you was Volume III, which I understand is still being printed. But they mistook my directions. If you can't make a talk out of the books you now have, what about reverting to our original idea and having one on *New Writing*. A similar anthology has just been published called *New Road*,[97] containing mostly the work of the writers who have come on since the New Writing group. If you would like this I can send it to you, and I think you said you already had a copy of *New Writing*. Please let me know as early as possible. I am sorry that there has been so much fuss.

E.M. Forster Esq.,	Yours sincerely,
West Hackhurst,	George Orwell
Abinger Hammer,	Talks Producer
Nr. Dorking, Surrey	Indian Section

07/ES/EB   3rd July 1943

Dear Mr. Forster,
Your letter of the 2nd has just arrived. Mr. Orwell is away from the office this morning, but I have obtained the pamphlet *Britain and India*, which you mentioned, and am sending it on right away, though I don't know whether it

---

[95] Lionel Fielden and Cedric Dover.
[96] The bibliography in Lionel Fielden, *Beggar my Neighbour* (1943), p. 127.
[97] *New Road, New Directions in European Art and Letters*, edited by Alex Comfort and John Bayliss and published by Grey Walls Press (1943).

will be of any use without the copy of the larger volume (III) which we were unable to send. If you are unable to use it could you kindly return it some time?

E.M. Forster Esq.,   Yours sincerely,
West Hackhurst,   Secretary to George Orwell
Abinger Hammer,   Talks Producer
Nr. Dorking, Surrey   Indian Section

Dear Orwell

Yes it is all a damned nuisance, but I had better make an attempt to get this talk about the political books through and revert to culture if it is turned down. Two volumes of Coupland's 'Report' have arrived from the publisher. Send me the third at once if you can, also any short books by him, also any publicity on him. (I have it on Brailsford).

Am in town tomorrow (Monday), and will ring you that afternoon, or Tuesday morning, in the hope of help.

Am also in town for the night on Thursday this week, and with luck might deliver the script then or Friday morning.

If it's banned, and I have to do a new talk, I may have to give it on the Sunday, live, for the sake of the extra time.

Yours ever
E.M. Forster
W.H.   Sunday

07/ES/EB   5th July 1943

Dear Forster,

Thanks for your letter. We cannot send the third volume of Coupland's book, as I understand it is not out yet. We are sending you the short pamphlet[98] on the Cripps Mission — a very painful subject, as you will appreciate.

As for stuff about Coupland, I really know little about him but on looking him up in *Who's Who*, find that he is a Fellow of All Souls, Editor for some time of *The Round Table*, and has held a number of official positions and seats on Royal Commissions in England and India. He sounds thoroughly dull all round, but perhaps you can make something of him. I am told that John S. Hoyland's book on India just published is good, and am endeavouring to

---

[98] I have not been able to identify this; it was presumably a Government publication.

procure that for you, as well. I hope you will find time to deal with all this.

E.M. Forster Esq.,   Yours,
West Hackhurst,   George Orwell
Abinger Hammer,   Talks Producer
Nr. Dorking, Surrey   Indian Section

07/ES/EB   9th July 1943

Dear Mr. Bowyer,
   Very many thanks for the copy of *The Future of British Air Transport*, which I
shall read with great interest.

E.C. Bowyer Esq.,   Yours sincerely,
Society of British Aircraft   George Orwell
   Constructors Ltd.,   Talks Producer
32 Savile Row, W.1   Indian Section

Dear Orwell,

   We never settled when we record on Friday. I will ring Friday morning to
find out, but should be glad if it could be not earlier than [3].30. – i.e. arrival
for timing etc. at 2.45 – as I am going out to lunch.
   Monkey[98a] only reached me this morning – will return it with the other books.

   Yours in haste
   EMF
W.H.   Wednesday

07/ES/EB   13th July 1943

Dear Darlington,
   We are sending you a copy of your script for your talk next week, so that
you will be able to run over it before then. The actual time of your broadcast
is at 12.15 to 12.30 (DBST) on Thursday next, the 22nd July. Could you
manage to be here (200 Oxford Street) at about 11.45 a.m. so that we may
have a short rehearsal beforehand?

Dr. C.D. Darlington   Yours sincerely,
John Innes Horticultural Institution,   George Orwell
Mostyn Road,   Talks Producer
Merton Park, S.W.19   Indian Section

[98a] A Chinese novel translated by Arthur Waley.

07/ES/EB   16th July 1943

Dear Stephens,

    I wonder whether you would like to do a talk on Bernard Shaw. I am not sure whether he is up your street, but if he is I would like to have the talk on him done by another Irishman. We have got a series coming on shortly dealing with modern prose writers to balance the one we have now got going dealing with 'Modern Poets'. These talks are of 13½ minutes, and unlike the one you did before don't include an acted extract. The date of this talk would be early in September. If you would like to do it would you let me know and I will send you further particulars.

James Stephens Esq.,   Yours sincerely,
Woodside Chapel,   George Orwell
Tunley, Sapperton,   Talks Producer
Near Cirencester, Glos.   Indian Section

07/ES/EB   23rd July 1943

Dear Stephens,

    Following on our hurried conversation in the entrance hall, I will explain just what kind of talk we want you to do on Bernard Shaw. We have a series coming on called 'Modern Men of Letters', dealing with modern English prose writers. In this case we are not having any extract from the writer's work as in the series you took part in before, but we just want a talk with such illustrations as you think necessary. The way we want to do it is to make each talk give some idea of the writer's work as a whole but to revolve ostensibly round one book or play in particular. You can choose whichever of Shaw's plays you like to talk about but I'd rather you did not choose *Arms and the Man* because we had that on the air fairly recently. The date of your talk would be Sunday, the 5th September, which means that I want the script in before the end of August. As it is a Sunday you can record it beforehand and we will fix up later a date convenient to you. These talks go out at 5.15 pm. They are of 13½ minutes, which means 15/1600 words.

James Stephens Esq.,   Yours sincerely,
Woodside Chapel,   George Orwell
Tunley, Sapperton,   Talks Producer
Nr. Cirencester, Glos.   Indian Section

[Postcard]   24.7.43
Yes – Friday Aug. 13 3.0. for recording.
Subject: French culture and the war (more or less).
    EMF   Sunday

07/ES/EB   29th July, 1943

Dear Dr. Fletcher,

   Mr. Brian Brooke suggested to me that you might be willing to do a talk
for the Indian Section of the BBC. We do, from time to time, series of popular
scientific talks and we wish shortly to do a series on recent discoveries in
drugs and recent advances in medical practice generally. We would like you,
if you would, to do us a talk on *penicillin*. This follows on a talk on the
sulphonamide group by Professor L.P. Garrod.[99] These talks are aimed at
the English speaking Indian students. In drafting the talk you can assume
that you are speaking to an educated audience, but not to people with much
scientific knowledge. These talks are of $13\frac{1}{2}$ minutes, which means 15 or 16
hundred words. We usually have them printed afterwards in India in
pamphlet form. I suppose you would not object to that? In addition to the fee
for the talk you would in theory get a royalty on the pamphlet, but you can
imagine that this is not likely to amount to much. The date of your talk
would be Thursday, 2nd September at 11.15 a.m., and I would like to have
the script by the 15th August. Could you be kind enough to let me know fairly
soon whether you would care to undertake this.

Dr C.M. Fletcher   Yours truly,
34 Church Crescent   Eric Blair
Whetstone, N.20.

From: Eric Blair, Indian Section, 200 Oxford Street   2nd August 1943
Subject: Recording of poem by Dylan Thomas – 31/7/43[100]
To: Miss Alexander (Prog. Copyright)

Will you please arrange for payment to be made to Mr. Dylan Thomas for his
recording of a poem written by himself entitled 'A Saint about to Fall' (the
first line). The duration of the recording was 3'38" and it took place on
Saturday, July 31st, in St. 2, Oxford Street, in the period 12.15 to 12.45
p.m.(DBST).
   This poem will be transmitted on Sunday, August 8th, at 1515-1530 GMT,
in the Eastern Service (Purple Network) in our series 'Calling All Students'
(Literary Series No.6) a talk on 'The Apocalyptic Poets' by Desmond
Hawkins.

   [99] Lawrence Paul Garrod (1895-1979), Professor of Bacteriology, University of London.
   [100] This recording has not survived. Many recordings at the time were only made on soft wax
discs which were wiped as soon as their purpose had been fulfilled – which is no doubt the
reason why none of Orwell's recordings have survived either.

07/ES/EB   3rd August, 1943

Dear Comfort,
   I will be dispatching the translations of the two stories by Prem Chand[101] in a few days time. Now that they are translated I am rather disappointed with them, at any rate they are not so good as the one which was in that Indian review I told you about, but you might care to have a look at them.
   Forster is doing his broadcast on Sunday, 15th August at 4.15 p.m. standard time. You might be able, if you are some distance from London, to pick him up on the 19.46 wavelength, but it is not usually easy to pick up these broadcasts at all in England. He is going to talk about *New Road*, the latest *New Writing* and Maurice Bowra's book on symbolism.[102]

Alex Comfort, Esq.,   Yours truly,
41 Robin Hood Road,   George Orwell
Brentwood, Essex.

07/ES/EB   4th August 1943

Dear Dr. Fletcher,
   Many thanks for your letter of August 3rd and for the specimen article, which I am returning herewith.
   I think Professor Garrod will probably have made a few brief introductory remarks on chemotherapy in his talk about the sulphonamide group. At any rate I should plan your talk as though he had done so. If necessary we can always make a few last-minute modifications.
   I think the article you sent is at about the right level for our audience, except that we ought not to assume that they have a working knowledge of the various groups of bacteria.
   I look forward to seeing your script.

Dr. C.M. Fletcher,   Yours truly,
34 Church Crescent,   Eric Blair
Whetstone, N.20.

---

[101] Prem Chand, *pseud*. Dhanpat Rai Srivastava (1881-1936). Few of his works were published in English. A volume of short stories, including 'The Chess Players', was put out by an English-language publishing house in Bombay in 1946.
[102] C.M. Bowra, *The Heritage of Symbolism* (1943), a study of Valéry, Rilke, George, Blok and Yeats.

07/ES/MB   5th August 1943

Dear Mr. Hawkins,

Thank you for your P.C. Here is a Book – *The Royal Observatory Greenwich – its History & Work*. I do hope this will be of some use to you.

'Backward Glance' No.1 went off well and was really slick and entertaining. The only sad thing was that while Mr. Blair's secretary was actually typing the script for Mr. Cleverdon to produce,[103] she murmured vaguely that she thought that the Recording of L.A.G. Strong's talk had been destroyed! And it had! The script was altered (only slightly) accordingly, and we didn't actually refer to L.A.G. Strong's voice, as though he were himself speaking again. This won't happen again. We have already carefully checked that all the talks which have been sent to you, marked 'As Recorded' are actually recorded and the discs really available.

Desmond Hawkins Esq.,   Yours sincerely,
Todds Farm,   Mary Blackburn
Saxtead,   Assistant (Programmes)
Woodbridge, Suffolk.

07/ES/EB   10th August, 1943

Dear Comfort,

Thanks for your letter of the 9th August. I am glad you succeeded in picking up Hawkins's broadcast. Forster's will be at the same time etc. The BBC retain copyright of broadcast material for 28 days, after which it reverts to the author, so you have only to fix it up with Hawkins about reprinting. I can let you have a copy if Hawkins hasn't got one.

Our audience in India, i.e. for English language stuff, is very small, a question of thousands at most, but we do find that literary stuff is more listened to than anything else, except of course the news and some of the music. I try to aim exclusively at the students, but I fancy there is a possible subsidiary audience among the British troops which is why I am circularising people likely to be interested. In my experience it is no use trying to push this kind of broadcast on to the Home Service – they will never look at any of our stuff.

I have sent the two Prem Chand stories, but am also procuring the one which was previously printed (in India only) and will send that.

Yours sincerely,
George Orwell

[103] Douglas Cleverdon produced a number of Orwell's scripts and others put out by the Indian Section. See above p. 56.

07/ES/EB   20th August 1943

Dear Eliot,
   Very many thanks for the talk which will do very well and covers the
ground we wanted. I will ring up your secretary and find out a day convenient
to you for recording. If you come here half an hour before the actual
recording time that would be all right for rehearsal, I should say. It is about
the right length.

T.S. Eliot, Esq.,   Yours sincerely,
c/o Faber and Faber Ltd.,   George Orwell
24 Russell Square, W.C.1.

07/ES/EB   21st August 1943

Dear Desmond,
   I am enclosing another batch of scripts for the next Backward Glance
programme to be broadcast on Wednesday, September 1st. I shall be glad if
you will include an extract from the featurised short story 'Crainquebille'
broadcast on the 11th August.

Desmond Hawkins, Esq.,   Yours,
Todds Farm,   for George Orwell
Saxtead,
Framlingham, Suffolk.

From: Eric Blair, Indian Section, 200 Oxford Street   24th August 1943
Subject: Copyright for 'The Fox' by Ignazio Silone
To: Prog. Copyright, Miss Alexander

On Wednesday, 8th September we intend to broadcast a featurised
adaptation of the short story 'The Fox' by Ignazio Silone which is published
in *Penguin New Writing*, No.2. This programme will go on the air in the Purple
Network, Eastern Service, between 1000-1030 GMT.
   Would you kindly cover the copyright for this story.
                                                    Eric Blair

07/ES/EB   26th August 1943

Dear Desmond,
   I suggest the following might be suitable for the September anniversary:

General Wolfe (died at Quebec – 13.9.1759)
Buffon (naturalist) (born – 7.9.1707)
Zola (died 29.9.1902)
The Nuremberg Laws (passed – 15.9.1935)
G.D. Fahrenheit (died 16.9.1736)
Rudolf Diesel (diesel engines) (died 30.9.1913)
Torquemada (died 16.9.1498)

   Could you let me know fairly soon which one you fix on.

Desmond Hawkins, Esq.,   Yours sincerely,
Todds Farm,   George Orwell
Saxtead,
Framlingham, Suffolk.

[Postcard]   30-8-43
In reply, I had better record on the Friday preceding as usual. It had better be
mix of books. Please could you send me *at once* Edward Thompson[104] on the
Indian Princes. Also anything else new that occurs to you.
   E.M. Forster.
   Monday   W.H.

07/ES/EB   2nd September, 1943

Dear Hawkins,
   I am going away this week for a fortnight's holiday so I shall not be here for
the next Backward Glance. Your anniversary programme will also be coming
off just after I get back. Could you please let us have the scripts a bit earlier. In
the case of today's programme I didn't get the script until yesterday – only
one day before production. This can make a lot of trouble: if there is any
censorship difficulty or in the case of today's cast when they had to come and
do their stuff live unexpectedly. I am going to try and make quite sure that in
future it is quite clear whether the scripts are recorded or live. If it is a live
script it is better not to write the programme so that people have to do their

---

[104] Edward Thompson (1886-1946), friend of Tagore, Nehru and Gandhi, author of *An Indian
Day* (1927) and *These Men Thy Friends* (1927), lecturer in Bengali at Oxford. He was father of
the historian E.P. Thompson.

piece again, which entails paying them over again as well as bringing them to the studio at short notice.

D. Hawkins, Esq.,   Yours sincerely,
Todds Farm,   George Orwell
Saxtead,
Woodbridge, Suffolk

P.S. I shall be glad if you will return the books on Greenwich Observatory as soon as possible.

07/ES/EB   3rd September 1943

Dear Mr. Forster,
    I have arranged a recording for your next 'Some Books' talk on Friday, 10th September at 3.00 p.m. and I shall be very glad if you could be here at 2.30 to run through and time it. I am enclosing *The Making of the Indian Princes* by Edward Thompson and *Reflections on the Revolution of our Time* by Harold Laski.

E.M. Forster, Esq.,   Yours sincerely,
West Hackhurst,   for George Orwell
Abinger Hammer,
Nr. Dorking, Surrey.

[Postcard]
Thank you for letter and books. Though dated Sept. 3 they only reached me this morning. I will, if possible, post the script off Wednesday, but if it is not ready will leave it by hand Thursday evening, and hope you can get it typed and censored Friday morning. Will call Friday 2.30. as requested, to run through.
    EMF
    W.H.   6-9-43

07/ES/EB   6th September 1943

Dear Mr. Hawkins,
    I am enclosing a copy of the *Radio Times* which gives some information about the six pips.
    With regard to the Anniversary of the Month programme on September 21st. Mr. Cleverdon is going to Bristol on the 13th and will be producing it

from there. I understand you will be in Bristol during that time, so perhaps you could get in touch with him there and let him know about the cast etc. Could you also give him a copy of the script and let us have one too, if possible by Monday the 13th.

D. Hawkins, Esq.,   Yours sincerely,
Todds Farm,   for George Orwell
Saxtead,
Woodbridge, Suffolk.

W.H.   24-9-43

Dear Orwell,

I rang yesterday, but no answer. I hope you had a good holiday.

I suggest recording for the Strachey broadcast on Friday afternoon, the 1st, at about 3.0. and for the normal book talk on Friday the 8th.

Miss Blackburn did not know about the Strachey broadcast. It is to be on Queen Victoria isn't it – with but slight reference to the rest of his work, or to his personality?[105]

As for the book talk, I have John Morris[106] on Japan but have a further inspiration. J.M. Dent are bringing out Tom Sawyer and Huckleberry Finn together I think in Everyman. Could you get hold of this at once for me? I like Tom Sawyer very much, and Huckleberry Finn, which I have never got on with, is said to be better still. Anyhow they would make a nice extroversial change.

Please will you thank Bokhari for his letters and say that Thursday Nov. 4th will suit all right for the change back to 'live'. I had intended to write to him, but since I am writing to you will be obliged if you will transmit this message.

Yours ever
E.M. Forster

Can you put me wise on Roop and Mary Krishna, artists who have sent me their surrealist thoughts from Lahore – ? Their book must be mentioned some time, though it has failed to stir me.

[Postcard]
W.H.   26-9-43
Friday won't be very convenient, on the other hand I shall be up Sunday. So

---

[105] The broadcast based on Max Beerbohm's talk on Strachey and Strachey's book on Queen Victoria. See above, n.92.

[106] John Morris had recently joined the Eastern Service and was involved with some of Orwell's programmes. See above, pp. 49-50.

please may I do the Lytton Strachey live, and will you cancel the recording. I will let you have the script Saturday morning and will be round on Sunday the 3rd at about 3.30. for the 4.15. broadcast.

For the next broadcast (Oct. 10th) I should like to record as arranged.

– Please drop a p.c. confirming this change.

E.M. Forster

[Postcard]

West Hackhurst. Abinger Hammer. Dorking   26-9-43

Could you please send me at once *Huckleberry Finn* as before: have been ringing you without success.

EMF

07/ES/EB   27th September 1943

Dear Forster,

Thank you for your letter and post-card. It will be quite all right for you to do the Lytton Strachey talk live on Sunday, 3rd October. I have arranged a recording for the Some Books talk on Friday, 8th October at 3.0 p.m. I am enclosing copies of *Huckleberry Finn* and *Tom Sawyer*.

E.M. Forster, Esq.,   Yours sincerely,
West Hackhurst,   George Orwell
Abinger Hammer,
Nr. Dorking, Surrey.

07/ES/EB   28th September 1943

Dear Spender,

This is to confirm the telephone conversation this morning. We are doing a series called Great Dramatists, which are half hour programmes consisting of an acted extract from a play preceded by a ten minutes talk on it. I want you to say something about Ibsen's work in general, using *The Enemy of the People* as a pretext. We usually start by broadcasting a few lines from the play as a trailer and that gives you your cue to start off 'Those lines you have just heard come from An Enemy of the People by Henrik Ibsen'. The date of the broadcast is Sunday, October 24th, at 4.15 p.m. I shall want the script by October 17th.

Stephen Spender, Esq.,   Yours sincerely,
Flat 4,   George Orwell
2 Maresfield Gardens, N.W.3

From: Eric Blair, Indian Section, 200 Oxford Street   4th October 1943
Subject: Approaching M.P.s
To: Norman Collins   [WAC: R51/257/2]

When Parliament reopens we shall be approaching some more M.P.s for The
Debate Continues series, and would like to know whether Aneurin Bevan
and Sir Richard Acland are off the black list yet. When we proposed to
approach Acland before I was told that he had a vote of censure tabled and
that we could not use him while this was still sub judice.
EB/JEL   Eric Blair

07/ES/EB   8th October 1943

Dear Eliot,
   With reference to our brief conversation yesterday. I do not know whether
you would like to do another talk in the Great Dramatists series, similar to
the one you did before. The date of the talk would [be] November 21st, which
would mean having the script in about November 14th. It would be a ten
minutes talk.
   You probably remember how these programmes go. They are half hour
programmes consisting of an extract from a play and a talk about the play and
as far as possible about the author's work. We haven't yet fixed the play for
November 21st, and you could choose anyone you like, but I would prefer it to
be a contemporary play because we are doing these more or less in
chronological order. The other five in the series are *Macbeth, An Enemy of the
People, Doctor's Dilemma, Cherry Orchard*, and *R.U.R.*

                                         Yours sincerely,
                                         George Orwell

From: General Overseas Services Manager   10th October 1943
Subject: Approaching M.P.s Aneurin Bevan, Richard Acland.
To: Mr Eric Blair   [WAC: R51/257/2]

Before you approach either could I please have a note of the brief you are
proposing to give these two speakers. It would be undesirable, for instance, for
Acland to talk about the Commonwealth as such, if he is being introduced in
the series on the basis of his being an M.P. – I will clear up about *both*
speakers as soon as I get your note.
   Could you please let me have a list of the M.P.s who have already spoken in
these series?
NC/MAJ   Norman Collins

[Handwritten reply from Orwell on the back]
i. We have not fixed dates for these two speakers (Bevan & Acland) yet but
   wished to know whether we could add them to our repertory. It is difficult
   to fix subjects e.g. in advance because they arise out of the week's debate,
   e.g. if there is a coal bill we might get them to talk about the mining
   industry, etc. There would of course be no question of getting Acland to
   talk about Common Wealth (I should think he might talk on agriculture
   for instance). I know both these people & could handle them.
ii. MPs who have spoken are Winterton, Quintin Hogg, Hugh Molson,
   Hinchingbrooke, Brian Brooke, Sorensen, Gallacher, Ellen Wilkinson,
   Edith Summerskill, King-Hall, V. Bartlett, Butler (Education), Strauss,
   Laws, & one or two others.

E[ric] B[lair]   19.10.43

07/ES/EB   16th October 1943

Dear Hawkins,
   The last 'Backward Glance' programme went off very smoothly and was an
extremely good programme, I thought. I liked the use of the man and woman,
two voices. Could you make the same treatment in your next programme,
which goes on the air on Wednesday, the 27th October, from 11 to 11.30 a.m.
Douglas Cleverdon is again producing this programme, this time from
London and not from Plymouth, thank goodness. We have already booked
Freda Falconer and Arthur Bush to take part in it and Douglas Cleverdon is
having a rehearsal on the Tuesday afternoon, the 26th October, so if you
could possibly let us have the script a little earlier than usual this time, say the
Thursday or Friday in advance, it would be a great help.

Desmond Hawkins Esq.,	Yours truly,
Todds Farm,	George Orwell
Saxtead,	dispatched in his absence by
Framlingham, Suffolk.	

From Guy Burgess   19/10/43
To Registry

Please attach to file.
I have written to E.M. Forster and received a discouraging reply. I have also
talked to him personally and have been equally discouraged. He says that he
is quite happy broadcasting in the Indian Service which, he says, gives him
more freedom to say what he wants than would the Home Service.

for Mr. Burgess

07/ES/EB   11th November 1943

Dear Ivor Brown,[107]
    I think you wanted some particulars of the talk we should like you to do on
Thunder Rock[108] for December 19th. These are half hour programmes and
consist of an acted extract from the play with a talk on the play and sometimes
on the author's work in general by some qualified person. The programme
starts off with a short trailer from the play itself then the speaker follows (so
that your talk should start 'Those lines you have just heard come from
Thunder Rock,' or words to that effect) and after that comes the extract from
the play. The length would be about ten minutes or twelve hundred words. I
would like to have the script a week before the date of transmission. As these
programmes go out on Sunday you will probably prefer to record your talk
beforehand, and we can arrange a recording anytime convenient to you.

                              Yours sincerely,
                              George Orwell

[Postcard]
Didn't know you were still there. Yes please send a [batch(?)] of Burmese
books with Indian bearings. Also the 3rd. vol. of Coupland, which had better
be mentioned, and isn't there somebody's banned book on India: there never
seems any objections to these. – Finally I have a novel here, *Breakfast with the
Nikolides*, which can be dragged in if needed.[109]
    EMF.
21-11-43   W.H.

07/ES/ZAB   14th July 1944

My dear Blair,
    May I again approach you for a talk in our series New Writing which is
scheduled for September 12th? Would you like to discuss in it new
tendencies, or new books, or the lack of new books – and you know here what
I mean by new books? Can real creative work be done while the world

---

[107] Ivor Brown (1891-1974), author and journalist, editor of the *Observer* 1942-8.
[108] A play by the American Robert Ardrey, first produced in England at the Neighbourhood
Theatre, London, in 1940, with a cast which included Michael Redgrave and Bernard Miles.
[109] *Breakfast with the Nikolides* (1941) by Rumer Godden.

consists of partisans? Why haven't we been able to produce a Rupert Brooke? Why are the creative writers turning into literary commentators? These are just vague suggestions, and I am sure you will be able to improve upon them considerably. Perhaps you will drop me a line in reply.[110]

George Orwell, Esq.,   Yours sincerely,
c/o The Tribune,   Z.A. Bokhari
222 Strand, W.C.2.   Indian Programme Organiser

---

[110] Orwell was by this time completely absorbed in his work as Literary Editor of *Tribune* and declined to contribute.

Appendix A
Censorship at the BBC in wartime

The question of censorship of broadcasts in wartime is a complex one. The BBC was subject to extensive censorship controlled by the Ministry of Information which was located, during the war, in the University of London's headquarters building, Senate House, Malet Street. The building bears a close resemblance to the Ministry of Truth in *Nineteen Eighty-Four* and acted as a direct model for it. The BBC's practice in the matter was admirably summed up in a minute, reproduced below, which was sent by J.B. Clark, Controller Overseas Services, to his opposite number in the Broadcasting Division of the Ministry of Information in November 1941. The original purpose of the letter was to provide an explanation of how the system operated for Canada House which had earlier asked for information.

To: Mr Latham, Broadcasting Division, MOI.   14 November 1941
From: Mr J.B. Clark, Controller (Overseas Services), BBC
Subject: Broadcasting Services: Wartime Operations

I much regret the delay in replying to your memo of November 6th on the Canada House enquiry to the Dominions Office. I hope, however, that the following rather fuller formula than the one embodied in your note will prove helpful.

    It seems that the wartime operation of broadcasting services in this country could be covered, subject to your Ministry's agreement, by a statement on the following lines:

On any political question affecting the war effort, guidance is provided by the Government, primarily through the Minister of Information, the Minister responsible to Parliament for BBC activities. In specialised political fields, other Government Departments concerned make direct contact with the BBC; these include the recently established Political Warfare Executive (European Services), the Foreign Office (all services), and the Dominions, Colonial and India Offices (the Empire Services). The Fighting Service Departments maintain close contact with service matters of all kinds – in greater or less detail according to circumstances. The Ministers of Economic Warfare, War Transport, and the Home Departments similarly are closely in touch with all broadcasts bearing on their responsibilities. The execution of policy in the fields of broadcasting technique and the actual preparation of material for programmes remains in the hands of the Corporation.

On censorship matters, responsibility as delegate censors is vested in appropriate officers (i.e. editorial and talks staff, etc.,) of the BBC, who receive by teleprinter, direct from the Censorship Division, copies of all security notices circulated to other executive censors. Doubtful points about security censorship or policy, are referred, when necessary, to or through the main censorship bureau in the Ministry of Information, or to the Service or other department concerned in special cases.

The BBC Overseas Services (other than European) are divided geographically into Latin-American, Near East (Arabic, Persian and Turkish) and Empire (or World) Services, comprising North American, Eastern, African and Pacific Services. For the USA aspect of the North American Service the main Government contact is the American Division of the Ministry of Information, but the Foreign Office has direct contact with the Corporation from time to time.

For the Latin-American Service, the Latin-American Section of the Ministry similarly provides the main Governmental focus of policy.

As a convenient and authoritative means of canalising this political direction, the Corporation has appointed to its staff advisers on Foreign, and Home and Empire affairs respectively. These advisers maintain appropriate contact with all sections of the Corporation for two-way traffic between the Corporation and Government Departments.

The fact that the lowest rank of censor, 'delegate censors', were not from the Ministry of Information but colleagues within the BBC, indeed within one's own department, could make life tense in the sort of situation in which people like Orwell often found themselves. More serious matters, defined by precise instructions cabled every day from the Ministry of Information, were referred to the Ministry either for censorship there or for further consideration by other experts. In effect everyone could be seen as checking on everyone else, just as Orwell describes Comrade Tillotson in *Nineteen Eighty-Four* doing the same task as Winston Smith. It has often been suggested that the censorship was of a negative character and confined to refusal of permission without specific reason. This comforting delusion must have made day-to-day life within broadcasting departments easier, but the few surviving scripts in the BBC Written Archives which have the censor's comments attached from the MOI show that this was not the case. The most severe verdicts were often given, and they could and did seriously affect people's careers with the BBC.

As an example of detailed censorship we show here a Ministry of Information report on a talk (by Barbara Ward) which was banned. The criticisms that follow it give a general reason for rejection and then a detailed line-by-line criticism. In this case there was also correspondence which showed that the author was not to be told of what had happened other than in general terms.

G.R. Barnes, Esq.,   4.3.42
Director of Talks
British Broadcasting Corporation, W.1

Dear Barnes,

Thank you very much for submitting the script by Barbara Ward entitled 'British Colonial Policy'. This has been very carefully considered, and in view of the conclusions reached, we must ask you to cancel this broadcast. I have attached some notes on the script, headed by a general statement by Sir Donald Cameron as to its complete unsuitability.

Sorry to cause you this trouble, but we know that you will appreciate how important it is to avoid any ill considered criticism of British Administration being put over the air at the present time.

Yours sincerely,
H.V. Usill
Colonial Section

British Colonial Policy by Barbara Ward

General criticism
Sir Donald Cameron after reading the MS says: 'It would be impossible for me to revise this so as to present a truer picture. I do not defend our Colonial Policy through thick and thin, but at least it should be correctly presented. I fear that the writer has insufficient knowledge of British Colonial Policy and Colonial affairs generally to equip her for the delicate task she has undertaken. The paper would have to be recast almost entirely and the Malay slander should not be repeated.'

Specific criticisms
Page one, para two: Burma is not a Colony.
Page two, top: The less said about India at the present time the better. In any case, the Indian problem is not related to Colonial problems.
Page two, para two: The whole of the paragraph beginning 'Now this way ...' gives an entirely false picture. The alternate aim has been declared and we have been working consistently towards it, and with a large measure of success.
Page three, top: No countenance whatever must be given to this. It is at present mere rumour, and in any case, the events in Malaya and Singapore can be demonstrated quite conclusively to have little relation to British Colonial policy. Both were military disasters which in due course will doubtless be related to Vichy selling out on Indo China, the events at Pearl Harbour, etc. Until an official explanation in relation to all the facts can be given the less said the better.
Page three, para two: This paragraph is grossly inaccurate. To which territories does the author intend this figment of her imagination to apply? Goebbels would welcome this paragraph.
Page four: The attempt on this page to catch up on the previous material is too

thin to have the desired effect. Whereas there is much to explain about our Colonial Empire, on balance there is surprisingly little of which we need to be ashamed.

Page five, top: Here again the author deals with Singapore.

Page five, bottom: This is just pernicious nonsense. It has been no part of British Colonial Policy to consider any members of the British Colonial Empire as 'racially inferior'. As for the 'colour bar' this has been fought wherever it has reared its ugly head.

Page five, para one: Our patience is nearly exhausted. When has Great Britain taken 'riches out of the Colonies'? Surely the writer must know that the Colonial Development and Welfare Act was an advance on previous policy in relation to the encouragement of social enterprises. Prior to this reform it was considered that territories should be encouraged to indulge in social development schemes with the assistance of the British exchequer on condition that they could guarantee maintenance. However, this insistence upon ability to maintain, which is the basis of British Local Government, had a hampering effect upon development in Colonial territories where the local exchequer could not meet running costs. Consequently the British tax payer has been asked to find additional monies to help certain Colonies over these difficulties, not a penny of which, be it remembered, will find its way into the pockets of the mythical 'foreign exploiters'.

Page seven: Yes, we are our brother's keeper, and it is unfair to suggest that 'we have not cared a fig in the past for their (the Colonial people's) welfare'. By all means let us be frank in our admissions that much still remains to be done, and to appeal to people in Britain to take a more intelligent interest in the problem of administrating such a vast Colonial Empire. But, surely, it is better to stimulate a justifiable pride in past efforts and a sincere desire to do even better when we have rid the world of the menace of Hitlerism?

H.V. Usill

There was another form of censorship operating within the BBC, again directly controlled from the Ministry of Information, which it is more difficult to get information about even now. It involved the banning of people from the air at certain times, or for certain talks, or completely; that is, a denial of the right of free speech. Orwell frequently found himself in difficulty here. As a rather complete example we show here the papers that led up to a simple request from Orwell to the well-known scientist J.B.S. Haldane to do an innocuous talk. Orwell first indicated to his superior, Rushbrook-Williams, that he would like to use Haldane. Rushbrook-Williams sent a confidential memorandum to R.A. Rendall, Assistant Controller (Overseas):

BBC internal circulating memo.   Private and Confidential
Subject: J.B.S. Haldane.   16 November 1942

I should so much like to get JBSH to talk upon the obstacles which science encounters under the Nazi and Fascist regimes. His script would of course be scrutinised for ideological unorthodoxy. Is he banned? I can't find out whether he is actually a member of the C[ommunist] P[arty] or not – no one quite seems to know. [His membership had been announced at the National Conference of the CP on 24 May.] But if he is he is a very unorthodox one!

This question was considered serious enough to be referred to J.B. Clark and his minute appended to the note states the case:

   i. There is no general ban on anyone, each case being judged on its merits.
   ii. There's no blacklist [Rushbrook-Williams hadn't said there was].
   iii. In this case are we really sure that JBSH is the *best* man for this subject? I have personal doubts.
   iv. Having regard to past difficulties, are we satisfied that this is a case in which we want to deal with temperamental difficulties over script? [Haldane did not take kindly to censorship.]

Rendall then conveyed this reply, on the same sheet of paper, in manuscript, no carbon copies being kept, to Rushbrook-Williams:

Please see C(OS)'s minute. We have had many cases of trouble with Haldane in the past – seldom for any good reason. If you want to press this suggestion I can probably secure agreement but I am not convinced that there is an outstanding case. C(OS) suggests that some German refugee scientist might make the point most tellingly. I do not myself know of one. If you want to proceed with the Haldane suggestion please let me know.

The ground having been cleared, Orwell then wrote requesting permission to use Haldane and at the same time sent a letter to Haldane. There were no problems. But this procedure was followed repeatedly throughout the time that Orwell was with the Eastern Service. Many times he was refused speakers; at other times he pressed the matter and obtained permission to use them for certain subjects. At the very end of his period with the BBC Orwell requested permission to use Sir Richard Acland and the Labour politician Aneurin Bevan, claiming that both were on a black list (see above, p. 274). Permission was obtained for Acland on anything other than his party, the Commonwealth Party; Bevan was refused completely. As the minute put it, 'I thought that Aneurin Bevan would be better left alone', with no mention, of course, of a black list.

An influential outsider's view at the time can be seen in Cardinal Heenan's record of the problems of Cardinal Hinsley, who had also effectively been banned:

The Corporation is a formidable example of the English Way. It ... is independent of the Government. It makes its own arrangements and appointments. But, on occasion, the Ministry of Information, the Home or Foreign Office may give a hint to the BBC regarding the kind of person or thing it likes to hear or, more often, does not like to hear. The Cardinal could never discover precisely who controlled this most powerful single influence on the intellectual life of the British public. (J.C. Heenan, *Cardinal Hinsley* (1944), p. 211.)

Appendix B
Indian Section programmes produced by George Orwell

The Indian Section of the Eastern Service was unique among the BBC's overseas services for the wide range of programmes it produced. Much of the material was available nowhere else at all in the BBC. Until the coming of the Third Programme the Indian Section was almost alone in providing regular programmes dealing with political and literary matters in the highest intellectual context. To make clear the full range of this work we print here two sets of programme notes by Orwell which have survived. The first is a very detailed listing of all the speakers for his programmes in a single week at the end of 1942; the second is a broadcast talk outlining the highlights of three months' broadcasting which also gives an idea of the personal approach Orwell took with the programmes. It is amusing to note that in the first of these 'Eric Blair' refers to 'George Orwell's' regular weekly news summary.

(i)

Speakers for Week 51   7th December 1942

On Sunday, the 13th December, as usual, the Brains Trust will answer questions sent in by listeners. Those taking part will be Dr Malcolm Sargent, Leslie Howard, Dr C.E.M. Joad, the guest speakers being Captain E.J. Bellanger MP and Dr C.H. Waddington. Dr Waddington has already broadcast a talk in the series 'Literature Between Wars', on science and literature, and also took part in a discussion with Professor J.B.S. Haldane, on the subject of scientific research in the series 'I'd Like it Explained' in the Eastern Service.

On Monday, the 14th, at 1115 GMT, Princess Indira continues her usual weekly review of events in Parliament 'The Debate Continues'. This is followed by Radio Theatre, in which John Burrell presents a selection from Nelson, featuring Leslie Howard.

On Tuesday, the 15th, we have the third in the series 'Science and the People', dealing with Plastics, the new synthetic substances which have revolutionised the light industries all over the world. The talk is delivered by Dr V.K. Yarsley. After the last war Dr Yarsley graduated in the Honours School of Chemistry, at Birmingham University and was awarded a Research Fellowship

284

by the Salters Institute of Industrial Chemistry which he held at the Eidgenossische Technische Hochschule in Zürich. Returning to England he was engaged as Chief Chemist in the manufacture of non-inflammable cinefilm, and had the somewhat unique experience of producing this film right from the raw cotton minters to the production on the screen. Twelve years ago commenced practice as an independent consulting chemist, specialising in cellulosic plastics and products. Was Chairman of the Plastics Group of the Society of Chemical Industry and a member of the Council of the Institute of Plastics Industry, having particular interest in the establishment of schemes for education in plastics. Dr Yarsley is co-author with a colleague (E.G. Couzens) of *Plastics* in the Pelican series, which is published by Penguin Books Ltd. This talk will, we hope, be followed at 1145 GMT by Noel Sirkar's film commentary in which he tells listeners in India about films shortly to be released.

On Wednesday the 16th, at 1115 GMT, Shridhar Telkar is at the microphone, as usual, with 'Behind the Headlines', in which he explains to listeners the importance of some or other current event which may have escaped general notice. This is followed by quarter of an hour of violin solos by F. Grinke, and then by Lady Grigg's usual Wednesday programme 'Women Generally Speaking'. The speaker will be Mrs Eugenie Fordham, and the title of her talk is 'Tessa – a Polish Baby'. Mrs Eugenie Fordham is Assistant Director of British Survey at the British Association for International Understanding. She read law at Cambridge, is married to a barrister and has a son aged 8.

On Thursday, at 1115 GMT, Dr Shelvankar will give the seventh and last talk in the series 'The Story of Fascism' and will deal with the Nazi invasion of Soviet Russia. Dr Shelvankar has been a frequent speaker in this service and has usually talked about Russian and central Asian affairs.

At 1130 GMT the feature programme 'Behind the Battlefront' appears as usual.

On Friday, the 18th, at 1115 GMT, listeners will hear an imaginary interview between William Pitt, the younger, Britain's Prime Minister during the darkest days of the Napoleonic war and Wickham Steed. Wickham Steed is a frequent broadcaster in this service and is almost too well known to need any introduction. He was for many years Editor of *The Times* and is probably the most respected figure in British journalism. This is followed at 1130 GMT by the sixth and last interview in the series 'Let's Act it Ourselves', when Norman Marshall, the well-known theatrical producer answers questions on stage technique put to him by Balraj and Damyanti Sahni.

At 1145 GMT Mulk Raj Anand conducts the seventh and last interview in his series 'A Day in My Life' in which he interviews war workers of various kinds. This time the speaker is a canteen worker, Lady Peel. Lady Peel is the wife of Sir William Peel who is a member of the Club Committee (Victoria League Club Committee) and also a member of the Victoria League Central Executive Committee. He was a Governor and Commander in Chief Hong-Kong. Lady Peel herself is one of the oldest commandants and workers of the Victoria League Club. She has been with the Victoria League Club since it opened. She looks after and organises entirely three midday shifts of meals a week, one of the busiest times of course which the Club has to cope with. The

Victoria League is run entirely for the benefit of men from overseas and many Indians serving in the forces in England go there regularly when on leave.

On Saturday the 19th, at 1145 GMT, George Orwell gives his usual weekly News Commentary. This is followed by Princess Indira's musical programme, Favourite Movements. This week she's presenting a selection from various French composers.

Eric Blair

(ii)

'Thro' Eastern Eyes': The Next Three Months   1st February 1942

Today for the first time – and I think it will probably be the only occasion – we are breaking our rule of having only Oriental speakers in this series. The reason is that today we are starting Through Eastern Eyes on its new schedule, and we wanted to give a sort of preliminary talk to let you know what the new schedule will be like and what subjects it will cover. I have been picked out to do this because I have had a good deal to do with arranging the schedule. But I should like to let you know in passing that I am the only European in this Indian section of the BBC. All the others are Indians, and the section is presided over by Z.A. Bokhari, whose voice I think you all know.

Well, we are retaining the general idea of Through Eastern Eyes, but we are altering the scope somewhat. Anyone who has listened in to these talks before will know that Through Eastern Eyes is a series of talks in the English language given entirely by Orientals, in most cases Indians. The general idea is to interpret the West, and in particular Great Britain, to India, through the eyes of people who are more or less strangers. An Indian, or a Chinese perhaps, comes to this country, and because everything is more or less new to him he notices a great deal which an Englishman or even an American would take for granted. So we have given you a series of talks on British institutions of every kind, from the Houses of Parliament to the village pub, all of them delivered by Orientals and most of them by people who have been only a few years in this country. We hope that in doing so we have brought the East and the West a little nearer together. This general plan will continue, with the difference that several talks each week are going to have a wider scope and to be more directly connected with the war and the political situation of the world. But I had better start by telling you which series of talks we are *not* altering.

First of all, we are going to continue every Monday with our Parliamentary commentary, which we call 'The Debate Continues'. This gives you a summing-up of the proceedings in the House of Commons during the current week. Tomorrow the speaker in this series will be Sir Hari Singh Gour, whom you have heard giving the talks before. We are also keeping on with our News Commentary every Saturday. This is a weekly discussion of the strategy of the world war, and it is nearly always given by Mr Z.A. Bokhari. And we are also keeping the series we call 'The Man in the Street', on Fridays, which tells you about the reactions of ordinary private people to the war. We have had a good many women speakers in this series, and I think we shall continue with that practice. There are some exceptionally talented broadcasters among the Indian women now in this country, and we like to have at least one talk a week with a special appeal to women.

On the next three Sundays following this one you are going to hear the results of the Indian students' competition which was set some time back by the BBC. After the results of the competition have been announced the three top entries will be read over the air on three successive Sundays by Indian members of our department. We only wish the winners were here to read them for themselves. But now I want to say something about the three series of talks which are a new departure.

The first of these, on Tuesdays, will be called 'These Names Will Live'. These talks are short sketches – more or less biographical sketches, but giving you an idea of their work and what they stand for – of the outstanding personalities of our time. We aren't sticking only to British personalities – for instance the first talk in the series, which will be given by Mr Appaswami, the London correspondent of *The Hindu*, is on President Roosevelt, and we are having others on Stalin and Chiang-Kai-Shek. Also, we shan't only talk about politicians and people of that kind – on the contrary, we want to concentrate rather on scientists, artists and literary men. I ask you particularly to listen in two or three weeks' time to Mulk Raj Anand, the Indian novelist – author of *Untouchable, Two Leaves and a Bud* and so on – who is going to give several talks about some of the best-known English writers.

The next new series, on Wednesdays, is called 'Today and Yesterday'. These talks are discussions of the social changes that are taking place in Britain as a result of the war. There has been considerable and very rapid change in the structure of our life here, often happening in a rather indirect way as the result of measures forced on us by the air raids, by the need for a much bigger mobilisation of labour, and so on. For example, the Excess Profits Tax, food rationing and the fact that there is no longer any unemployment have gone some distance towards equalising the various standards of living in Britain. Again, English agriculture has expanded enormously owing to the need to grow our own food, and as a result of evacuation hundreds of thousands of children who would normally be growing up in big towns are growing up in the country. Or again, the English educational system is being very markedly altered by the redistribution of population, by the fact that fewer people than before can afford to send their children to boarding schools, and by the need to train great numbers of young men as airmen or technicians of one kind and another. Then there are the changes that are occurring in the press and in popular literature, and in the political outlook of the average man. These are the kind of subjects that we shall be discussing in 'Today and Yesterday'.

The third new series is called 'What it Means to Me'. These talks, which will be given every Thursday, are discussions of the abstract ideals for which the anti-Fascist powers are fighting. We constantly hear words and phrases flung to and fro – democracy, liberty, national sovereignty, economic security, progress, international law. What do they mean in concrete terms? Is democracy simply a matter of dropping your vote into a ballot box? Is liberty any use without economic security? Can any nation in the modern world be really independent? Is progress a reality? These are some of the questions that our speakers are going to discuss.

As to who these speakers will be, they will all be Orientals – I mean people whose native land is somewhere East of Suez. Apart from Indians, we have already brought Chinese and Burmese speakers to the microphone in this series, and we shall bring others, as well as Malays, Thais, Turks and Indonesians, I hope. We are particularly anxious to bring you as many Chinese speakers as possible because of the enormous importance, especially at this moment, of solidarity between India and China. Asia, no less than Europe, is fighting for its life against Fascism, and the more that the two greatest nations of Asia – I mean India and China – know about one another, the better. For that reason we may occasionally interrupt our programme, which is supposed to deal mostly with the West, to give you some specially topical talks by Chinese speakers. I ask you particularly to listen for two talks by Mr Hsiao Ch'ien, a Chinese student now in London, who has been in various parts of Japanese-occupied China. He will tell you something of what it means to live under Japanese rule, and of the ways in which the Japanese try to corrupt as well as conquer their victims.

But of course most of our speakers will be Indians. Some of these will be from the regular staff of the BBC – I think you already know the voices of Balraj Sahni, and I.B. Sarin, and Venu Chitale, as well as Z.A. Bokhari himself – but most of them will be independent speakers. There is not a very large number of Indians now in England, but the ones who are here are a very varied and very talented body of people. They include doctors, students, correspondents of Indian papers such as *The Hindu* and the *Amrita Bazar Patrika*, writers like Mulk Raj Anand and J.M. Tambimuttu, technical trainees under the Bevin scheme, lawyers, airmen and civil servants. I think I can promise that the subjects on our list will be discussed exhaustively and from many different angles.

This series of talks, Through Eastern Eyes, will be going on for three months, always at the same time of day, that is, 8.30 p.m., Indian Standard Time. We hope anyone who listens and who has any suggestions to make, or any criticisms to offer, will write to us about it, and not be put off by the fact that letters take rather a long time to get here. We are very grateful to the various people in India who have written to us about this series already.

And finally, may I say how happy it makes me to be helping to organise these broadcasts – broadcasts which I believe can be really helpful and constructive at a time like this – to the country in which I was born and with which I have many personal and family ties.

Appendix C
The principles of Axis & Allied propaganda

The three documents that follow are: a formal appraisal of the strength of German broadcasts in Hindustani, dating from the early part of the war; an analysis of counter propaganda written at the time of the abortive Cripps mission to India in 1942; and lastly an example of Japanese propaganda which particularly annoyed Orwell at the time (see above, *Letters*, p. 237.).

(i)

Note on development of German broadcasts in Hindustani

As remarked in previous analyses there have been indications of a development in the 'Hindustani section' of German radio propaganda.

We know that, on the outbreak of war, the Germans underwent difficulties, owing to the shortage of Hindustani broadcasters. For a certain period broadcasts in Hindustani ceased. The Germans then started a regular service on 22nd November of a quarter of an hour's daily broadcast, which has continued up to the present date.

At first the German broadcasts in Hindustani were largely mere translations of portions of items from their news bulletins in German and English. Latterly, although a large proportion of the Hindustani broadcasts are still culled from the broadcasts in English and German, the system seems to be undergoing a change. More individual items are appearing in the Hindustani broadcasts, and these items have shown a tendency towards increased length and more careful preparation.

Avoiding tedious quotation one instance may be given. The perusal of the daily summaries of 14th and 15th March will reveal the fact that far more forceful treatment was accorded to the Caxton Hall murder [of Sir Michael O'Dwyer] in Hindustani than in German and English.

In assessing the potential effect of radio-propaganda, the listening public to any broadcast can be divided in two different ways:

1. By mentality
   (a) Educated
   (b) Semi-educated
   (c) Uneducated

2. By sentiment
   (d) Persons predisposed towards the sentiments or the type of broadcast
   (e) Persons predisposed against the sentiments or the type of broadcast
   (f) Persons who have no personal bias either way

The only type of broadcast which may be taken to have a general appeal to all of the above groups is a pure news item of topical interest which affects all listeners; and even then, the amount of interest aroused in the listener depends largely on the phraseology and presentation.

German broadcasts in Hindustani seem to be divided into two 'compartments':

(1) The translation of items from other German broadcasts. These, by reason of their remoteness from Indian affairs, are probably extremely tedious to uneducated listeners.
(2) Items specially written for the consumption of Hindustani-speaking listeners. Both are couched in simple language, and are plain statements of fact or fiction, whichever suits German propaganda at the moment: but the noticeable difference between the two 'compartments' lies in the sentiments expressed. German broadcasts are never dulcet in tone, and are usually reminiscent of the hymn of hate of the last war. But their special items in Hindustani by reason of their poisoned malice, as exemplified in their comments on the murder of Sir Michael O'Dwyer, can only offend most Indian opinion.

German broadcasters are nothing if not systematic and methodical, even in their contradictions. Hitler and Dr Goebbels maintain that contradictions do not matter, provided the content is sufficiently damaging to their opponents.

There is no doubt that German radio-propagandists follow a pre-ordered routine, that the contents of their broadcasts are carefully studied from the point of view of comparative stress to be laid on the various subjects selected for the week. This is probably worked out with arithmetical exactitude. But we are frankly doubtful how far the Germans consider the types of listener to which they are appealing.

What we consider the major faults of German radio propaganda are well exemplified in their broadcasts in Hindustani, namely – lack of subtlety, pre-supposition of anti-British sentiment and a contradictory attitude towards the mentality of British statesmen and officials. One example of lack of subtlety in German radio is their attitude towards British and French propaganda. Their usual method of refutation is to say: 'Mr Churchill's (or Lord Zetland's) statement is merely ridiculous, etc., etc.' A far more effective method is to point out the cleverness of enemy propaganda and then refute it by dialectics. The German method is apt to defeat itself with the intelligent listener.

The pre-supposition of anti-British sentiment is probably a considered basis of German propaganda: but it has a special significance when applied to the Indian listener. The Indian listening public may be divided (as in Group 2 above) into two comparatively small sections (d) anti-British (e) pro-British and the majority (f) who, either through lack of thought or lack of interest, hold no strong opinion: any suggestion made over the air that the listener feels something he does not feel, at once creates hostility in the listener towards the broadcaster.

Possibly the greatest psychological error of German radio is their consistent contradiction of British policy as exemplified in British leaders, whom they state in one breath to be stupid old men 'ignorant of the political signs of the times', and in the next to be positively Machiavellian in their oppression of subjugated peoples and in their method of spreading communal dissension in India, so that they may maintain their hold over the starving millions. Once again German radio tends to defeat itself in the minds of the intelligent.

One of the strong points of German radio, emanating from their unscrupulousness, lies in their ability to twist news items to their own advantage and Britain's disadvantage. An example of this appears in a statement on 'Satyagraha' in the German news in Hindustani of Friday, 5th April, and is discussed under the paragraph 'Broadcasts in Hindustani' below.

Remembering the two 'compartments' of German broadcasting in Hindustani and taking the above factors into account, it would seem that, either by design or accident, these broadcasts at present direct their appeal to the Anti-British (d) and semi-educated (b) sections of Indian listeners. In fact we believe most of the 'special' items of German Hindustani news bulletins are designed to supply ammunition to Indian agitators.

By reason of the excellent reception from German transmitters, the entertainment value of the colourful content of their broadcasts and the pleasure afforded by the comparison of German and British versions of news items, they undoubtedly attract many listeners in groups (c) and (f): but because of their inherent faults the broadcasts do not have as much effect as they easily might. One might imagine that group (f) would be the one group German radio propagandists are the most anxious to contaminate. And if German propaganda in Hindustani improves, as it may well do, here lies the greatest potential danger.

As regards the educated and pro-British sections of the Indian public, the effect is probably detrimental to Germany, except among educated Indians with an anti-British bias, who can only be affected through their own 'wishful thinking'.

Two important facts, however, must not be overlooked:

(1) The German 'Hindustani' announcers are excellent broadcasters. Their delivery is well-timed, and the language employed easily understood. Given better material they are undoubtedly potentially dangerous.
(2) German broadcasts in Asiatic languages are in a state of development, and we are still waiting to see what will emerge from the chrysalis. But the foregoing may, at least, place before those of our readers, who are interested in German broadcasts in Hindustani, some of the potentialities of enemy radio propaganda directed to India and the Indians.

(ii)

Counter-propaganda on Indian themes   Private & Confidential
                                                          9th April, 1942

This will confirm our telephone conversation of yesterday when I asked you to get in touch with Burton Leach of the Empire Division of the MOI about counter-propaganda on Indian themes.

The India Office are, it appears, most anxious that special attention should be paid, not only now but after the conclusion of the Cripps mission, to countering Axis propaganda about India directed to parts of the world other than India. They have asked the MOI to conduct a campaign, and Lord Dufferin has asked that there should be one focal point in the BBC for distribution of material to all departments concerned with propaganda overseas. Only the European and Overseas Services Divisions are concerned and C.(Eur.S.) has asked that any material should be sent to D.Eur.B. for distribution within the European Services Division.

Incidentally, I pointed out to Lord Dufferin that it did not seem to me likely that European Services would be able to give very much attention to this theme or that occupied countries would normally be very greatly interested in the question of India, except when it was headline news as at present. Dufferin and Burton Leach agreed to this and explained that they were mainly concerned about the rest of the Empire (particularly South Africa), the USA and, in somewhat less degree, Latin-America. I said that we would do what we could in all such cases and added that, in my view, the Near East (particularly from the point of view of Muslim opinion) was likely to be more important than America.

Will you please arrange to distribute any material that may be received from the MOI to the recipients of this memorandum, and will you also arrange, if you think fit, that Burton Leach should discuss ways and means of conducting such a campaign with those who will be primarily concerned? I suggested, for instance, that Burton Leach should meet Fergusson, because 'Listening Post' is especially important in this respect.

In our general preliminary discussion with Dufferin and Burton Leach yesterday, the following points emerged:

(a) Negative propaganda, consisting of denials of Axis lies, was in this instance, as in most others, undesirable.
(b) Whatever the result of the Cripps mission, we should not allow ourselves to be forced back on the defensive in speaking of British/Indian relations.
(c) Discrediting, by pointing out inconsistencies and analysing intentions, on the lines of 'Listening Post', was helpful.
(d) Comment from overseas, particularly the United States, should be used whenever possible.

No doubt you will be able to devise other less obvious lines of guidance.
How far this can really be developed into a 'campaign' depends on many at

present unknown factors, including the capacity of the MOI, with the help of the India Office, to provide material, as well as the result of the Cripps mission. In any case, it will be for each Service on its own initiative to decide the amount of attention to be paid to it. For the present it clearly cannot be regarded as having a separate existence, as a propaganda campaign from the more important question of our treatment of the Cripps mission. I suggest, therefore, that anything that you may wish to circulate on the counter-propaganda theme for the present be regarded as part of the guidance that you are supplying throughout the Corporation on the handling of the Cripps mission. When that is over, you can begin to circulate counter-propaganda material to the smaller list of people.

R.A. Rendall

(iii)

News Commentary: 'More Jews to Oust the Arabs from Palestine'   28.12.42
Palestine Already Overcrowded

The demand that every Jew saved from Europe should be sent to Palestine, which, it is said, could support 50,000 more people, is likely to be acceded to by the British Government. It is a threat to the lawful Arab population of Palestine, which is so closely populated that a further influx would mean that more Arabs would lose their homes and land.

During the last war, Britain needed help from the Arabs against the Turks and promised them an Arab State. Palestine was withdrawn from the promised State to placate the Jews, from whom Britain needed financial assistance. A National Home in Palestine, not a Jewish State, was promised, and Churchill declared that this did not mean expropriation of the Arabs. But under the British Mandate, that is what happened. Jews from Europe flocked to the promised land, and Arabs were thrown off the soil which they had tilled for hundreds of years. There can never be any cooperation between the two races. The Jews will not employ Arabs, and will not even permit them to enter Tel Aviv. Arab feeling against the Jews runs very high and the war has increased the Jewish problem a hundredfold. In addition to the authorised entry of Jews into Palestine, thousands have come in illegally; now a further large influx is proposed. These Jews will not be welcomed even by fellow-Jews already established there. Palestine is already overcrowded and there is terrific poverty among the dispossessed Arabs. Many lower-class Jews cannot get enough to eat in the land supposed to be flowing with milk and honey. The slums of the Jewish cities are more overcrowded than anywhere in Europe or U.S.A. If more Jews are sent there will be bloody trouble. The Palestine Arabs will be supported by Arabs of Syria, Iraq and Saudi Arabia. Britain should refuse to countenance the shipping of more Jews to Palestine. She will be playing with fire if she makes the Arabs' lot any harder.

Appendix D
Kingsley Martin and the BBC

For much of the war Kingsley Martin was effectively banned from the BBC. This stemmed from an 'incident' connected with his appearance on a programme called 'Answering You' directed at American audiences.

Complaints were made both by the Home Office and the Ministry of Information, which produced the courageous response printed here from R.A. Rendall defending the BBC strongly against the encroachments of other Government departments. Despite this effort Martin was not used again, and there are letters from him in his BBC file saying that he feels he has offended in some way. Orwell decided to approach him in the summer of 1943, and matters had cooled sufficiently for permission to be given to make contact with him. He did two programmes before J.B. Clark realised that he was being used again and wrote with a formal enquiry about his exact position. Within a few days Martin had obliged his critics within the MOI by broadcasting without warning a totally uncensored and unscheduled talk on British education. The other letters here show the result. The programme did not make Orwell's position any easier. His first mention that he was definitely leaving the BBC dates from this time.

For an excellent account of Kingsley Martin ('in politics ... a mixed-up Peter Pan') see the article by Frank Hardie in the *Dictionary of National Biography* (d. 1969).

(i)

'Answering You': Kingsley Martin on 18B Regulations   Private & Confidential
                                                          23rd December, 1941

I think you will wish to know about a recent incident connected with the 'Answering You' programme for North America. Amongst the questions selected for answering from London were three from the Editor of the Toronto *Saturday Night*, of which one dealt with 18B. In accordance with the principle of making effective use of opposition speakers that we have always tried to observe, when possible, in propaganda programmes for the United States and elsewhere, Mrs Adams approached Mr Kingsley Martin and asked him if he would be willing to prepare an answer. Mrs Adams made it clear to Kingsley Martin that she approached him on the understanding that, even though he was critical of the principle lying behind 18B, he would come down effectively in favour of it, and that she was approaching him because of our belief that a critical question of this nature could most effectively be answered by one who was known for his liberal outlook.

Mr Kingsley Martin supplied an answer which seemed to Mrs Adams satisfactory (copy attached). This answer was submitted to Mr Cummings for advice, as is the usual practice. Cummings agreed to it, indicating the possible cuts, but suggested that the Home Office ought to be consulted about the script. N.A.S.D. consulted C.(N.C.) about this and C.(N.C.) confirmed that the Home Office should be consulted. In accordance with the usual procedure in regard to this programme, N.A.S.D. passed the script to Darvall at the Ministry of Information and asked him to take the matter up with the Home Office. Darvall subsequently informed Gorham that the Home Office (Mr Griffiths) and the MOI had approved the script, subject to the cuts suggested by us. He added, however, that the Home Office registered a protest against the BBC's 'failure to consult them earlier and determination to use only left-wing critics of H.M.G. when dealing with 18B'.

In the meantime, the delay involved in the final submission had made the talk too late to be included in the immediately succeeding series of answers, which did not disturb us greatly, since we felt happy to carry the answer forward for a week. But this delay did arouse Kingsley Martin's curiosity and some sort of explanation had to be given to him. Meanwhile, the question of the Gibbs 18B broadcast had been raised in the House, and Kingsley Martin subsequently wrote saying that, when originally asked to answer the American question on 18B, he had been unaware of the 'Gibbs incident', but that he now thought it better to withdraw his own broadcast since 'it is quite impossible for me or any independent person to broadcast any such case; anyone who now defends 18B on the wireless will be assumed by American listeners to be merely a yes-man of the Home Office.'

It seems to me that the Home Office protest against the use of Kingsley Martin for the purpose of answering a question on 18B, on the grounds that he is a left-wing critic of H.M.G., raises a serious point. It was, of course, just because he was known (as well as any potential answerer can be said to be known in Canada and the United States) for his left-wing tendencies – just as the *New Statesman* is known as being a periodical that is critical of the Government on this type of issue – that he was chosen to answer this question. He was in fact, according to our function as propagandists in general and in this particular programme, an ideal speaker, provided that he was prepared to come down in favour of the Government's attitude. Mrs Adams assured herself on this latter point at the moment of approaching Kingsley Martin, and that his answer was satisfactory is evident to anyone who reads it and was confirmed by the attitude of the Home Office themselves.

I have not spoken to Darvall about this matter, but I feel sure that the MOI agree with us as to the desirability of making use of opposition speakers when dealing with awkward questions. An important point of principle seems, therefore, to be at issue between ourselves and the Home Office, who have elected to protest without, it seems, any proper grounds for such action. If the 'Answering You' programme is to be carried on effectively, it is essential that we should have some assurance that we shall be able to continue on the same lines as in the past without laying ourselves open to criticism or interference from departments who are not concerned with propaganda.

There remains the question of earlier reference claimed by the Home Office. The effective execution of the plan made in agreement with the MOI for the 'Answering You' programme has presented innumerable difficulties. Throughout Mrs Adams has kept in the closest touch with the American Division of the MOI and has used the ordinary Corporation channels for consultation and guidance. Nearly all the more difficult questions involve the work of some Government department or other, but in practice the helpfulness of these departments has varied very greatly; some have seen the significance of the programme and have helped to give us answers, but in many other cases the attitude has been unhelpful and obscurantist because the departments have been more concerned with self-justification than with giving the most effective answer to the North American audience. For these reasons it has not been made a regular principle that Government departments should be consulted in every case, because, had we done so, the programme would have resembled nothing so much as a succession of answers to Parliamentary questions and have done little to elucidate or to persuade the questioners and listeners in general. Moreover, the time factor (questions selected by the British Information Services often come in by cable from New York with little time to prepare answers and we have always been on the edge of running out of material) has made detailed consultation in all cases quite impracticable.

In this particular instance, Mrs Adams was not aware, at the time of receiving the script, of the 'Gibbs incident' in the Home Service. The dangers of consultation at an early stage are well shown by this case, since it is quite clear that, had the Home Office been consulted earlier, they would have prevented, or done their best to prevent, the use of a left-wing critic, thereby seriously impairing the value of the answer without gaining any equivalent advantage in the effectiveness of its actual content.

R.A. Rendall

(ii)

From: Eastern Services Organiser   Private & Confidential
Subject: Mr Kingsley Martin: Broadcasting activities
        in the Eastern Service
To: Controller (Overseas Services)   23rd July 1943

The position with regard to Kingsley Martin is that he is down to give one talk in every fourth week. In other weeks this period is filled by (1) Joad on philosophical subjects, (2) the High Commissioner talking about Indians in Britain, and (3) a short 'Anniversary of the Month' feature, written by Desmond Hawkins.

The basis of Kingsley Martin's contribution is that he should talk each time on some matter of current political interest (not necessarily domestic) and should give his purely personal reactions. The method is that a week or so before the talk he has a preliminary discussion with Blair and they decide between them what subjects are available for treatment within this framework. The policy is then agreed with E.S.D., and Blair gives Martin a clear brief on the chosen subject.

It is felt that though Martin is not a good broadcaster for European audiences his voice and manner are not unacceptable to Indians, and the audience for whom we are specially catering in this period is, in broad terms, the left-wing student intelligentsia among whom the *New Statesman* enjoys a reputation considerably higher than might be judged from its very limited circulation.

So far, Martin has done two talks: one with Princess Indira on the Labour Party Conference, and one on the exiled governments in Britain. No subjects have yet been decided for future talks, but the sort of thing which he might treat would be the Beveridge unemployment enquiry, the political aspects of the coal-mining problem, and the annual conference of the Liberal Party.

C. Lawson-Reece

(iii)

From: Controller (Overseas Services)   5th August, 1943
Subject: Mr Kingsley Martin's talk July 30th
To: Eastern Services Director   Private

In following up a point raised at the Oxford Street programme meeting last week I agreed the proposal that Mr Kingsley Martin should deal in his talk to be recorded last Friday with the Norwood Report, 'assuming that the subject was judged to be of interest to the Indian audience'. I also asked that A.C.(H) should be consulted about the script in view of his expert knowledge and experience of the education machine in this country. After the talk had been recorded I discovered (a) that the talk was entitled 'Education in England' and in fact did not mention the Norwood Report. Was the change of subject agreed by you or was it unauthorised? (b) that Blair on consulting A.C.(H) seemed to show scant respect for the normal courtesy and discipline appropriate to an organisation such as ours over some points that were raised by A.C.(H).

I would personally not have thought that Kingsley Martin was a suitable speaker on the broader subject with which he dealt. Moreover, I feel critical of the script attached which strikes me as both superficial and ill-balanced – possibly as a result of too hurried work. For example, Martin falls into the very trap which he says at the outset catches so many people, by having far too much to say about Public Schools. Equally at the top of page 3 there is a confused statement which does not put the Secondary Schools into the right perspective, and the sort of desirable re-wording I had in mind will I think be obvious. Thirdly, in the middle of page 4 surely the point which Martin wanted to make was that the public generally were less divided, or less concerned, with purely denominational aspects of the religious background to the teaching in schools.

There are several other questions of actual drafting which will I think be obvious to you and which make me regard the script as it stands as a rather poor and inadequate effort. In brief, a talk which was supposed to deal with the

Norwood Report (on Secondary Schools), but which makes considerable reference to the Government White Paper, drags in a lot of personal views and reminiscences with a disturbing result.

Would you please let me have your views on the talk as a whole and especially on (a) and (b) above.

J.B. Clark

(iv)

BBC internal circulating memo
From: Eastern Services Director   Private & Confidential
Subject: Mr Kingsley Martin's talk July 30th
To: Controller (Overseas Services)   11th August 1943

Your memo of 5th August. I am sorry for the delay in replying, but a thorough enquiry has been necessary!

I must first explain that Mr Kingsley Martin broadcasts a monthly Topical Talk, for which a subject is agreed between him and this Department. At our request he avoids the more controversial subjects. His general approach to present-day problems, and his position as editor of the *New Statesman* combine to make him respected by Indian intellectuals. He does not mind being 'briefed' and permits cheerfully a good deal of modification in his scripts. But he is interested in India, knows a good deal about its current problems, and can generally hit off what we want pretty well.

On this occasion, unfortunately, after agreeing to deal with the Norwood Report, he switched over, without telling us, to the general topic of educational reform: and increased (from our point of view) his delinquency by sending in his script just before he was due to record it.

Blair (instructed by E.S.O. at, I understand, your instance) immediately got into touch with A.C.(H): but was uncertain in what capacity A.C.(H) entered the picture at all. A.C.(H), according to Blair, could not be induced to surmount an initial objection to Kingsley Martin being asked to deal with an educational topic. Blair tried in vain to explain that Kingsley Martin had not been selected as an educational expert: but as a writer on current political affairs whose topic on this occasion happened to be an educational one. The exchange between A.C.(H) and Blair never recovered from the initial misunderstanding: although Blair did succeed in elucidating A.C.(H)'s principal objections to some of Kingsley Martin's expressions, which were modified in the 'as broadcast' script (this had further been 'touched up' by Weymouth). Blair has expressed his regrets that his treatment of A.C.(H) lacked the normal courtesies: but pleads that he did, under conditions of great urgency, find it very difficult indeed to reach a common basis of approach.

I agree that the script is disappointing in its balance. The stress laid upon denominational difficulties, and the personal reminiscences, are in fact just right for the particular audience: but I admit that this may be the result of accident rather than of *expertise*!

In future, I have arranged that the scripts of this series shall come to me personally in ample time to ensure that the agreed topic is in fact dealt with, and dealt with as we should like.

L.F. Rushbrook-Williams

(v)

From: Controller (Overseas Services)   15th August 1943
To: Eastern Services Director

Thank you for your memo of August 11th. Experience in this instance does, as I am sure you will realise, yield valuable guidance for the future over one or two important principles:

(a) As you know, I am constantly emphasising the extreme importance of clear briefs to speakers. These are essential if we are, in fact, to direct and control our own services and if we are to choose the right speakers for a given subject. It is one thing for a journalist of distinction, like Kingsley Martin, to deal in a topical talk with a published report (for example the Norwood Report) but the changing of the brief or subject as in this case must not recur. I am glad to have your assurance on this point in your final paragraph, but of course the same principle does apply to all talks or series.

(b) I made it quite clear in my short manuscript note to E.S.O. that A.C.(H) should be consulted 'as an expert within the BBC on education'. Blair should therefore have been under no misapprehensions as to the capacity in which he was to consult A.C.(H). There was nothing new about this and I was merely re-stating a situation explained to the Oxford Street Services many months ago. Just as it is valuable for people in other services to consult your Department on Eastern and Far Eastern affairs, it is from a Corporation angle justifiable for A.C.(H) to be consulted on all doubtful matters in broadcasts about education in this country, or on other educational questions where expert advice is necessary.

J.B. Clark

[MS note to Sir Malcolm Darling on (v)]

Please see C(O.S.)'s note above. Would you please keep a fatherly eye on this matter of briefing?

We cannot risk any more trouble over Kingsley Martin; and I'd be grateful if you would get Blair's co-operation to ensure that the suggested precautions are in fact observed.

L.F.R-W. 16/8

Index

(illustrations not included)